Shojo Beat

OTOMEN

Story & Art by
Aya Kanno

Volume
ONE

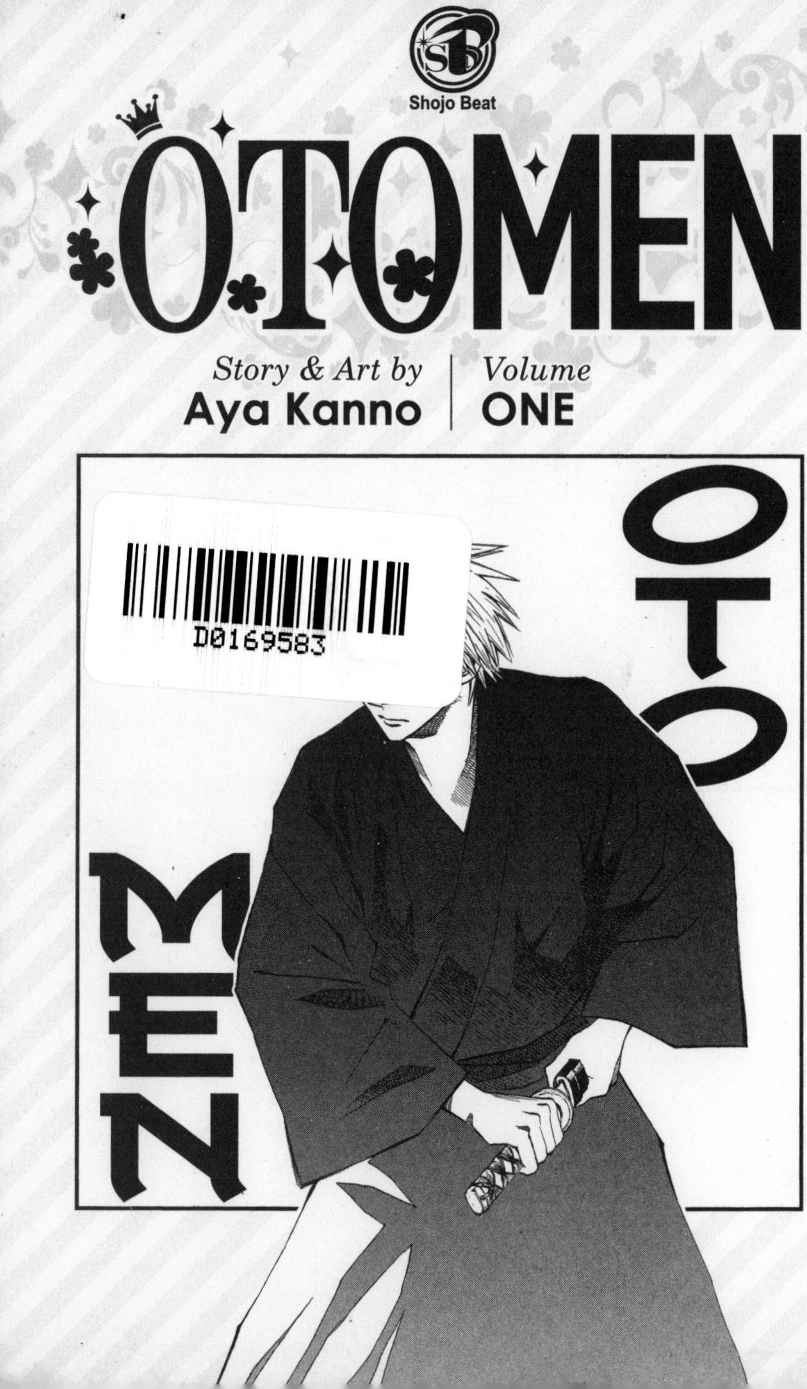
OTO
MEN

OTOMEN

volume 1
CONTENTS

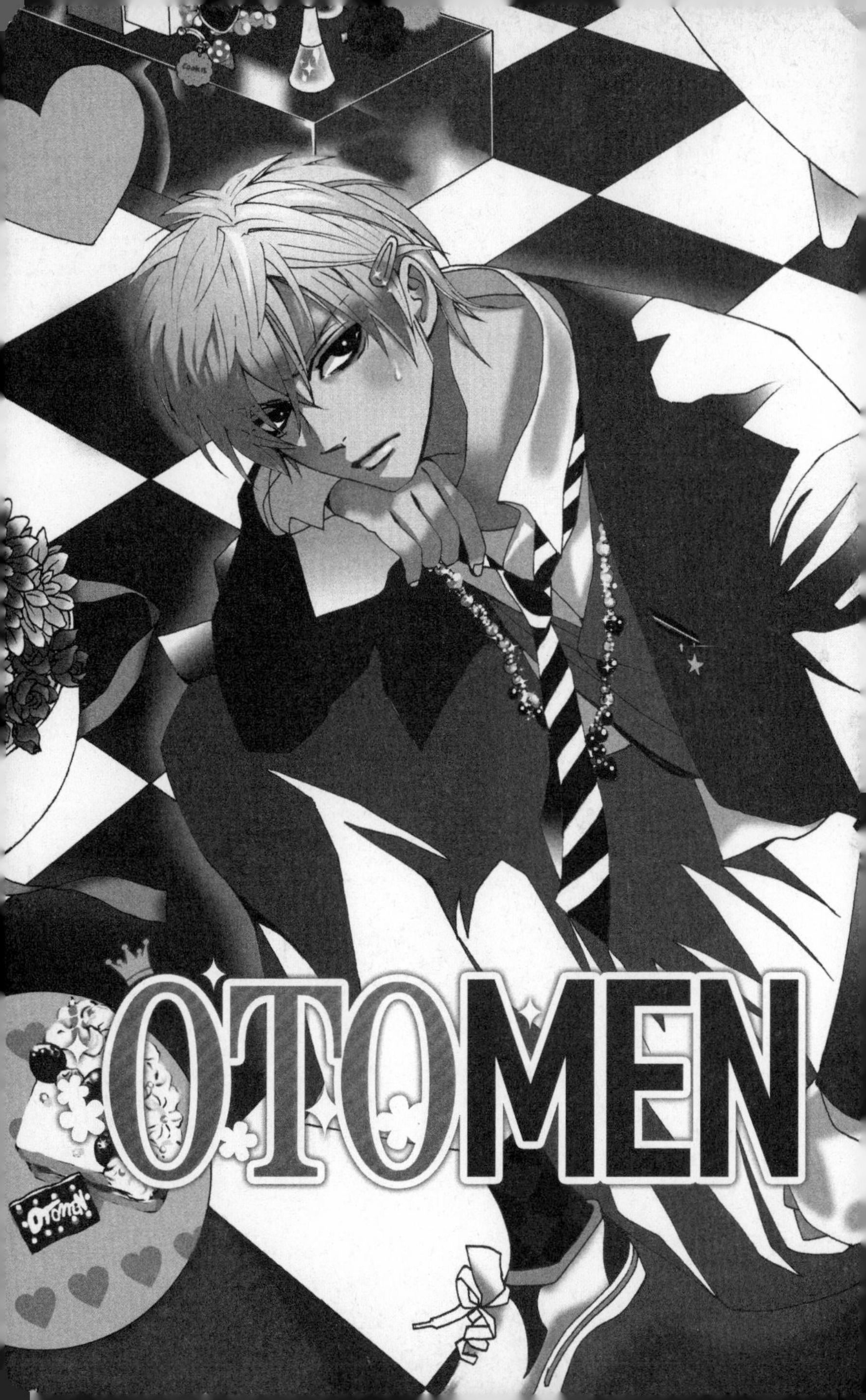
OTOMEN

OTOMEN

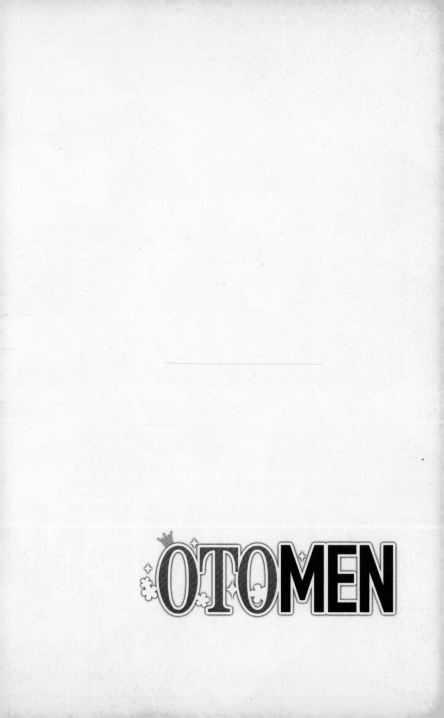

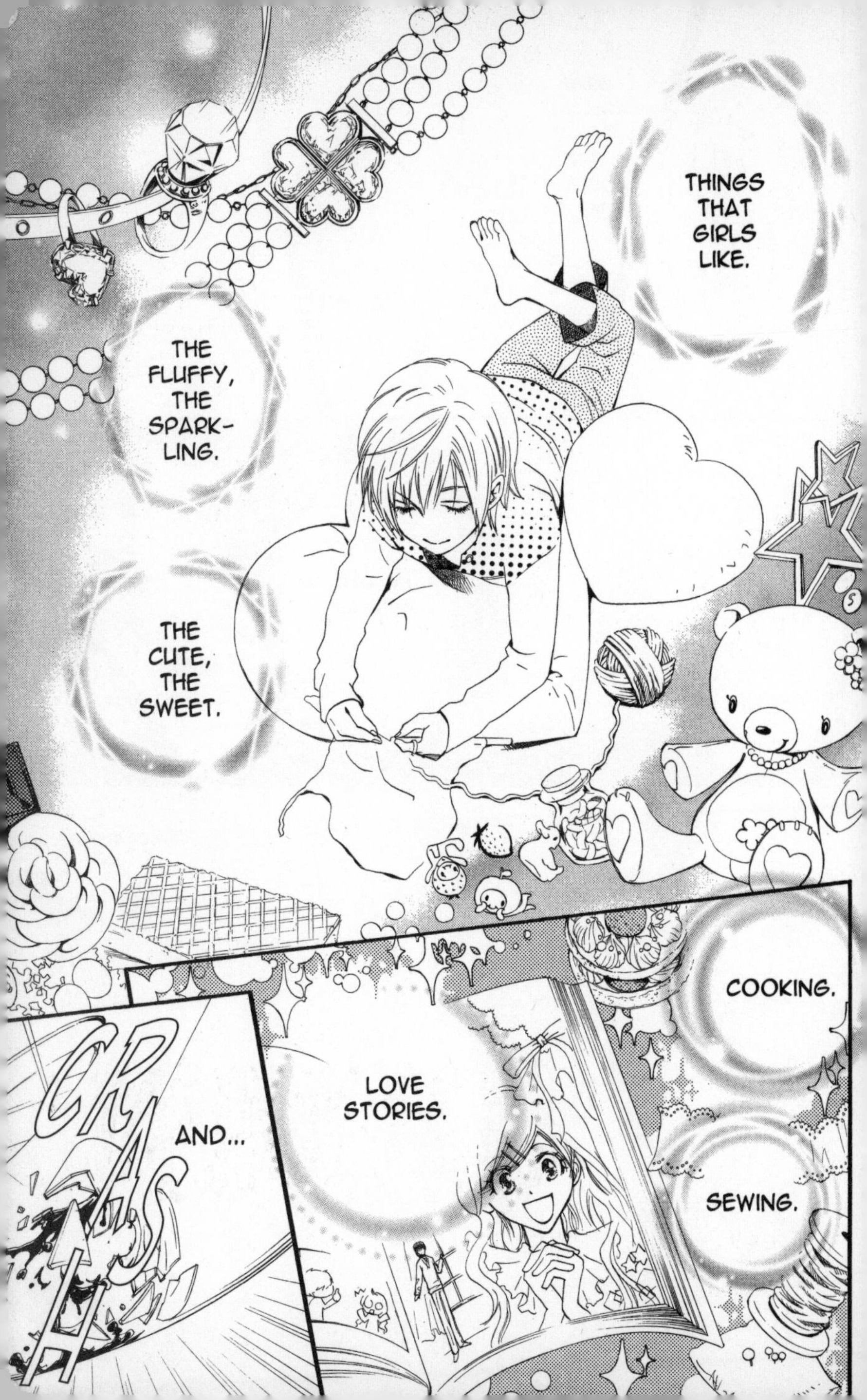
THINGS THAT GIRLS LIKE.
THE FLUFFY, THE SPARK-LING.
THE CUTE, THE SWEET.
COOKING.
SEWING.
LOVE STORIES.
AND...
CRASH

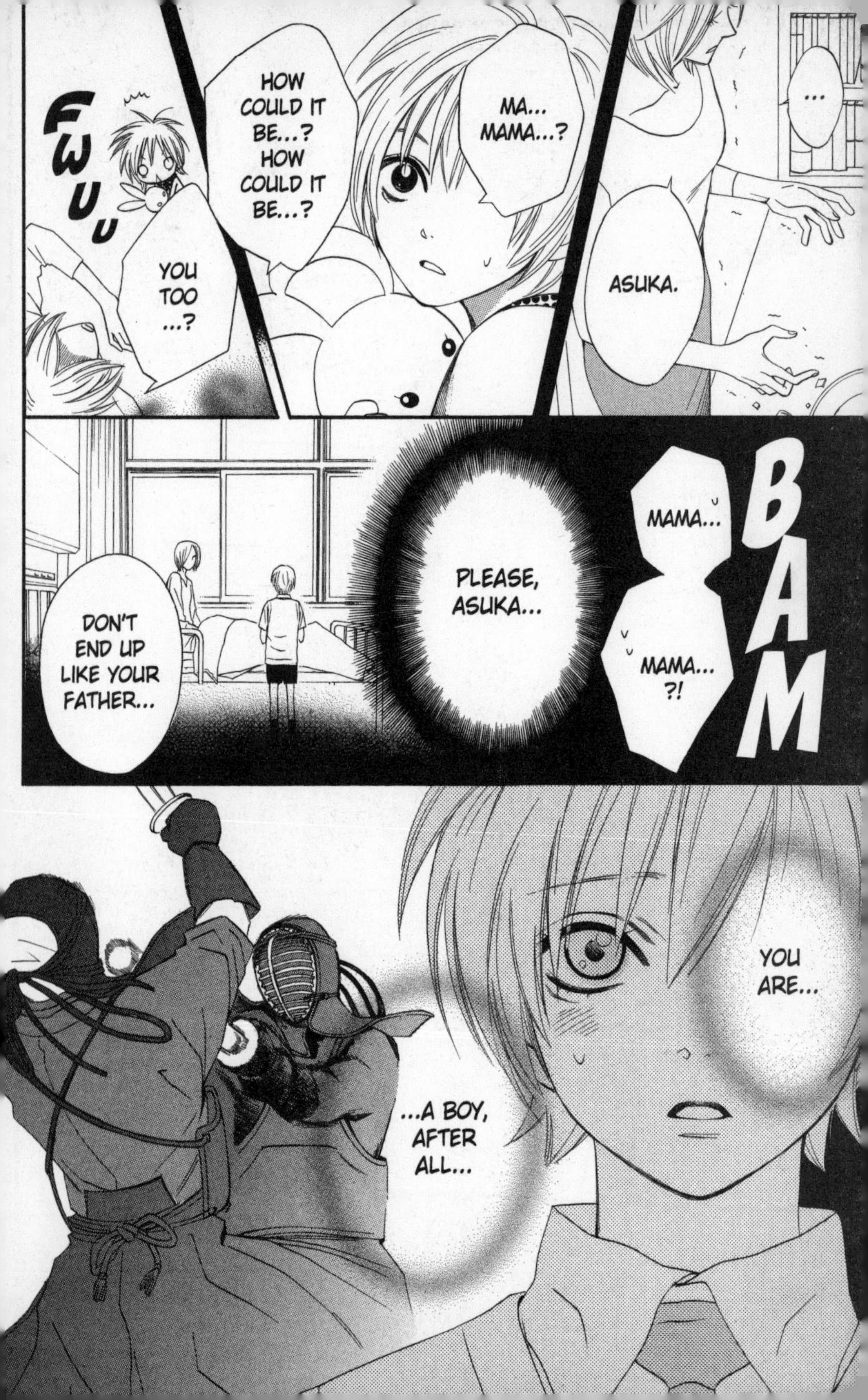
...
ASUKA.
MA... MAMA...?
HOW COULD IT BE...? HOW COULD IT BE...?
FWUU
YOU TOO ...?
BAM
MAMA...
MAMA... ?!
PLEASE, ASUKA...
DON'T END UP LIKE YOUR FATHER...
YOU ARE...
...A BOY, AFTER ALL...

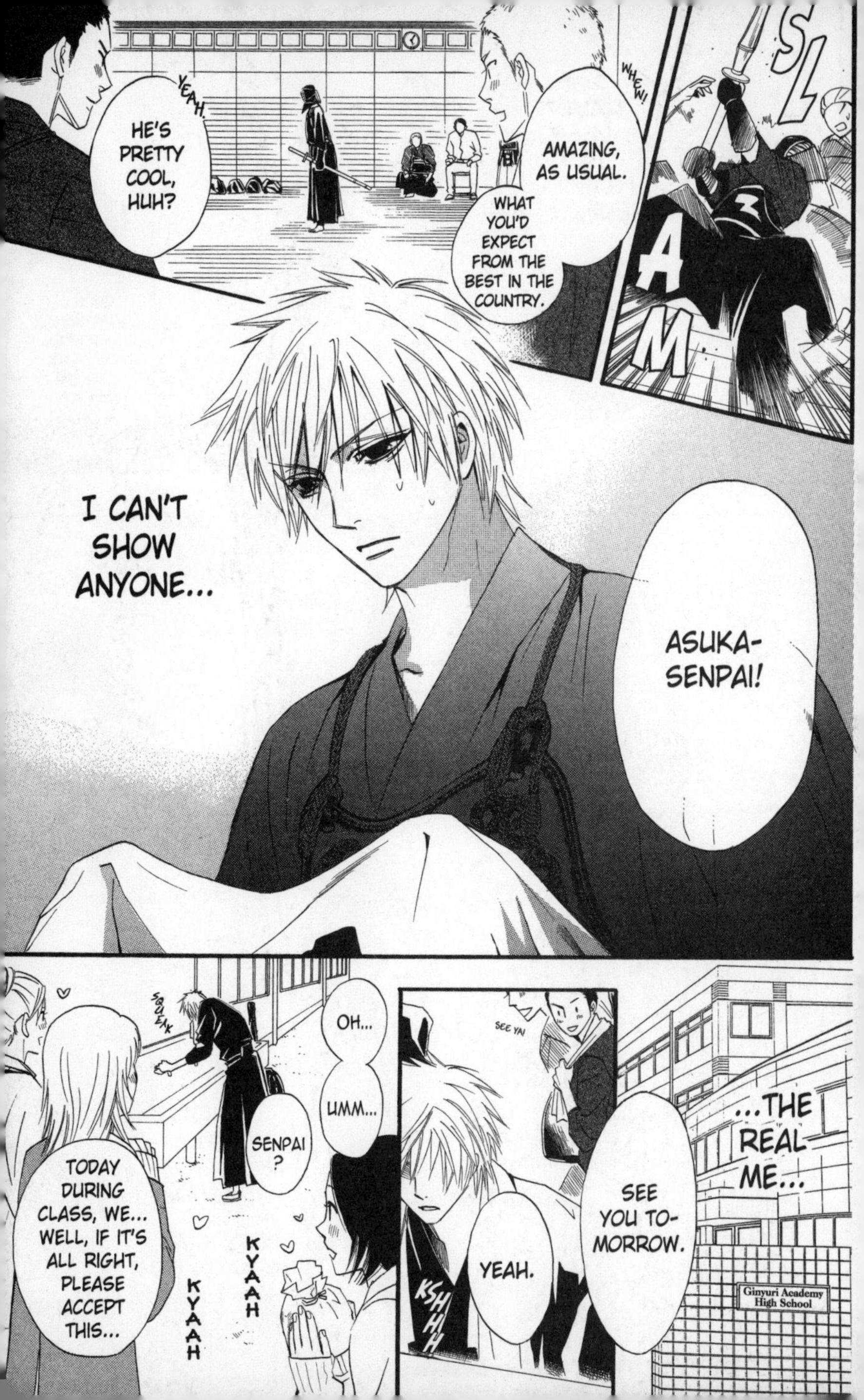
SLAM
WHEW!
AMAZING, AS USUAL.
WHAT YOU'D EXPECT FROM THE BEST IN THE COUNTRY.
YEAH.
HE'S PRETTY COOL, HUH?
ASUKA-SENPAI!
I CAN'T SHOW ANYONE...
...THE REAL ME...
Ginyuri Academy High School
SEE YA!
SEE YOU TO-MORROW.
YEAH.
KSHHH
SQUEAK
OH...
UMM...
SENPAI?
TODAY DURING CLASS, WE... WELL, IF IT'S ALL RIGHT, PLEASE ACCEPT THIS...
KYAAH
KYAAH

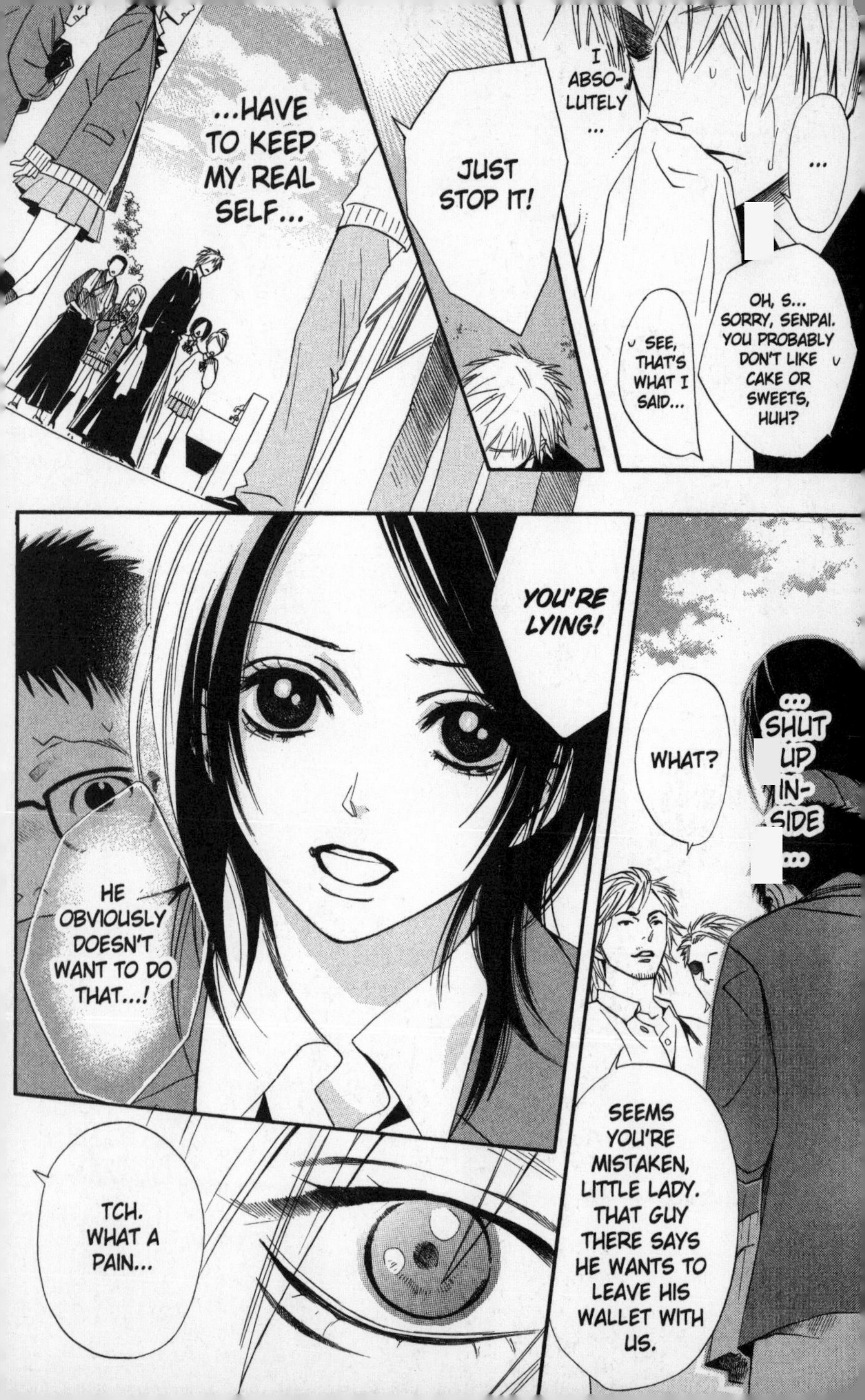

I ABSOLUTELY...
...
OH, S... SORRY, SENPAI. YOU PROBABLY DON'T LIKE CAKE OR SWEETS, HUH?
SEE, THAT'S WHAT I SAID...
JUST STOP IT!
...HAVE TO KEEP MY REAL SELF...
...SHUT UP INSIDE...
WHAT?
SEEMS YOU'RE MISTAKEN, LITTLE LADY. THAT GUY THERE SAYS HE WANTS TO LEAVE HIS WALLET WITH US.
YOU'RE LYING!
HE OBVIOUSLY DOESN'T WANT TO DO THAT...!
TCH. WHAT A PAIN...

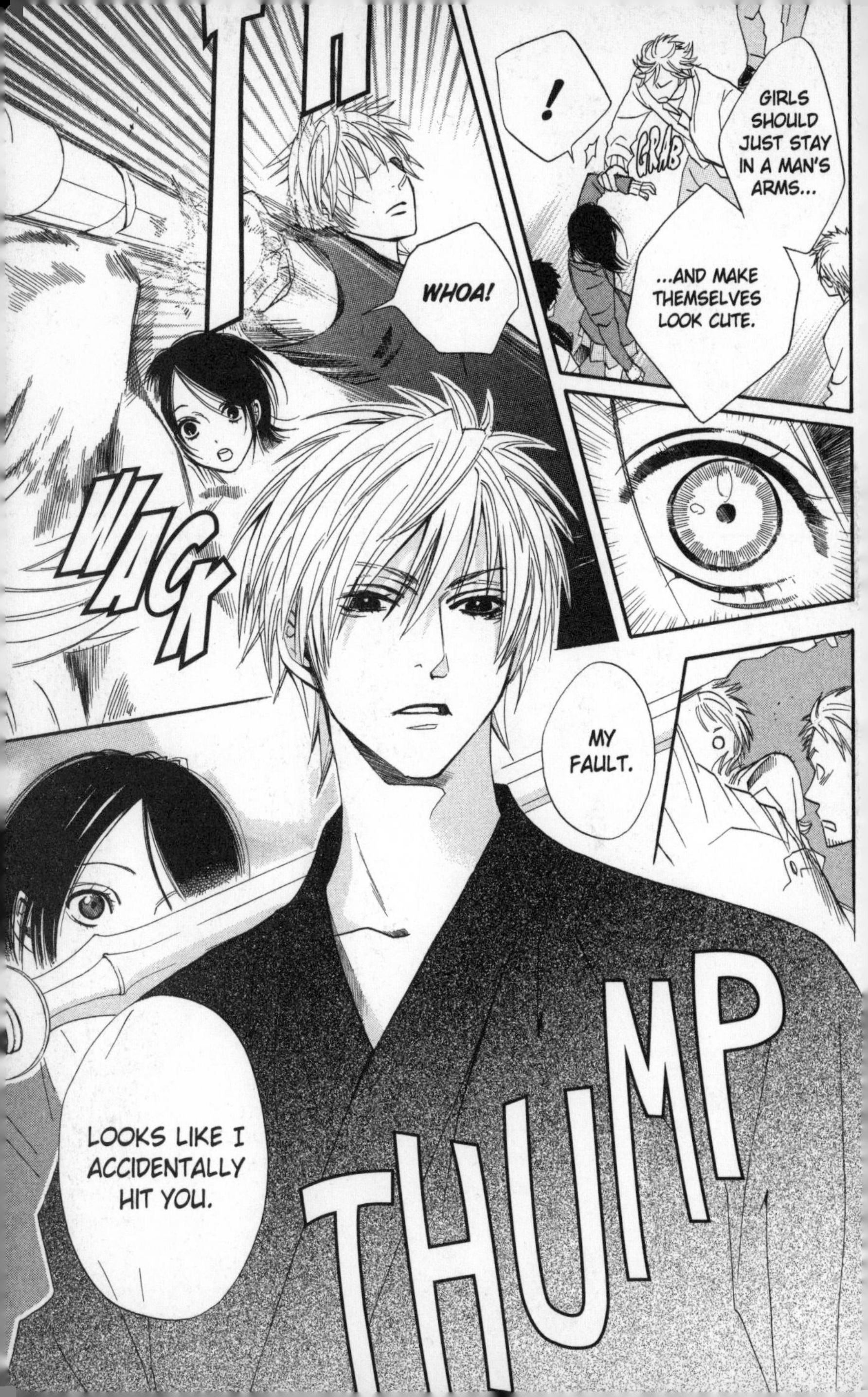
!
GRAB
GIRLS SHOULD JUST STAY IN A MAN'S ARMS...
...AND MAKE THEMSELVES LOOK CUTE.
WHOA!
WACK
MY FAULT.
LOOKS LIKE I ACCIDENTALLY HIT YOU.
THUMP

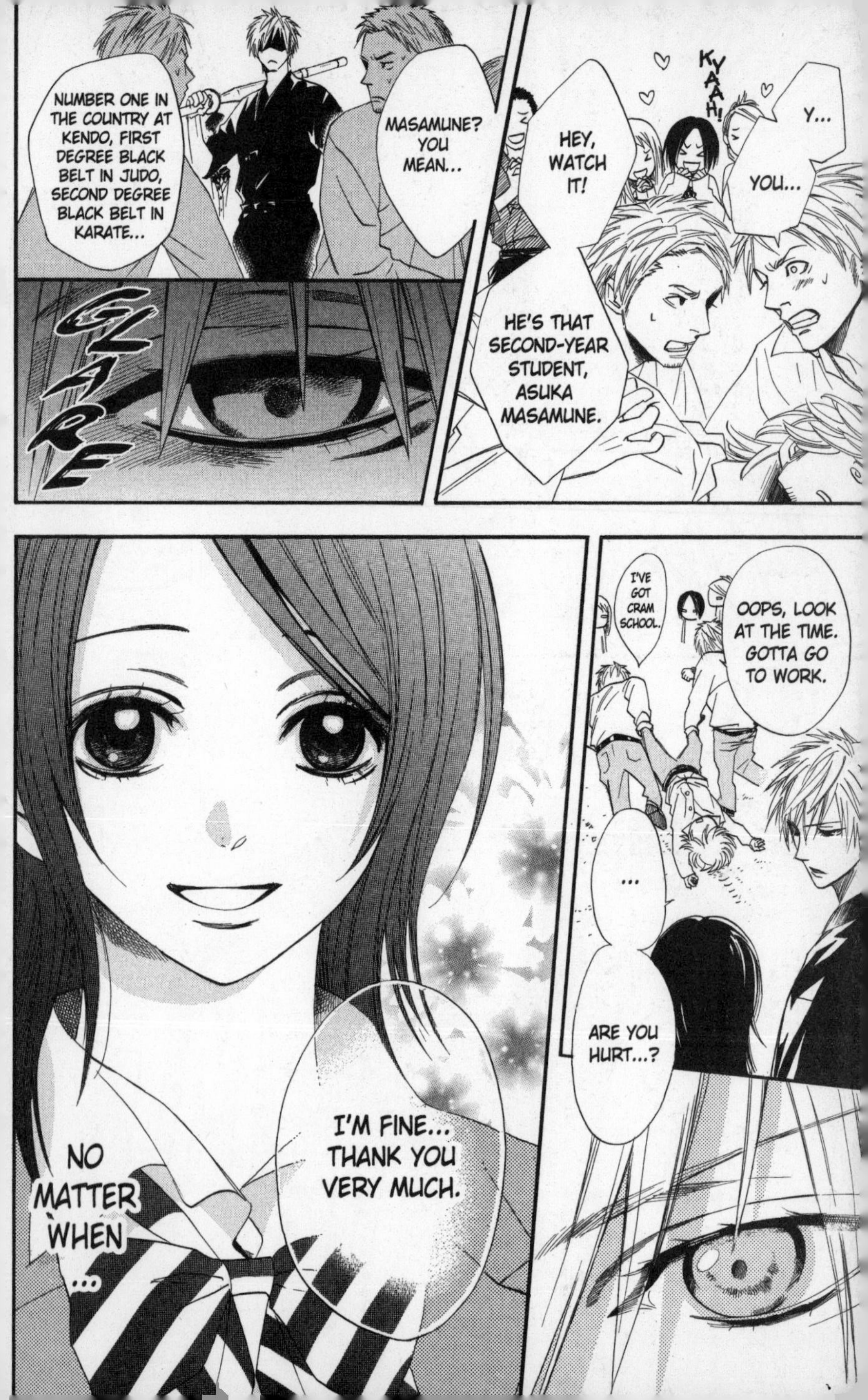
Y...
YOU...
KYAAH!
HEY, WATCH IT!
HE'S THAT SECOND-YEAR STUDENT, ASUKA MASAMUNE.
MASAMUNE? YOU MEAN...
NUMBER ONE IN THE COUNTRY AT KENDO, FIRST DEGREE BLACK BELT IN JUDO, SECOND DEGREE BLACK BELT IN KARATE...
GLARE
OOPS, LOOK AT THE TIME. GOTTA GO TO WORK.
I'VE GOT CRAM SCHOOL.
...
ARE YOU HURT...?
I'M FINE... THANK YOU VERY MUCH.
NO MATTER WHEN...

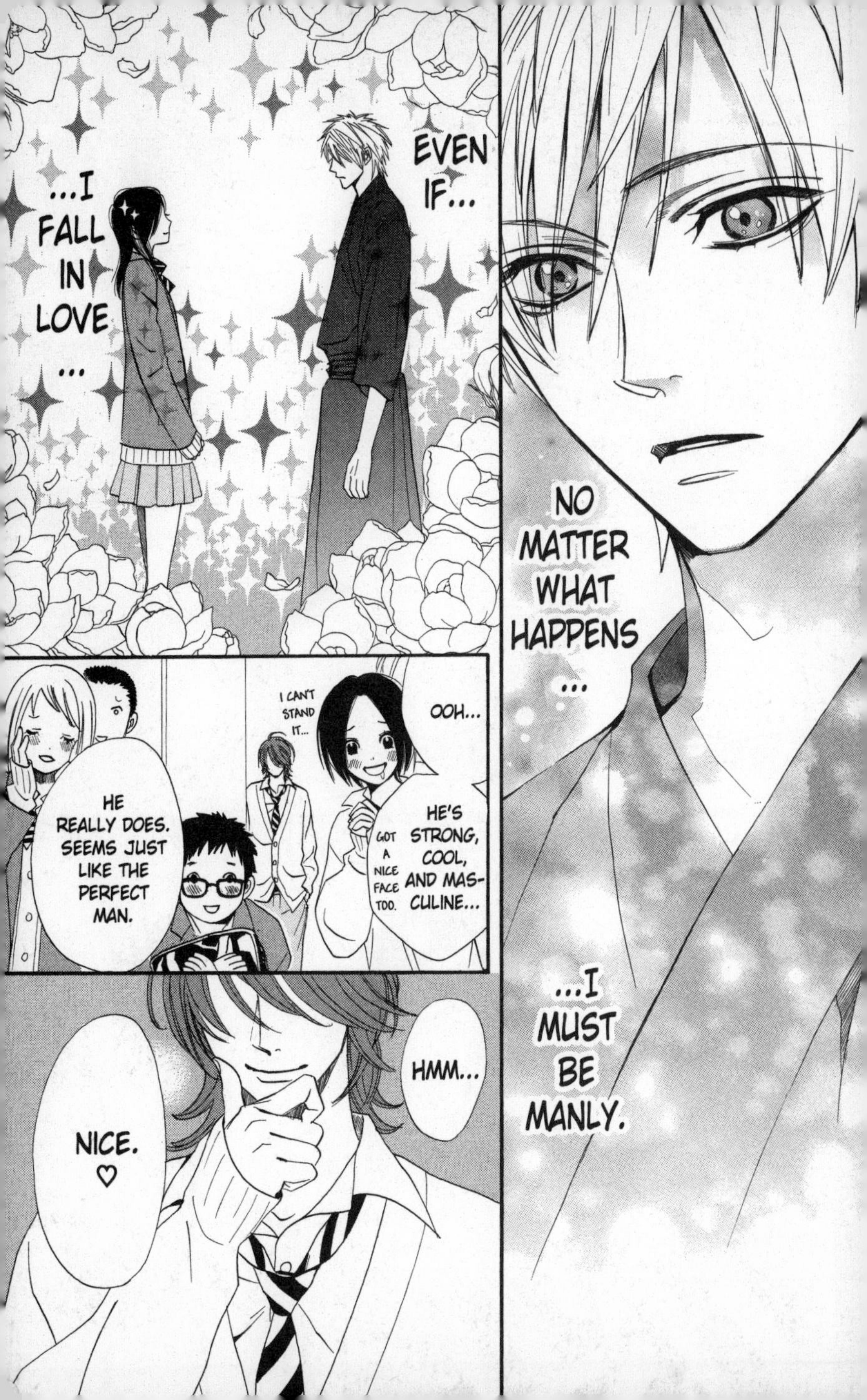
NO MATTER WHAT HAPPENS ...
...I MUST BE MANLY.
EVEN IF...
...I FALL IN LOVE ...
OOH...
I CAN'T STAND IT...
HE'S STRONG, COOL, AND MAS-CULINE...
GOT A NICE FACE TOO.
HE REALLY DOES. SEEMS JUST LIKE THE PERFECT MAN.
HMM...
NICE. ♡

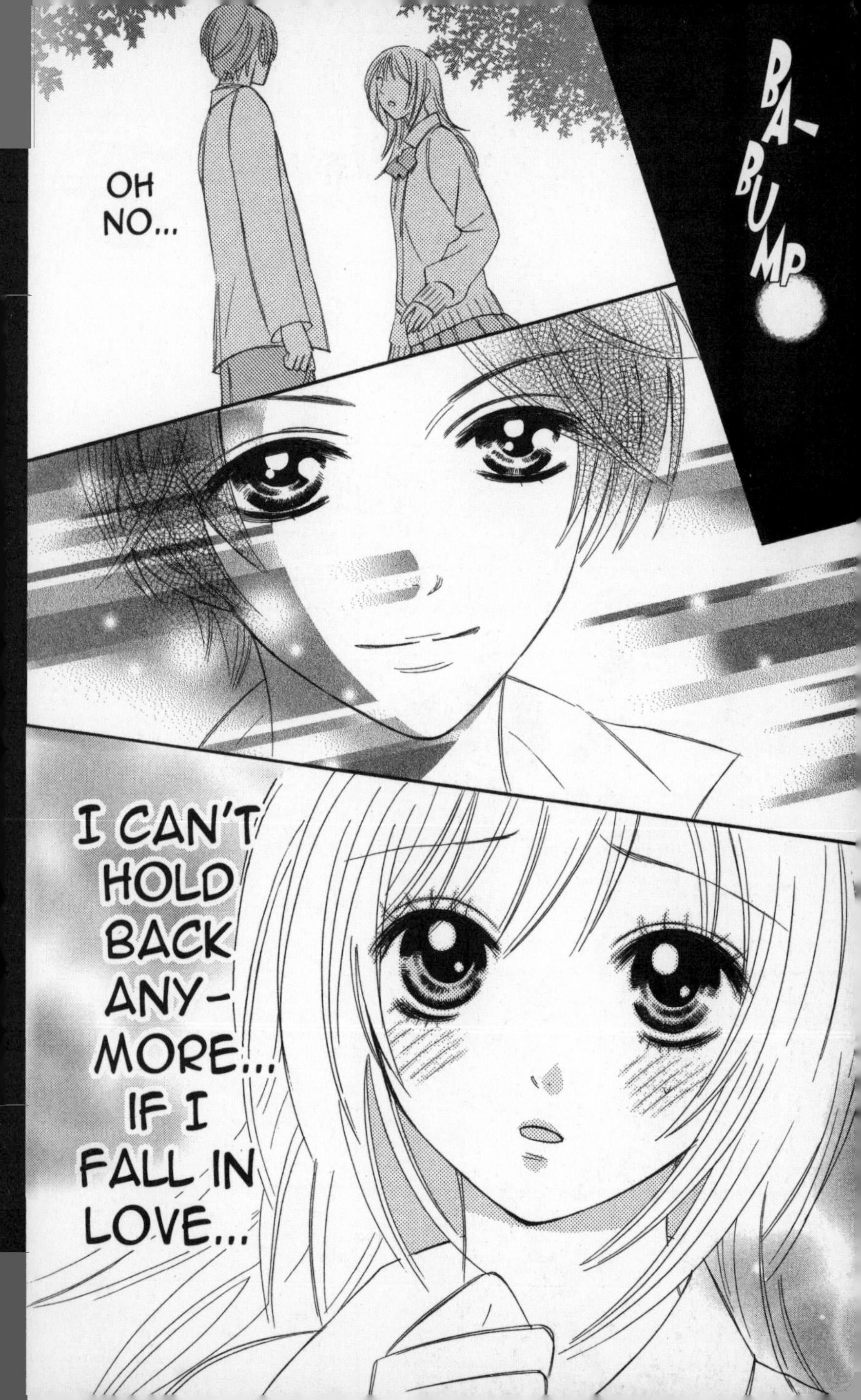
BA-BUMP
OH NO...
I CAN'T HOLD BACK ANY-MORE... IF I FALL IN LOVE...

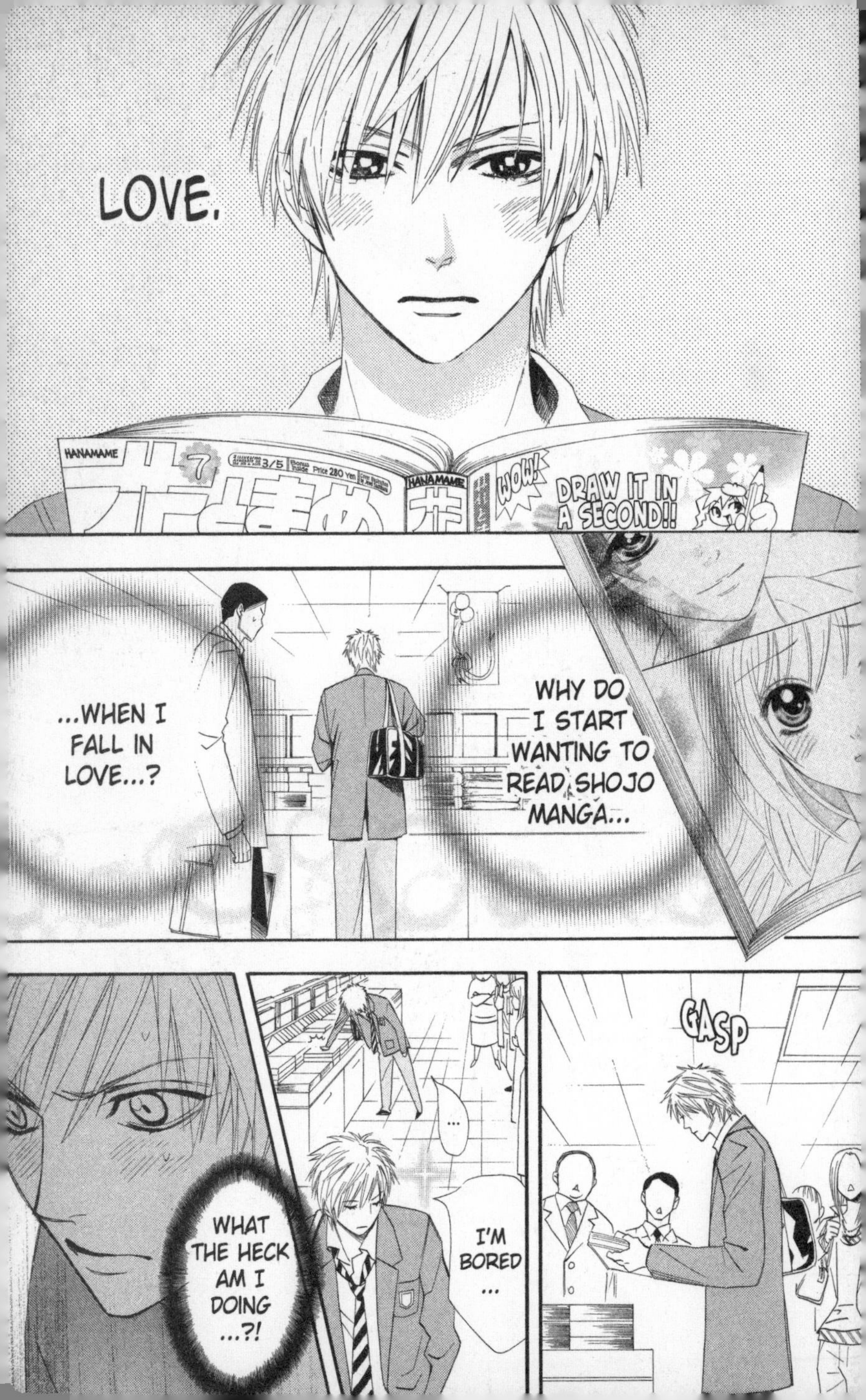
LOVE.
HANAMAME
7
3/5
Bonus Inside
Price 280 Yen
HANAMAME
WOW!
DRAW IT IN A SECOND!!
WHY DO I START WANTING TO READ SHOJO MANGA...
...WHEN I FALL IN LOVE...?
GASP
...
I'M BORED ...
WHAT THE HECK AM I DOING ...?!

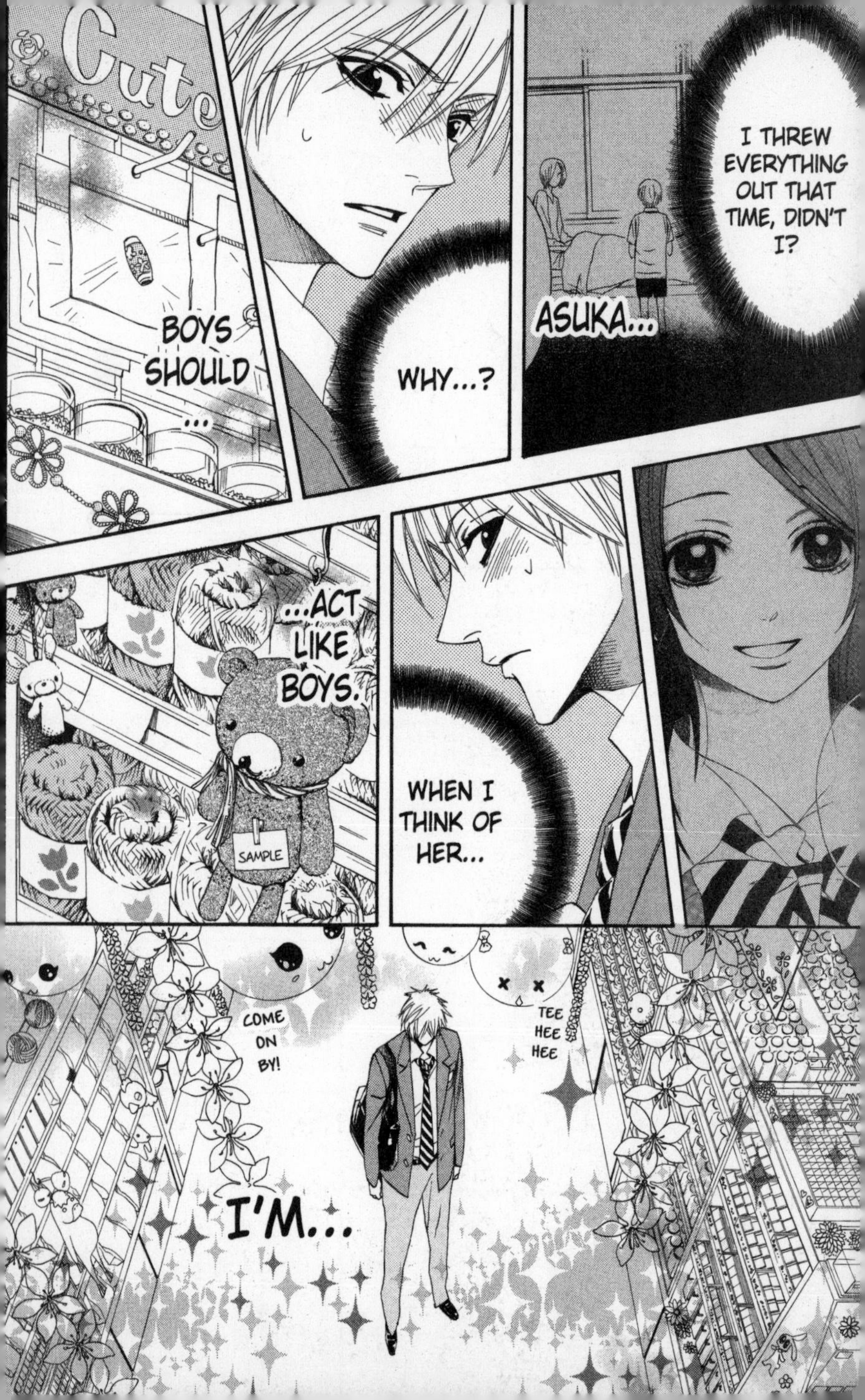
I THREW EVERYTHING OUT THAT TIME, DIDN'T I?
ASUKA...
WHY...?
Cute
BOYS SHOULD ...
WHEN I THINK OF HER...
...ACT LIKE BOYS.
SAMPLE
TEE HEE HEE
COME ON BY!
I'M...

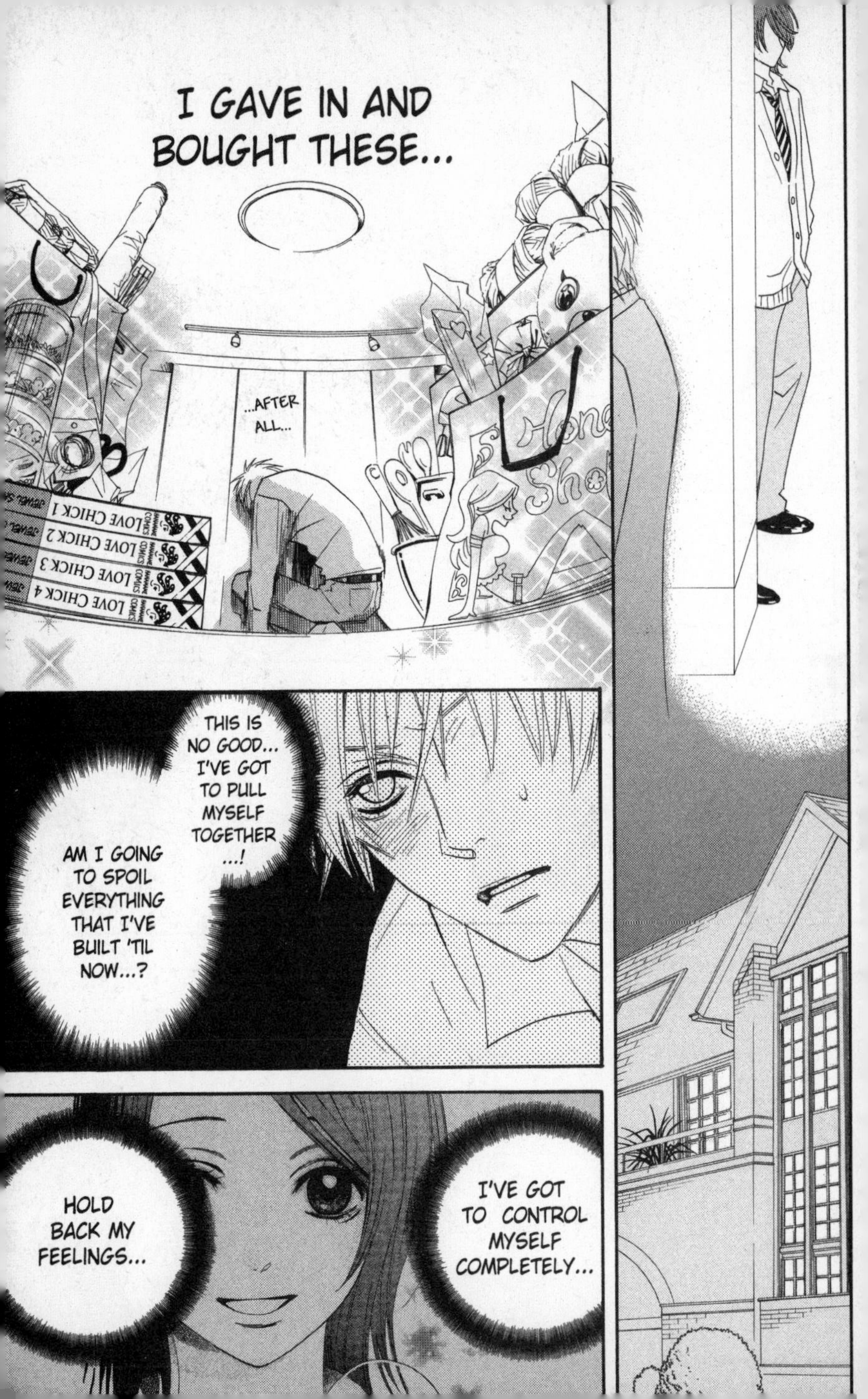
I GAVE IN AND BOUGHT THESE...
...AFTER ALL...
LOVE CHICK 1
LOVE CHICK 2
LOVE CHICK 3
LOVE CHICK 4
THIS IS NO GOOD... I'VE GOT TO PULL MYSELF TOGETHER ...!
AM I GOING TO SPOIL EVERYTHING THAT I'VE BUILT 'TIL NOW...?
I'VE GOT TO CONTROL MYSELF COMPLETELY...
HOLD BACK MY FEELINGS...

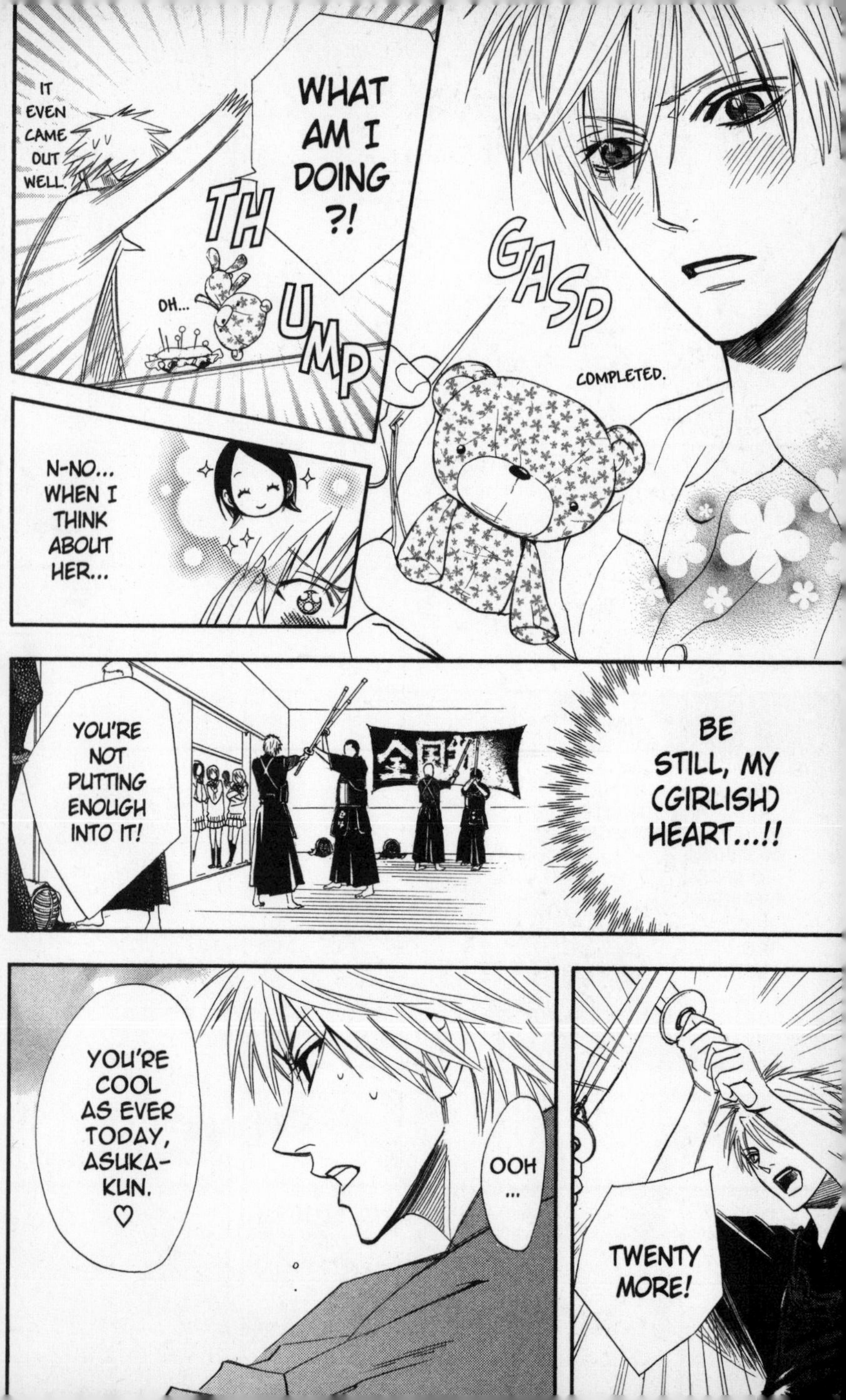
GASP
COMPLETED.
WHAT AM I DOING?!
IT EVEN CAME OUT WELL.
THUMP
OH...
N-NO... WHEN I THINK ABOUT HER...
BE STILL, MY (GIRLISH) HEART...!!
YOU'RE NOT PUTTING ENOUGH INTO IT!
TWENTY MORE!
OOH...
YOU'RE COOL AS EVER TODAY, ASUKA-KUN. ♡

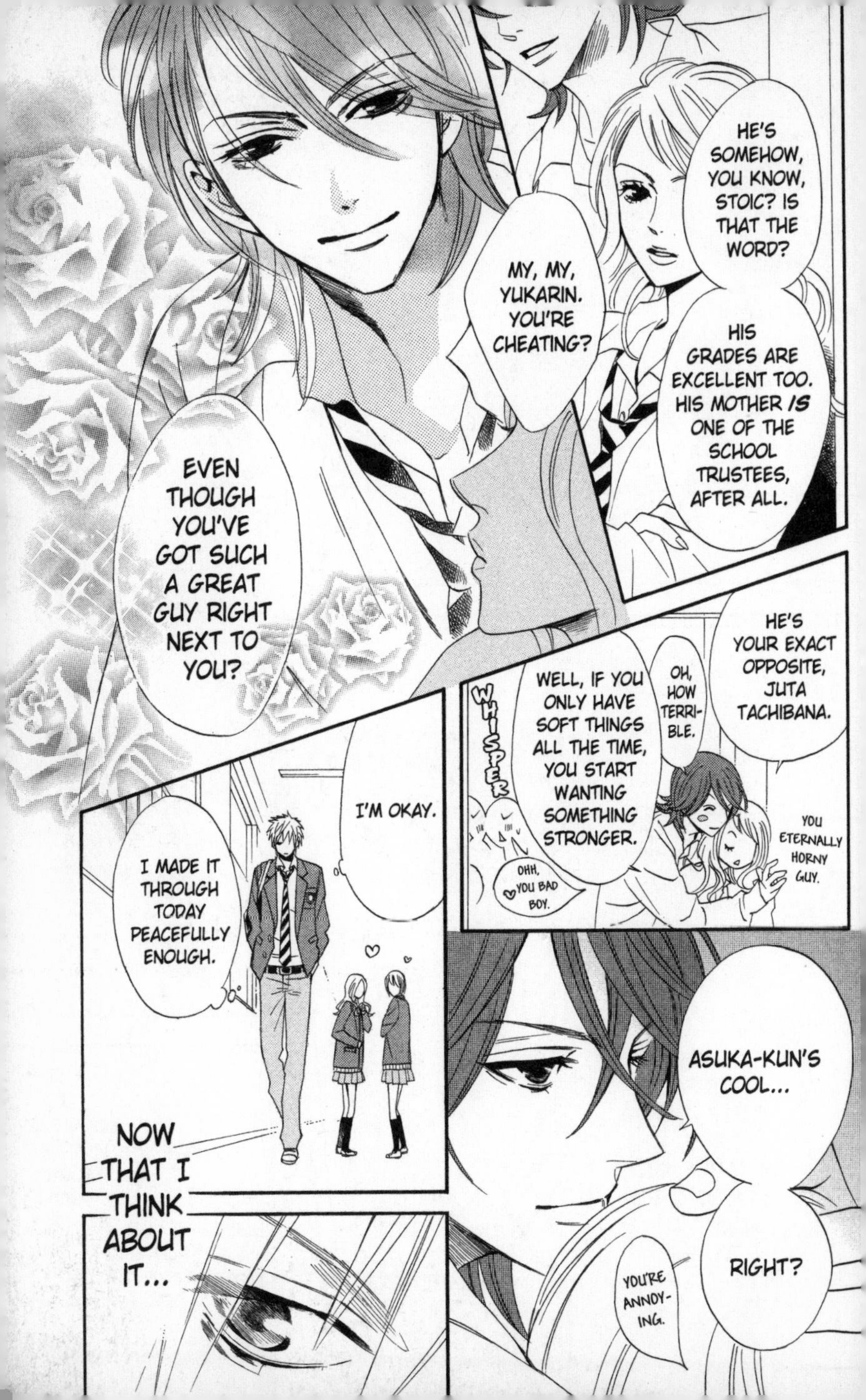
HE'S SOMEHOW, YOU KNOW, STOIC? IS THAT THE WORD?
HIS GRADES ARE EXCELLENT TOO. HIS MOTHER *IS* ONE OF THE SCHOOL TRUSTEES, AFTER ALL.
MY, MY, YUKARIN. YOU'RE CHEATING?
EVEN THOUGH YOU'VE GOT SUCH A GREAT GUY RIGHT NEXT TO YOU?
HE'S YOUR EXACT OPPOSITE, JUTA TACHIBANA.
OH, HOW TERRI-BLE.
WELL, IF YOU ONLY HAVE SOFT THINGS ALL THE TIME, YOU START WANTING SOMETHING STRONGER.
YOU ETERNALLY HORNY GUY.
OHH, YOU BAD BOY.
WHISPER
ASUKA-KUN'S COOL...
RIGHT?
YOU'RE ANNOY-ING.
I'M OKAY.
I MADE IT THROUGH TODAY PEACEFULLY ENOUGH.
NOW THAT I THINK ABOUT IT...

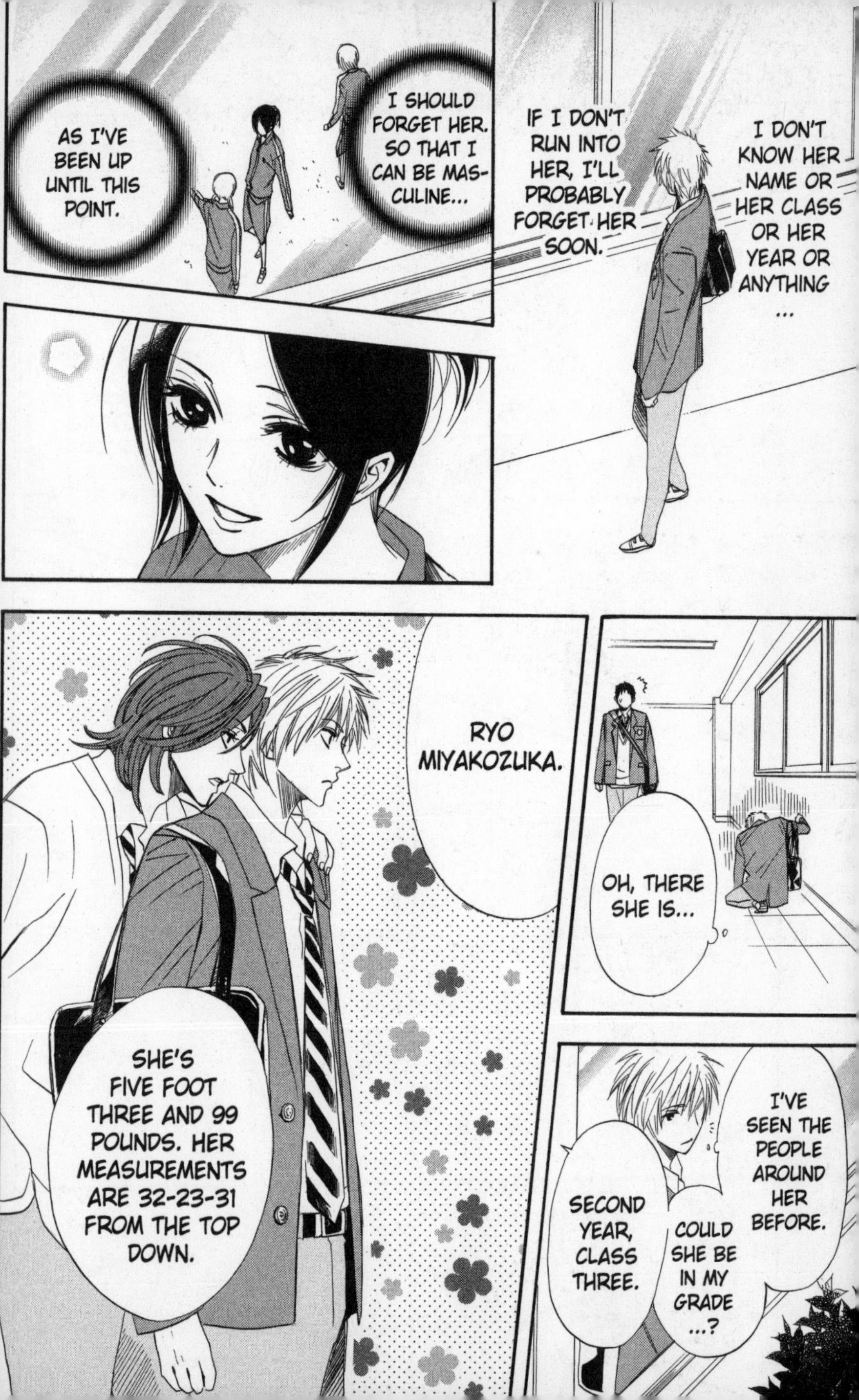
I DON'T KNOW HER NAME OR HER CLASS OR HER YEAR OR ANYTHING ...
IF I DON'T RUN INTO HER, I'LL PROBABLY FORGET HER SOON.
I SHOULD FORGET HER. SO THAT I CAN BE MAS-CULINE...
AS I'VE BEEN UP UNTIL THIS POINT.
OH, THERE SHE IS...
I'VE SEEN THE PEOPLE AROUND HER BEFORE.
COULD SHE BE IN MY GRADE ...?
SECOND YEAR, CLASS THREE.
RYO MIYAKOZUKA.
SHE'S FIVE FOOT THREE AND 99 POUNDS. HER MEASUREMENTS ARE 32-23-31 FROM THE TOP DOWN.

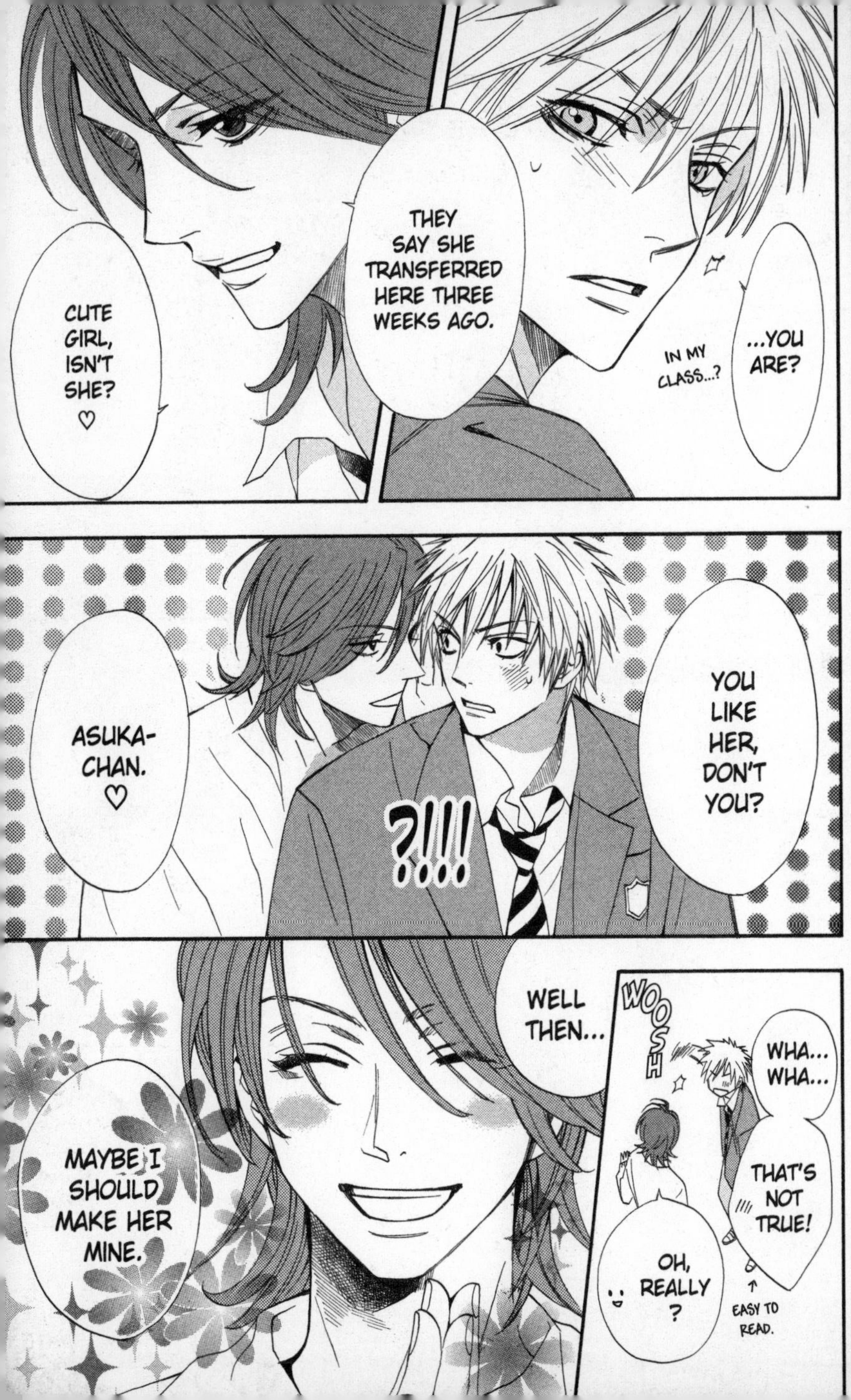
...YOU ARE?
IN MY CLASS...?
THEY SAY SHE TRANSFERRED HERE THREE WEEKS AGO.
CUTE GIRL, ISN'T SHE? ♡
YOU LIKE HER, DON'T YOU?
?!!!
ASUKA-CHAN. ♡
WOOSH
WHA... WHA...
THAT'S NOT TRUE!
EASY TO READ.
OH, REALLY?
WELL THEN...
MAYBE I SHOULD MAKE HER MINE.

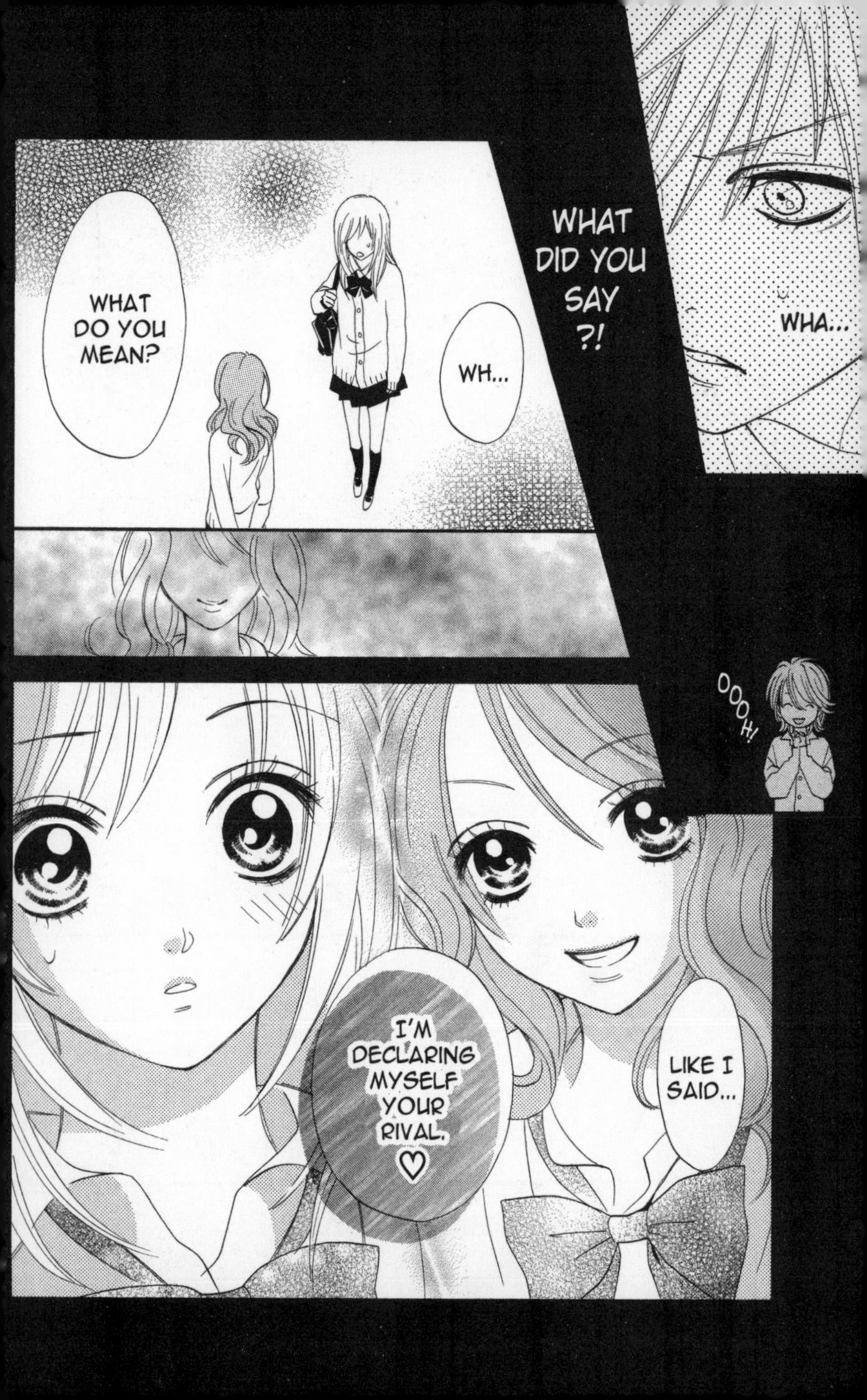
WHA...
WHAT DID YOU SAY ?!
WH...
WHAT DO YOU MEAN?
OOOH!
LIKE I SAID...
I'M DECLARING MYSELF YOUR RIVAL. ♡

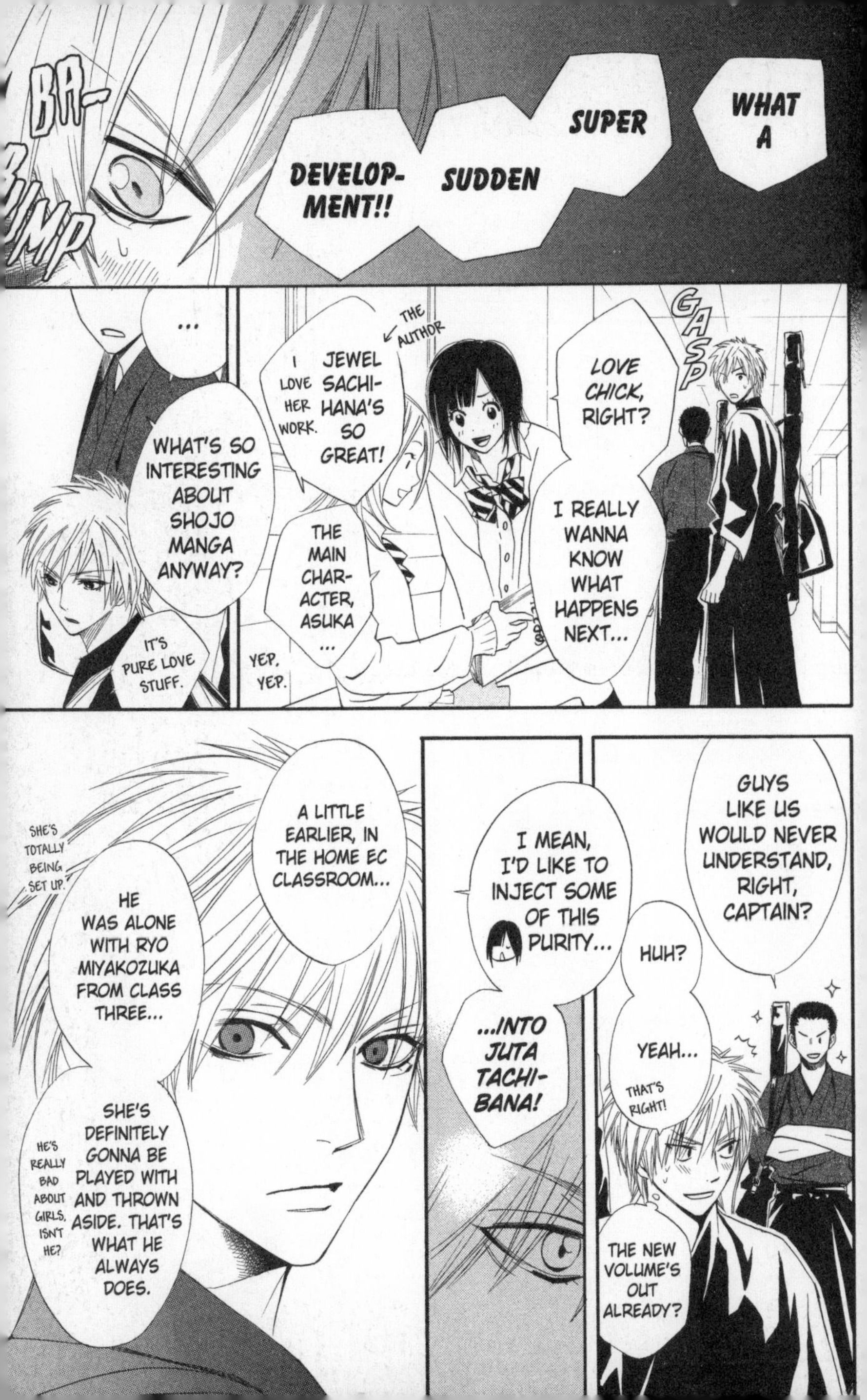

WHAT A SUPER SUDDEN DEVELOPMENT!!
BA-BUMP
GASP
LOVE CHICK, RIGHT?
I REALLY WANNA KNOW WHAT HAPPENS NEXT...
JEWEL SACHIHANA'S SO GREAT!
THE AUTHOR
I LOVE HER WORK.
THE MAIN CHARACTER, ASUKA...
YEP, YEP.
...
WHAT'S SO INTERESTING ABOUT SHOJO MANGA ANYWAY?
IT'S PURE LOVE STUFF.
GUYS LIKE US WOULD NEVER UNDERSTAND, RIGHT, CAPTAIN?
HUH?
YEAH...
THAT'S RIGHT!
THE NEW VOLUME'S OUT ALREADY?
I MEAN, I'D LIKE TO INJECT SOME OF THIS PURITY...
...INTO JUTA TACHIBANA!
A LITTLE EARLIER, IN THE HOME EC CLASSROOM...
HE WAS ALONE WITH RYO MIYAKOZUKA FROM CLASS THREE...
SHE'S TOTALLY BEING SET UP.
SHE'S DEFINITELY GONNA BE PLAYED WITH AND THROWN ASIDE. THAT'S WHAT HE ALWAYS DOES.
HE'S REALLY BAD ABOUT GIRLS, ISN'T HE?

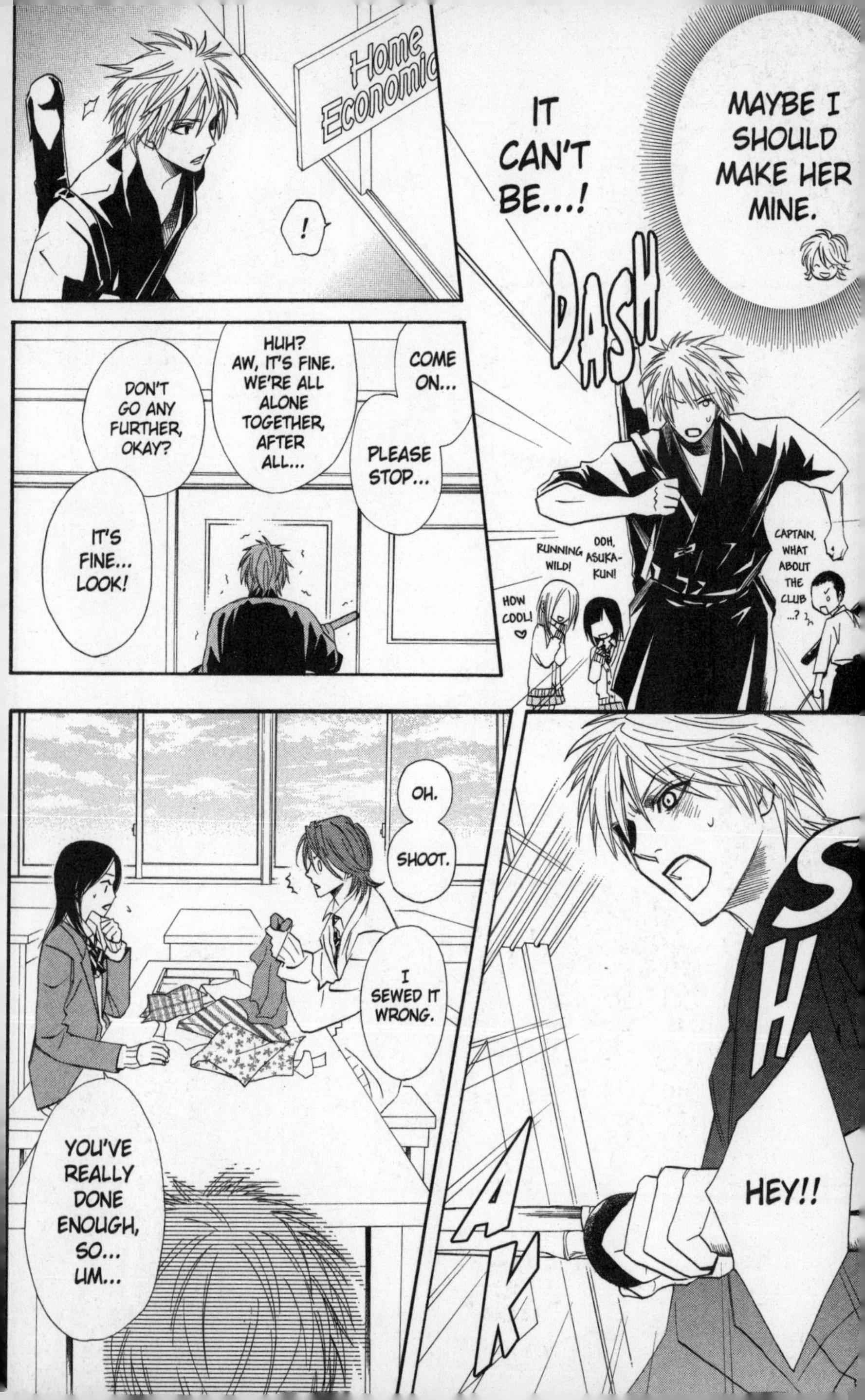
MAYBE I SHOULD MAKE HER MINE.
IT CAN'T BE...!
DASH
CAPTAIN, WHAT ABOUT THE CLUB ...?
OOH, ASUKA-KUN!
RUNNING WILD!
HOW COOL!
Home Economic
!
COME ON...
HUH? AW, IT'S FINE. WE'RE ALL ALONE TOGETHER, AFTER ALL...
DON'T GO ANY FURTHER, OKAY?
PLEASE STOP...
IT'S FINE... LOOK!
SH
HEY!!
AK
OH.
SHOOT.
I SEWED IT WRONG.
YOU'VE REALLY DONE ENOUGH, SO... UM...

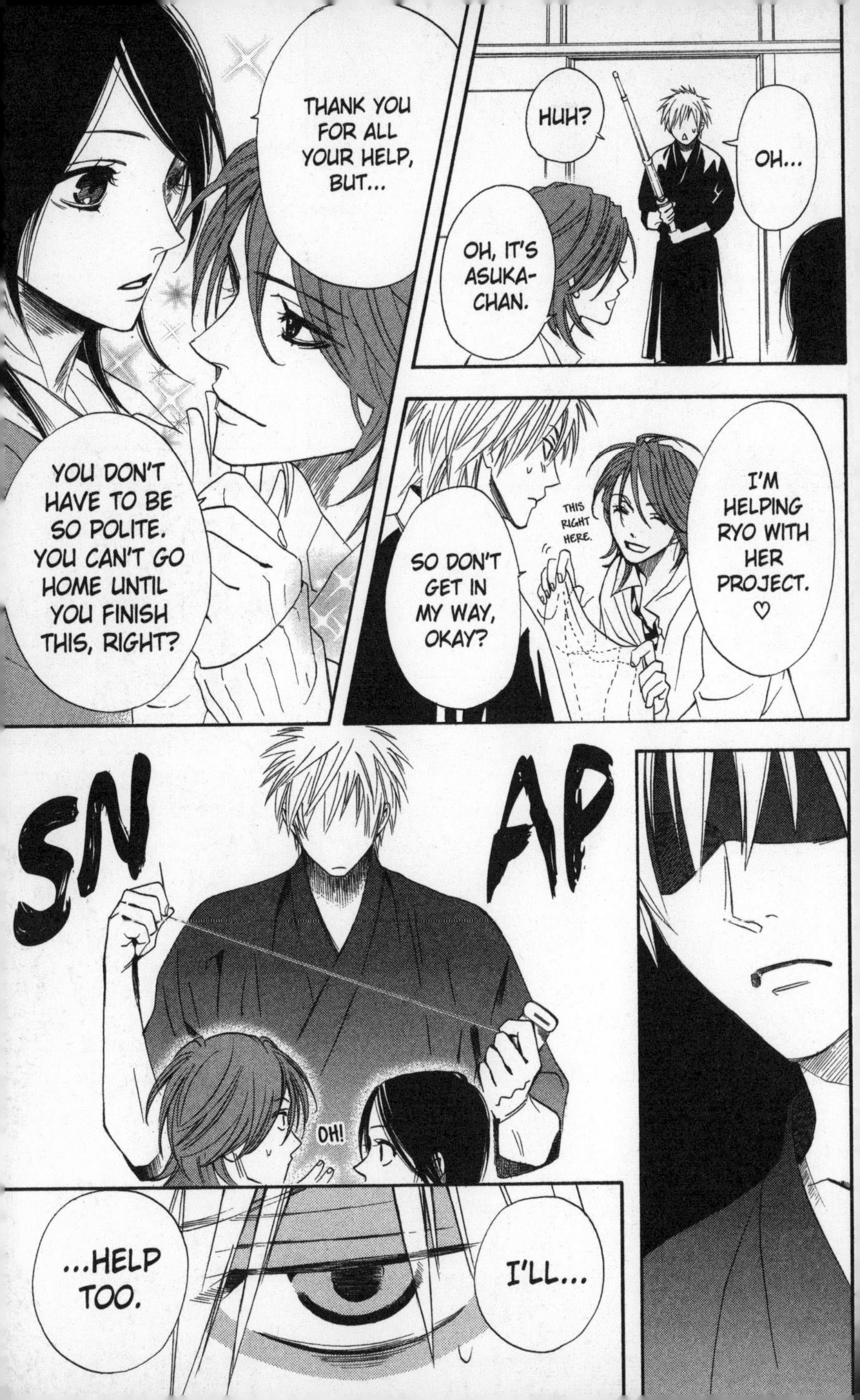
OH...
HUH?
OH, IT'S ASUKA-CHAN.
I'M HELPING RYO WITH HER PROJECT. ♡
THIS RIGHT HERE.
SO DON'T GET IN MY WAY, OKAY?
THANK YOU FOR ALL YOUR HELP, BUT...
YOU DON'T HAVE TO BE SO POLITE. YOU CAN'T GO HOME UNTIL YOU FINISH THIS, RIGHT?
SNAP
OH!
I'LL...
...HELP TOO.

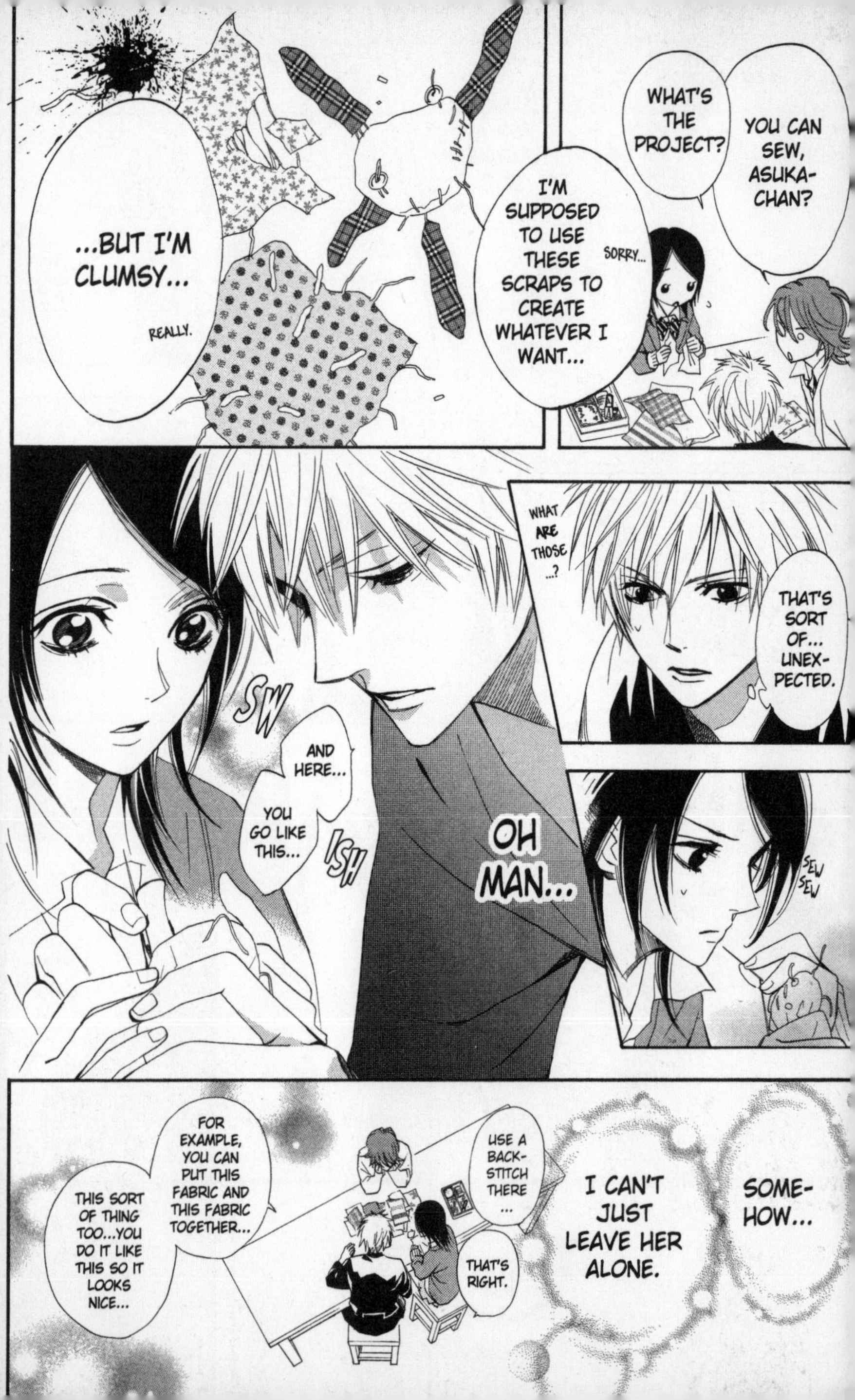
YOU CAN SEW, ASUKA-CHAN?
WHAT'S THE PROJECT?
SORRY...
I'M SUPPOSED TO USE THESE SCRAPS TO CREATE WHATEVER I WANT...
...BUT I'M CLUMSY...
REALLY.
WHAT ARE THOSE ...?
THAT'S SORT OF... UNEXPECTED.
SEW SEW
OH MAN...
AND HERE...
SW
YOU GO LIKE THIS...
ISH
SOME-HOW...
I CAN'T JUST LEAVE HER ALONE.
USE A BACK-STITCH THERE ...
THAT'S RIGHT.
FOR EXAMPLE, YOU CAN PUT THIS FABRIC AND THIS FABRIC TOGETHER...
THIS SORT OF THING TOO...YOU DO IT LIKE THIS SO IT LOOKS NICE...

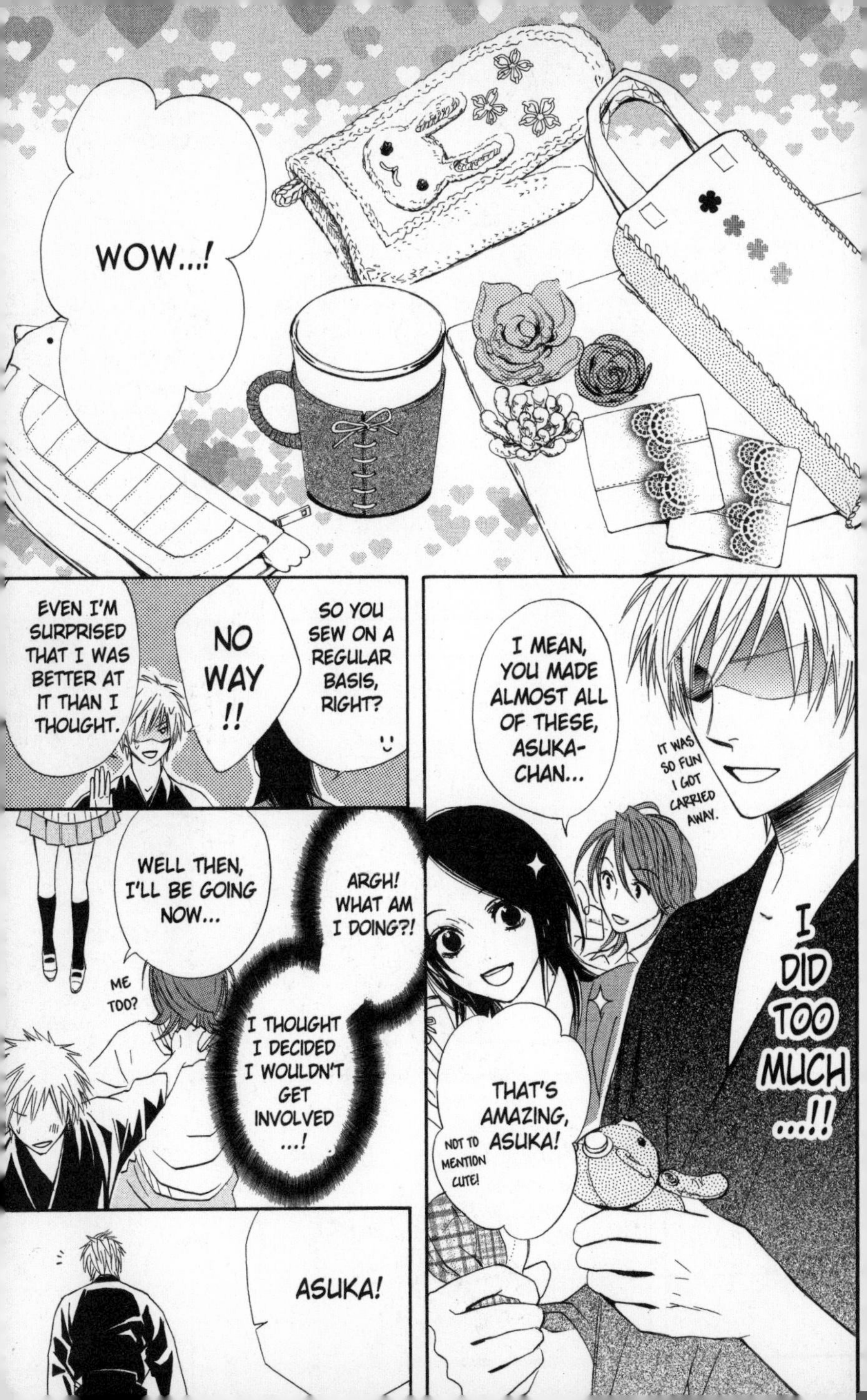
WOW...!
I MEAN, YOU MADE ALMOST ALL OF THESE, ASUKA-CHAN...
IT WAS SO FUN I GOT CARRIED AWAY.
I DID TOO MUCH ...!!
THAT'S AMAZING, ASUKA!
NOT TO MENTION CUTE!
SO YOU SEW ON A REGULAR BASIS, RIGHT?
NO WAY !!
EVEN I'M SURPRISED THAT I WAS BETTER AT IT THAN I THOUGHT.
ARGH! WHAT AM I DOING?!
WELL THEN, I'LL BE GOING NOW...
I THOUGHT I DECIDED I WOULDN'T GET INVOLVED ...!
ME TOO?
ASUKA!

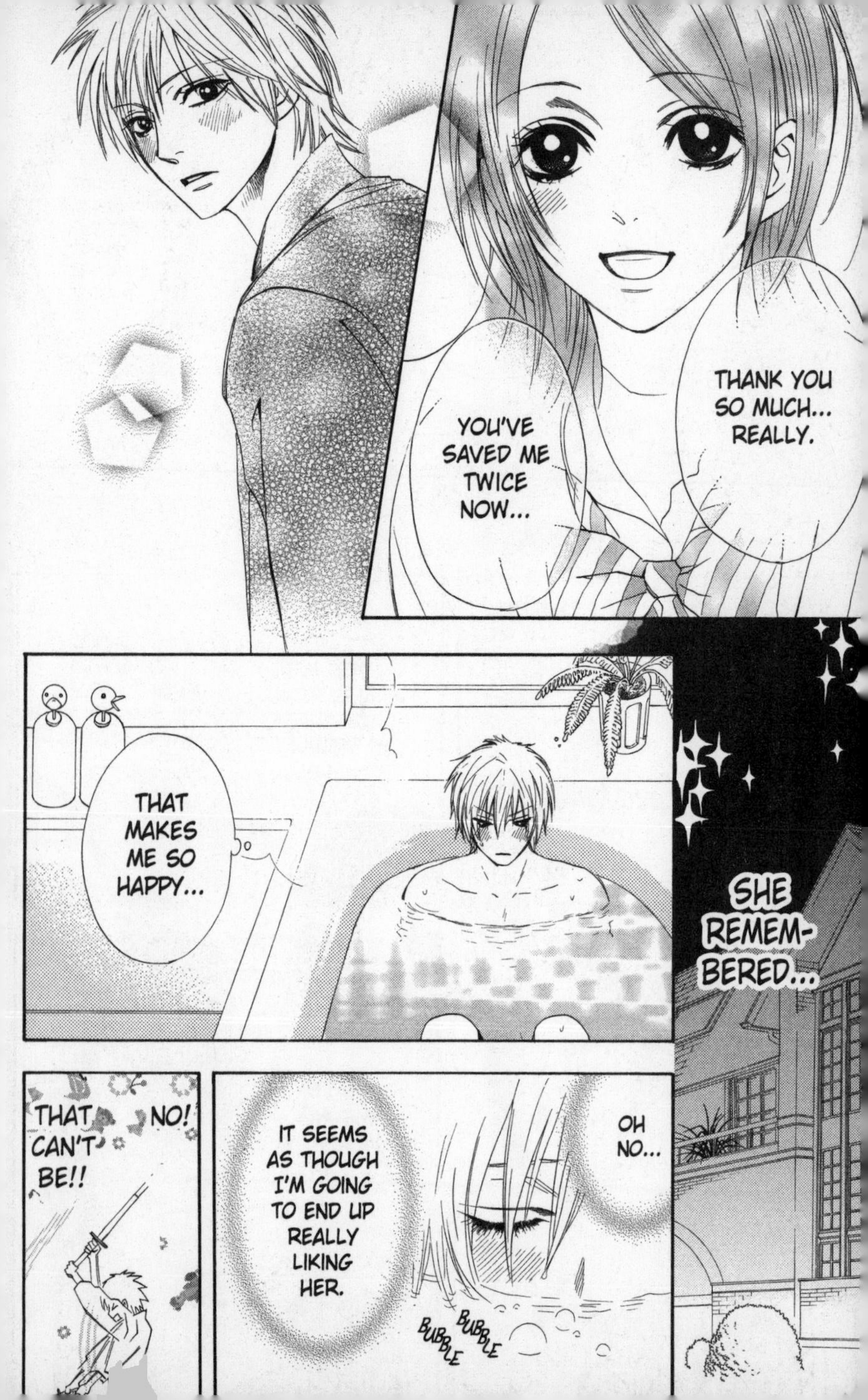
THANK YOU SO MUCH... REALLY.
YOU'VE SAVED ME TWICE NOW...
SHE REMEM-BERED...
THAT MAKES ME SO HAPPY...
OH NO...
IT SEEMS AS THOUGH I'M GOING TO END UP REALLY LIKING HER.
BUBBLE
BUBBLE
NO!
THAT CAN'T BE!!

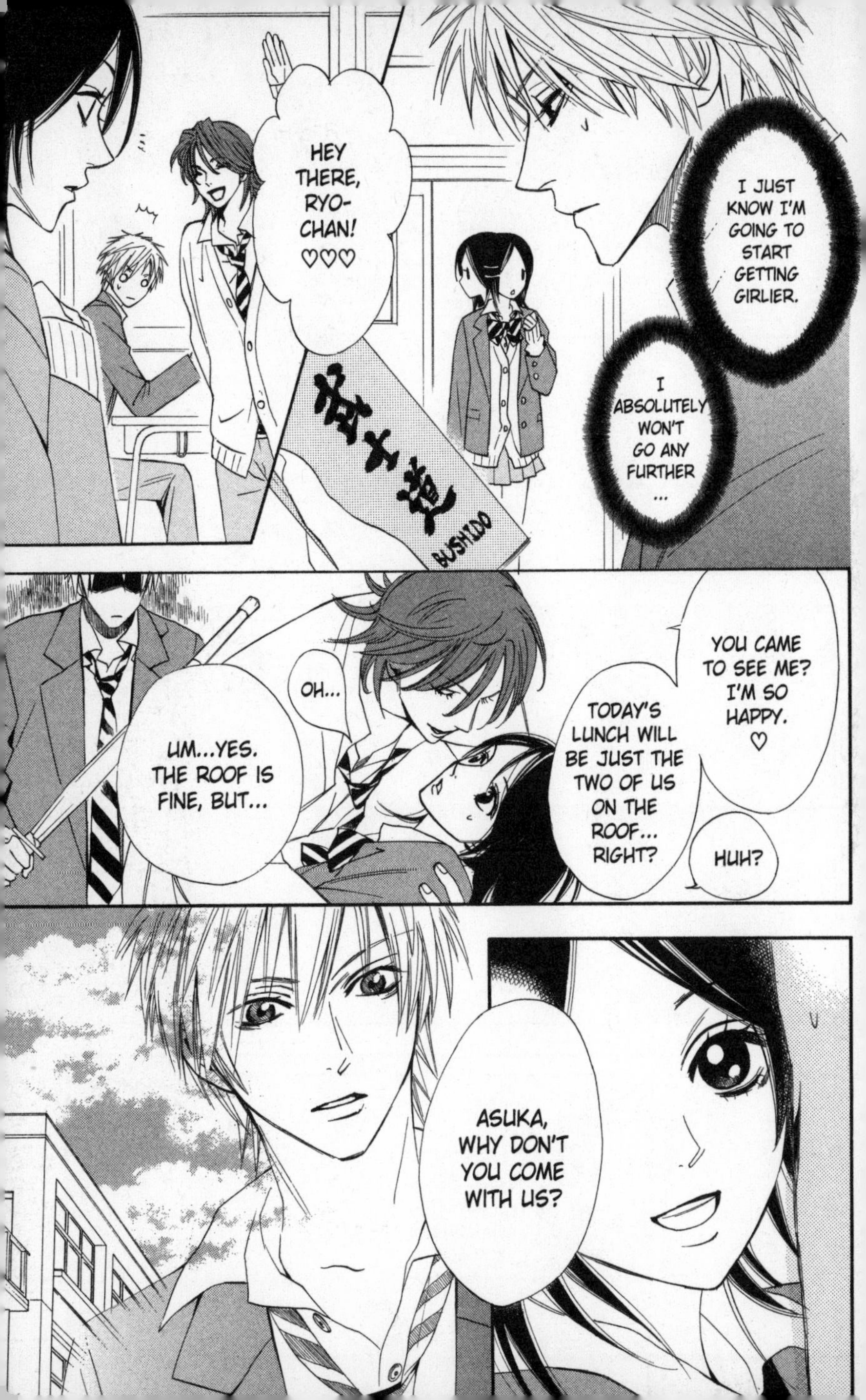
I JUST KNOW I'M GOING TO START GETTING GIRLIER.
I ABSOLUTELY WON'T GO ANY FURTHER ...
HEY THERE, RYO-CHAN! ♡♡♡
BUSHIDO
YOU CAME TO SEE ME? I'M SO HAPPY. ♡
HUH?
TODAY'S LUNCH WILL BE JUST THE TWO OF US ON THE ROOF... RIGHT?
OH...
UM...YES. THE ROOF IS FINE, BUT...
ASUKA, WHY DON'T YOU COME WITH US?

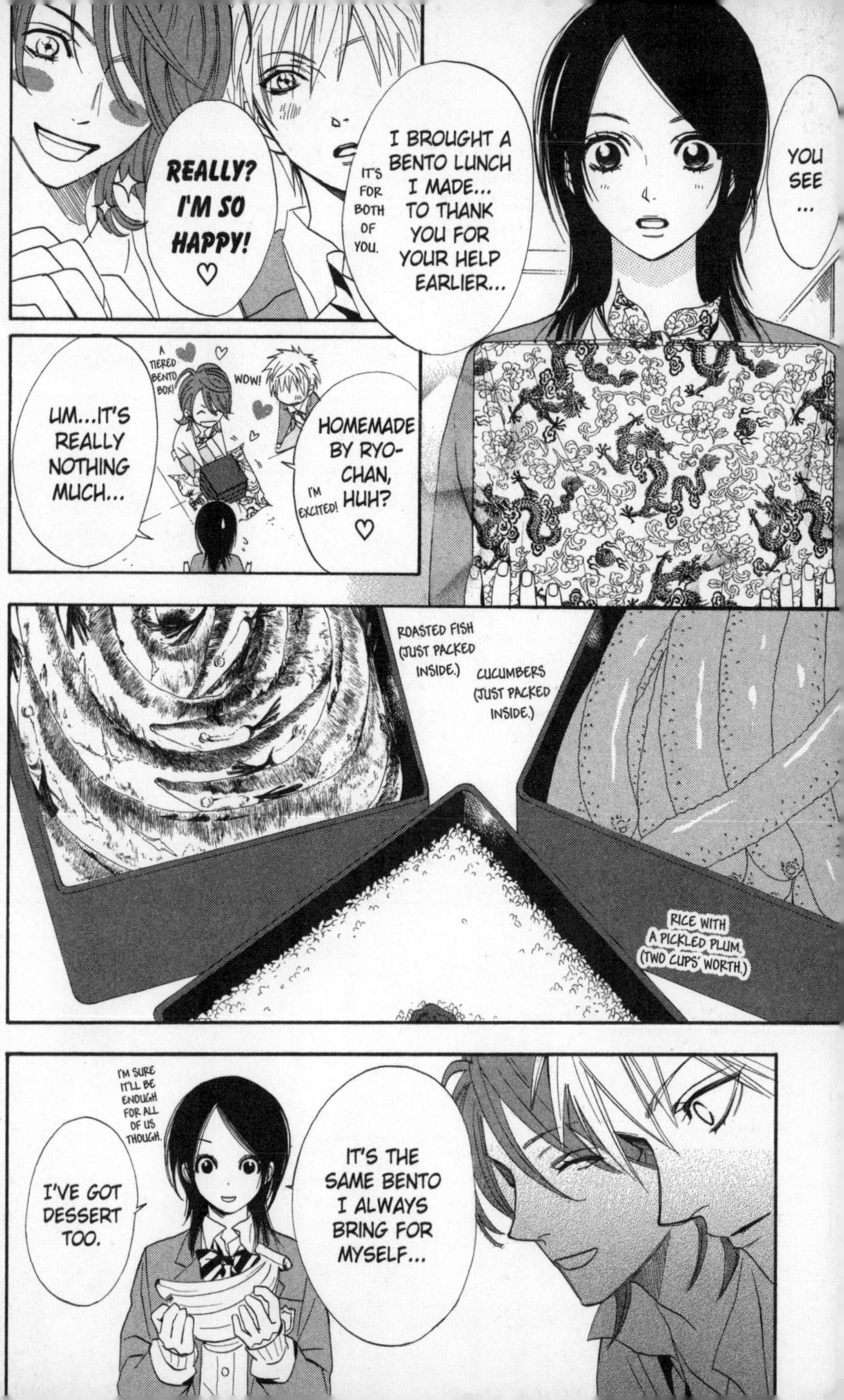
YOU SEE...
I BROUGHT A BENTO LUNCH I MADE... TO THANK YOU FOR YOUR HELP EARLIER...
IT'S FOR BOTH OF YOU.
REALLY? I'M SO HAPPY! ♡
HOMEMADE BY RYO-CHAN, HUH? ♡
I'M EXCITED!
WOW!
A TIERED BENTO BOX!
UM...IT'S REALLY NOTHING MUCH...
CUCUMBERS (JUST PACKED INSIDE.)
ROASTED FISH (JUST PACKED INSIDE.)
RICE WITH A PICKLED PLUM. (TWO CUPS' WORTH.)
IT'S THE SAME BENTO I ALWAYS BRING FOR MYSELF...
I'M SURE IT'LL BE ENOUGH FOR ALL OF US THOUGH.
I'VE GOT DESSERT TOO.

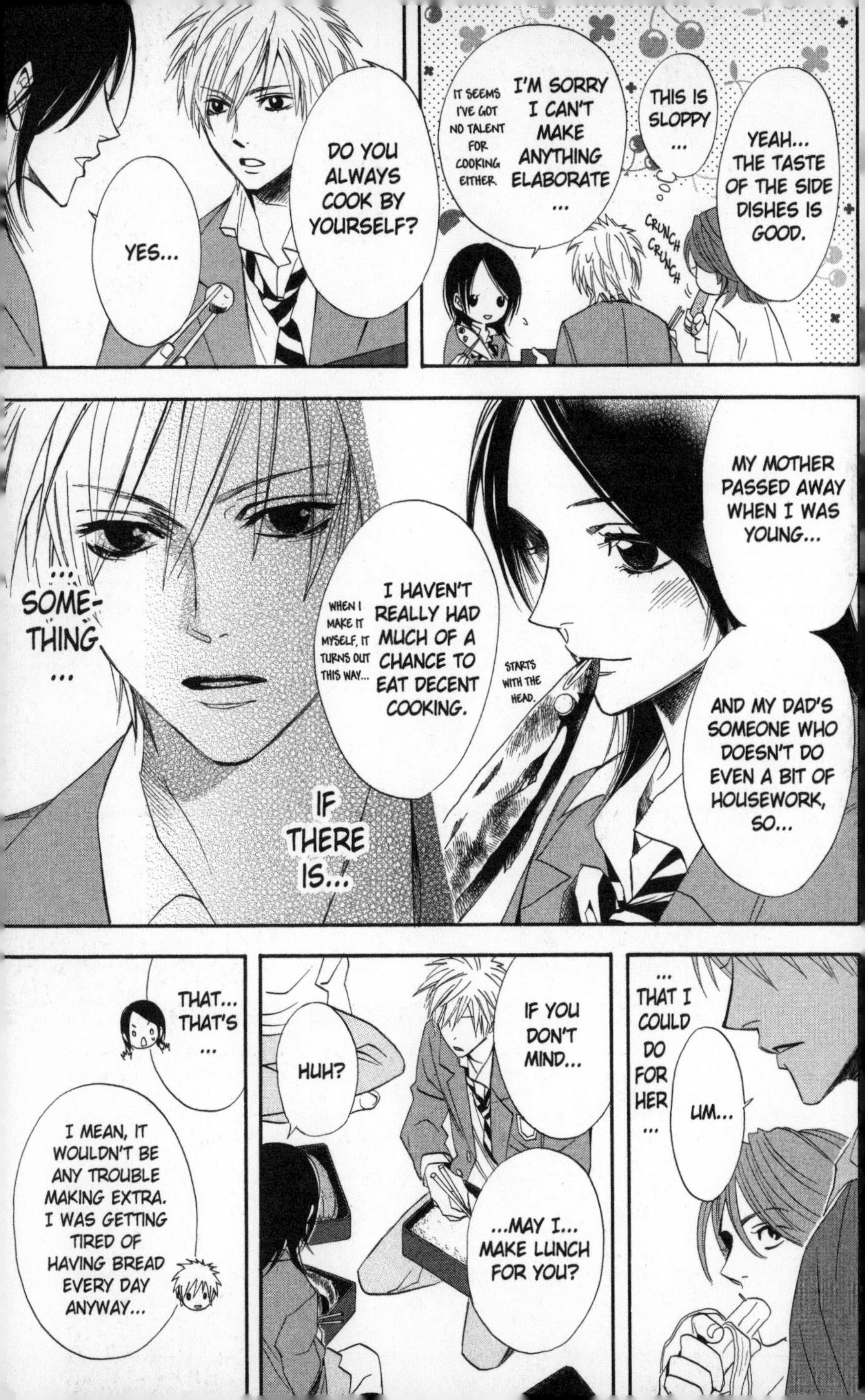
YEAH... THE TASTE OF THE SIDE DISHES IS GOOD.
CRUNCH CRUNCH
THIS IS SLOPPY...
I'M SORRY I CAN'T MAKE ANYTHING ELABORATE...
IT SEEMS I'VE GOT NO TALENT FOR COOKING EITHER.
DO YOU ALWAYS COOK BY YOURSELF?
YES...
MY MOTHER PASSED AWAY WHEN I WAS YOUNG...
AND MY DAD'S SOMEONE WHO DOESN'T DO EVEN A BIT OF HOUSEWORK, SO...
STARTS WITH THE HEAD.
I HAVEN'T REALLY HAD MUCH OF A CHANCE TO EAT DECENT COOKING.
WHEN I MAKE IT MYSELF, IT TURNS OUT THIS WAY...
...SOMETHING...
IF THERE IS...
...THAT I COULD DO FOR HER...
UM...
IF YOU DON'T MIND...
HUH?
...MAY I... MAKE LUNCH FOR YOU?
THAT... THAT'S...
I MEAN, IT WOULDN'T BE ANY TROUBLE MAKING EXTRA. I WAS GETTING TIRED OF HAVING BREAD EVERY DAY ANYWAY...

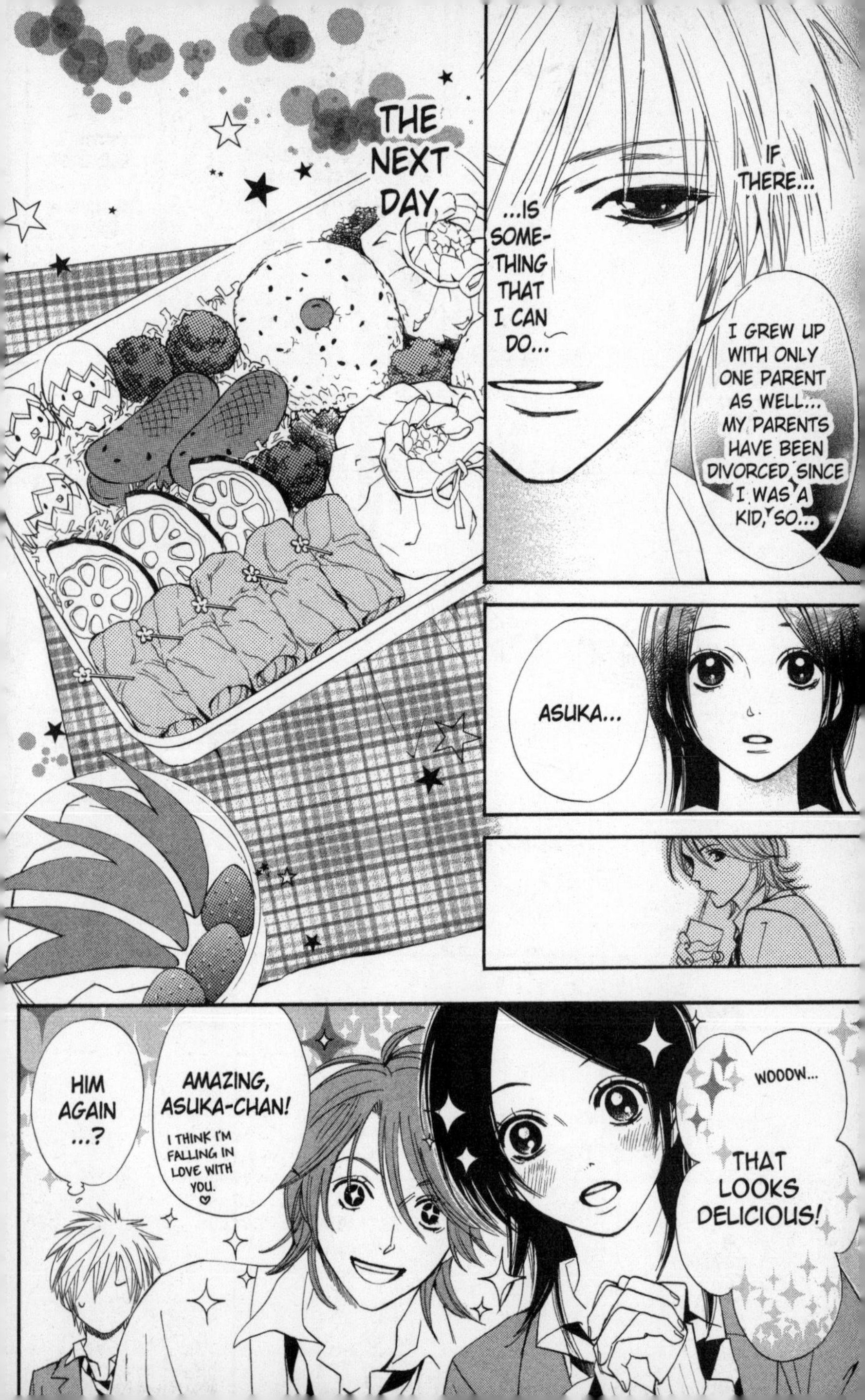
IF THERE...
...IS SOMETHING THAT I CAN DO...
I GREW UP WITH ONLY ONE PARENT AS WELL... MY PARENTS HAVE BEEN DIVORCED SINCE I WAS A KID, SO...
ASUKA...
THE NEXT DAY
WOOOW...
THAT LOOKS DELICIOUS!
AMAZING, ASUKA-CHAN!
I THINK I'M FALLING IN LOVE WITH YOU. ♡
HIM AGAIN ...?

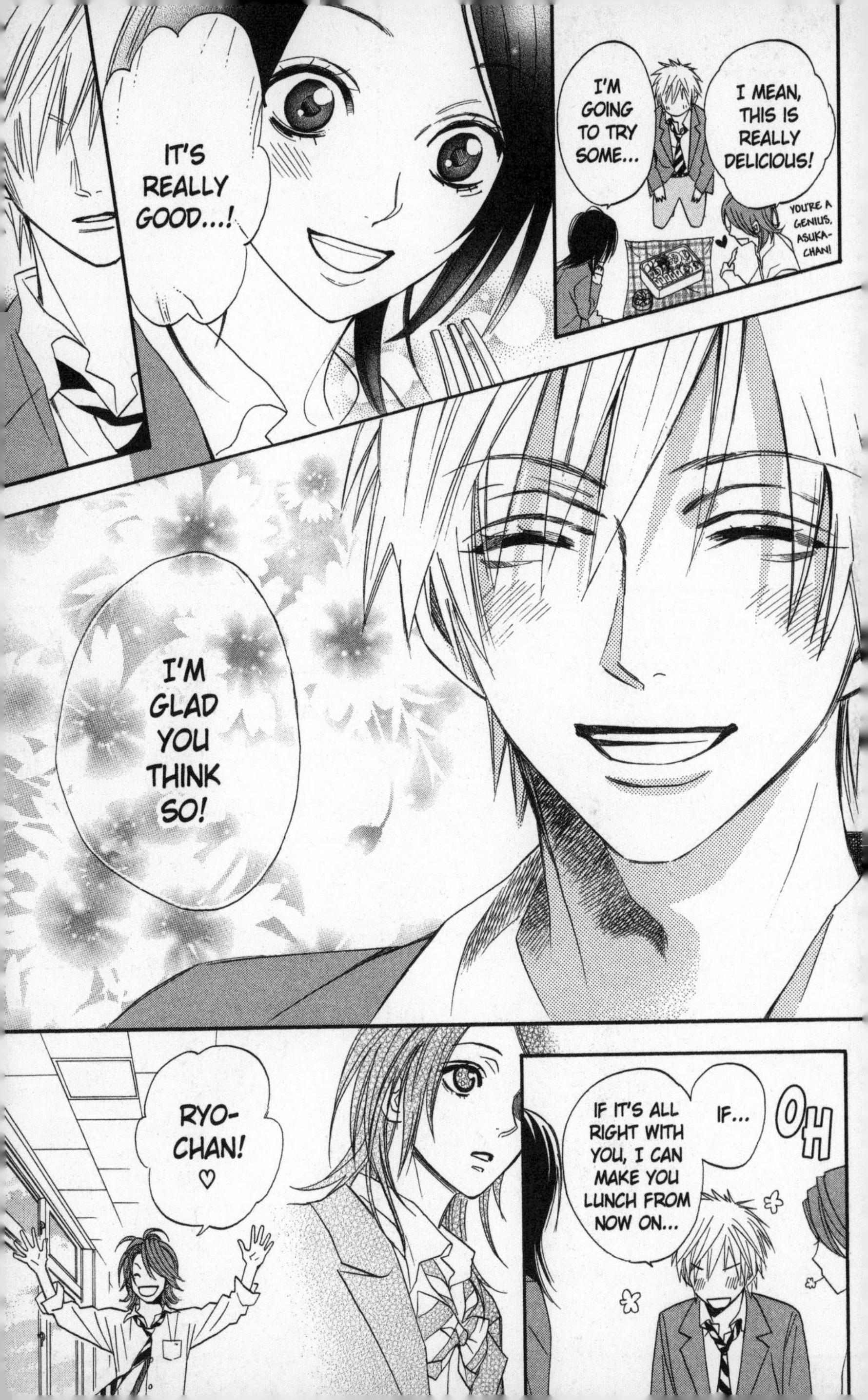
I MEAN, THIS IS REALLY DELICIOUS!
I'M GOING TO TRY SOME...
YOU'RE A GENIUS, ASUKA-CHAN!
IT'S REALLY GOOD...!
I'M GLAD YOU THINK SO!
OH
IF...
IF IT'S ALL RIGHT WITH YOU, I CAN MAKE YOU LUNCH FROM NOW ON...
RYO-CHAN! ♡

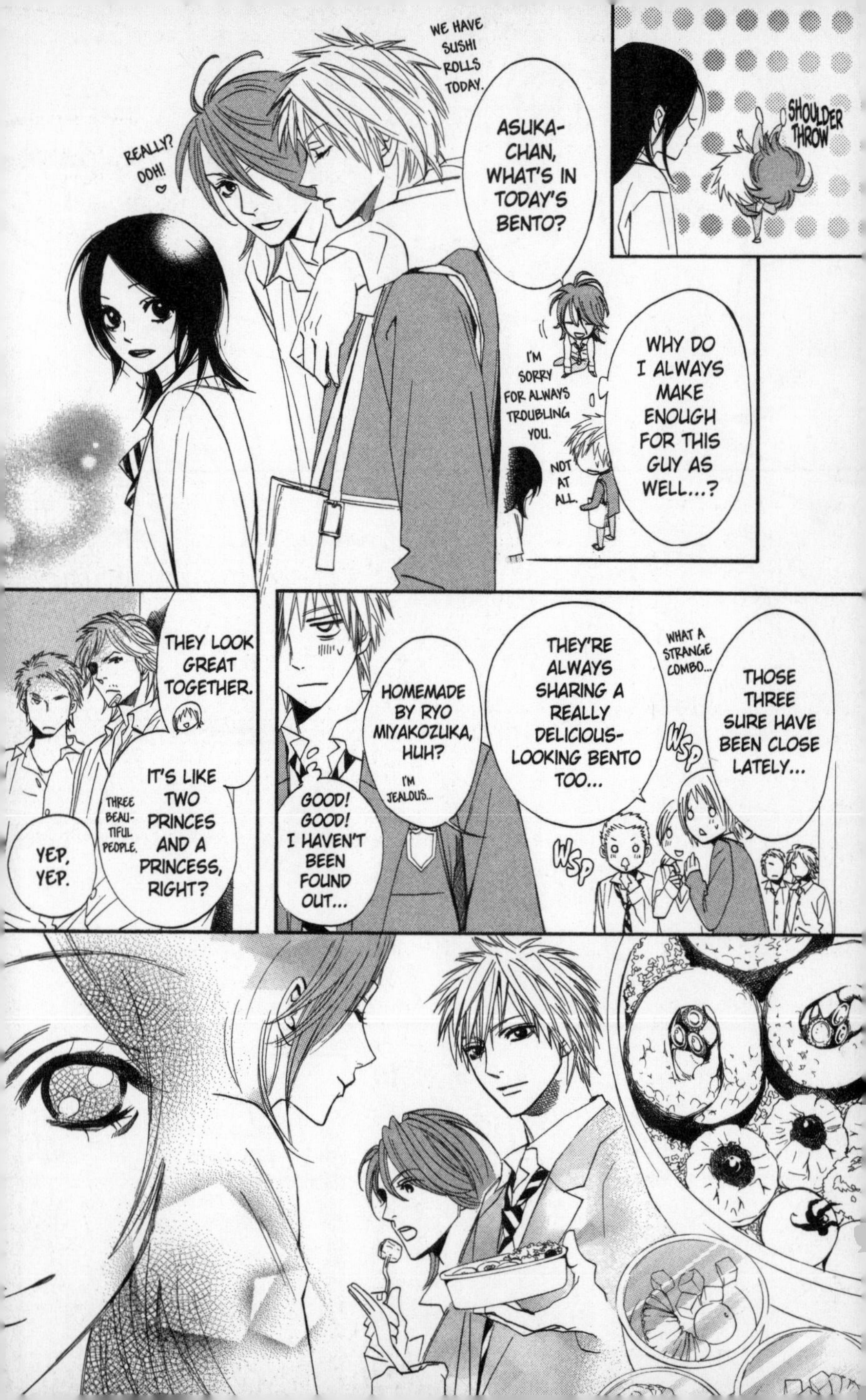
WE HAVE SUSHI ROLLS TODAY.
ASUKA-CHAN, WHAT'S IN TODAY'S BENTO?
REALLY? OOH!
SHOULDER THROW
I'M SORRY FOR ALWAYS TROUBLING YOU.
NOT AT ALL.
WHY DO I ALWAYS MAKE ENOUGH FOR THIS GUY AS WELL...?
THOSE THREE SURE HAVE BEEN CLOSE LATELY...
WHAT A STRANGE COMBO...
WSP
THEY'RE ALWAYS SHARING A REALLY DELICIOUS-LOOKING BENTO TOO...
WSP
HOMEMADE BY RYO MIYAKOZUKA, HUH?
I'M JEALOUS...
GOOD! GOOD! I HAVEN'T BEEN FOUND OUT...
THEY LOOK GREAT TOGETHER.
IT'S LIKE TWO PRINCES AND A PRINCESS, RIGHT?
THREE BEAUTIFUL PEOPLE.
YEP, YEP.

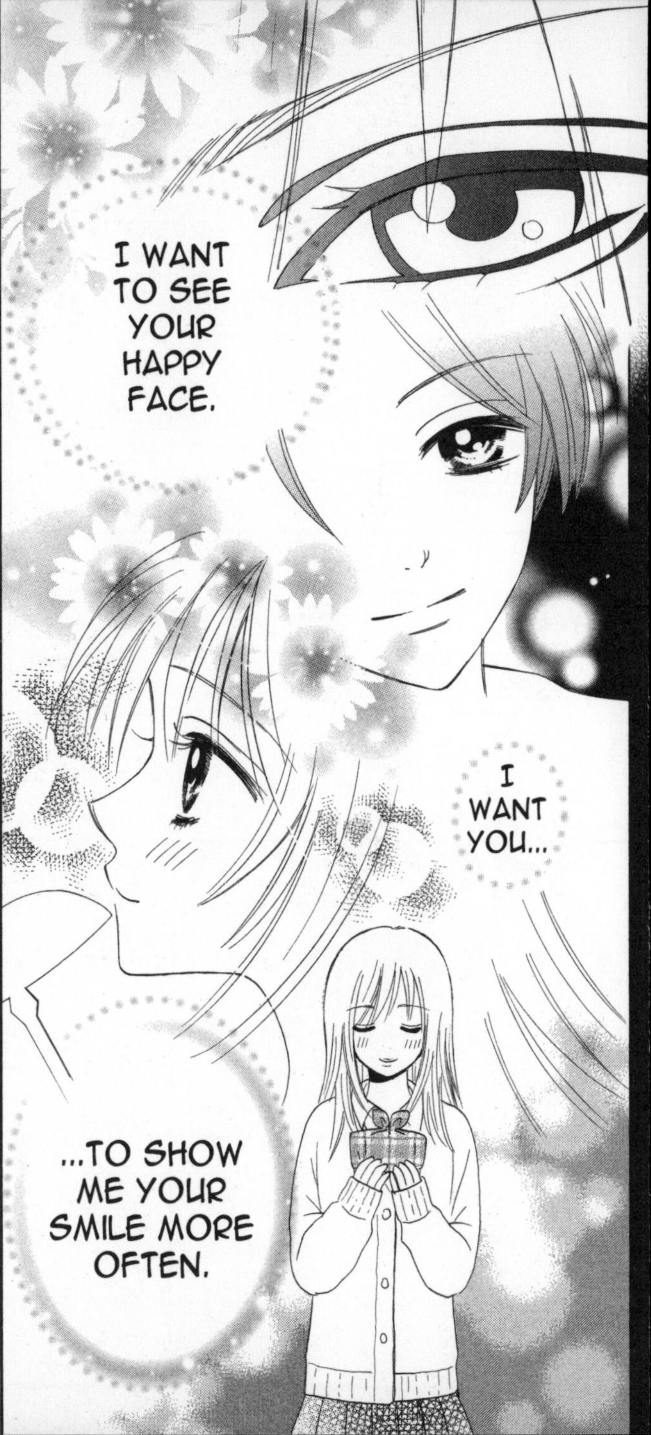
I WANT TO SEE YOUR HAPPY FACE.
I WANT YOU...
...TO SHOW ME YOUR SMILE MORE OFTEN.

Hello.
Or rather...
nice to meet you.
I'm Aya Kanno.

I am a far-from-girly author, so in order to draw this girlish world, I am doing my best to make sure that fact doesn't come through.

It's really fun to draw pictures like this one. →

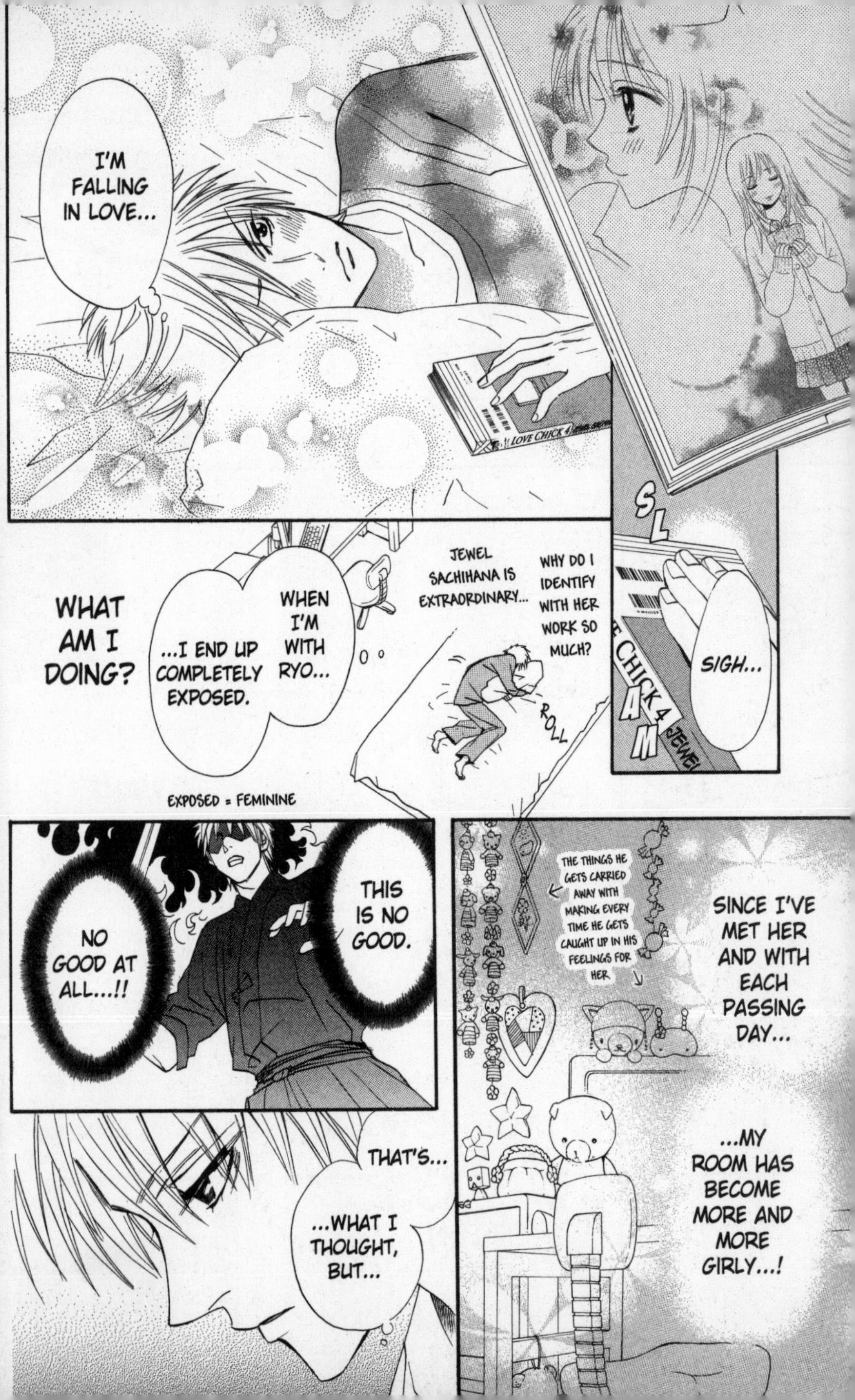

I'M FALLING IN LOVE...
LOVE CHICK 4
SLAM
SIGH...
JEWEL SACHIHANA IS EXTRAORDINARY...
WHY DO I IDENTIFY WITH HER WORK SO MUCH?
ROLL
WHEN I'M WITH RYO...
...I END UP COMPLETELY EXPOSED.
WHAT AM I DOING?
EXPOSED = FEMININE
SINCE I'VE MET HER AND WITH EACH PASSING DAY...
THE THINGS HE GETS CARRIED AWAY WITH MAKING EVERY TIME HE GETS CAUGHT UP IN HIS FEELINGS FOR HER
...MY ROOM HAS BECOME MORE AND MORE GIRLY...!
THIS IS NO GOOD.
NO GOOD AT ALL...!!
THAT'S...
...WHAT I THOUGHT, BUT...

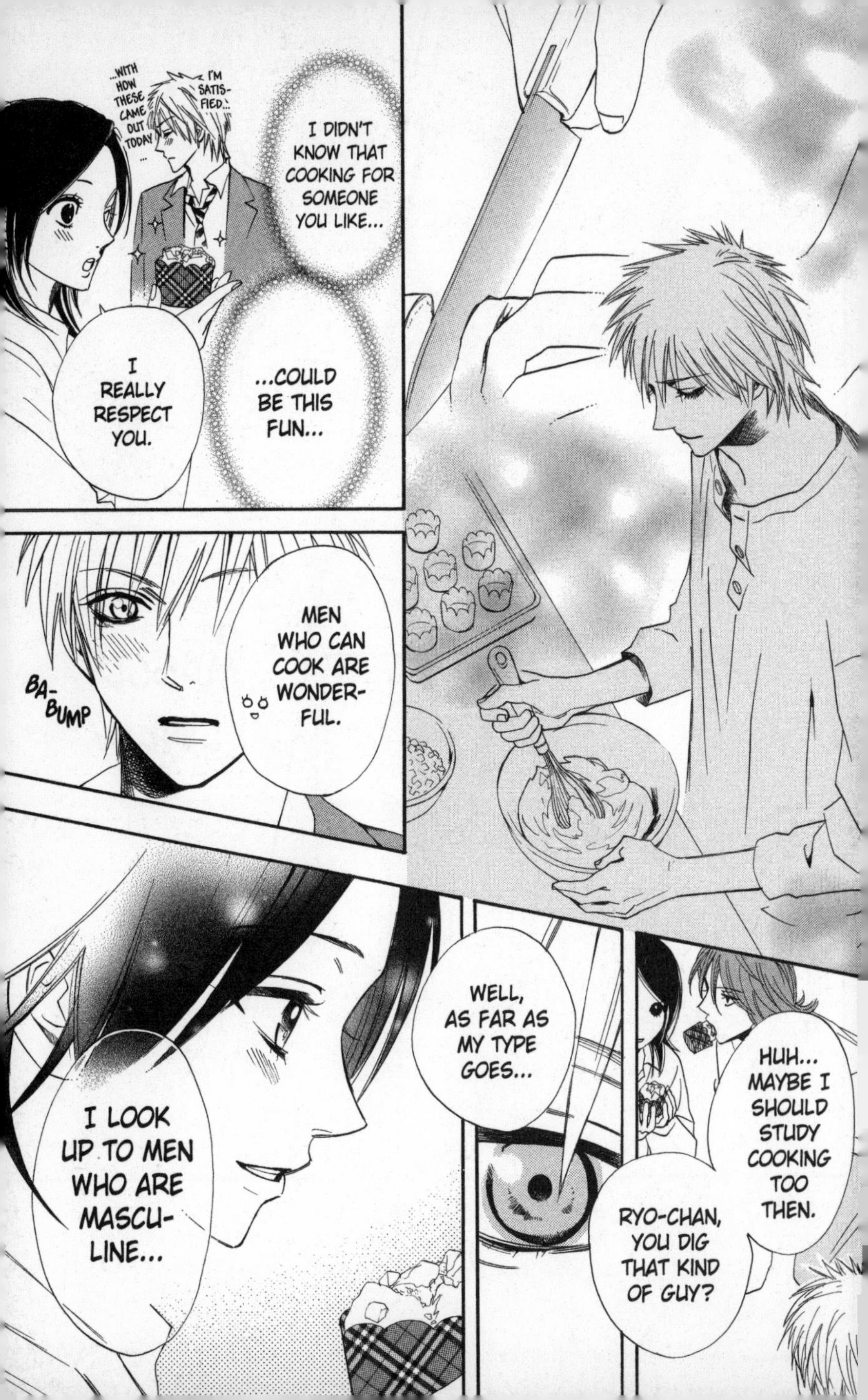
I DIDN'T KNOW THAT COOKING FOR SOMEONE YOU LIKE...
I'M SATIS-FIED...
...WITH HOW THESE CAME OUT TODAY...
...COULD BE THIS FUN...
I REALLY RESPECT YOU.
MEN WHO CAN COOK ARE WONDER-FUL.
BA-BUMP
HUH... MAYBE I SHOULD STUDY COOKING TOO THEN.
RYO-CHAN, YOU DIG THAT KIND OF GUY?
WELL, AS FAR AS MY TYPE GOES...
I LOOK UP TO MEN WHO ARE MASCU-LINE...

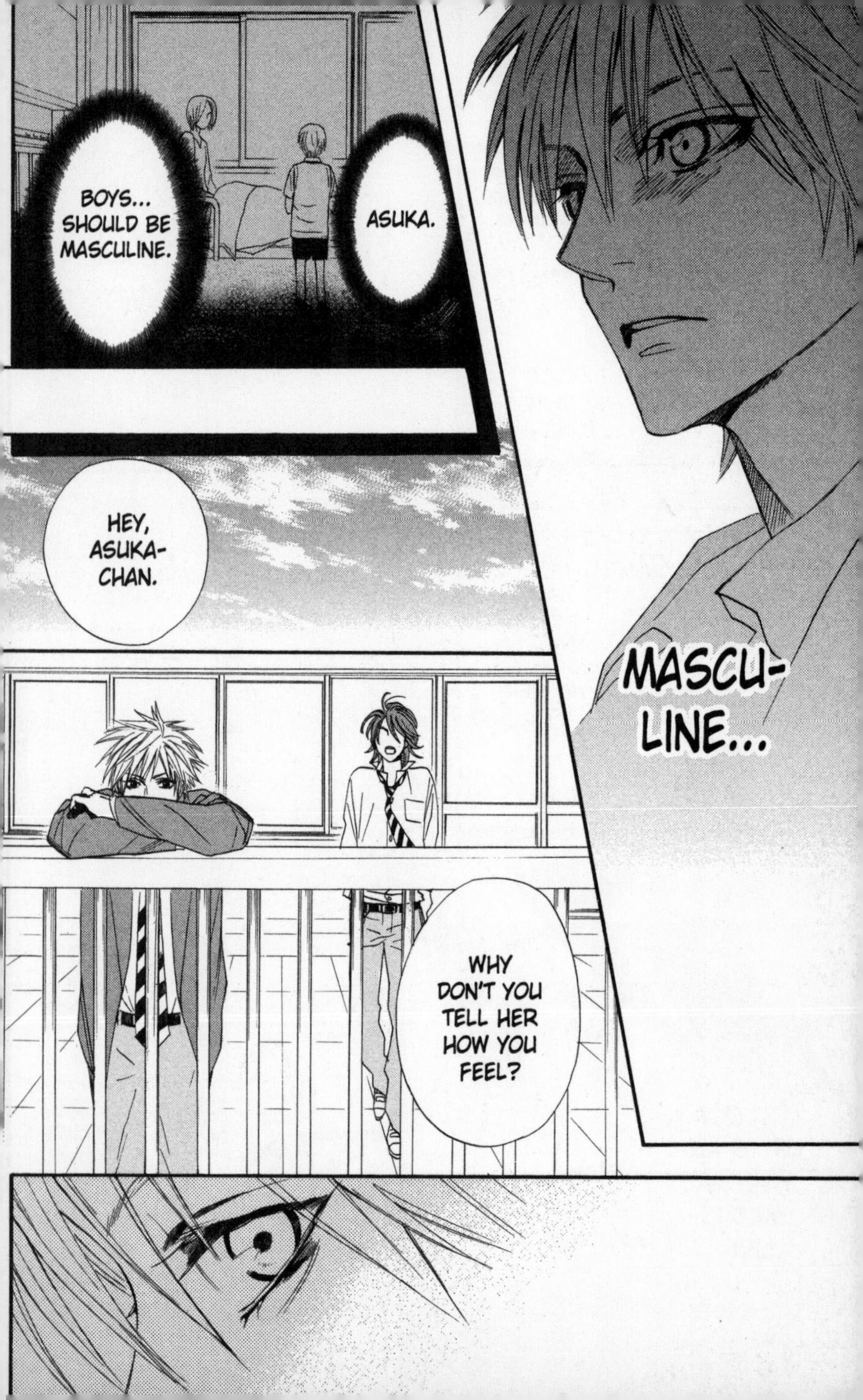
MASCU-LINE...
ASUKA.
BOYS... SHOULD BE MASCULINE.
HEY, ASUKA-CHAN.
WHY DON'T YOU TELL HER HOW YOU FEEL?

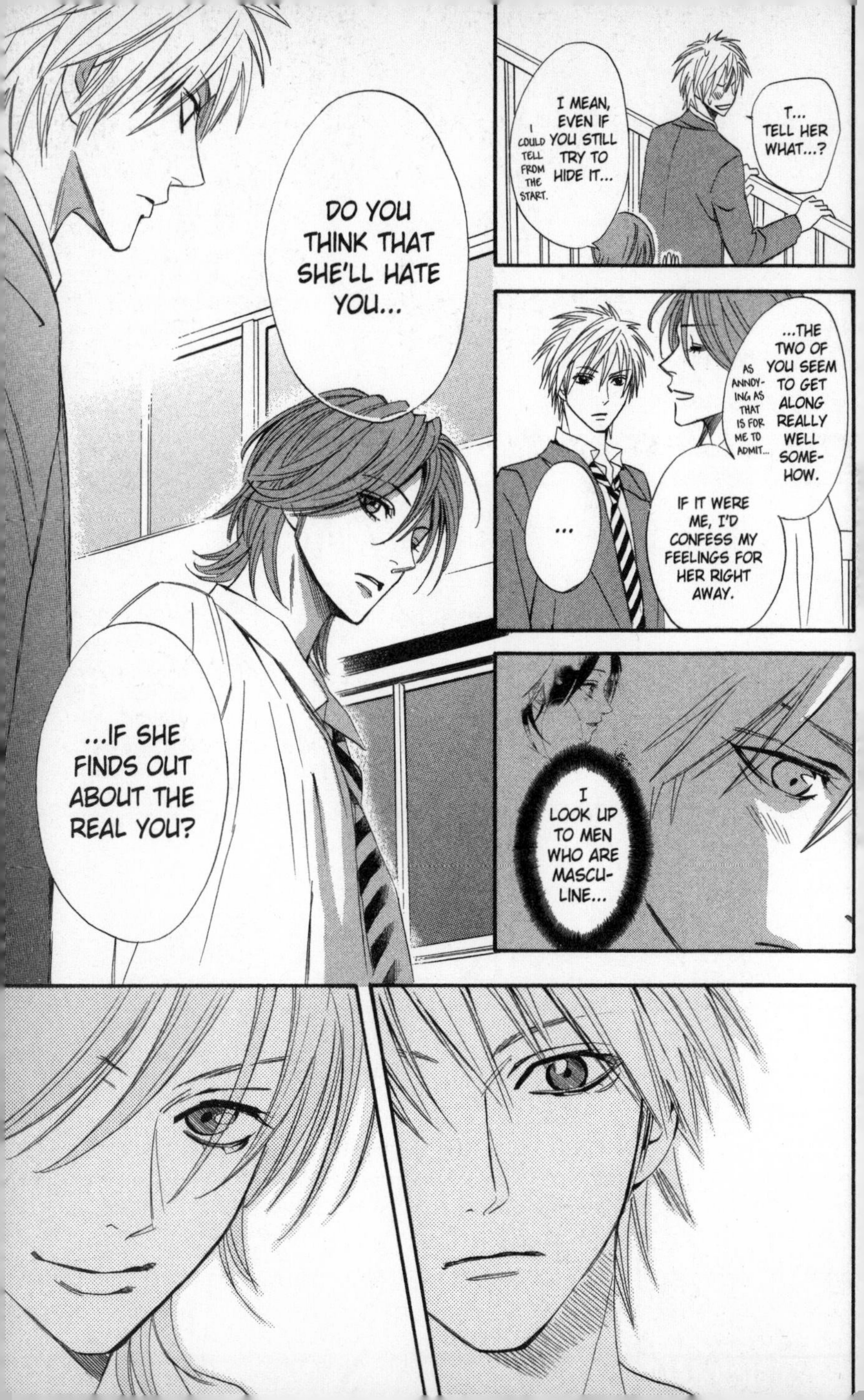
T... TELL HER WHAT...?
I MEAN, EVEN IF YOU STILL TRY TO HIDE IT...
I COULD TELL FROM THE START.
...THE TWO OF YOU SEEM TO GET ALONG REALLY WELL SOME-HOW.
AS ANNOY-ING AS THAT IS FOR ME TO ADMIT...
IF IT WERE ME, I'D CONFESS MY FEELINGS FOR HER RIGHT AWAY.
...
I LOOK UP TO MEN WHO ARE MASCU-LINE...
DO YOU THINK THAT SHE'LL HATE YOU...
...IF SHE FINDS OUT ABOUT THE REAL YOU?

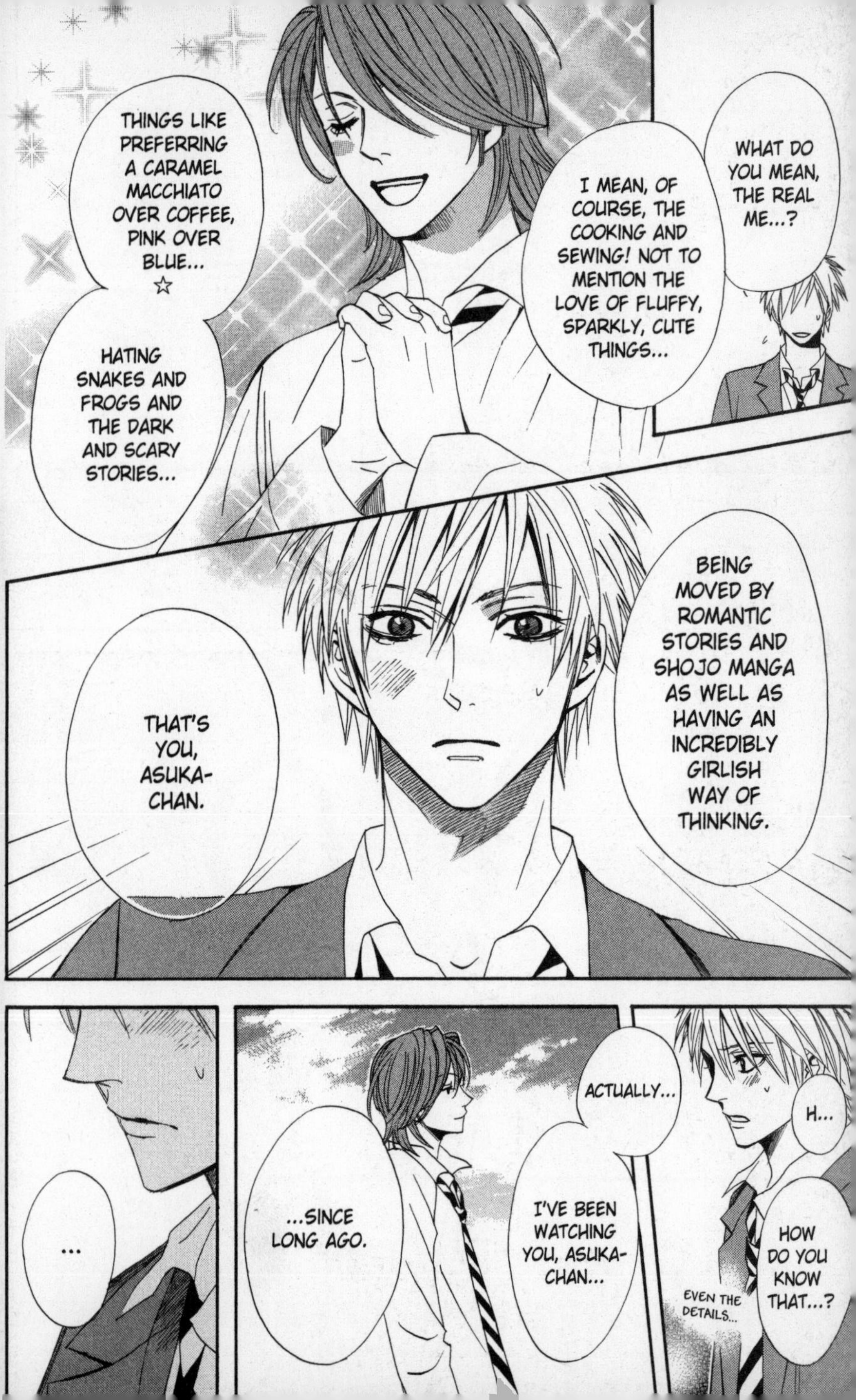
WHAT DO YOU MEAN, THE REAL ME...?
I MEAN, OF COURSE, THE COOKING AND SEWING! NOT TO MENTION THE LOVE OF FLUFFY, SPARKLY, CUTE THINGS...
THINGS LIKE PREFERRING A CARAMEL MACCHIATO OVER COFFEE, PINK OVER BLUE... ☆
HATING SNAKES AND FROGS AND THE DARK AND SCARY STORIES...
BEING MOVED BY ROMANTIC STORIES AND SHOJO MANGA AS WELL AS HAVING AN INCREDIBLY GIRLISH WAY OF THINKING.
THAT'S YOU, ASUKA-CHAN.
H...
HOW DO YOU KNOW THAT...?
EVEN THE DETAILS...
ACTUALLY...
I'VE BEEN WATCHING YOU, ASUKA-CHAN...
...SINCE LONG AGO.
...

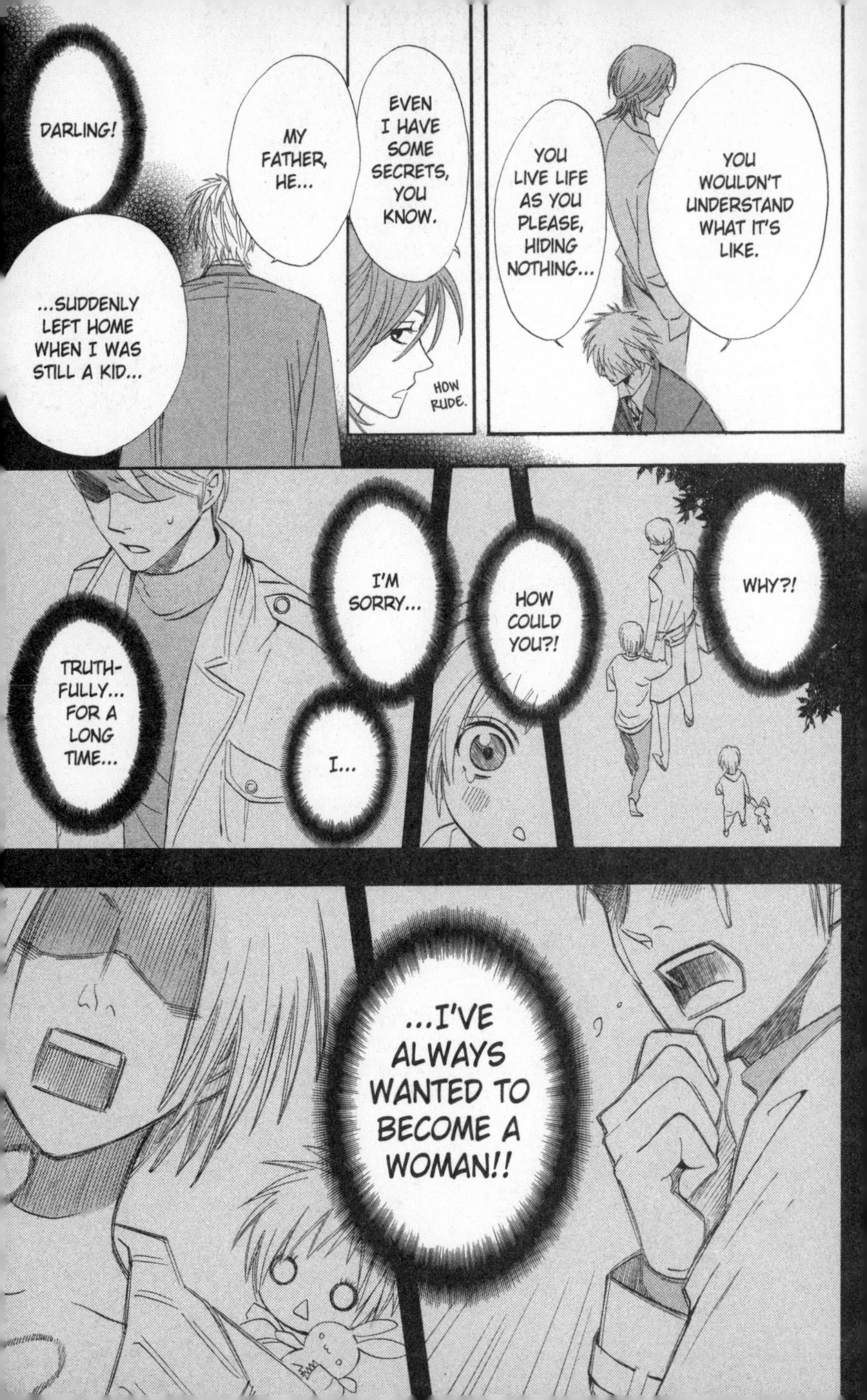
YOU WOULDN'T UNDERSTAND WHAT IT'S LIKE.
YOU LIVE LIFE AS YOU PLEASE, HIDING NOTHING...
EVEN I HAVE SOME SECRETS, YOU KNOW.
HOW RUDE.
MY FATHER, HE...
...SUDDENLY LEFT HOME WHEN I WAS STILL A KID...
DARLING!
WHY?!
HOW COULD YOU?!
I'M SORRY...
I...
TRUTH-FULLY... FOR A LONG TIME...
...I'VE ALWAYS WANTED TO BECOME A WOMAN!!

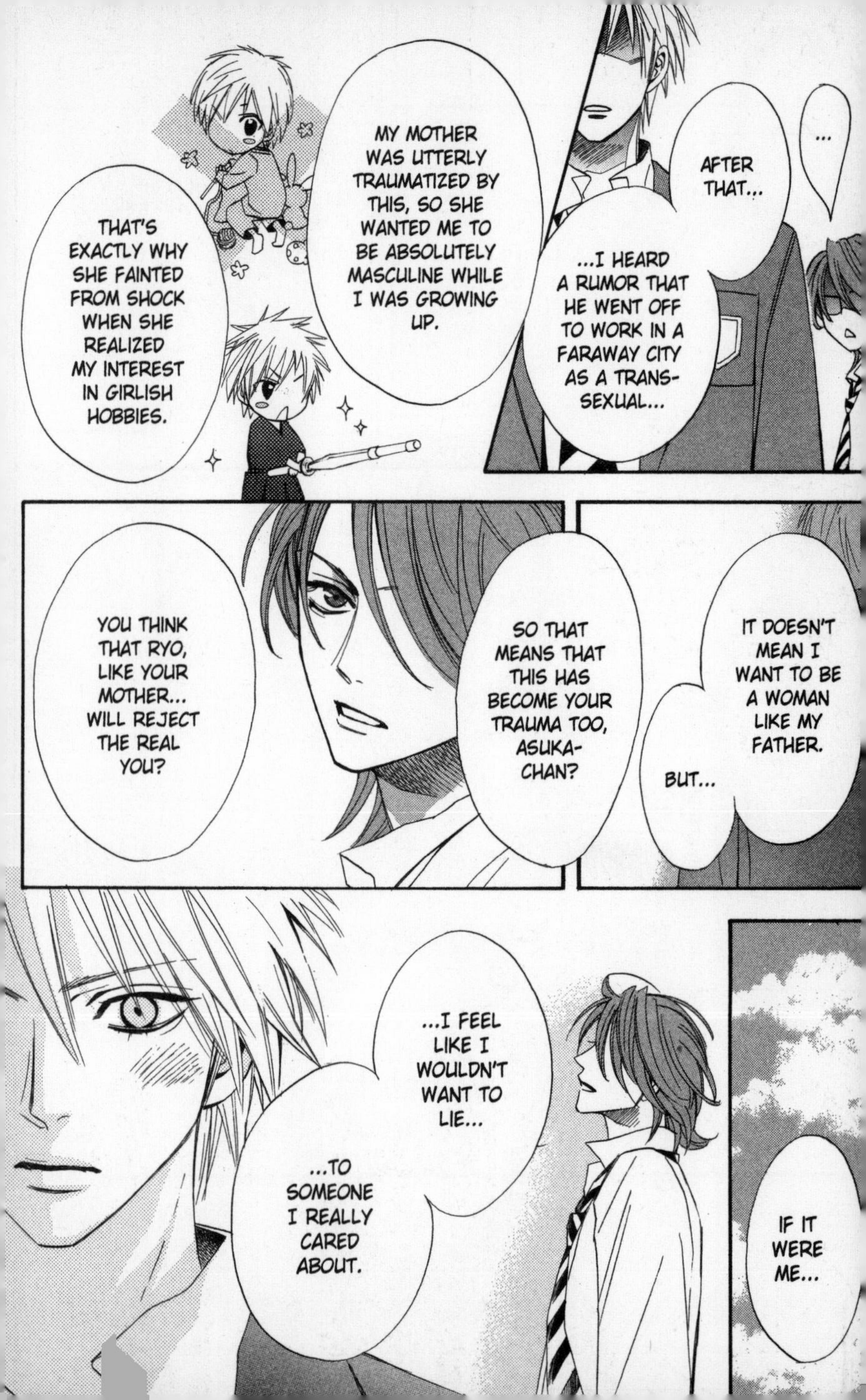
...
AFTER THAT...
...I HEARD A RUMOR THAT HE WENT OFF TO WORK IN A FARAWAY CITY AS A TRANS-SEXUAL...
MY MOTHER WAS UTTERLY TRAUMATIZED BY THIS, SO SHE WANTED ME TO BE ABSOLUTELY MASCULINE WHILE I WAS GROWING UP.
THAT'S EXACTLY WHY SHE FAINTED FROM SHOCK WHEN SHE REALIZED MY INTEREST IN GIRLISH HOBBIES.
IT DOESN'T MEAN I WANT TO BE A WOMAN LIKE MY FATHER.
BUT...
SO THAT MEANS THAT THIS HAS BECOME YOUR TRAUMA TOO, ASUKA-CHAN?
YOU THINK THAT RYO, LIKE YOUR MOTHER... WILL REJECT THE REAL YOU?
IF IT WERE ME...
...I FEEL LIKE I WOULDN'T WANT TO LIE...
...TO SOMEONE I REALLY CARED ABOUT.

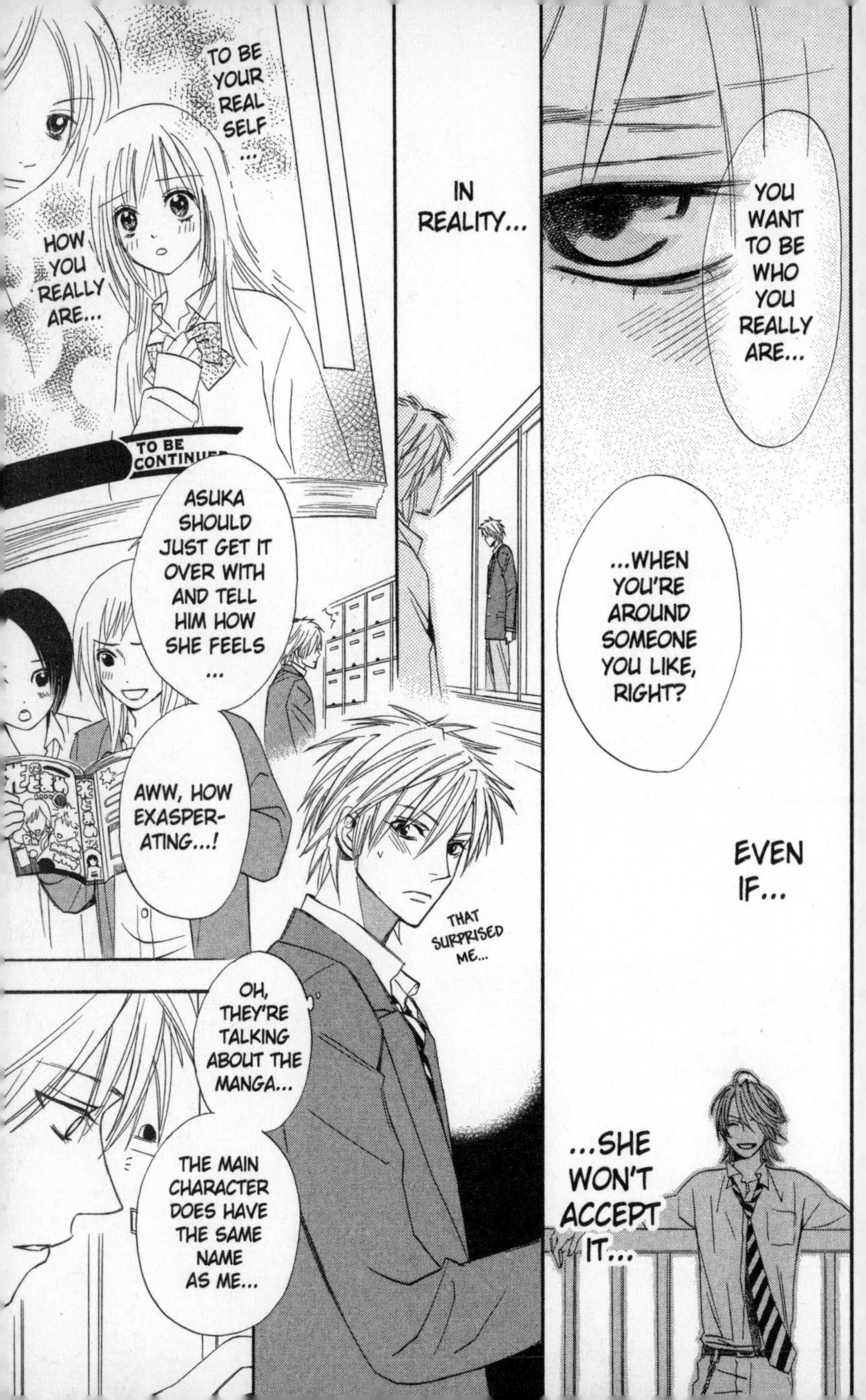
YOU WANT TO BE WHO YOU REALLY ARE...
...WHEN YOU'RE AROUND SOMEONE YOU LIKE, RIGHT?
EVEN IF...
...SHE WON'T ACCEPT IT...
IN REALITY...
TO BE YOUR REAL SELF...
HOW YOU REALLY ARE...
TO BE CONTINUED
ASUKA SHOULD JUST GET IT OVER WITH AND TELL HIM HOW SHE FEELS...
AWW, HOW EXASPER-ATING...!
THAT SURPRISED ME...
OH, THEY'RE TALKING ABOUT THE MANGA...
THE MAIN CHARACTER DOES HAVE THE SAME NAME AS ME...

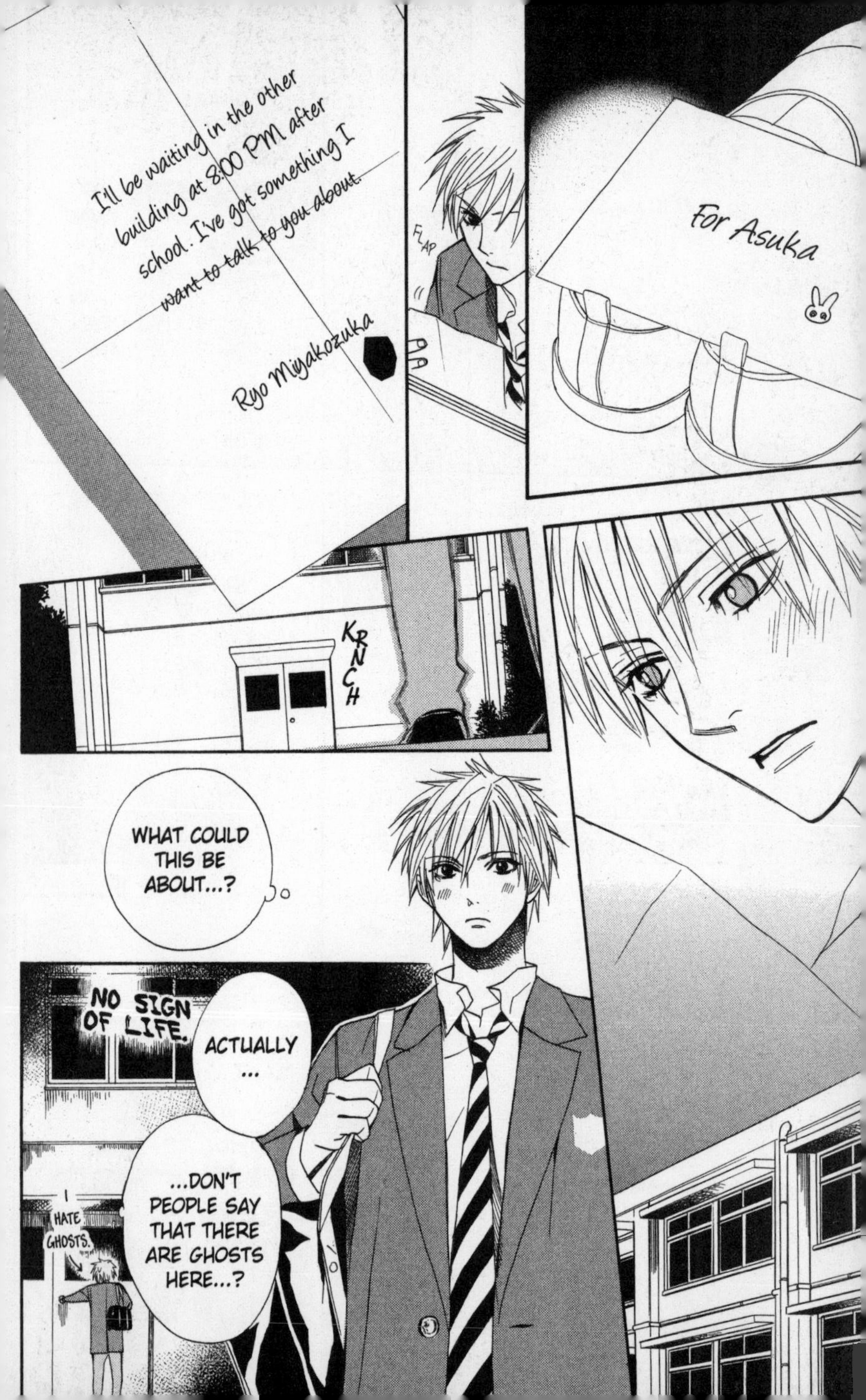
For Asuka
FLAP
I'll be waiting in the other building at 8:00 PM after school. I've got something I want to talk to you about.
Ryo Miyakozuka
KRNCH
WHAT COULD THIS BE ABOUT...?
ACTUALLY...
...DON'T PEOPLE SAY THAT THERE ARE GHOSTS HERE...?
NO SIGN OF LIFE.
I HATE GHOSTS.

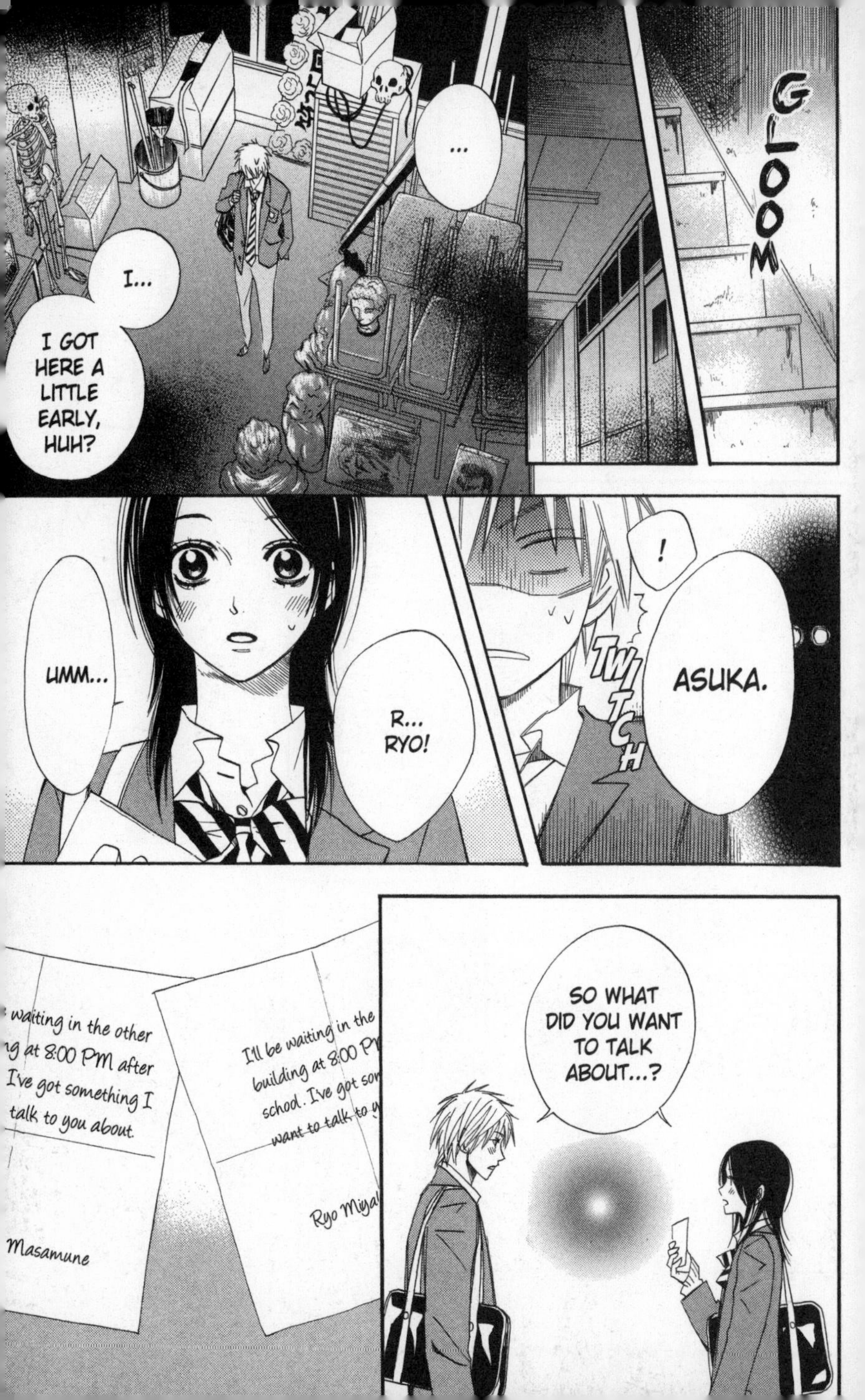
GLOOM
...
I...
I GOT HERE A LITTLE EARLY, HUH?
!
ASUKA.
TWITCH
R... RYO!
UMM...
SO WHAT DID YOU WANT TO TALK ABOUT...?
I'll be waiting in the
building at 8:00 P
school. I've got som
want to talk to y
Ryo Miyal
waiting in the other
g at 8:00 PM after
I've got something I
talk to you about.
Masamune

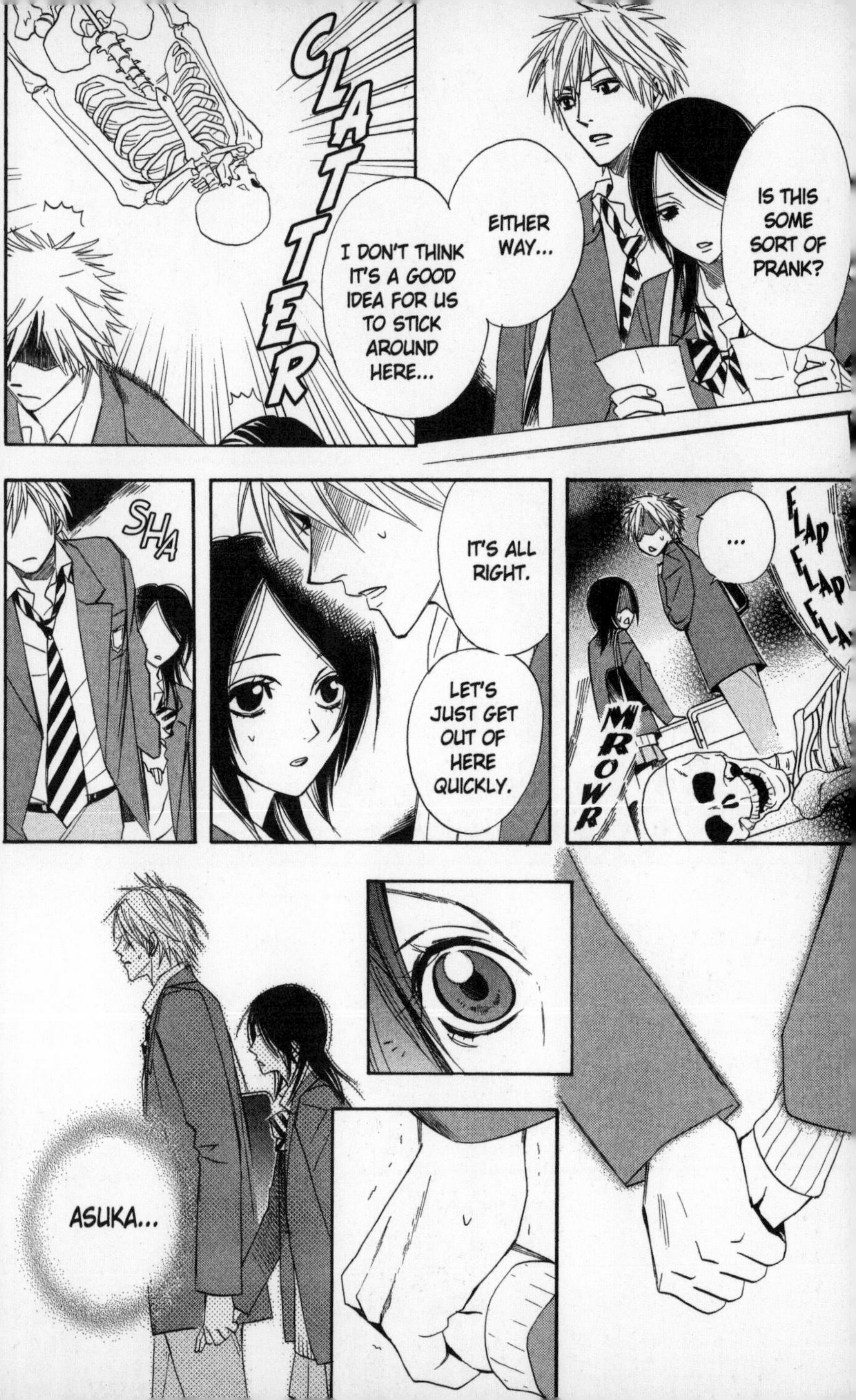
IS THIS SOME SORT OF PRANK?
EITHER WAY...
I DON'T THINK IT'S A GOOD IDEA FOR US TO STICK AROUND HERE...
CLATTER
...
FLAP FLAP FLA
MROWR
IT'S ALL RIGHT.
LET'S JUST GET OUT OF HERE QUICKLY.
SHA
ASUKA...

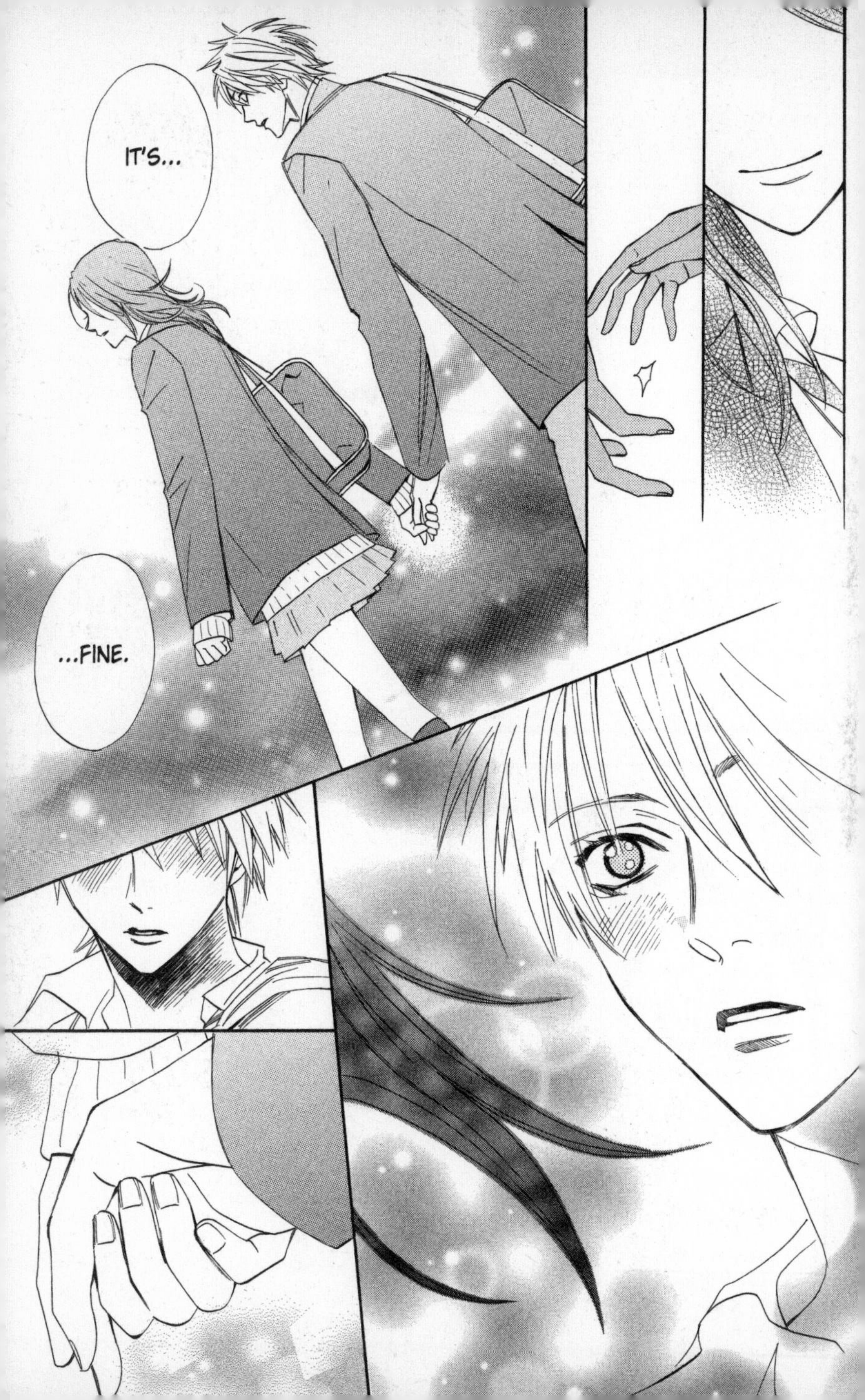
IT'S...
...FINE.

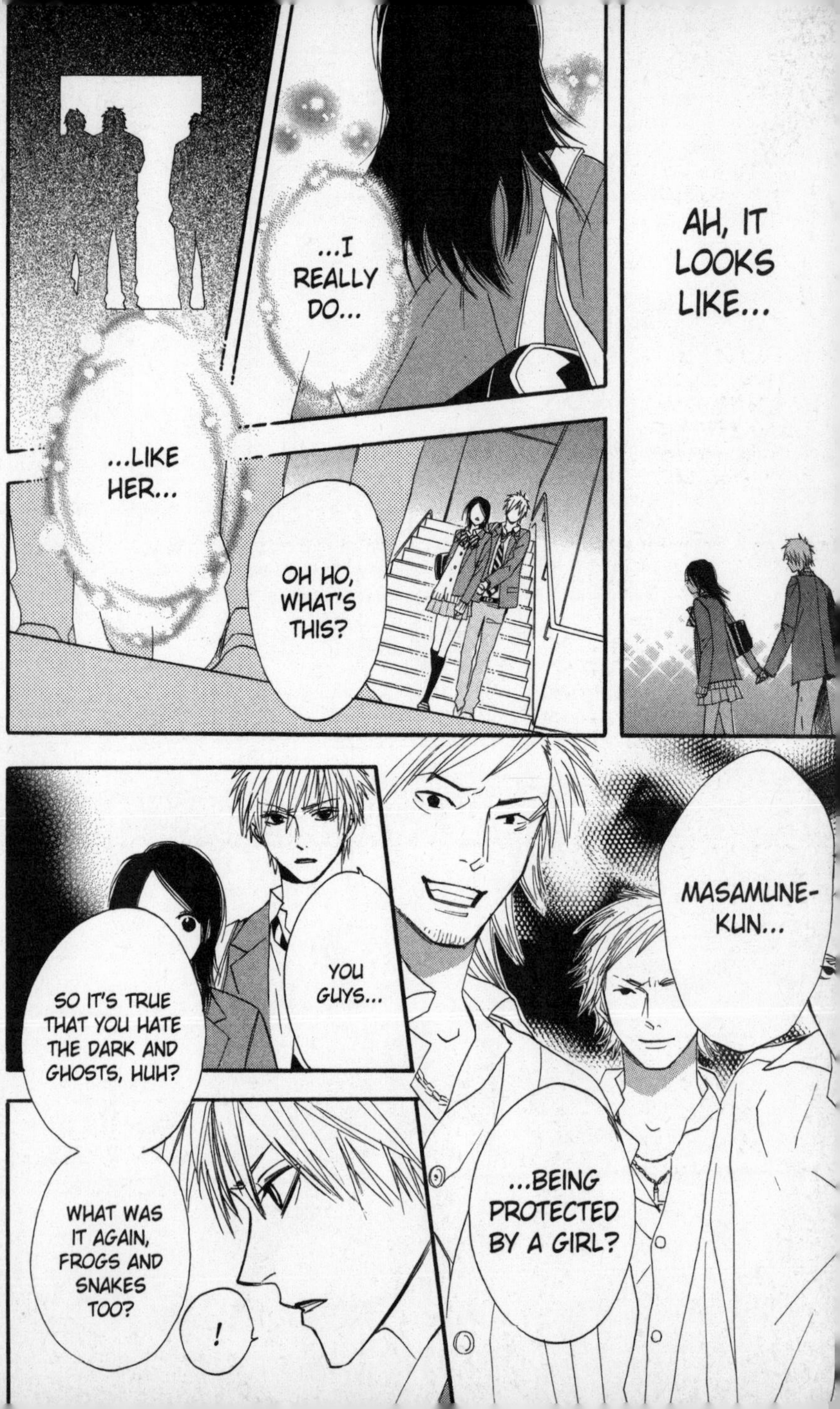
AH, IT LOOKS LIKE...
...I REALLY DO...
...LIKE HER...
OH HO, WHAT'S THIS?
MASAMUNE-KUN...
YOU GUYS...
SO IT'S TRUE THAT YOU HATE THE DARK AND GHOSTS, HUH?
...BEING PROTECTED BY A GIRL?
WHAT WAS IT AGAIN, FROGS AND SNAKES TOO?
!

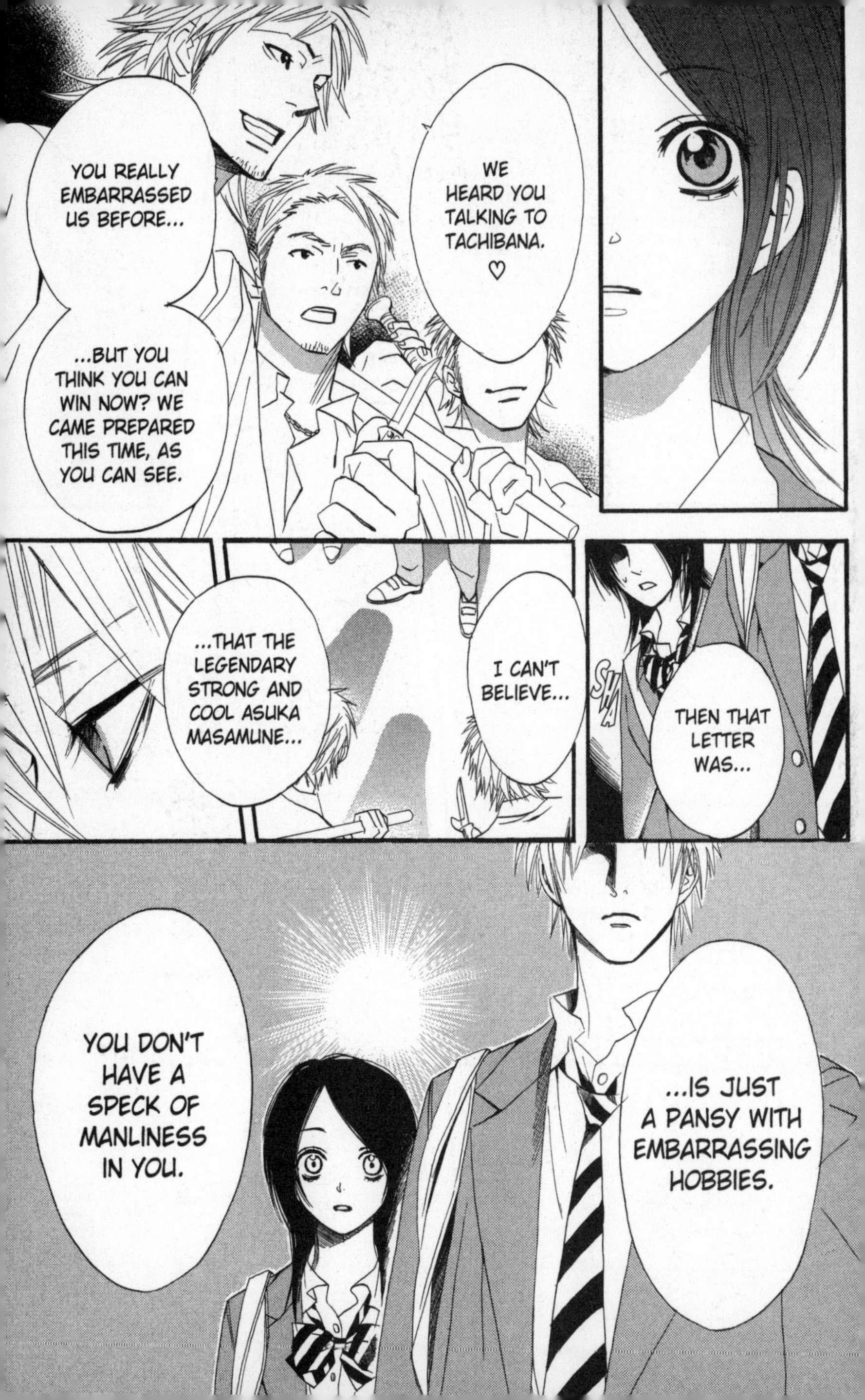
WE HEARD YOU TALKING TO TACHIBANA. ♡
YOU REALLY EMBARRASSED US BEFORE...
...BUT YOU THINK YOU CAN WIN NOW? WE CAME PREPARED THIS TIME, AS YOU CAN SEE.
SHA
THEN THAT LETTER WAS...
I CAN'T BELIEVE...
...THAT THE LEGENDARY STRONG AND COOL ASUKA MASAMUNE...
...IS JUST A PANSY WITH EMBARRASSING HOBBIES.
YOU DON'T HAVE A SPECK OF MANLINESS IN YOU.

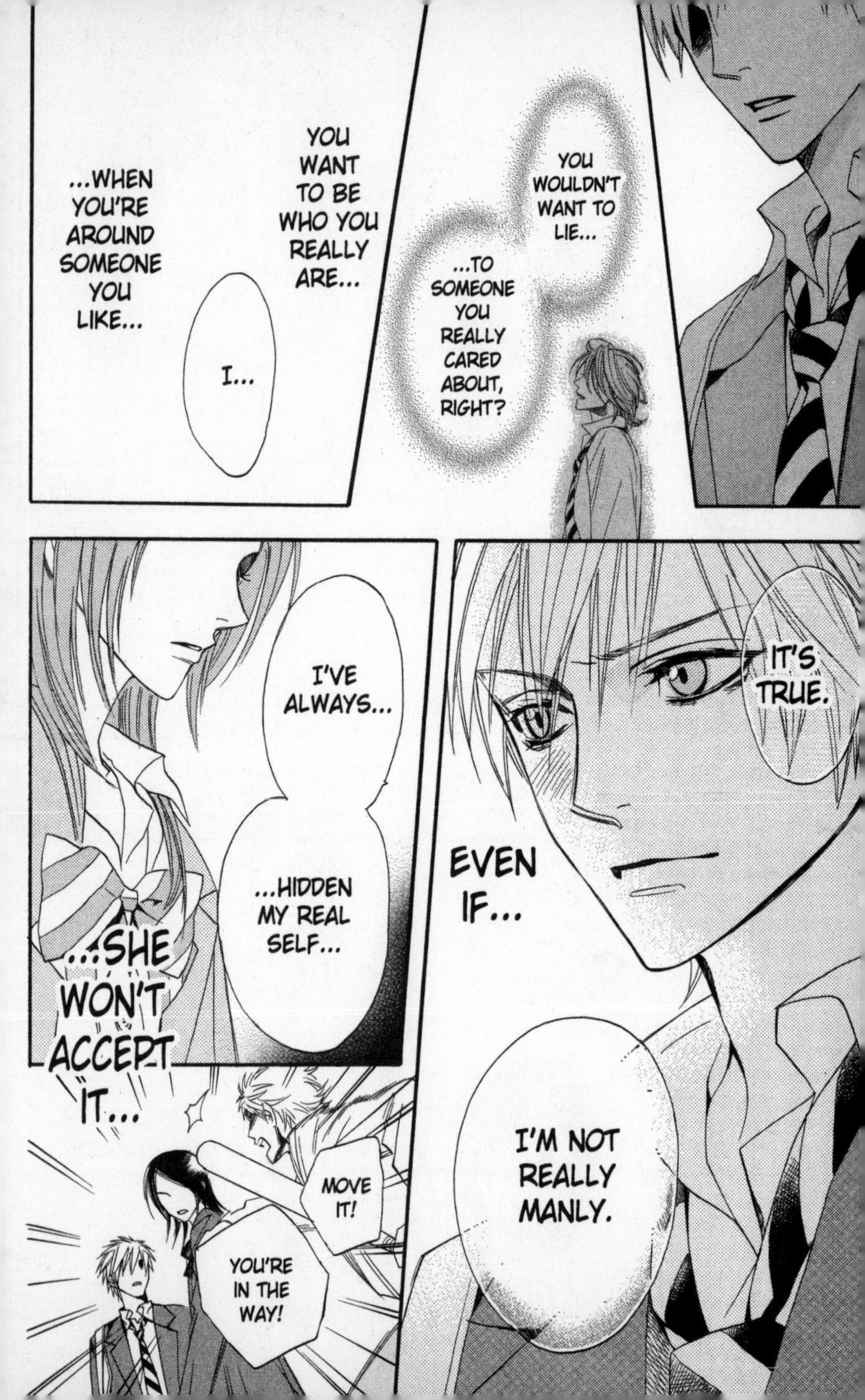

YOU WOULDN'T WANT TO LIE...
...TO SOMEONE YOU REALLY CARED ABOUT, RIGHT?
YOU WANT TO BE WHO YOU REALLY ARE...
...WHEN YOU'RE AROUND SOMEONE YOU LIKE...
I...
IT'S TRUE.
EVEN IF...
I'M NOT REALLY MANLY.
I'VE ALWAYS...
...HIDDEN MY REAL SELF...
...SHE WON'T ACCEPT IT...
MOVE IT!
YOU'RE IN THE WAY!

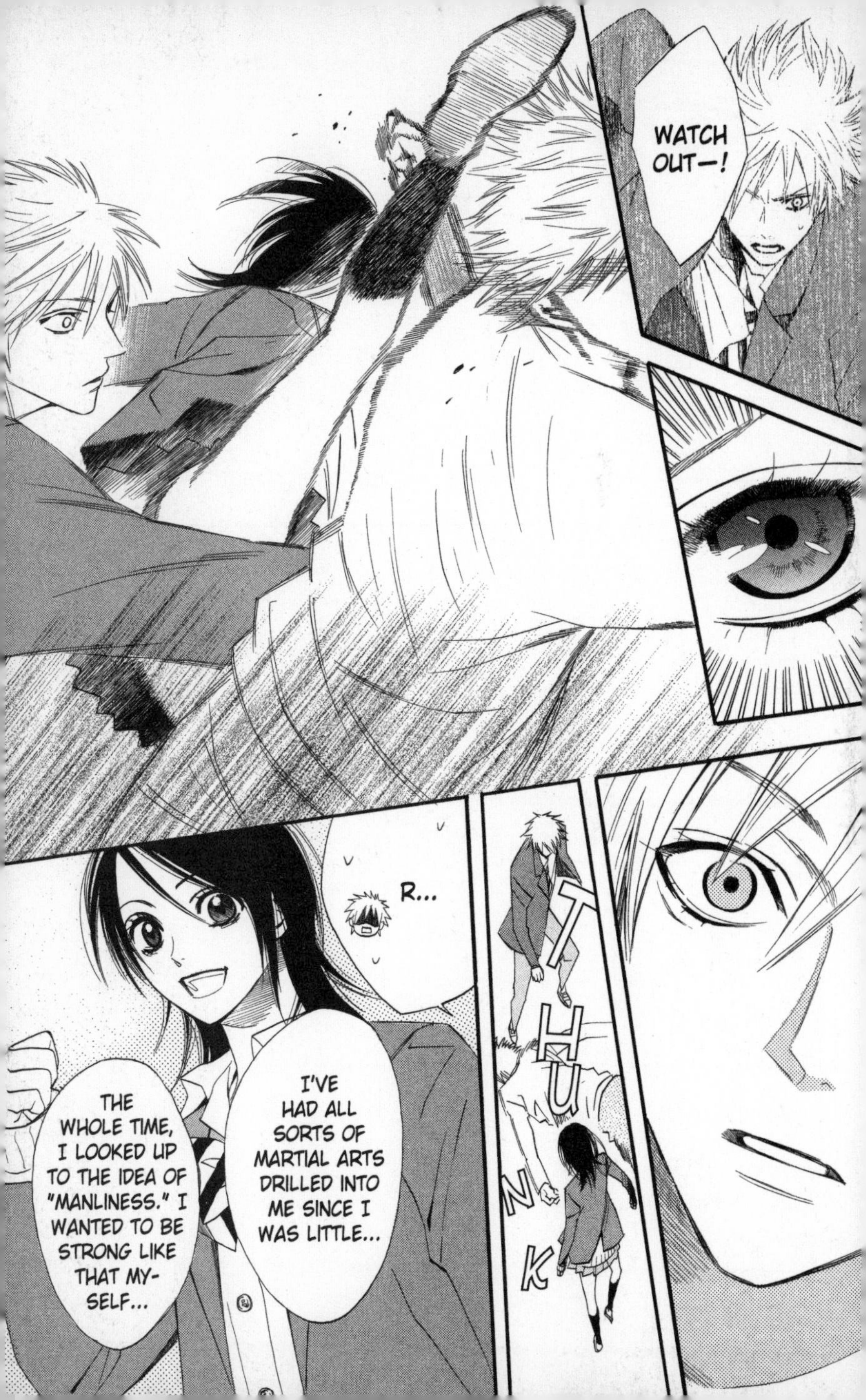
WATCH OUT—!
THUNK
R...
I'VE HAD ALL SORTS OF MARTIAL ARTS DRILLED INTO ME SINCE I WAS LITTLE...
THE WHOLE TIME, I LOOKED UP TO THE IDEA OF "MANLINESS." I WANTED TO BE STRONG LIKE THAT MY-SELF...

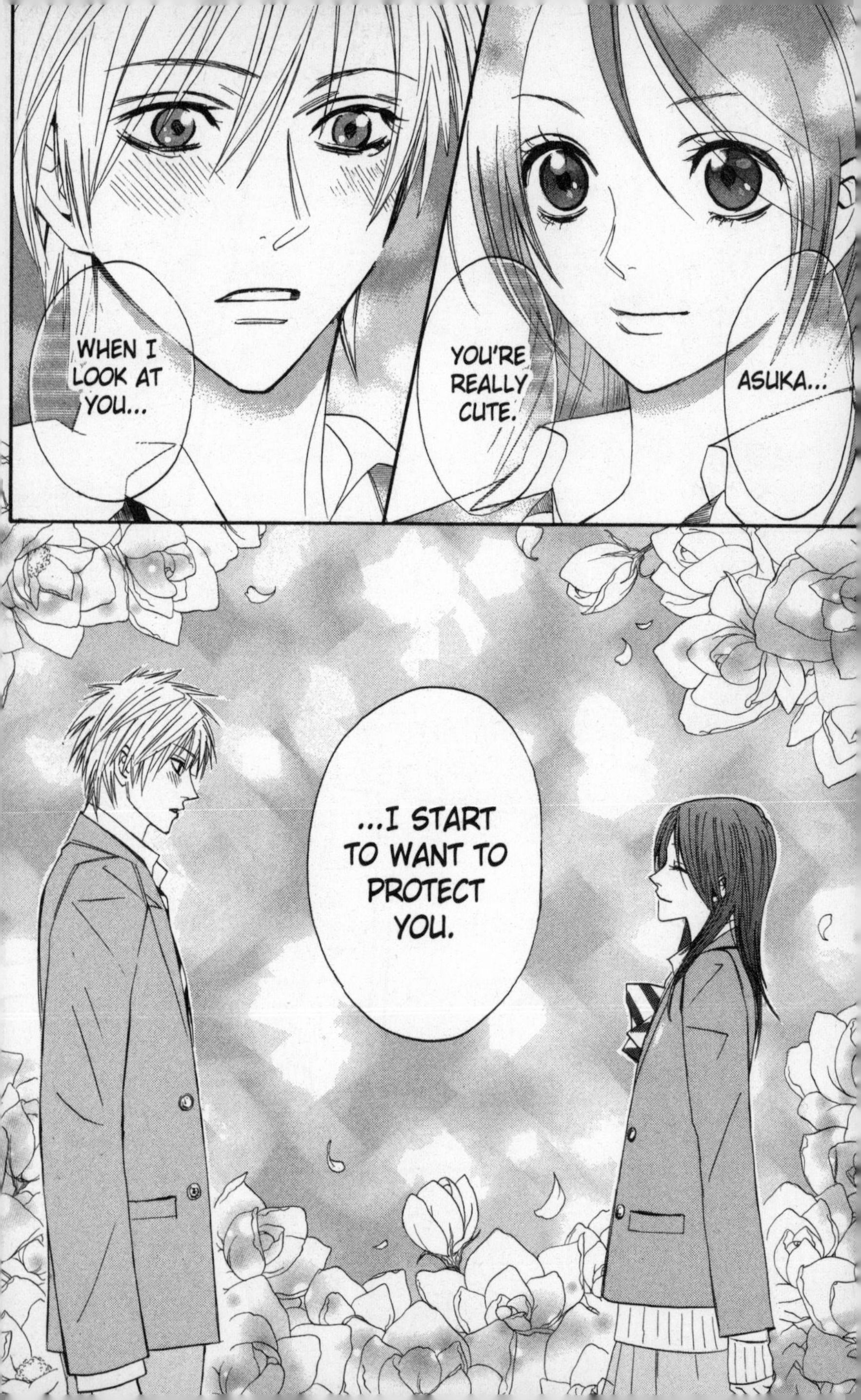
ASUKA...
YOU'RE REALLY CUTE.
WHEN I LOOK AT YOU...
...I START TO WANT TO PROTECT YOU.

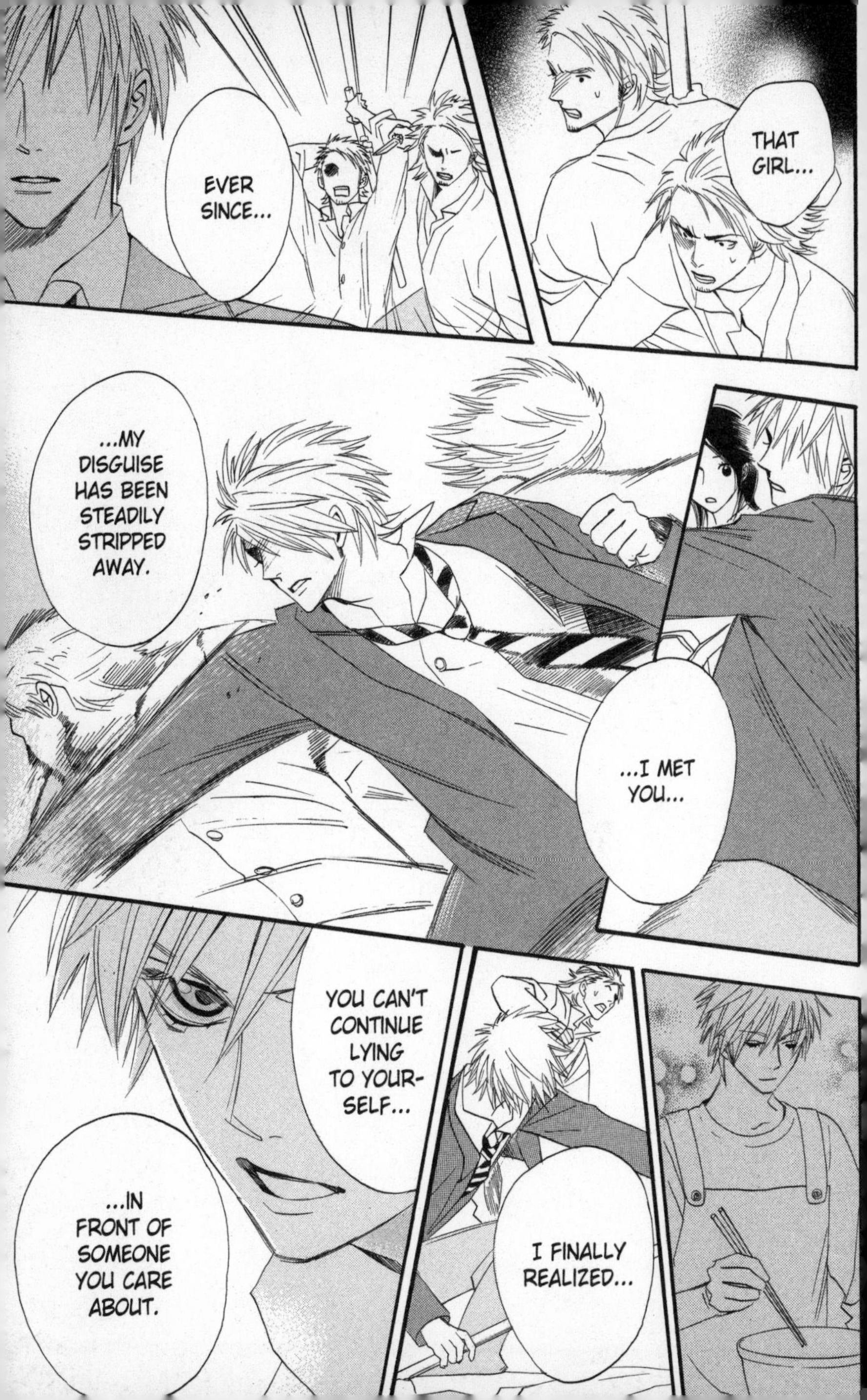
THAT GIRL...
EVER SINCE...
...I MET YOU...
...MY DISGUISE HAS BEEN STEADILY STRIPPED AWAY.
I FINALLY REALIZED...
YOU CAN'T CONTINUE LYING TO YOUR-SELF...
...IN FRONT OF SOMEONE YOU CARE ABOUT.

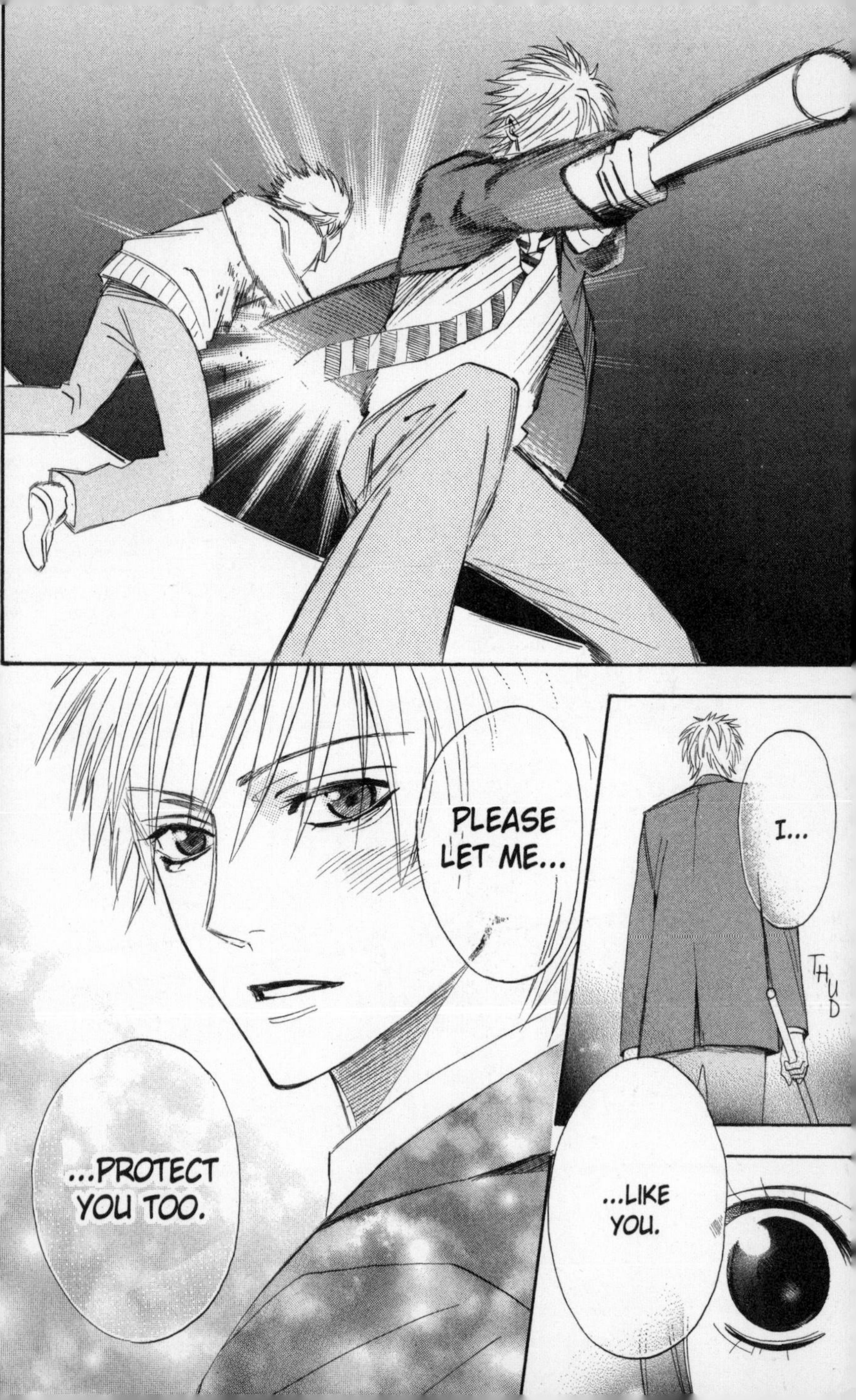
I...
THUD
...LIKE YOU.
PLEASE LET ME...
...PROTECT YOU TOO.

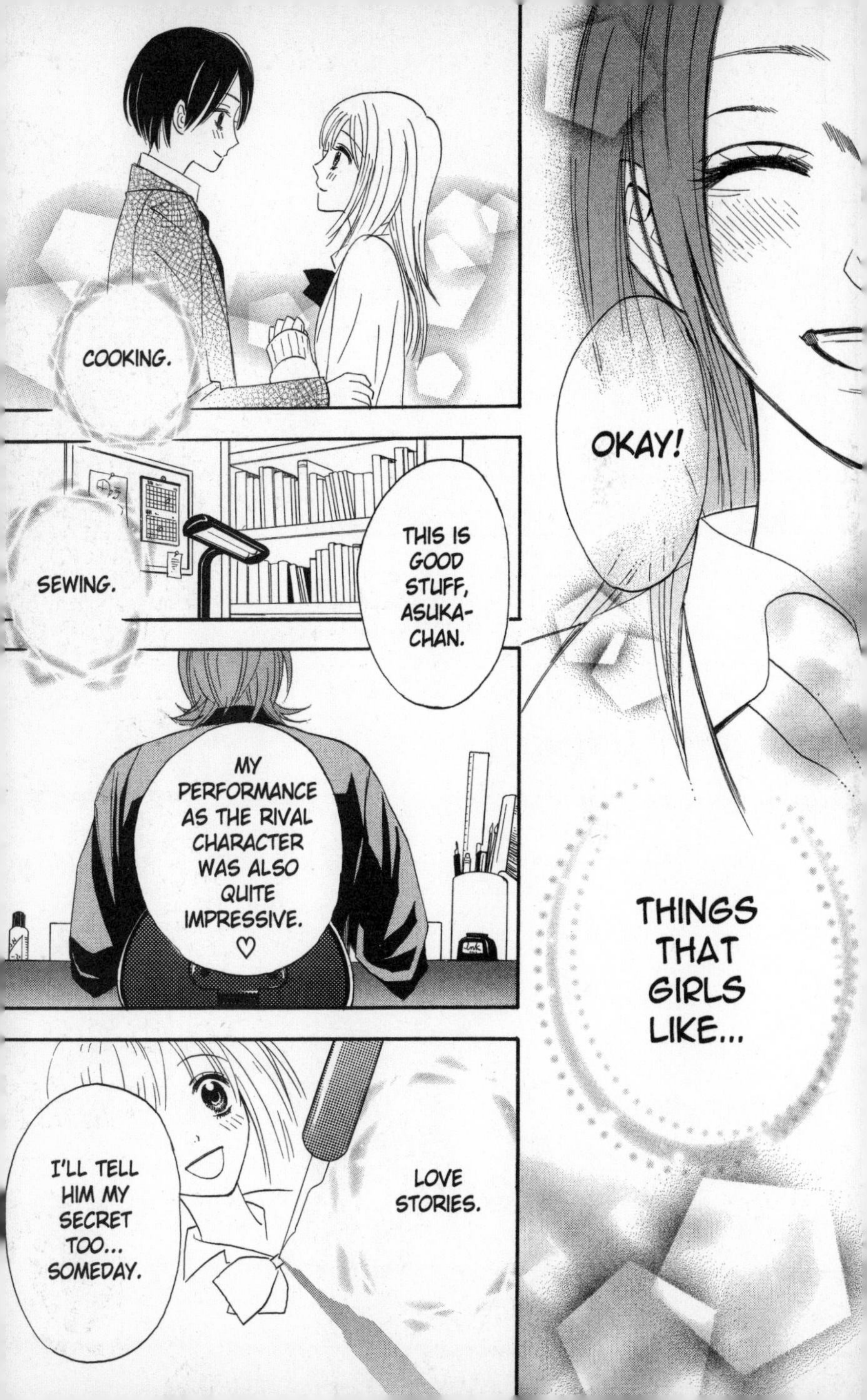
OKAY!
THINGS THAT GIRLS LIKE...
COOKING.
SEWING.
THIS IS GOOD STUFF, ASUKA-CHAN.
MY PERFORMANCE AS THE RIVAL CHARACTER WAS ALSO QUITE IMPRESSIVE. ♡
LOVE STORIES.
I'LL TELL HIM MY SECRET TOO... SOMEDAY.

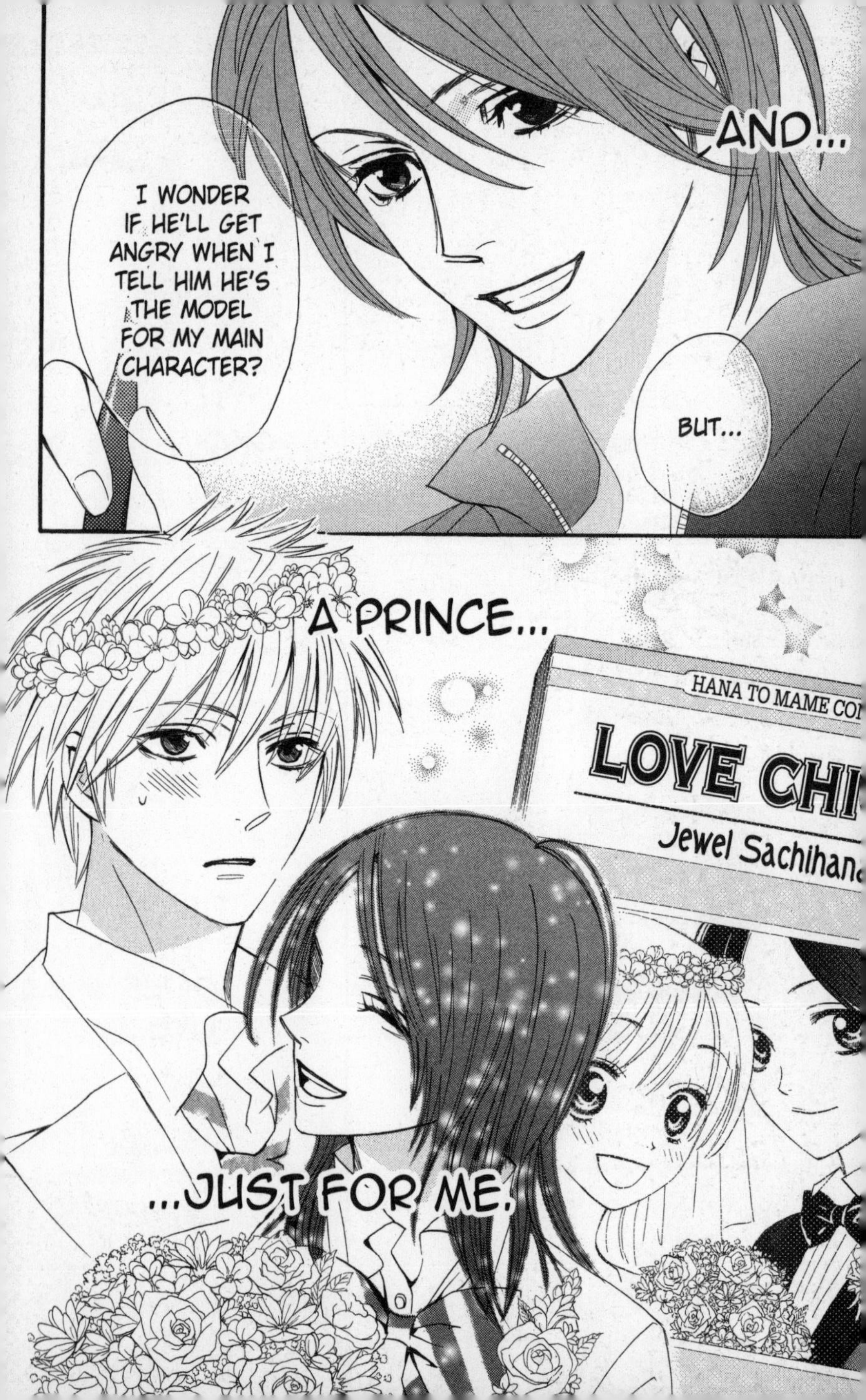
AND...
I WONDER IF HE'LL GET ANGRY WHEN I TELL HIM HE'S THE MODEL FOR MY MAIN CHARACTER?
BUT...
A PRINCE...
HANA TO MAME CO
LOVE CHI
Jewel Sachihan
...JUST FOR ME.

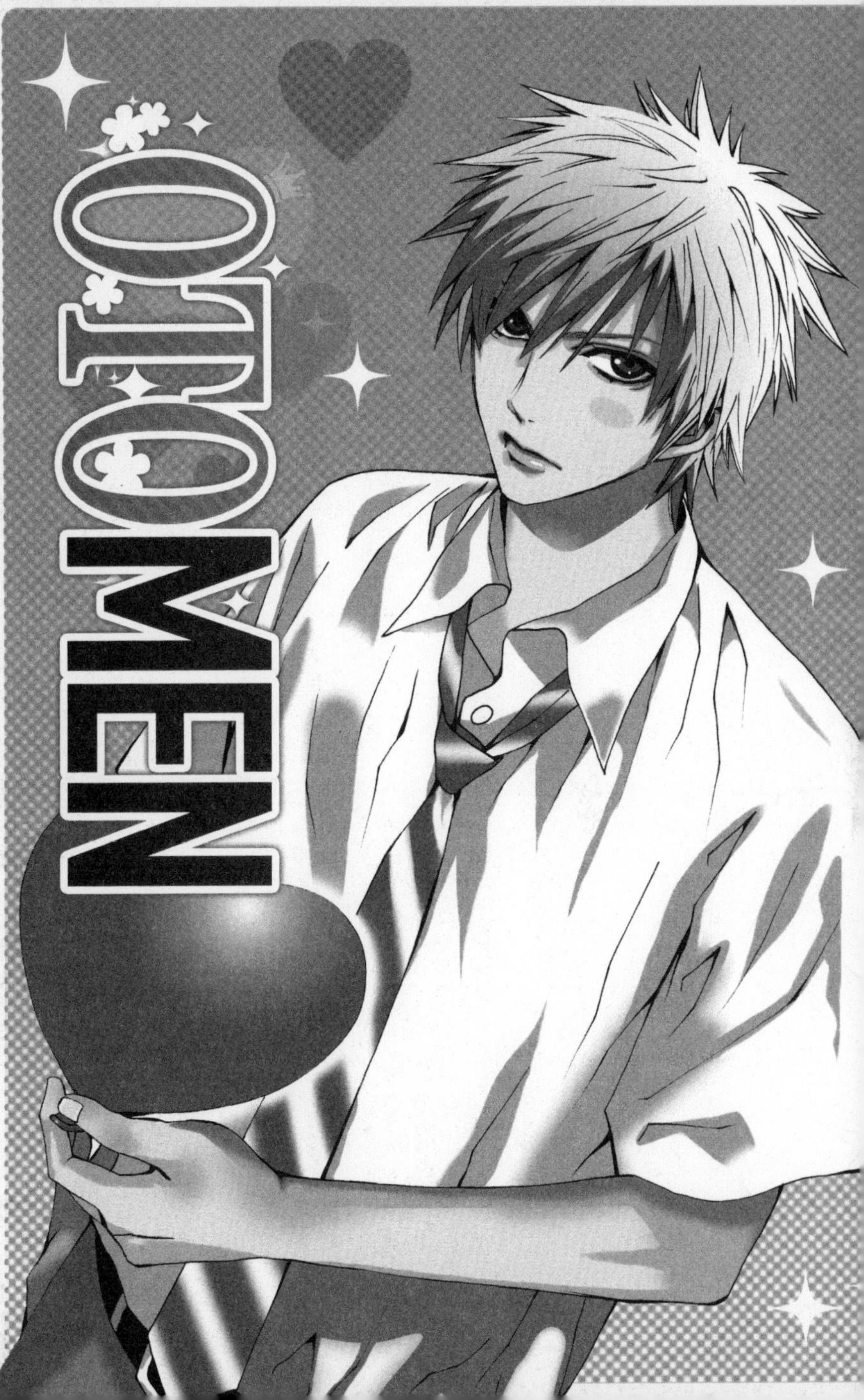
OTOMEN

OTOMEN

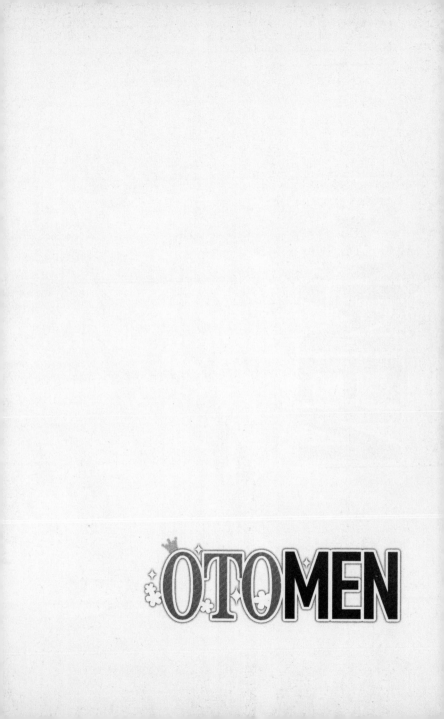

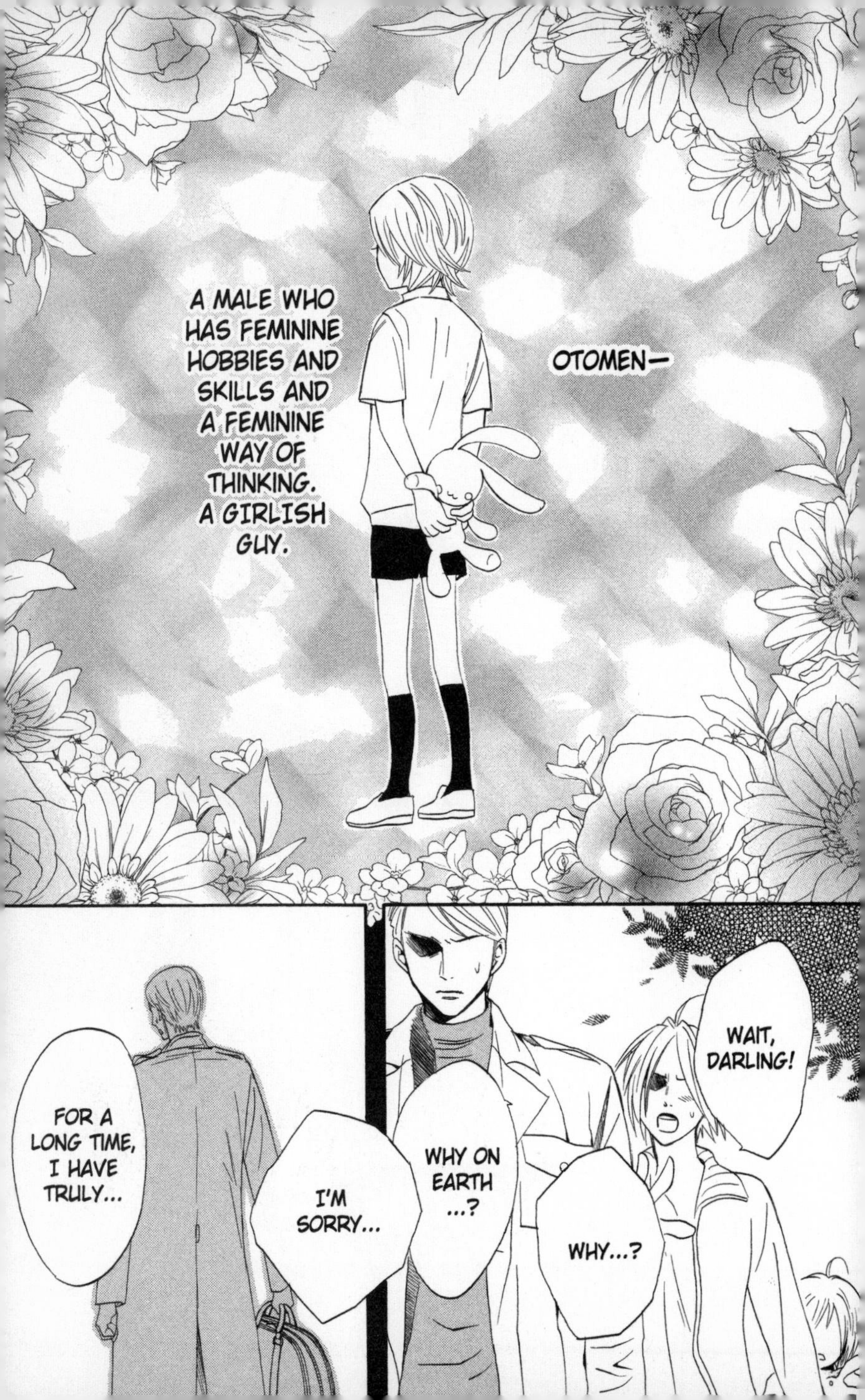
OTOMEN—
A MALE WHO HAS FEMININE HOBBIES AND SKILLS AND A FEMININE WAY OF THINKING. A GIRLISH GUY.
WAIT, DARLING!
WHY...?
WHY ON EARTH ...?
FOR A LONG TIME, I HAVE TRULY...
I'M SORRY...

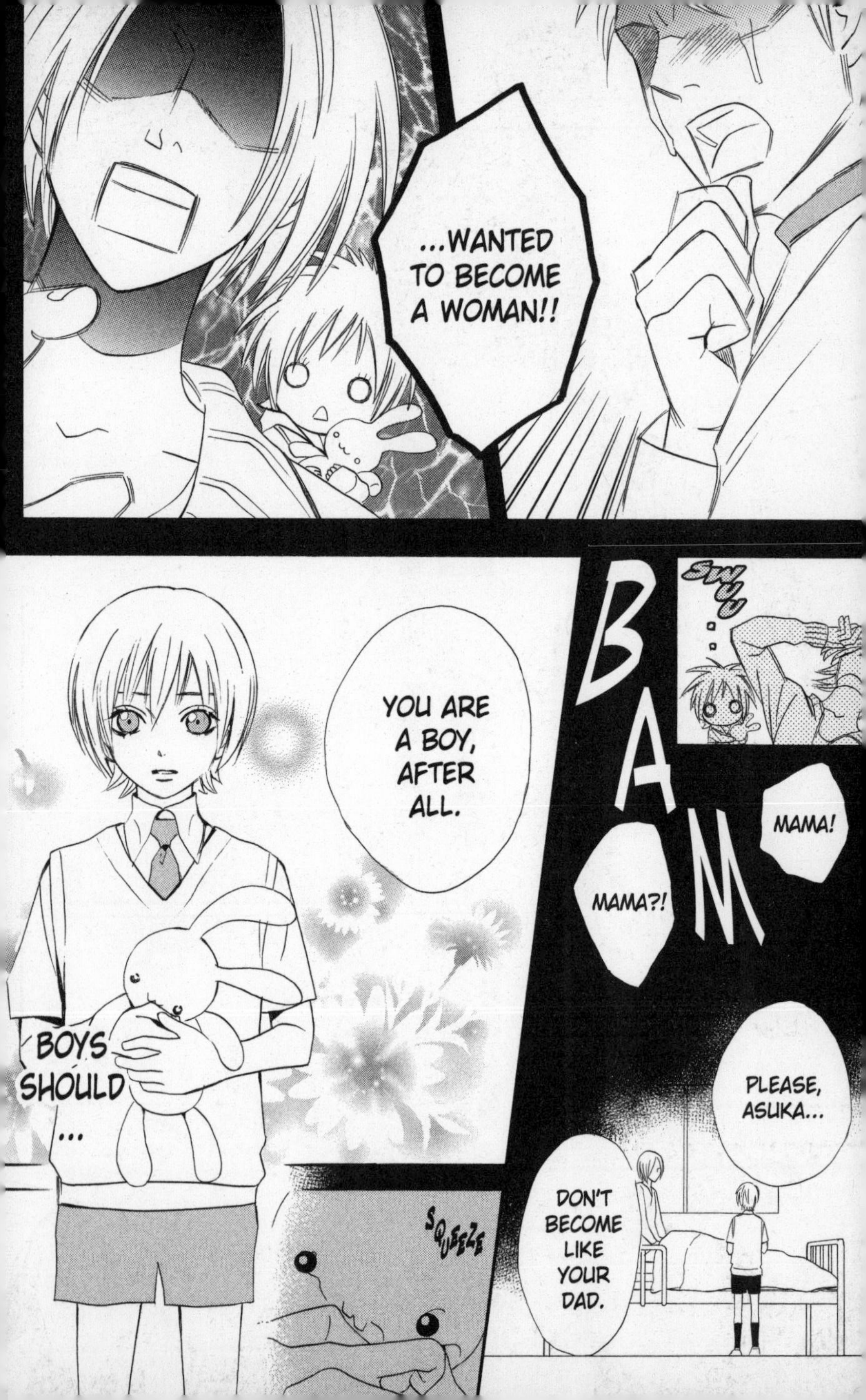
...WANTED TO BECOME A WOMAN!!
BAM
MAMA!
MAMA?!
PLEASE, ASUKA...
DON'T BECOME LIKE YOUR DAD.
YOU ARE A BOY, AFTER ALL.
BOYS SHOULD ...
SQUEEZE

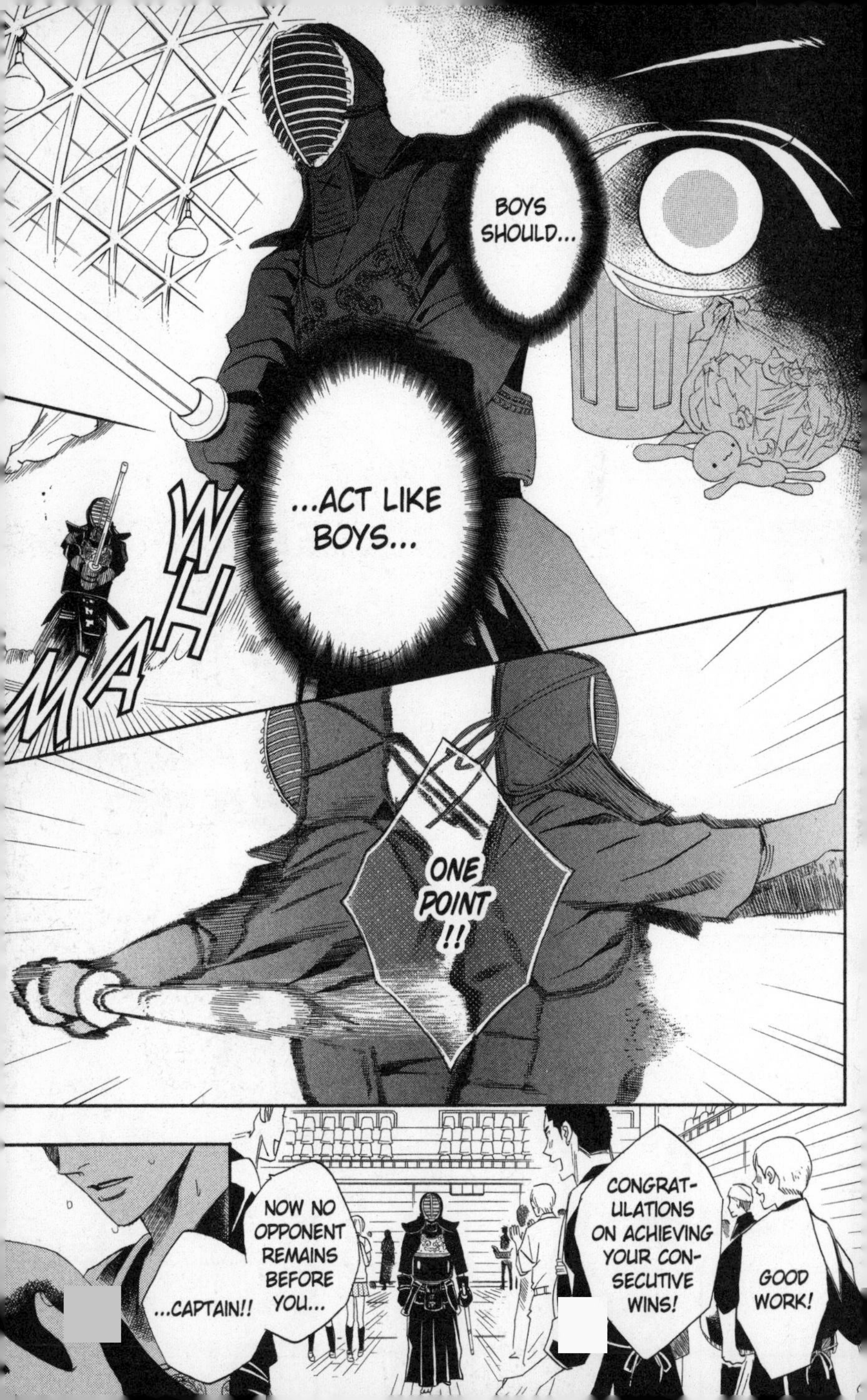
BOYS SHOULD...
...ACT LIKE BOYS...
ONE POINT !!
GOOD WORK!
CONGRAT-ULATIONS ON ACHIEVING YOUR CON-SECUTIVE WINS!
NOW NO OPPONENT REMAINS BEFORE YOU...
...CAPTAIN!!

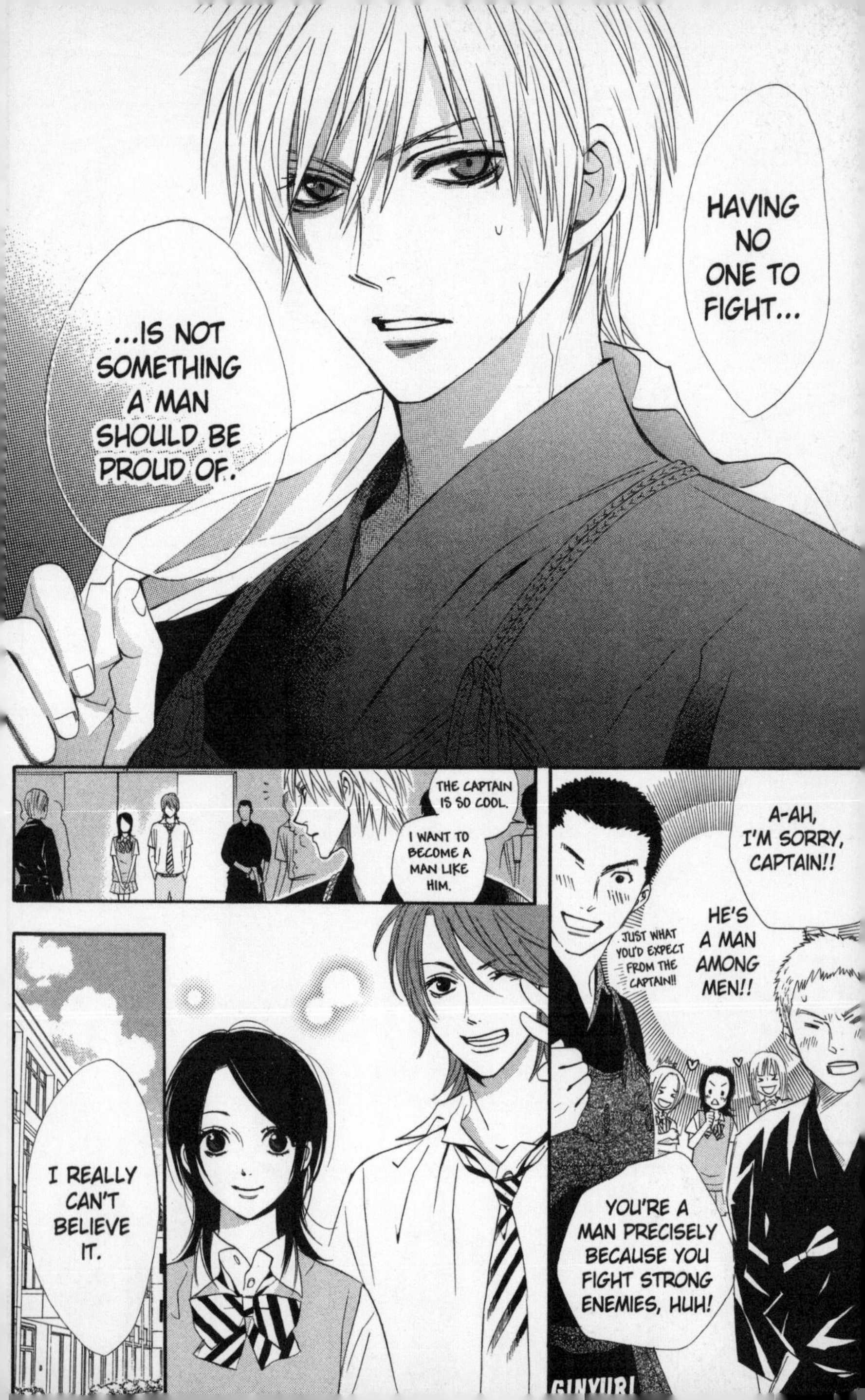
HAVING NO ONE TO FIGHT...
...IS NOT SOMETHING A MAN SHOULD BE PROUD OF.
A-AH, I'M SORRY, CAPTAIN!!
HE'S A MAN AMONG MEN!!
JUST WHAT YOU'D EXPECT FROM THE CAPTAIN!!
YOU'RE A MAN PRECISELY BECAUSE YOU FIGHT STRONG ENEMIES, HUH!
THE CAPTAIN IS SO COOL.
I WANT TO BECOME A MAN LIKE HIM.
I REALLY CAN'T BELIEVE IT.

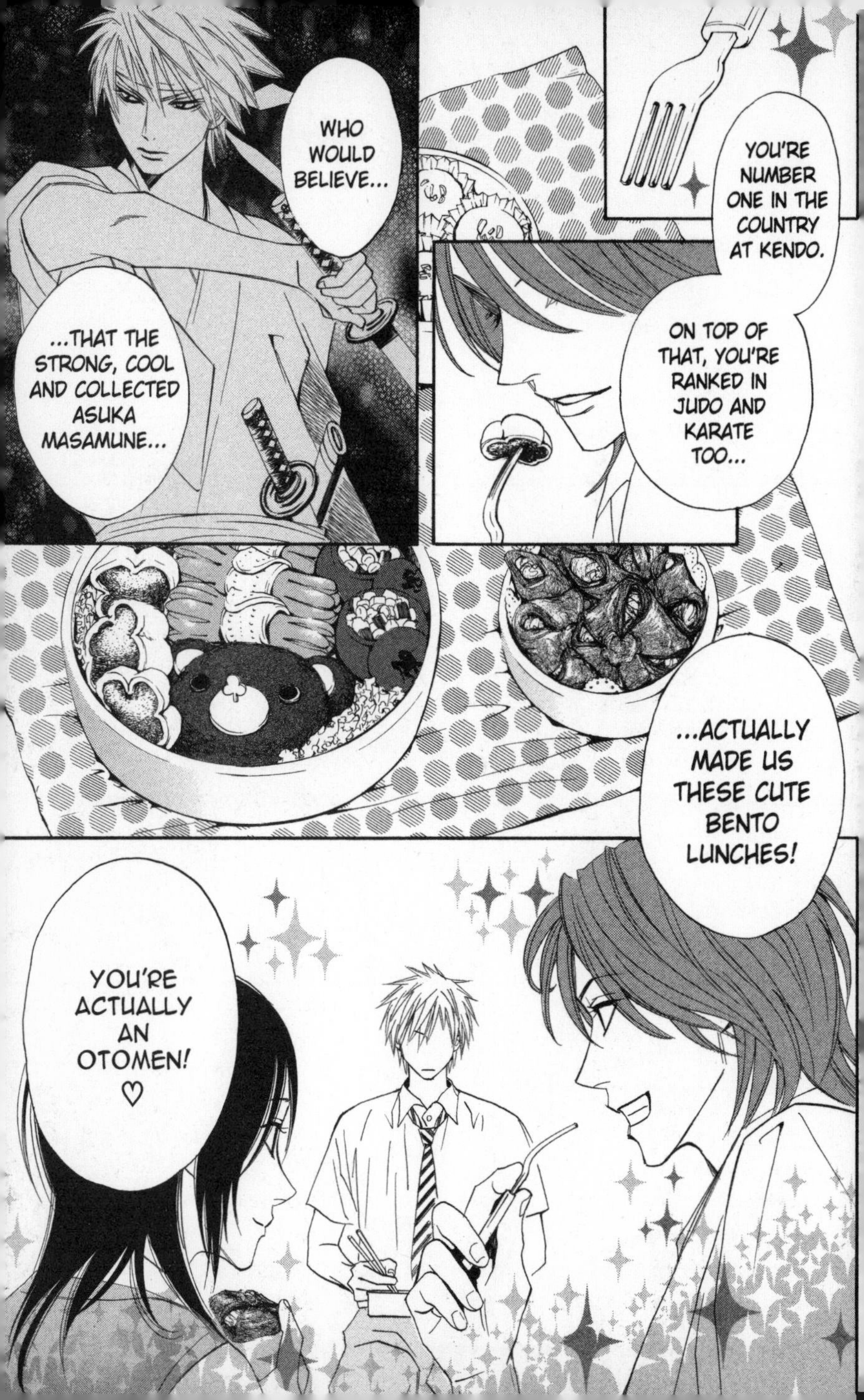
YOU'RE NUMBER ONE IN THE COUNTRY AT KENDO.
ON TOP OF THAT, YOU'RE RANKED IN JUDO AND KARATE TOO...
WHO WOULD BELIEVE...
...THAT THE STRONG, COOL AND COLLECTED ASUKA MASAMUNE...
...ACTUALLY MADE US THESE CUTE BENTO LUNCHES!
YOU'RE ACTUALLY AN OTOMEN! ♡

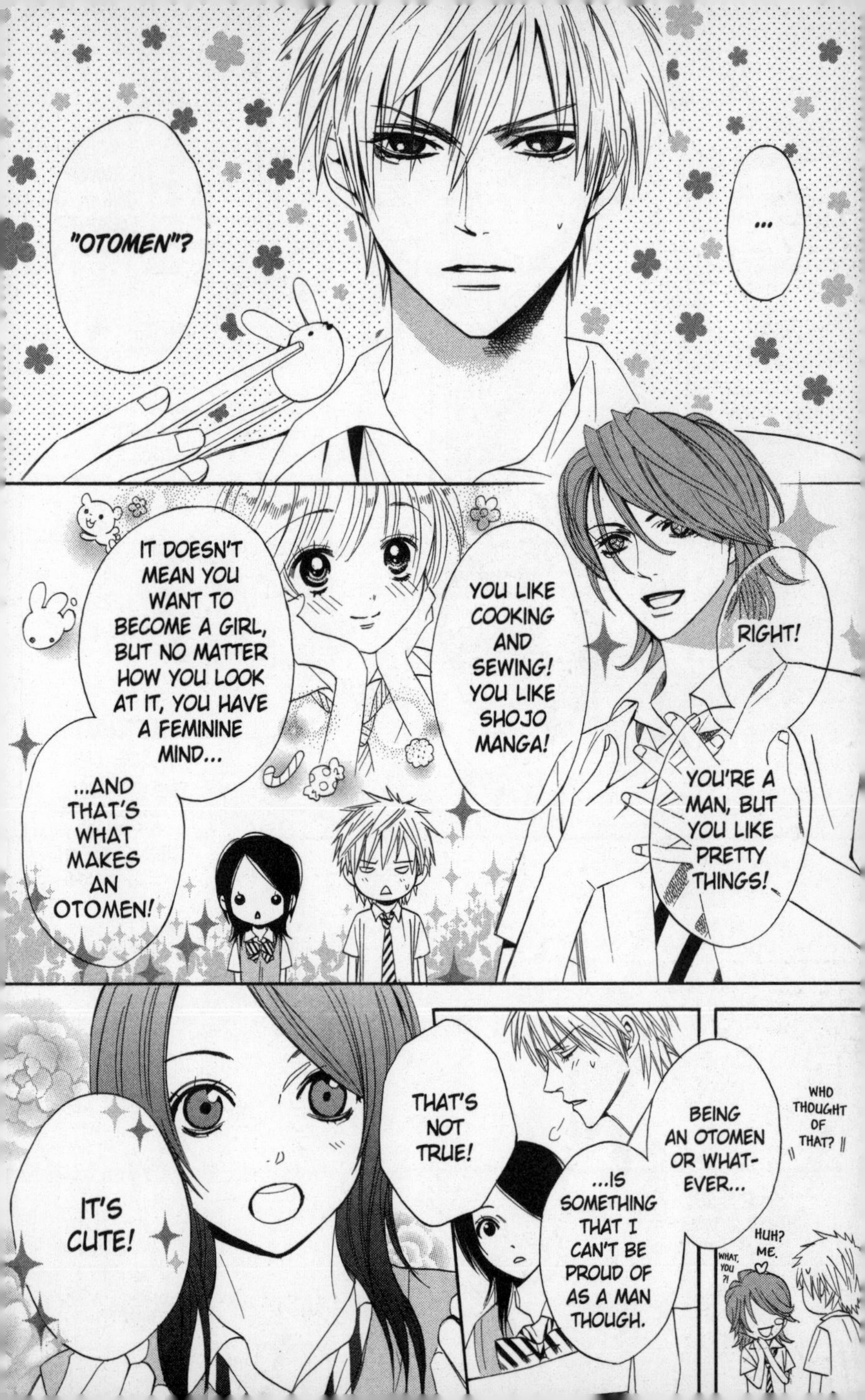
...
"OTOMEN"?
RIGHT!
YOU LIKE COOKING AND SEWING! YOU LIKE SHOJO MANGA!
YOU'RE A MAN, BUT YOU LIKE PRETTY THINGS!
IT DOESN'T MEAN YOU WANT TO BECOME A GIRL, BUT NO MATTER HOW YOU LOOK AT IT, YOU HAVE A FEMININE MIND...
...AND THAT'S WHAT MAKES AN OTOMEN!
WHO THOUGHT OF THAT?
HUH? ME.
WHAT, YOU?!
BEING AN OTOMEN OR WHATEVER...
...IS SOMETHING THAT I CAN'T BE PROUD OF AS A MAN THOUGH.
THAT'S NOT TRUE!
IT'S CUTE!

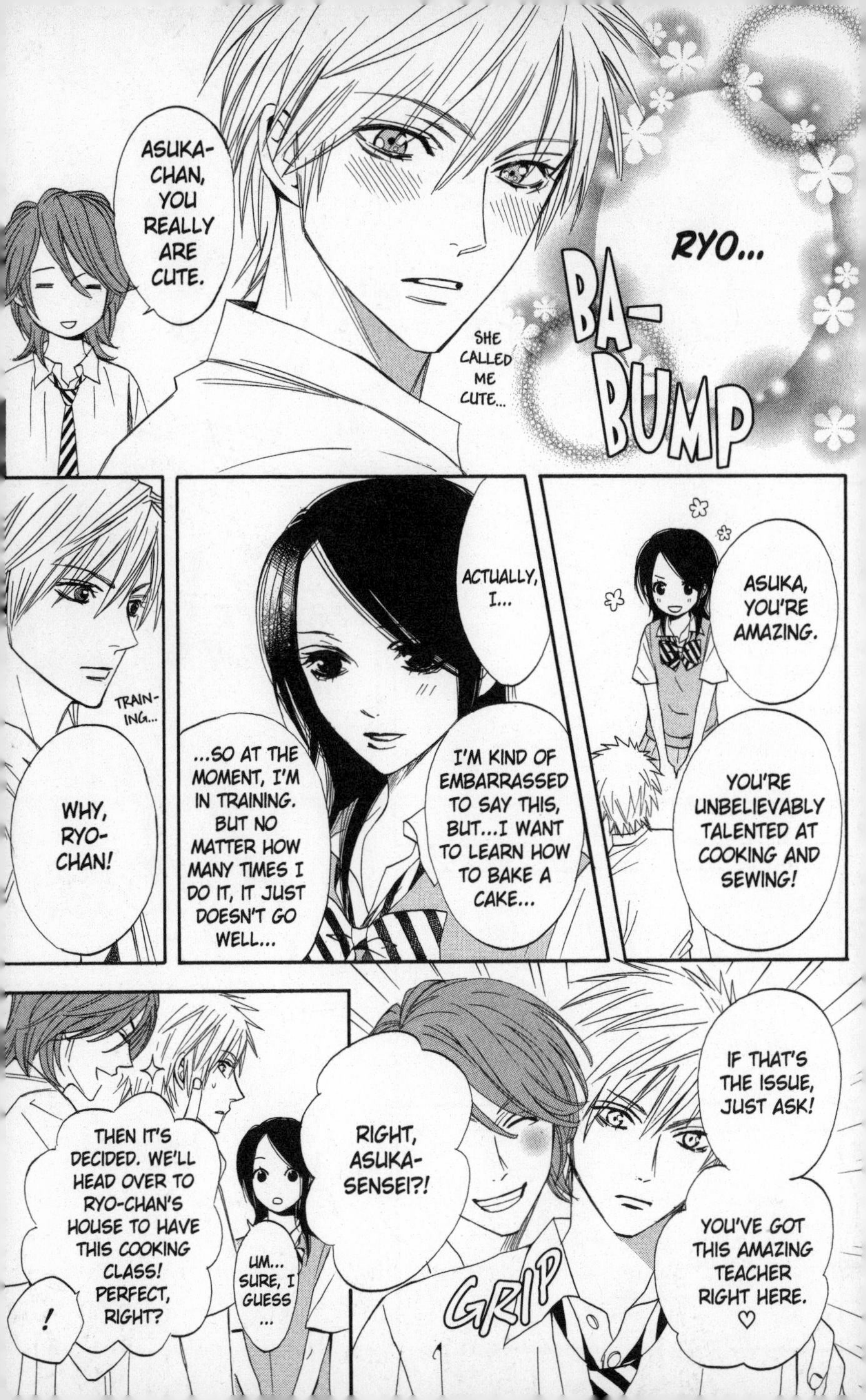
ASUKA-CHAN, YOU REALLY ARE CUTE.
RYO...
BA-BUMP
SHE CALLED ME CUTE...
ASUKA, YOU'RE AMAZING.
YOU'RE UNBELIEVABLY TALENTED AT COOKING AND SEWING!
ACTUALLY, I...
I'M KIND OF EMBARRASSED TO SAY THIS, BUT...I WANT TO LEARN HOW TO BAKE A CAKE...
...SO AT THE MOMENT, I'M IN TRAINING. BUT NO MATTER HOW MANY TIMES I DO IT, IT JUST DOESN'T GO WELL...
TRAINING...
WHY, RYO-CHAN!
IF THAT'S THE ISSUE, JUST ASK!
YOU'VE GOT THIS AMAZING TEACHER RIGHT HERE. ♡
RIGHT, ASUKA-SENSEI?!
GRIP
THEN IT'S DECIDED. WE'LL HEAD OVER TO RYO-CHAN'S HOUSE TO HAVE THIS COOKING CLASS! PERFECT, RIGHT?
UM... SURE, I GUESS...
!

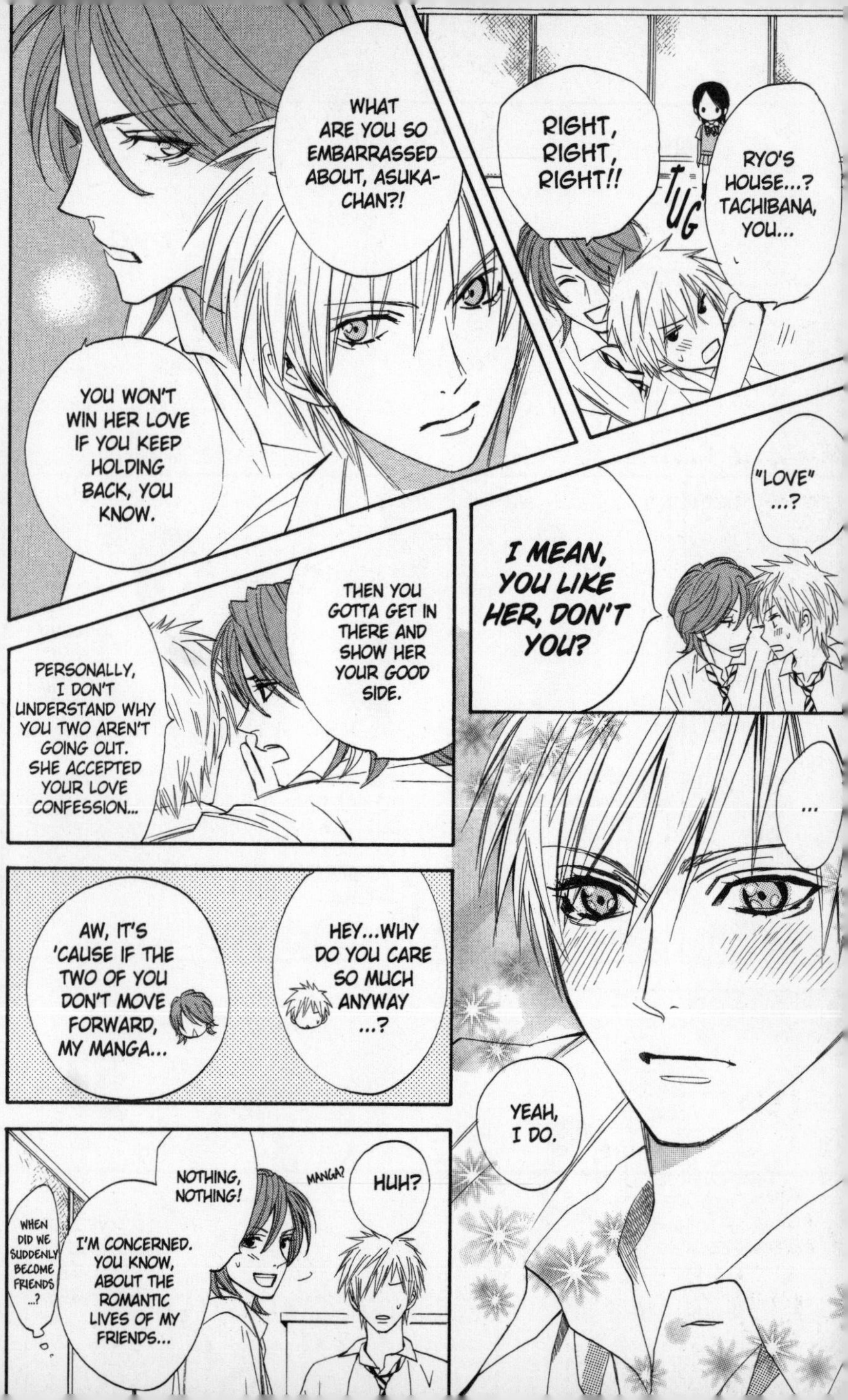
RYO'S HOUSE...? TACHIBANA, YOU...
TUG
RIGHT, RIGHT, RIGHT!!
WHAT ARE YOU SO EMBARRASSED ABOUT, ASUKA-CHAN?!
YOU WON'T WIN HER LOVE IF YOU KEEP HOLDING BACK, YOU KNOW.
"LOVE" ...?
I MEAN, YOU LIKE HER, DON'T YOU?
THEN YOU GOTTA GET IN THERE AND SHOW HER YOUR GOOD SIDE.
PERSONALLY, I DON'T UNDERSTAND WHY YOU TWO AREN'T GOING OUT. SHE ACCEPTED YOUR LOVE CONFESSION...
...
YEAH, I DO.
HEY...WHY DO YOU CARE SO MUCH ANYWAY ...?
AW, IT'S 'CAUSE IF THE TWO OF YOU DON'T MOVE FORWARD, MY MANGA...
HUH?
MANGA?
NOTHING, NOTHING!
I'M CONCERNED. YOU KNOW, ABOUT THE ROMANTIC LIVES OF MY FRIENDS...
WHEN DID WE SUDDENLY BECOME FRIENDS ...?

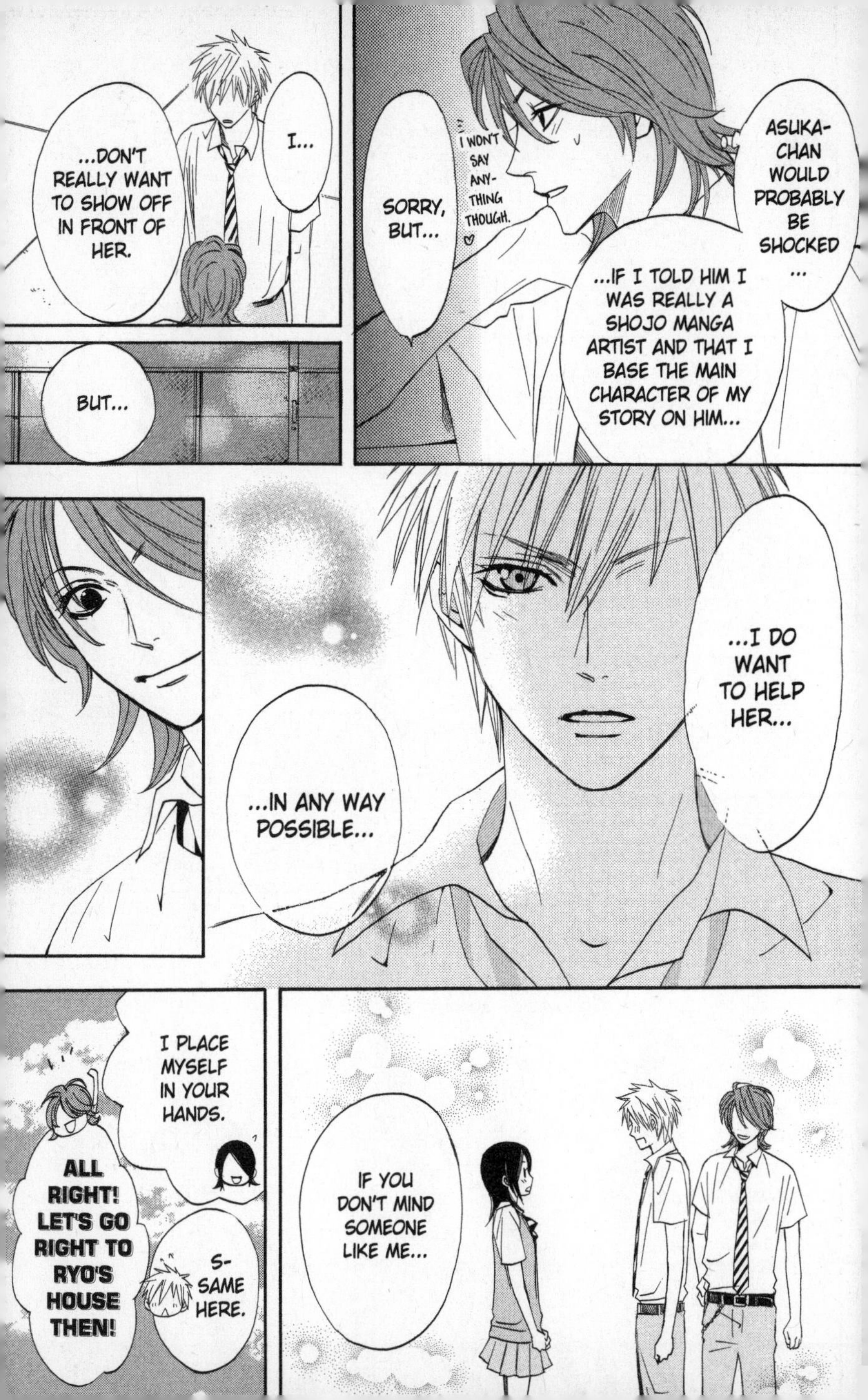
ASUKA-CHAN WOULD PROBABLY BE SHOCKED...
...IF I TOLD HIM I WAS REALLY A SHOJO MANGA ARTIST AND THAT I BASE THE MAIN CHARACTER OF MY STORY ON HIM...
I WON'T SAY ANY-THING THOUGH.
SORRY, BUT...
I...
...DON'T REALLY WANT TO SHOW OFF IN FRONT OF HER.
BUT...
...I DO WANT TO HELP HER...
...IN ANY WAY POSSIBLE...
IF YOU DON'T MIND SOMEONE LIKE ME...
I PLACE MYSELF IN YOUR HANDS.
ALL RIGHT! LET'S GO RIGHT TO RYO'S HOUSE THEN!
S-SAME HERE.

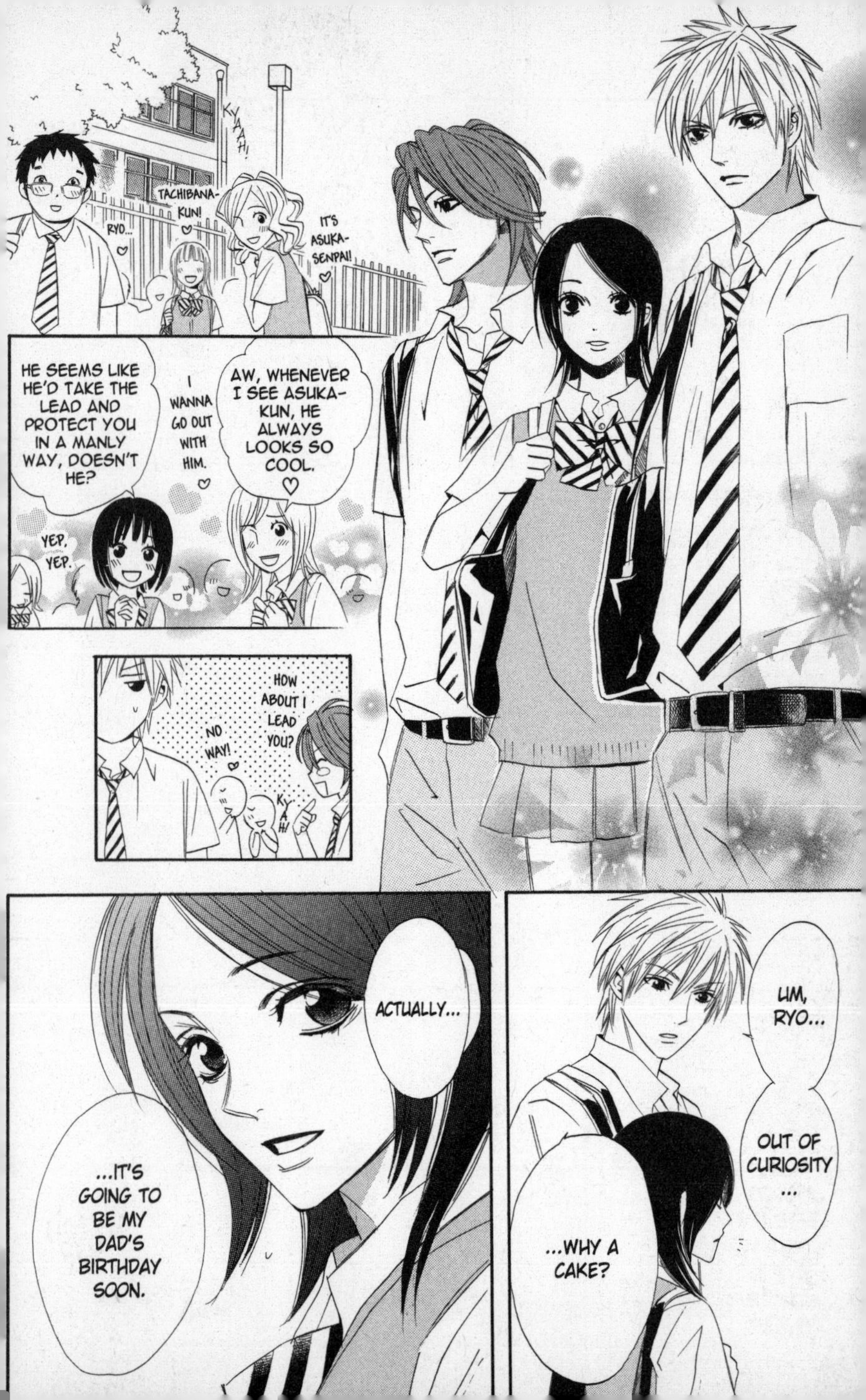
KYAAAH!
IT'S ASUKA-SENPAI!
TACHIBANA-KUN!
RYO...
AW, WHENEVER I SEE ASUKA-KUN, HE ALWAYS LOOKS SO COOL.
I WANNA GO OUT WITH HIM.
HE SEEMS LIKE HE'D TAKE THE LEAD AND PROTECT YOU IN A MANLY WAY, DOESN'T HE?
YEP, YEP.
HOW ABOUT I LEAD YOU?
KYAAH!
NO WAY!
UM, RYO...
OUT OF CURIOSITY...
...WHY A CAKE?
ACTUALLY...
...IT'S GOING TO BE MY DAD'S BIRTHDAY SOON.

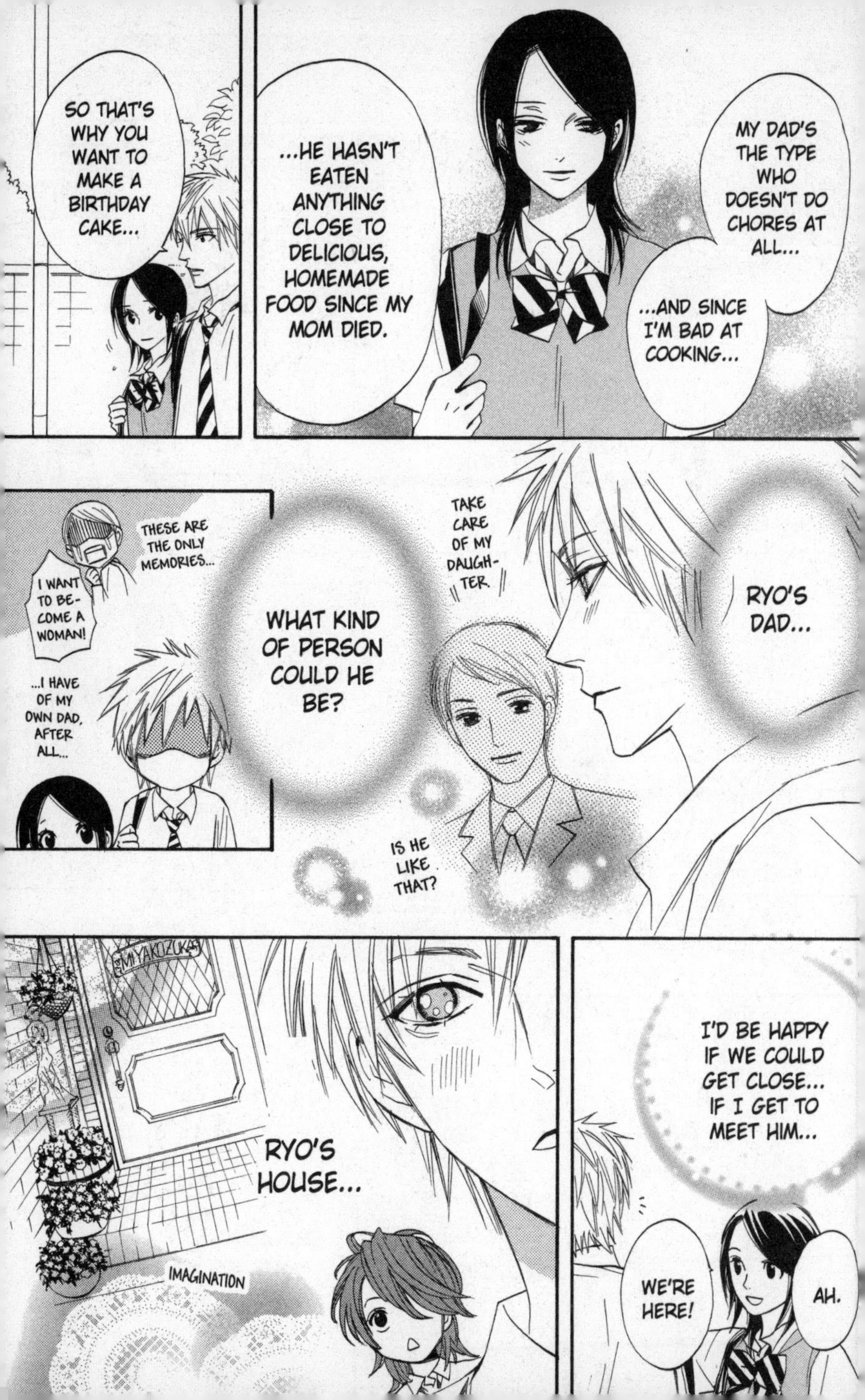
MY DAD'S THE TYPE WHO DOESN'T DO CHORES AT ALL...
...AND SINCE I'M BAD AT COOKING...
...HE HASN'T EATEN ANYTHING CLOSE TO DELICIOUS, HOMEMADE FOOD SINCE MY MOM DIED.
SO THAT'S WHY YOU WANT TO MAKE A BIRTHDAY CAKE...
RYO'S DAD...
TAKE CARE OF MY DAUGH-TER.
WHAT KIND OF PERSON COULD HE BE?
IS HE LIKE THAT?
THESE ARE THE ONLY MEMORIES...
I WANT TO BE-COME A WOMAN!
...I HAVE OF MY OWN DAD, AFTER ALL...
I'D BE HAPPY IF WE COULD GET CLOSE... IF I GET TO MEET HIM...
AH.
WE'RE HERE!
MIYAKOZUKA
RYO'S HOUSE...
IMAGINATION

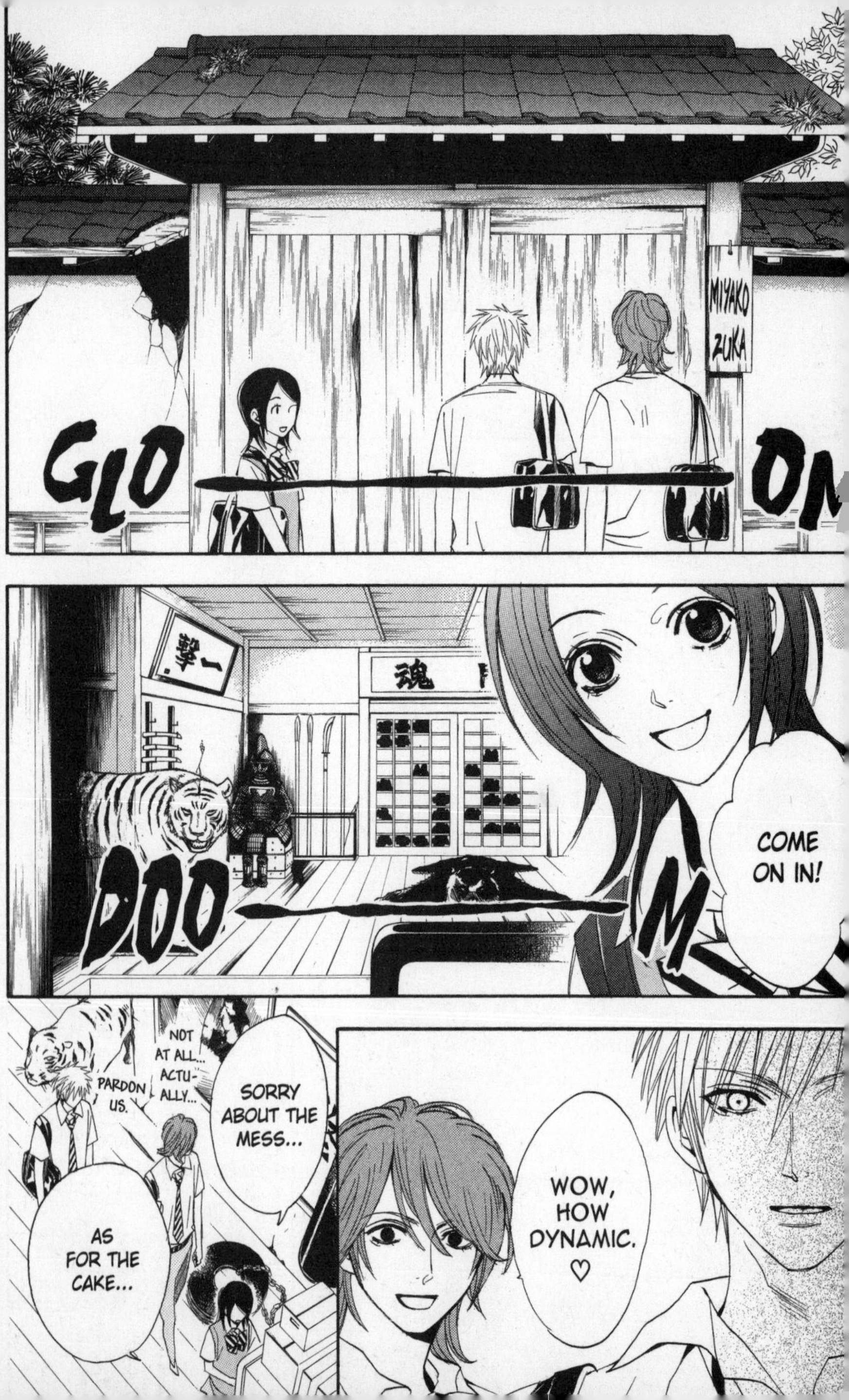
MIYAKO ZUKA
GLO
OM
一撃
魂
COME ON IN!
DOO
M
WOW, HOW DYNAMIC. ♡
SORRY ABOUT THE MESS...
NOT AT ALL... ACTU- ALLY...
PARDON US.
AS FOR THE CAKE...

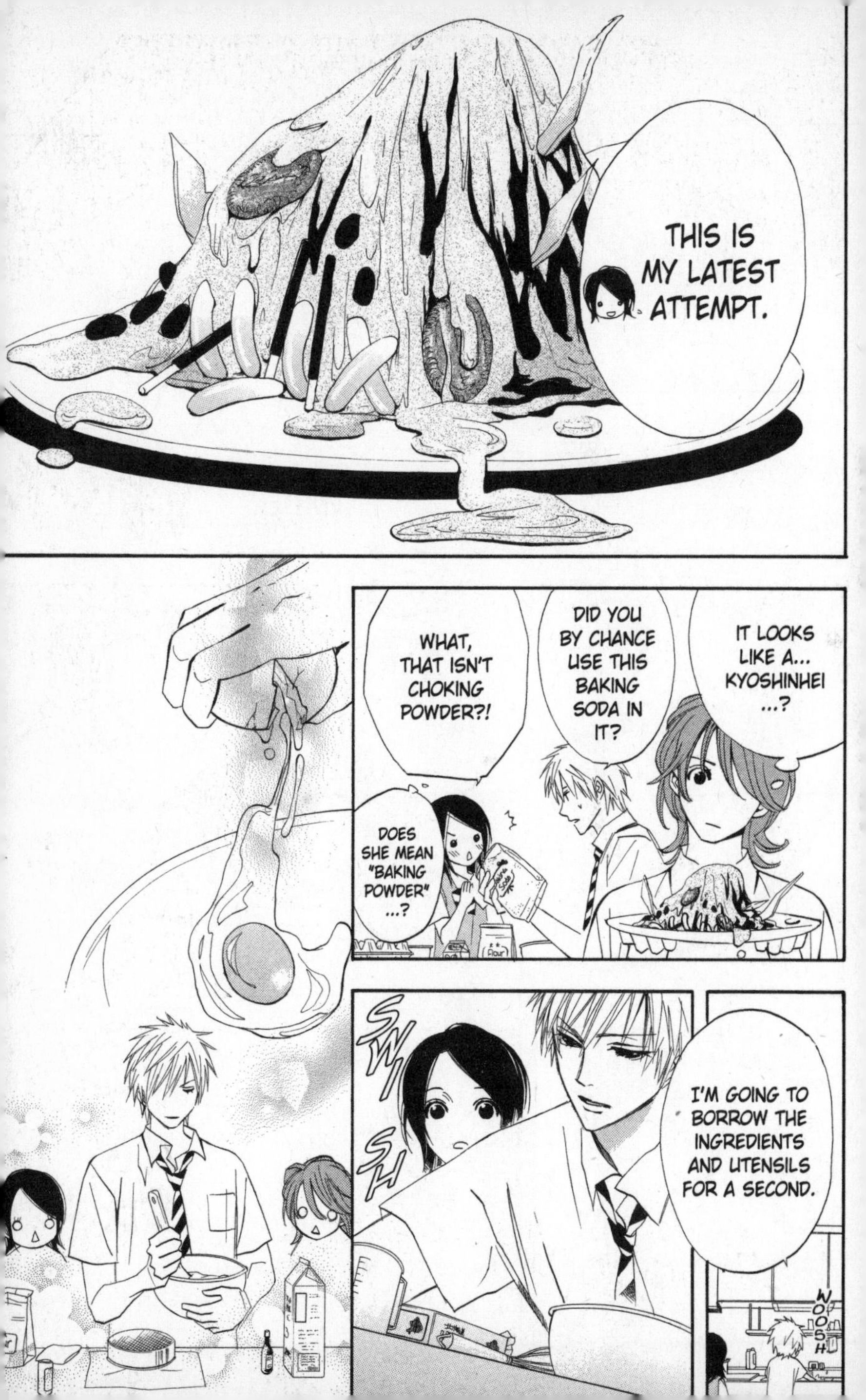
THIS IS MY LATEST ATTEMPT.
IT LOOKS LIKE A... KYOSHINHEI ...?
DID YOU BY CHANCE USE THIS BAKING SODA IN IT?
WHAT, THAT ISN'T CHOKING POWDER?!
DOES SHE MEAN "BAKING POWDER" ...?
I'M GOING TO BORROW THE INGREDIENTS AND UTENSILS FOR A SECOND.
WOOSH
SWISH

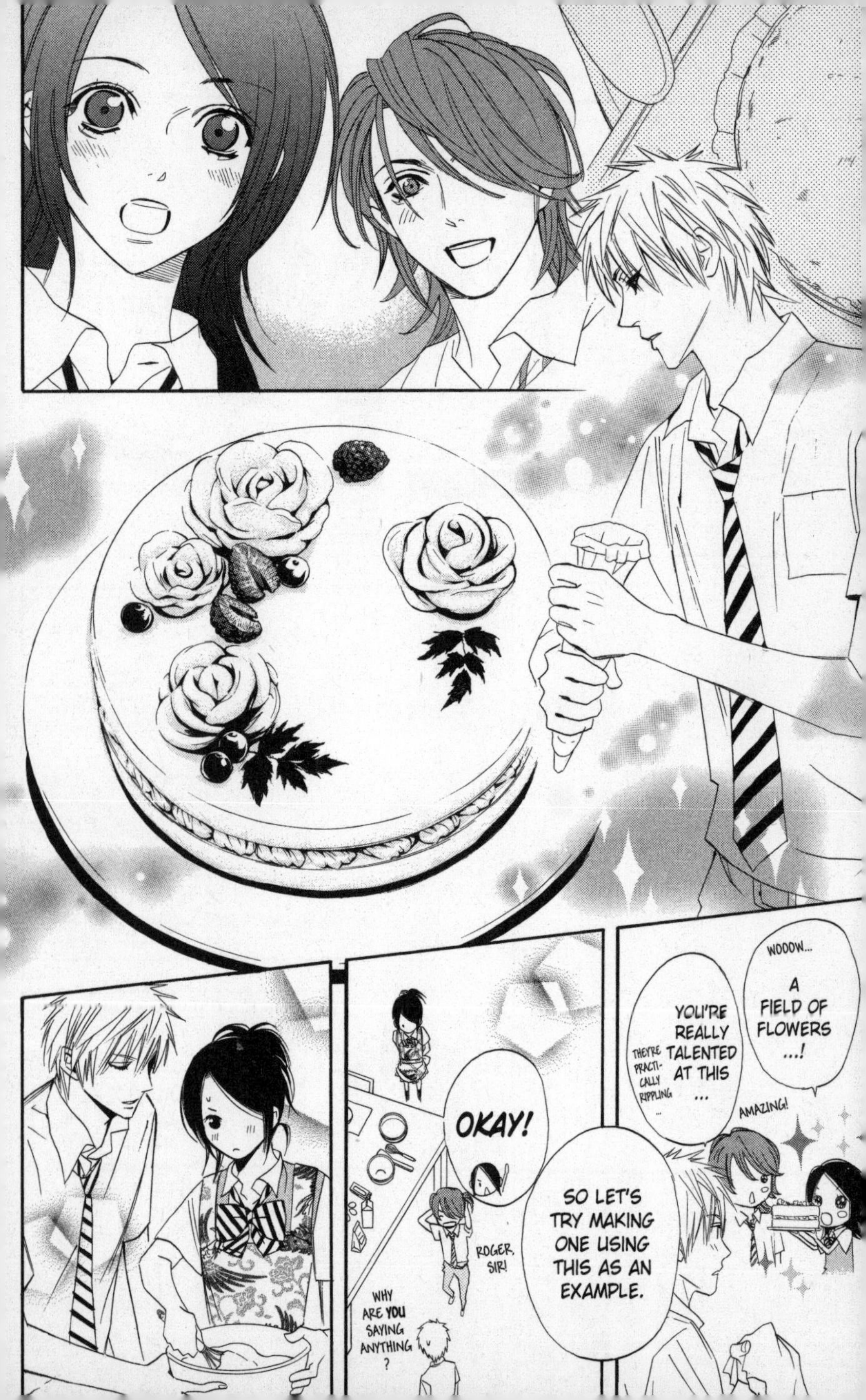

WOOOW...
A FIELD OF FLOWERS ...!
YOU'RE REALLY TALENTED AT THIS ...
THEY'RE PRACTI-CALLY RIPPLING ...
AMAZING!
SO LET'S TRY MAKING ONE USING THIS AS AN EXAMPLE.
OKAY!
ROGER, SIR!
WHY ARE YOU SAYING ANYTHING ?

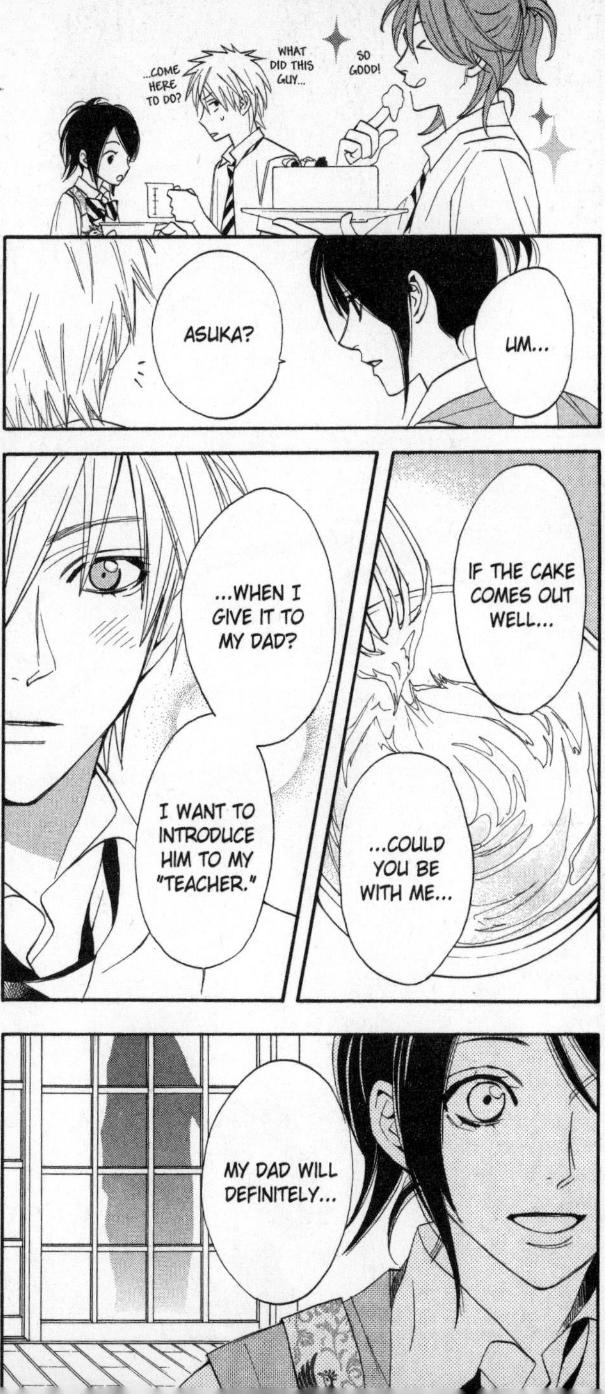
SO GOOD!
WHAT DID THIS GUY...
...COME HERE TO DO?
UM...
ASUKA?
IF THE CAKE COMES OUT WELL...
...COULD YOU BE WITH ME...
...WHEN I GIVE IT TO MY DAD?
I WANT TO INTRODUCE HIM TO MY "TEACHER."
MY DAD WILL DEFINITELY...

Since the main character Asuka has exactly the opposite hobbies and sensitivies as me, I always try to draw things as far from what I like as I can when drawing his dreams and the things he loves. When I do that, it naturally becomes feminine...or at least I think that it does.
The heroine Ryo is the exact opposite of Asuka, but even so, she likes masculinity in a slightly different way than what I like. Basically, I just think of her and draw her as "the extremely thick-skinned and clueless yet cool boy in shojo manga."

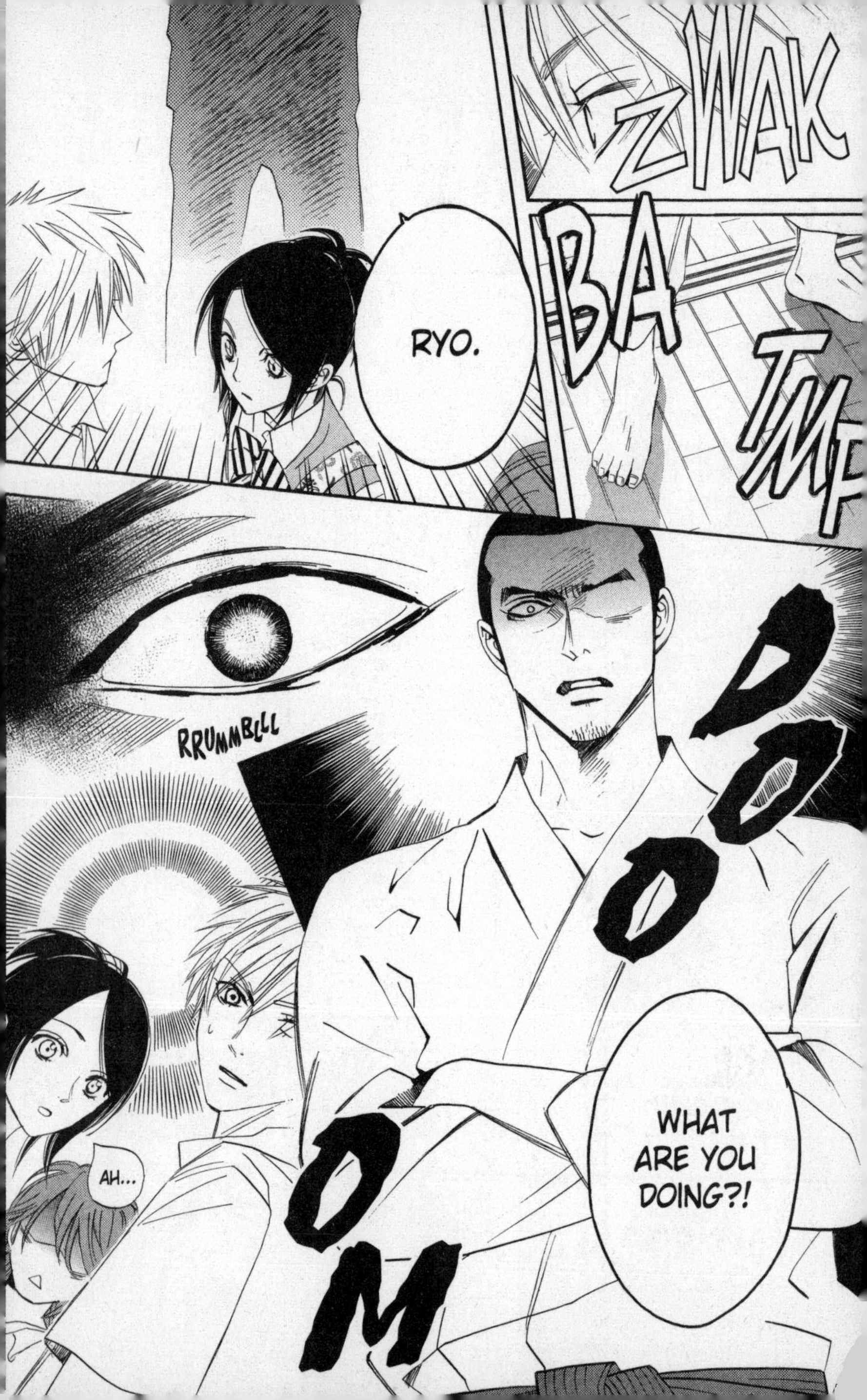
ZWAK
BA
TUMP
RYO.
DOOOOM
WHAT ARE YOU DOING?!
RRUMMBLLL
AH...

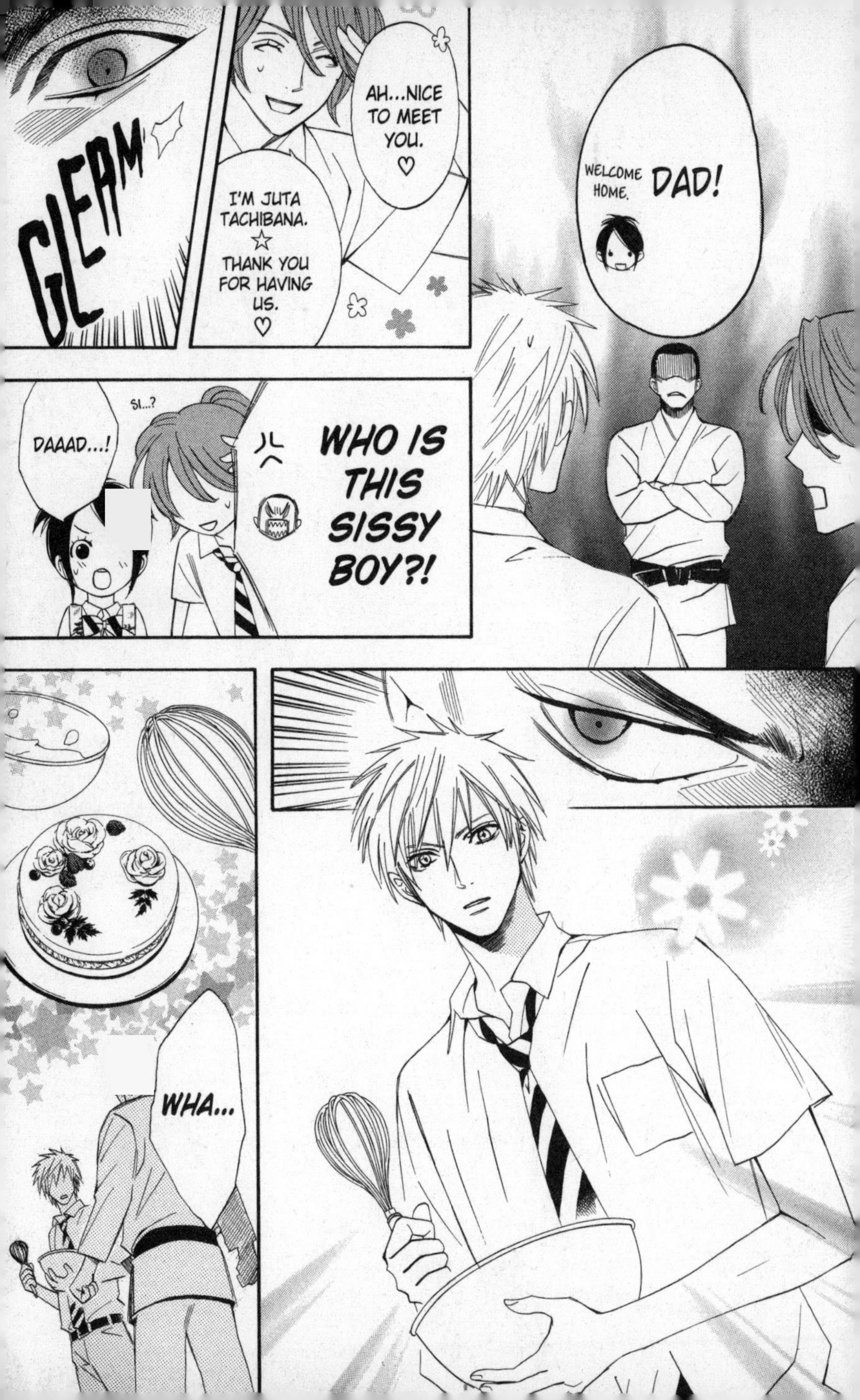
WELCOME HOME, DAD!
AH...NICE TO MEET YOU. ♡
I'M JUTA TACHIBANA. ☆ THANK YOU FOR HAVING US. ♡
GLEAM
WHO IS THIS SISSY BOY?!
SI...?
DAAAD...!
WHA...

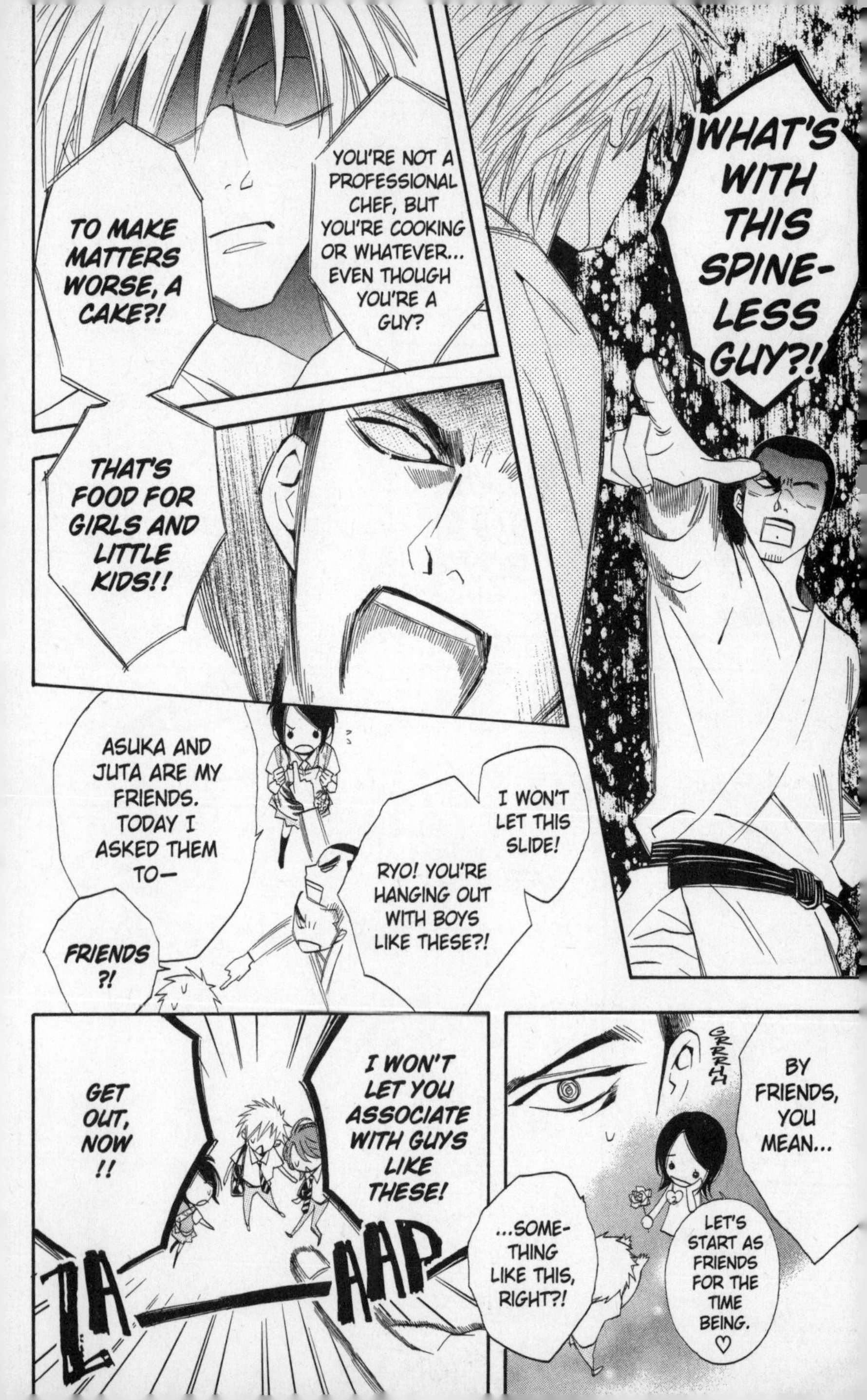
WHAT'S WITH THIS SPINE-LESS GUY?!
YOU'RE NOT A PROFESSIONAL CHEF, BUT YOU'RE COOKING OR WHATEVER... EVEN THOUGH YOU'RE A GUY?
TO MAKE MATTERS WORSE, A CAKE?!
THAT'S FOOD FOR GIRLS AND LITTLE KIDS!!
ASUKA AND JUTA ARE MY FRIENDS. TODAY I ASKED THEM TO—
FRIENDS ?!
I WON'T LET THIS SLIDE!
RYO! YOU'RE HANGING OUT WITH BOYS LIKE THESE?!
GRRRHH
BY FRIENDS, YOU MEAN...
LET'S START AS FRIENDS FOR THE TIME BEING. ♡
...SOME-THING LIKE THIS, RIGHT?!
I WON'T LET YOU ASSOCIATE WITH GUYS LIKE THESE!
GET OUT, NOW !!
ZLA——AAP

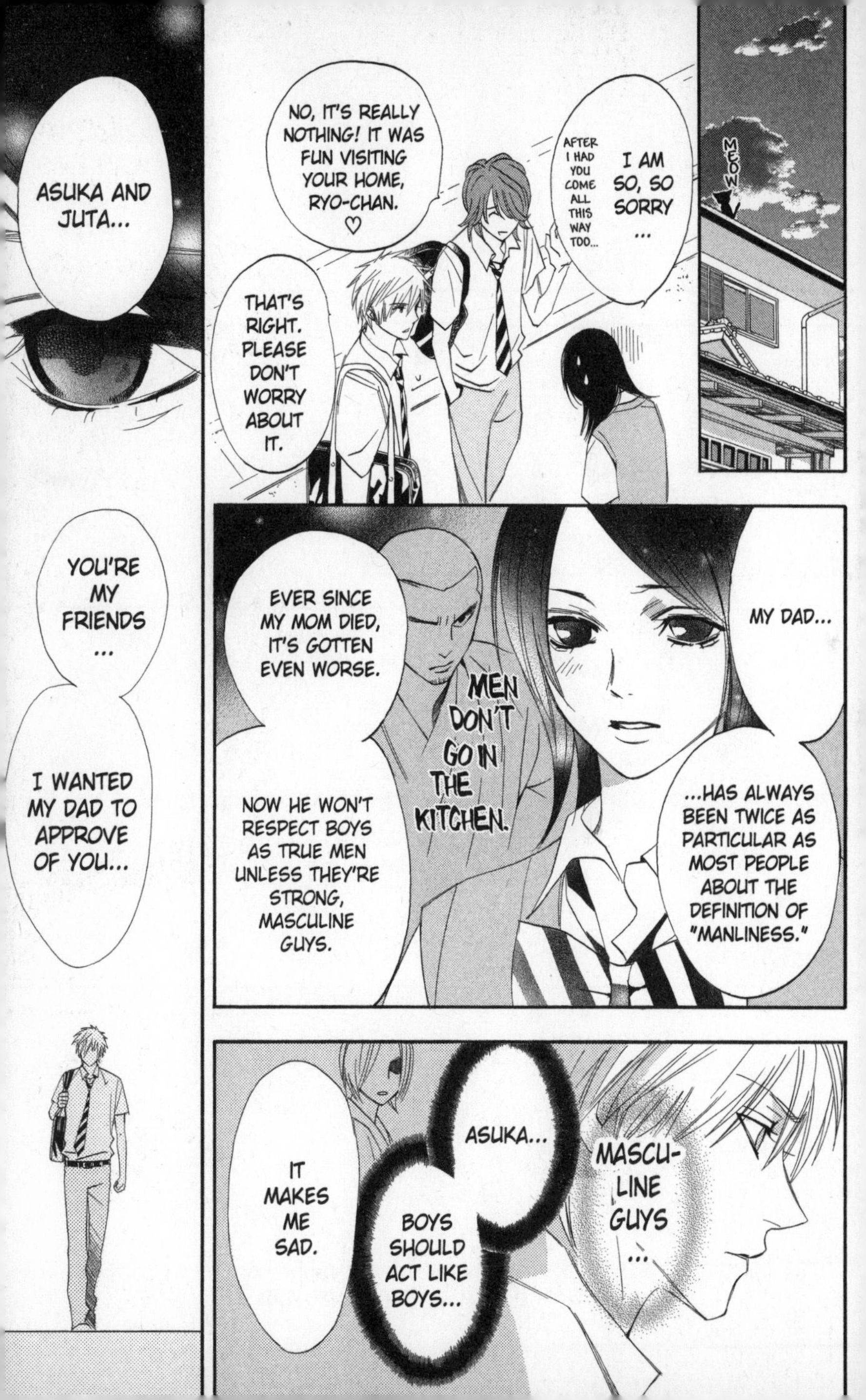
MEOW
I AM SO, SO SORRY...
AFTER I HAD YOU COME ALL THIS WAY TOO...
NO, IT'S REALLY NOTHING! IT WAS FUN VISITING YOUR HOME, RYO-CHAN. ♡
THAT'S RIGHT. PLEASE DON'T WORRY ABOUT IT.
MY DAD...
...HAS ALWAYS BEEN TWICE AS PARTICULAR AS MOST PEOPLE ABOUT THE DEFINITION OF "MANLINESS."
MEN DON'T GO IN THE KITCHEN.
EVER SINCE MY MOM DIED, IT'S GOTTEN EVEN WORSE.
NOW HE WON'T RESPECT BOYS AS TRUE MEN UNLESS THEY'RE STRONG, MASCULINE GUYS.
MASCU-LINE GUYS...
ASUKA...
BOYS SHOULD ACT LIKE BOYS...
IT MAKES ME SAD.
ASUKA AND JUTA...
YOU'RE MY FRIENDS...
I WANTED MY DAD TO APPROVE OF YOU...

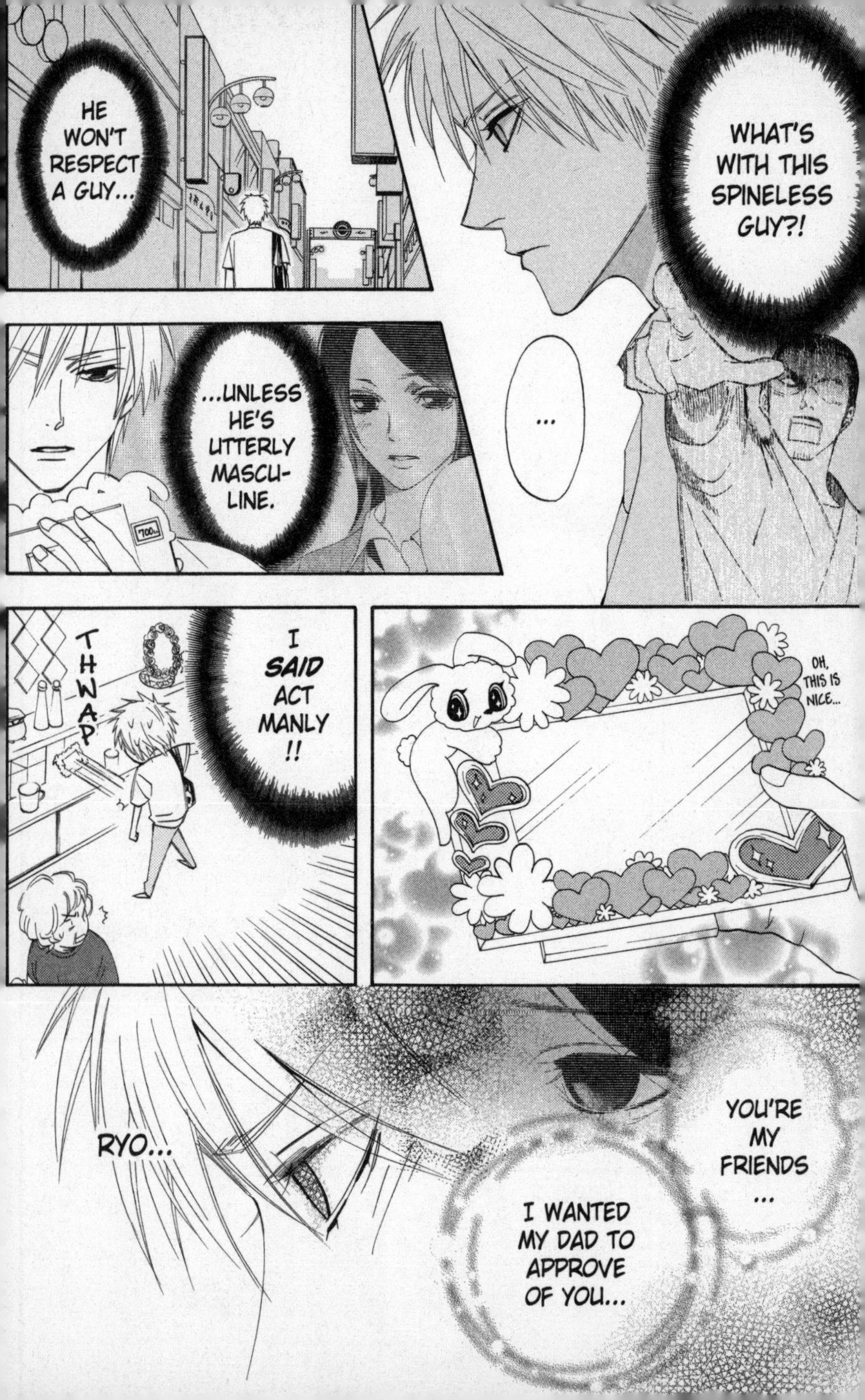
WHAT'S WITH THIS SPINELESS GUY?!
...
HE WON'T RESPECT A GUY...
...UNLESS HE'S UTTERLY MASCU-LINE.
OH, THIS IS NICE...
I SAID ACT MANLY!!
THWAP
YOU'RE MY FRIENDS...
I WANTED MY DAD TO APPROVE OF YOU...
RYO...

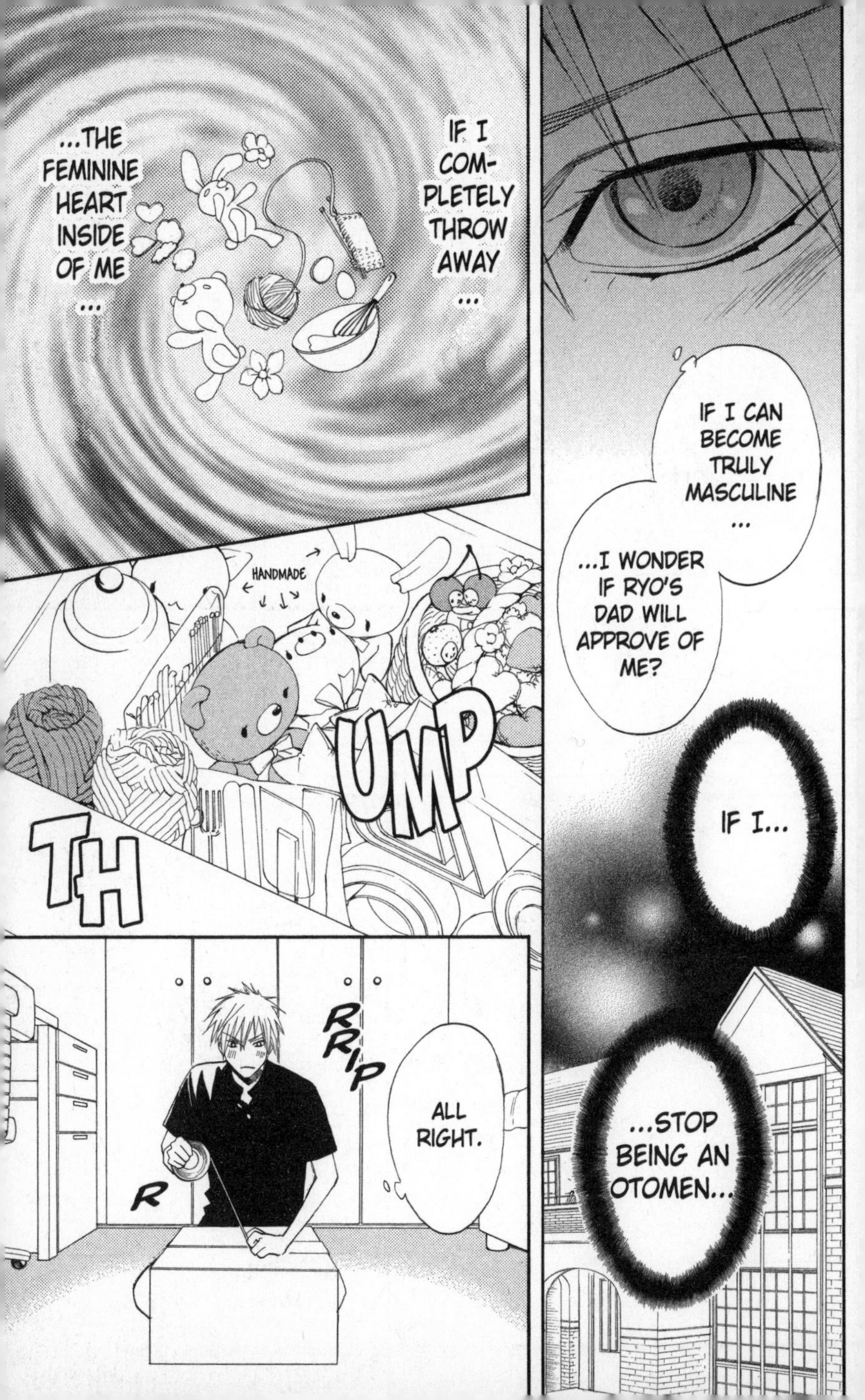
IF I CAN BECOME TRULY MASCULINE ...
...I WONDER IF RYO'S DAD WILL APPROVE OF ME?
IF I...
...STOP BEING AN OTOMEN...
IF I COM-PLETELY THROW AWAY ...
...THE FEMININE HEART INSIDE OF ME ...
HANDMADE
UMP
TH
RRIP
ALL RIGHT.
R

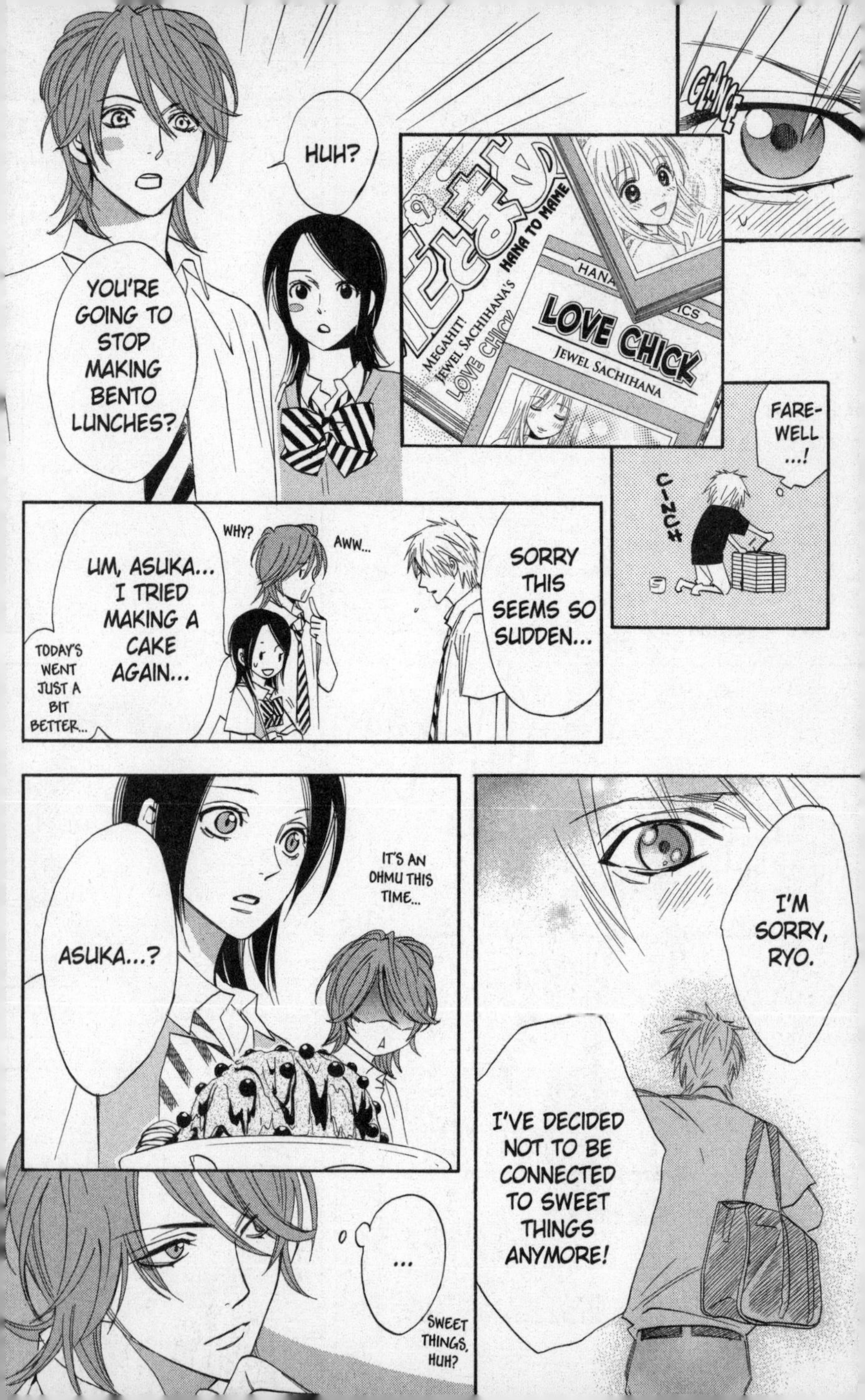
GLANCE
HANA TO MAME
MEGAHIT! JEWEL SACHIHANA'S LOVE CHICK
HANA
ICS
LOVE CHICK
JEWEL SACHIHANA
FARE-WELL ...!
CINCH
HUH?
YOU'RE GOING TO STOP MAKING BENTO LUNCHES?
SORRY THIS SEEMS SO SUDDEN...
AWW...
WHY?
UM, ASUKA... I TRIED MAKING A CAKE AGAIN...
TODAY'S WENT JUST A BIT BETTER...
I'M SORRY, RYO.
I'VE DECIDED NOT TO BE CONNECTED TO SWEET THINGS ANYMORE!
IT'S AN OHMU THIS TIME...
ASUKA...?
...
SWEET THINGS, HUH?

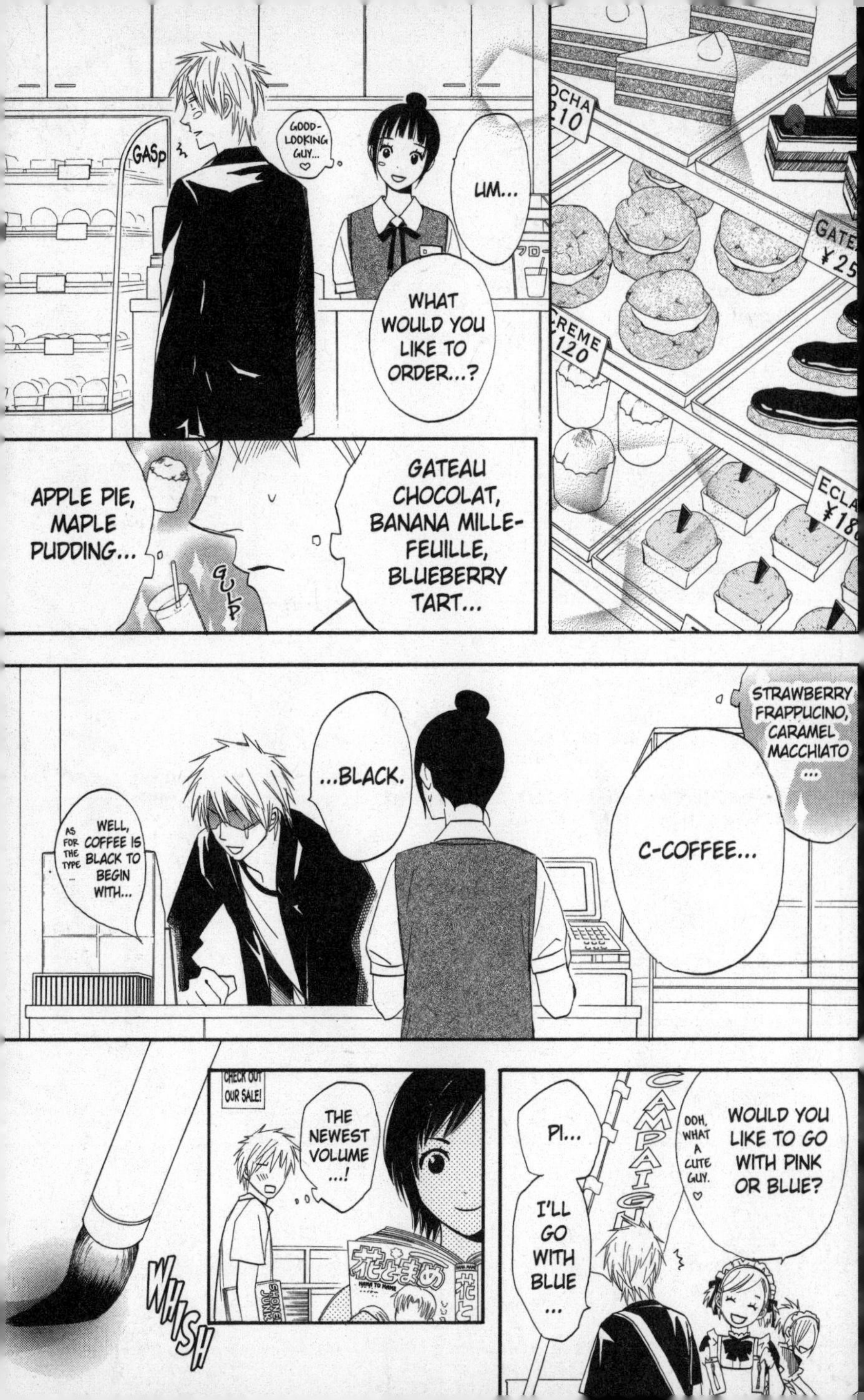
OCHA ¥210
GATE ¥25
CREME ¥120
ECLA ¥18
GASP
GOOD-LOOKING GUY...
UM...
WHAT WOULD YOU LIKE TO ORDER...?
GATEAU CHOCOLAT, BANANA MILLE-FEUILLE, BLUEBERRY TART...
GULP
APPLE PIE, MAPLE PUDDING...
STRAWBERRY FRAPPUCINO, CARAMEL MACCHIATO ...
C-COFFEE...
...BLACK.
WELL, COFFEE IS BLACK TO BEGIN WITH...
AS FOR THE TYPE ...
WOULD YOU LIKE TO GO WITH PINK OR BLUE?
OOH, WHAT A CUTE GUY.
CAMPAIGN
PI...
I'LL GO WITH BLUE ...
CHECK OUT OUR SALE!
THE NEWEST VOLUME ...!
WHISH

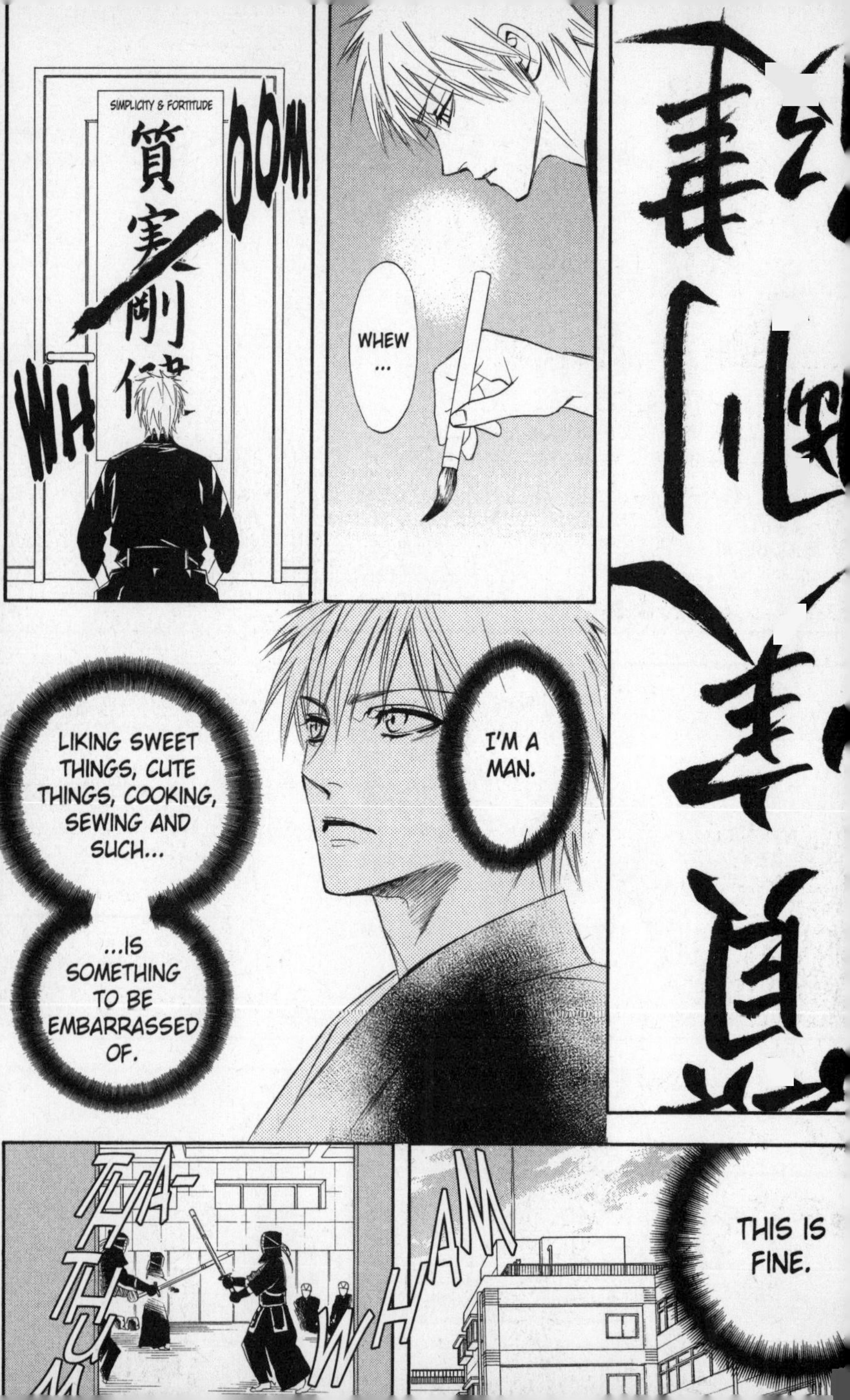
WHEW
...
DOOM
SIMPLICITY & FORTITUDE
質実剛健
WH
I'M A MAN.
LIKING SWEET THINGS, CUTE THINGS, COOKING, SEWING AND SUCH...
...IS SOMETHING TO BE EMBARRASSED OF.
THIS IS FINE.
WHAM
THA-THUM

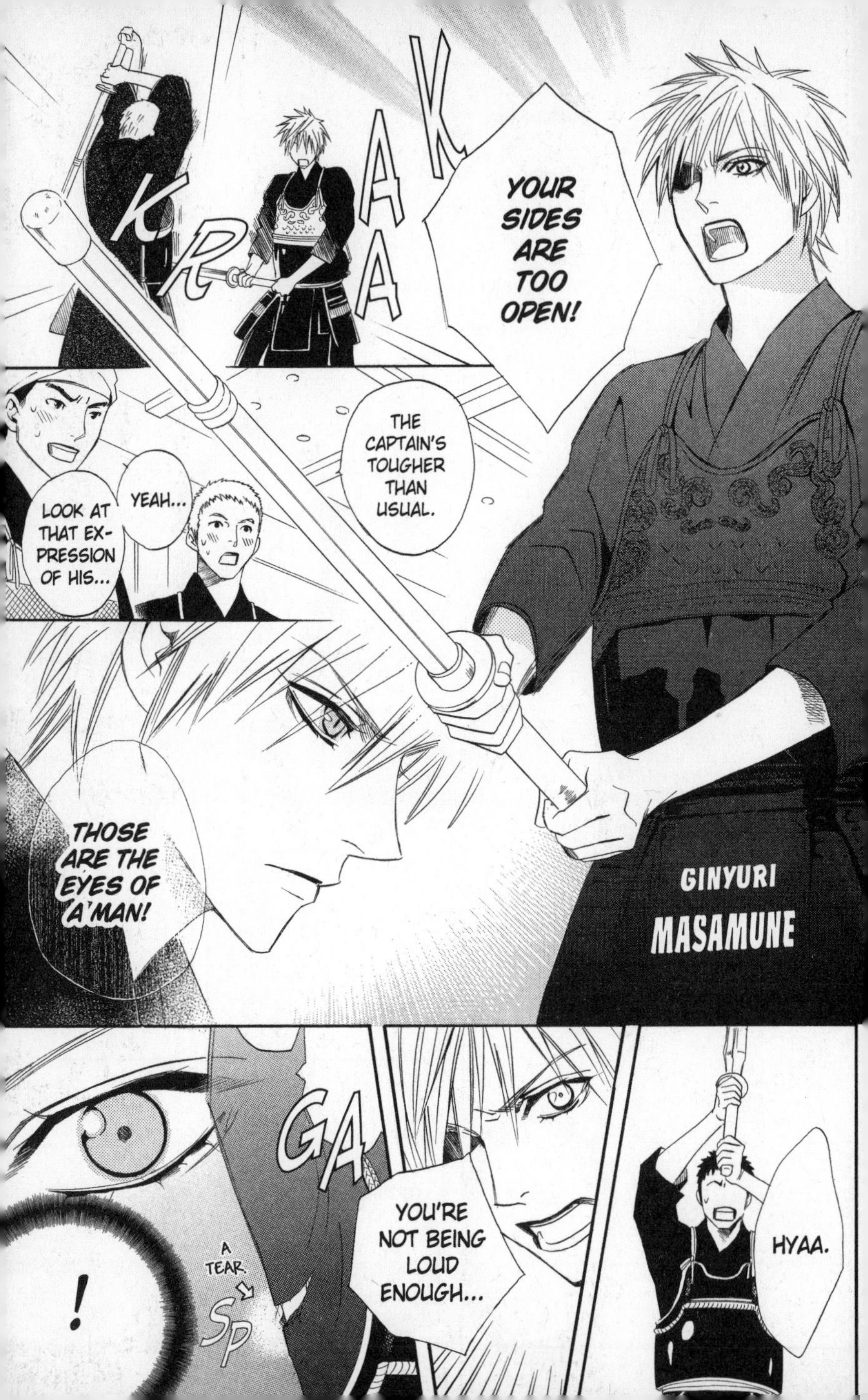
YOUR SIDES ARE TOO OPEN!
GINYURI MASAMUNE
KRAKAK
THE CAPTAIN'S TOUGHER THAN USUAL.
YEAH...
LOOK AT THAT EX-PRESSION OF HIS...
THOSE ARE THE EYES OF A MAN!
HYAA.
GA
YOU'RE NOT BEING LOUD ENOUGH...
A TEAR.
SP
!

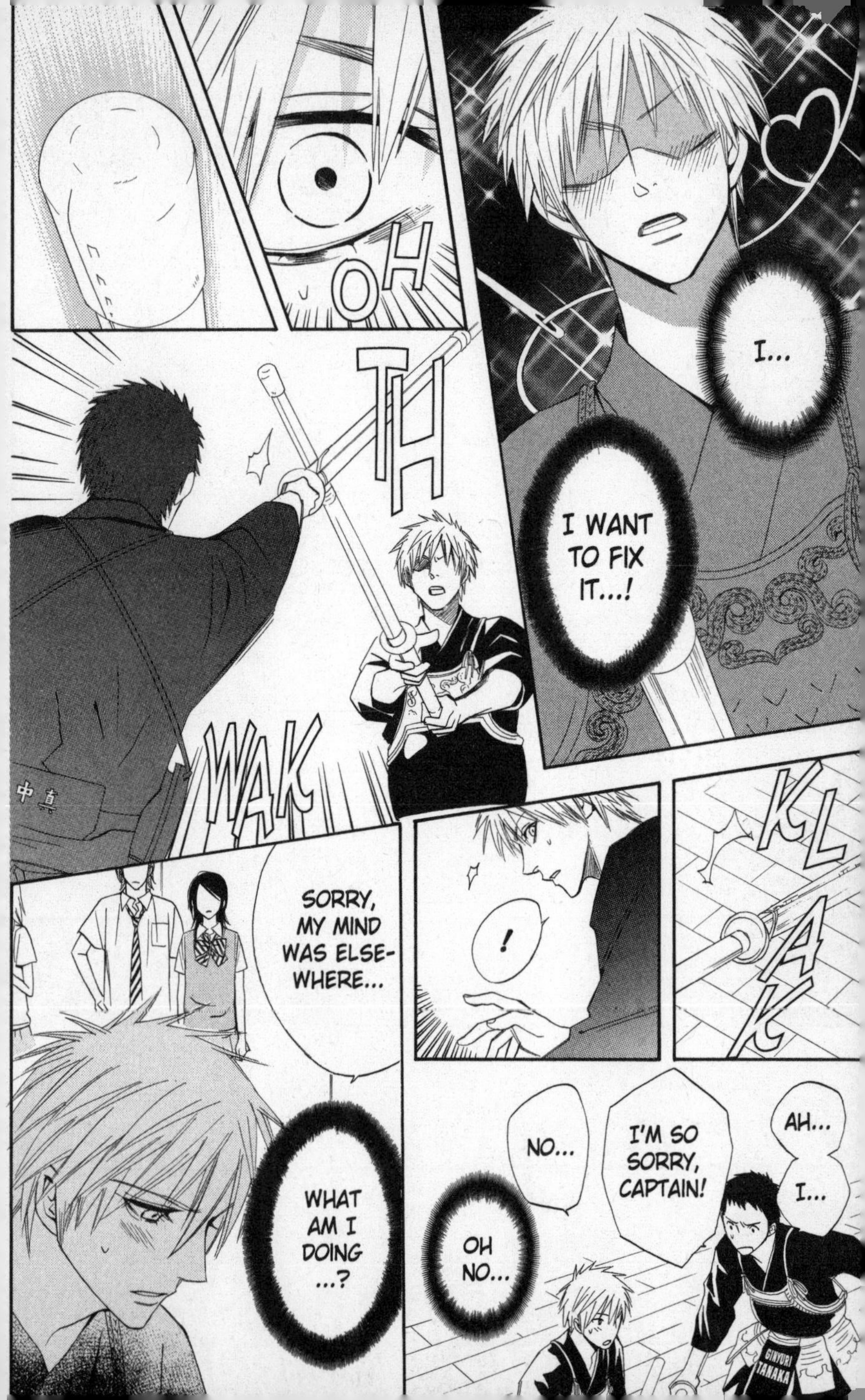
I...
I WANT TO FIX IT...!
OH
TH
WAK
中真
KLAK
!
SORRY, MY MIND WAS ELSEWHERE...
AH... I...
I'M SO SORRY, CAPTAIN!
NO...
GINYURI TANAKA
OH NO...
WHAT AM I DOING ...?

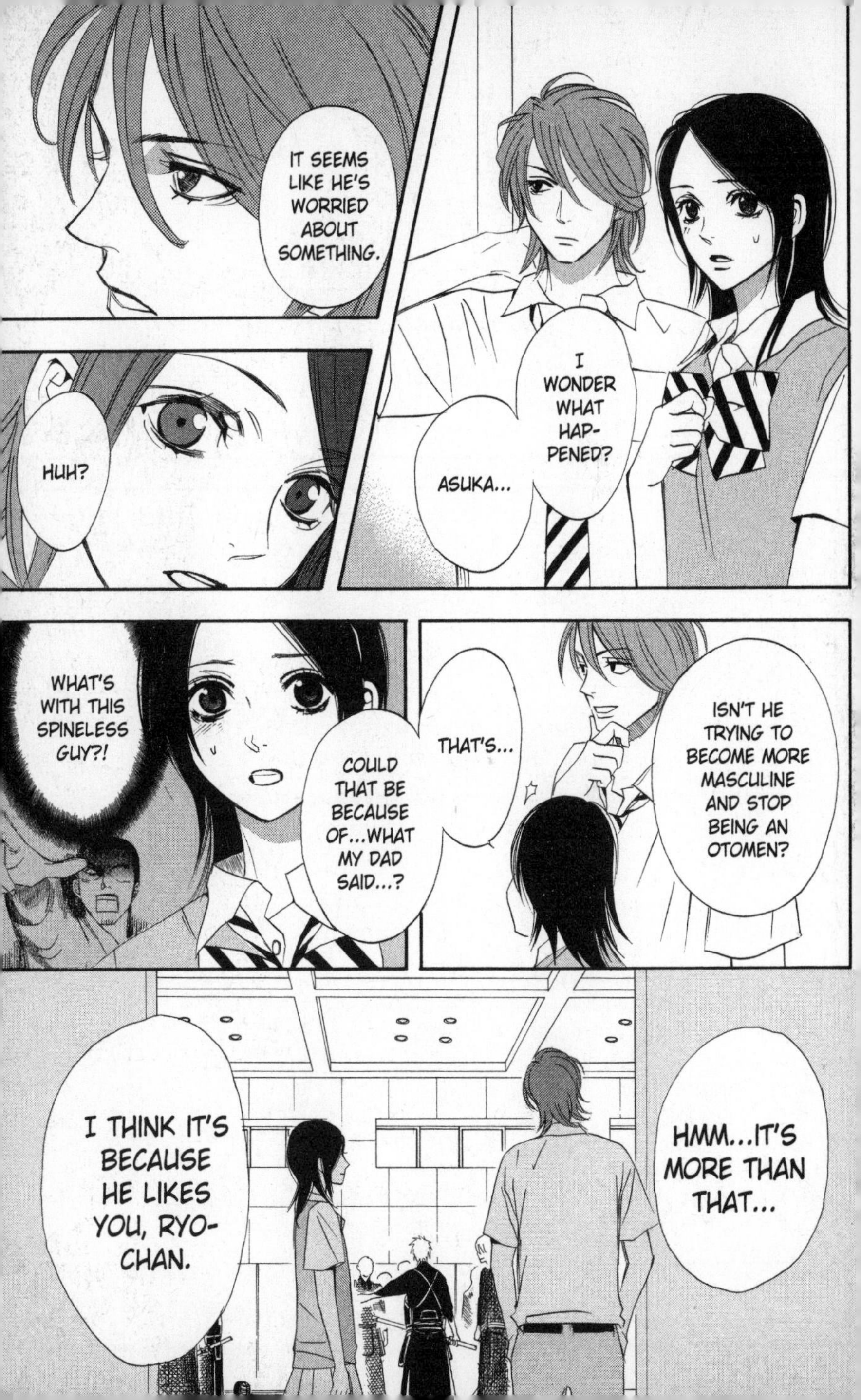
I WONDER WHAT HAP-PENED?
ASUKA...
IT SEEMS LIKE HE'S WORRIED ABOUT SOMETHING.
HUH?
ISN'T HE TRYING TO BECOME MORE MASCULINE AND STOP BEING AN OTOMEN?
THAT'S...
COULD THAT BE BECAUSE OF...WHAT MY DAD SAID...?
WHAT'S WITH THIS SPINELESS GUY?!
HMM...IT'S MORE THAN THAT...
I THINK IT'S BECAUSE HE LIKES YOU, RYO-CHAN.

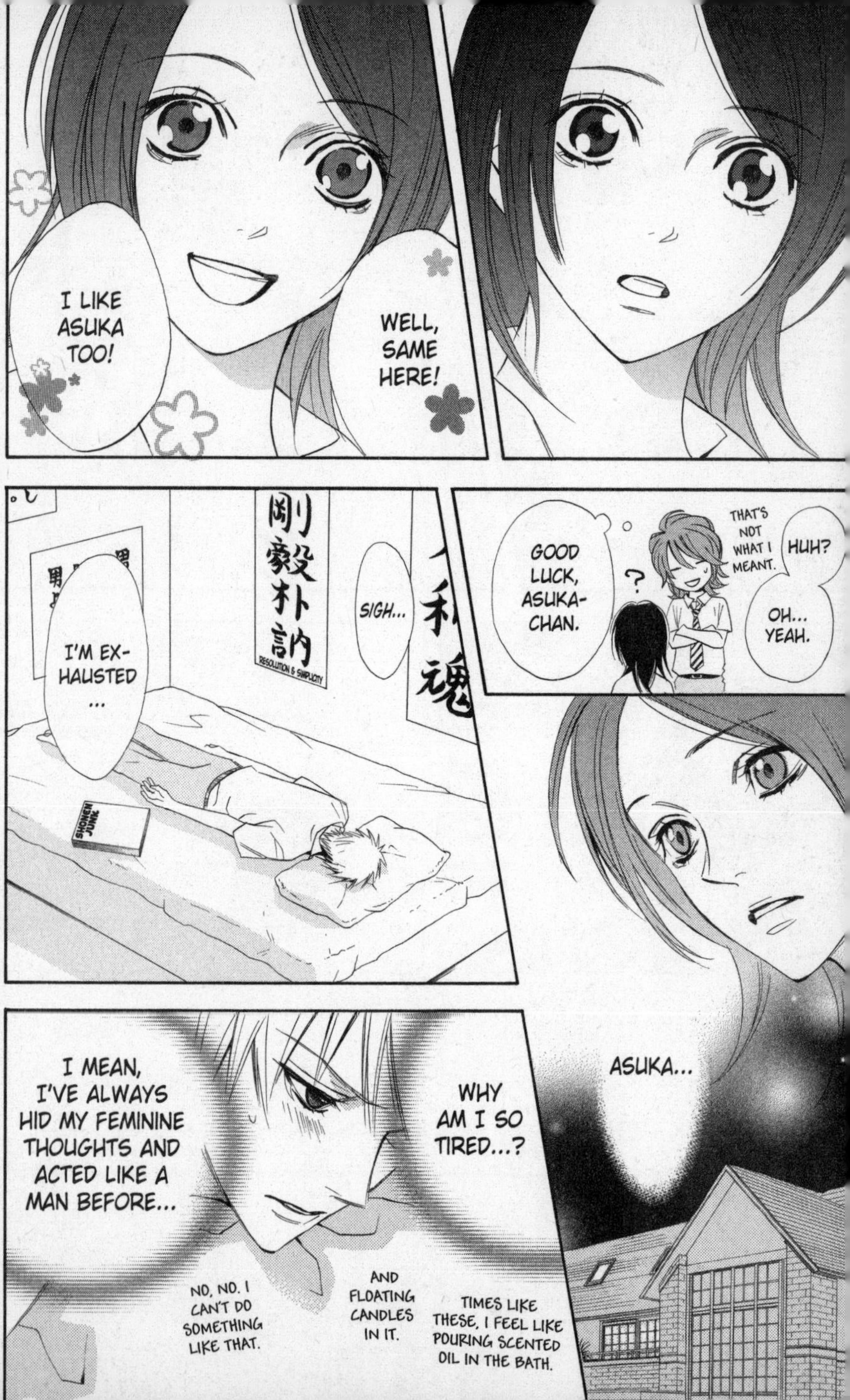
WELL, SAME HERE!
I LIKE ASUKA TOO!
HUH?
THAT'S NOT WHAT I MEANT.
OH... YEAH.
GOOD LUCK, ASUKA-CHAN.
ASUKA...
SIGH...
剛毅朴訥
RESOLUTION & SIMPLICITY
I'M EX-HAUSTED...
SHONEN JUMP
WHY AM I SO TIRED...?
I MEAN, I'VE ALWAYS HID MY FEMININE THOUGHTS AND ACTED LIKE A MAN BEFORE...
TIMES LIKE THESE, I FEEL LIKE POURING SCENTED OIL IN THE BATH.
AND FLOATING CANDLES IN IT.
NO, NO. I CAN'T DO SOMETHING LIKE THAT.

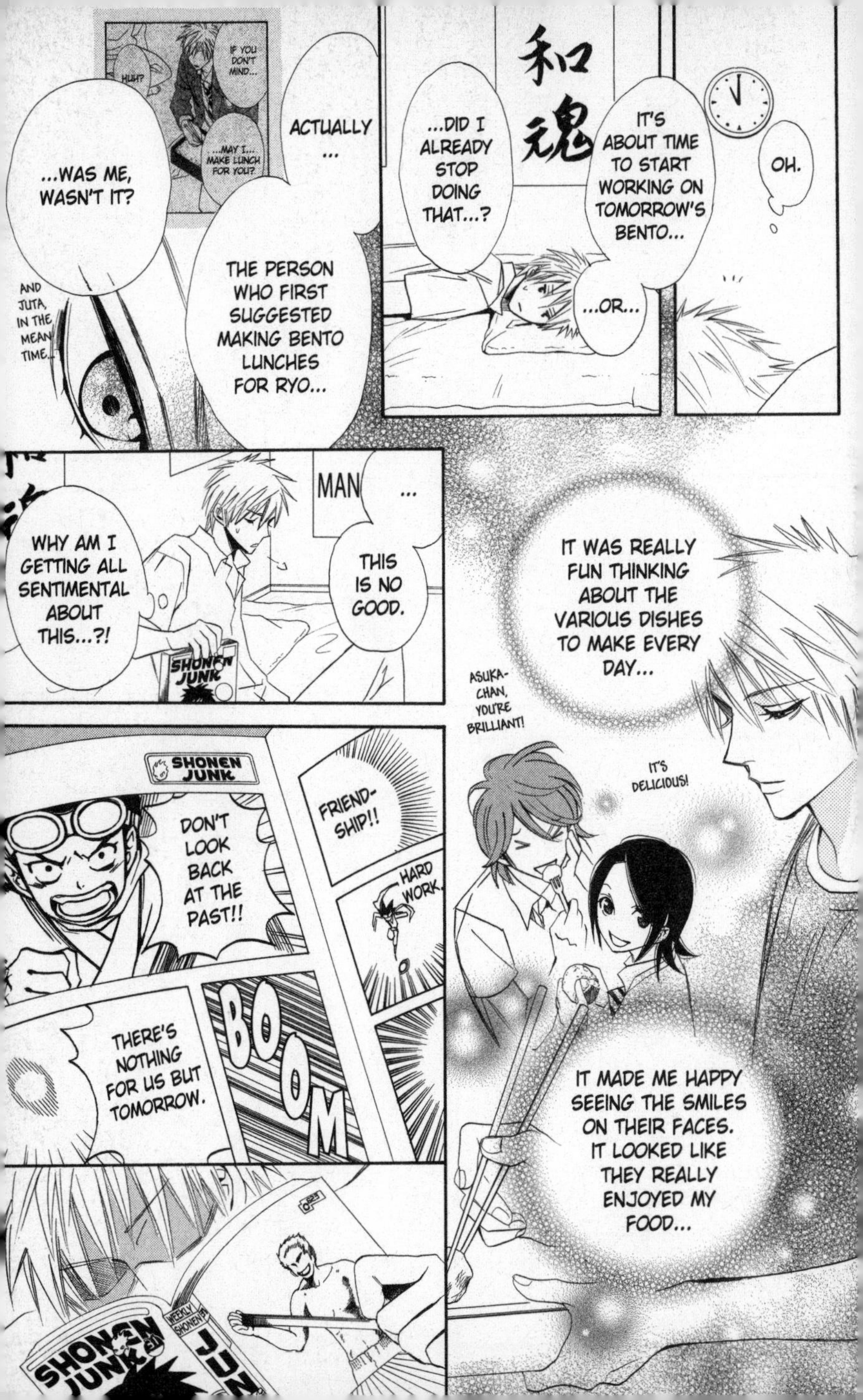
OH.
IT'S ABOUT TIME TO START WORKING ON TOMORROW'S BENTO...
...OR...
...DID I ALREADY STOP DOING THAT...?
和魂
ACTUALLY...
THE PERSON WHO FIRST SUGGESTED MAKING BENTO LUNCHES FOR RYO...
IF YOU DON'T MIND...
HUH?
...MAY I... MAKE LUNCH FOR YOU?
...WAS ME, WASN'T IT?
AND JUTA, IN THE MEAN TIME...
IT WAS REALLY FUN THINKING ABOUT THE VARIOUS DISHES TO MAKE EVERY DAY...
IT'S DELICIOUS!
ASUKA-CHAN, YOU'RE BRILLIANT!
IT MADE ME HAPPY SEEING THE SMILES ON THEIR FACES. IT LOOKED LIKE THEY REALLY ENJOYED MY FOOD...
MAN...
THIS IS NO GOOD.
WHY AM I GETTING ALL SENTIMENTAL ABOUT THIS...?!
SHONEN JUNK
FRIENDSHIP!!
HARD WORK.
SHONEN JUNK
DON'T LOOK BACK AT THE PAST!!
BOOM
THERE'S NOTHING FOR US BUT TOMORROW.
WEEKLY SHONEN JUN
SHONEN JUNK

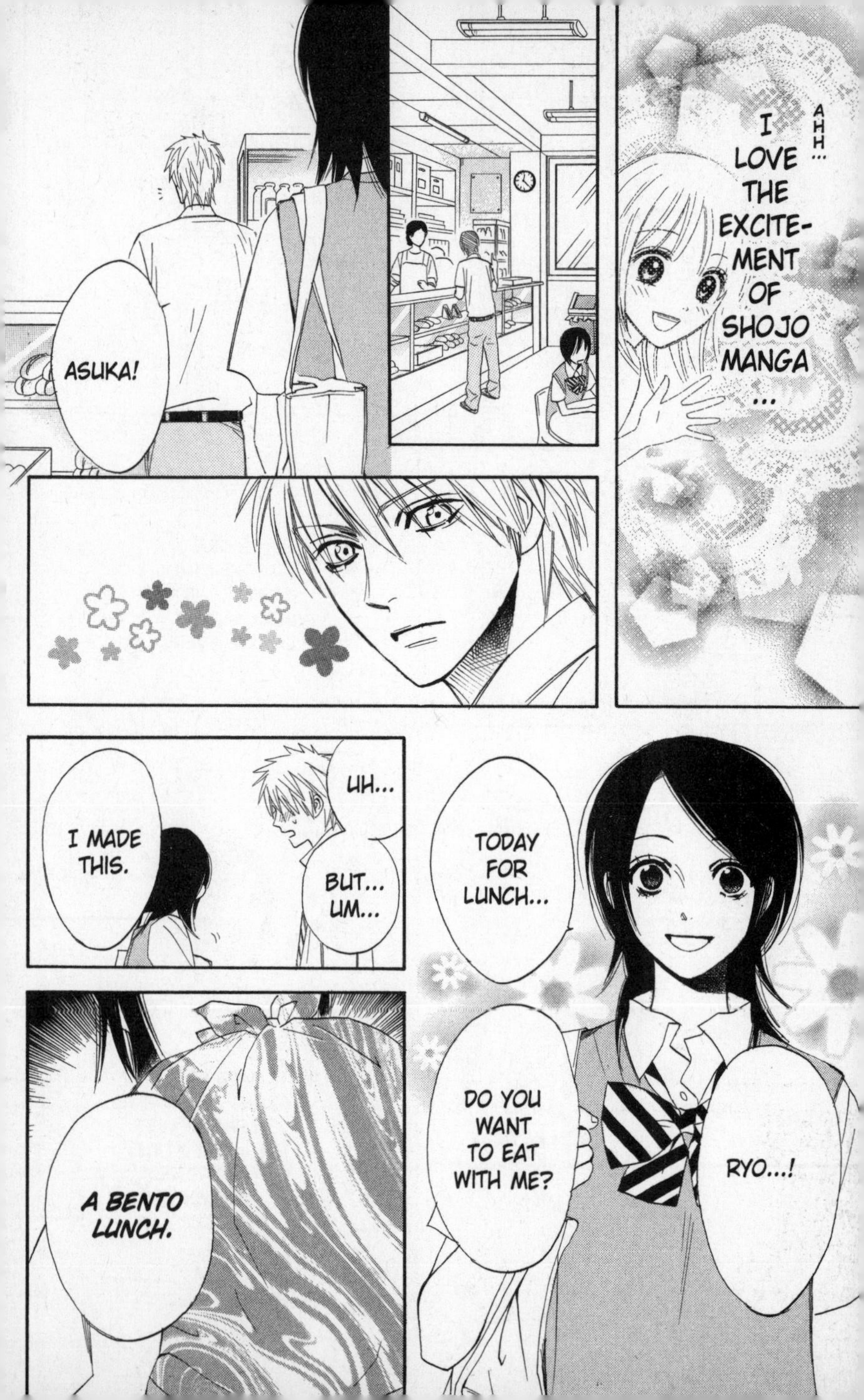
AHH...
I LOVE THE EXCITEMENT OF SHOJO MANGA...
ASUKA!
TODAY FOR LUNCH...
RYO...!
DO YOU WANT TO EAT WITH ME?
UH...
BUT... UM...
I MADE THIS.
A BENTO LUNCH.

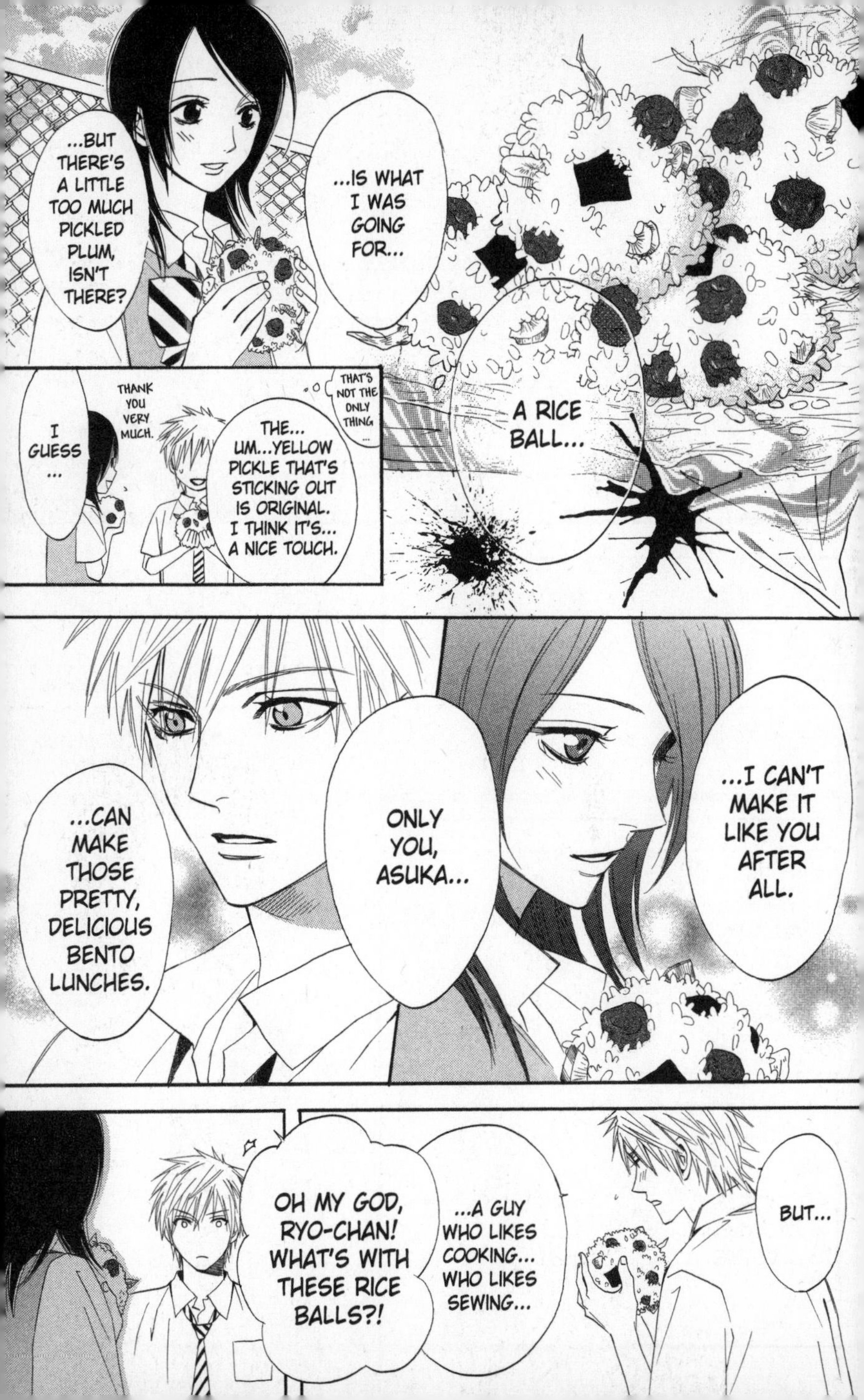
A RICE BALL...
...IS WHAT I WAS GOING FOR...
...BUT THERE'S A LITTLE TOO MUCH PICKLED PLUM, ISN'T THERE?
THAT'S NOT THE ONLY THING...
THE... UM...YELLOW PICKLE THAT'S STICKING OUT IS ORIGINAL. I THINK IT'S... A NICE TOUCH.
THANK YOU VERY MUCH.
I GUESS...
...I CAN'T MAKE IT LIKE YOU AFTER ALL.
ONLY YOU, ASUKA...
...CAN MAKE THOSE PRETTY, DELICIOUS BENTO LUNCHES.
BUT...
...A GUY WHO LIKES COOKING... WHO LIKES SEWING...
OH MY GOD, RYO-CHAN! WHAT'S WITH THESE RICE BALLS?!

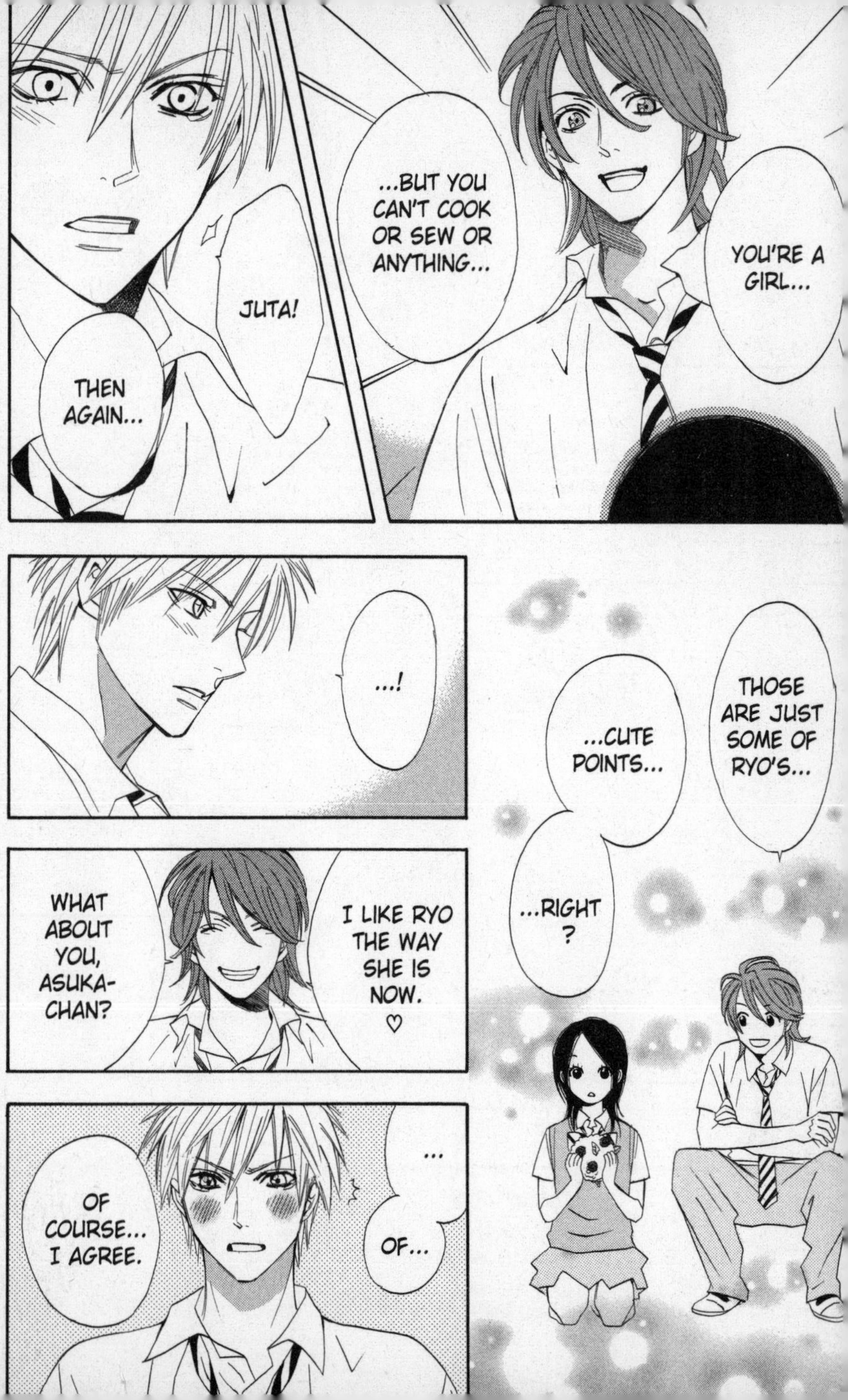
YOU'RE A GIRL...
...BUT YOU CAN'T COOK OR SEW OR ANYTHING...
JUTA!
THEN AGAIN...
THOSE ARE JUST SOME OF RYO'S...
...CUTE POINTS...
...RIGHT?
...!
I LIKE RYO THE WAY SHE IS NOW. ♡
WHAT ABOUT YOU, ASUKA-CHAN?
... OF...
OF COURSE... I AGREE.

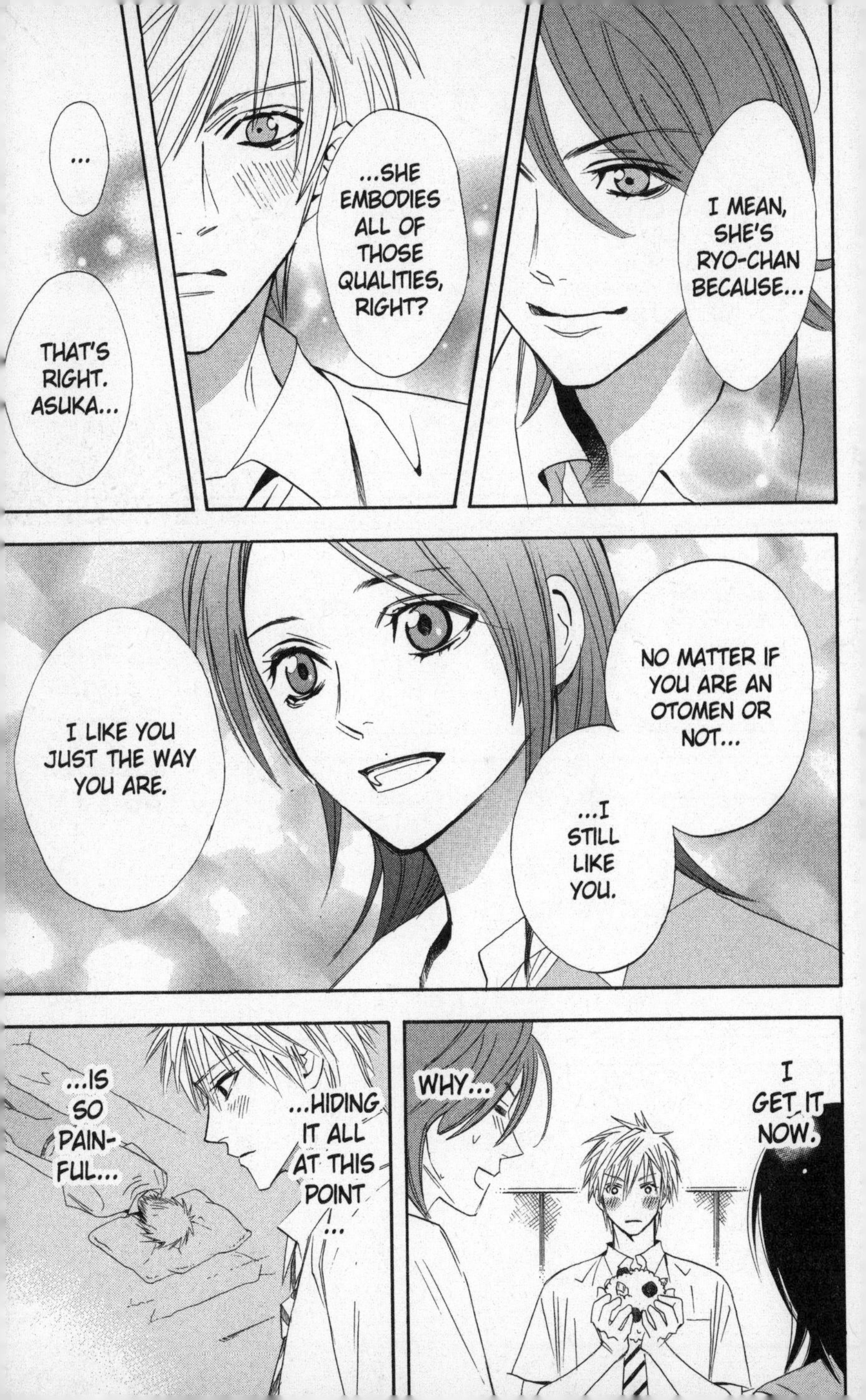
I MEAN, SHE'S RYO-CHAN BECAUSE...
...SHE EMBODIES ALL OF THOSE QUALITIES, RIGHT?
...
THAT'S RIGHT. ASUKA...
NO MATTER IF YOU ARE AN OTOMEN OR NOT...
...I STILL LIKE YOU.
I LIKE YOU JUST THE WAY YOU ARE.
I GET IT NOW.
WHY...
...HIDING IT ALL AT THIS POINT...
...IS SO PAIN-FUL...

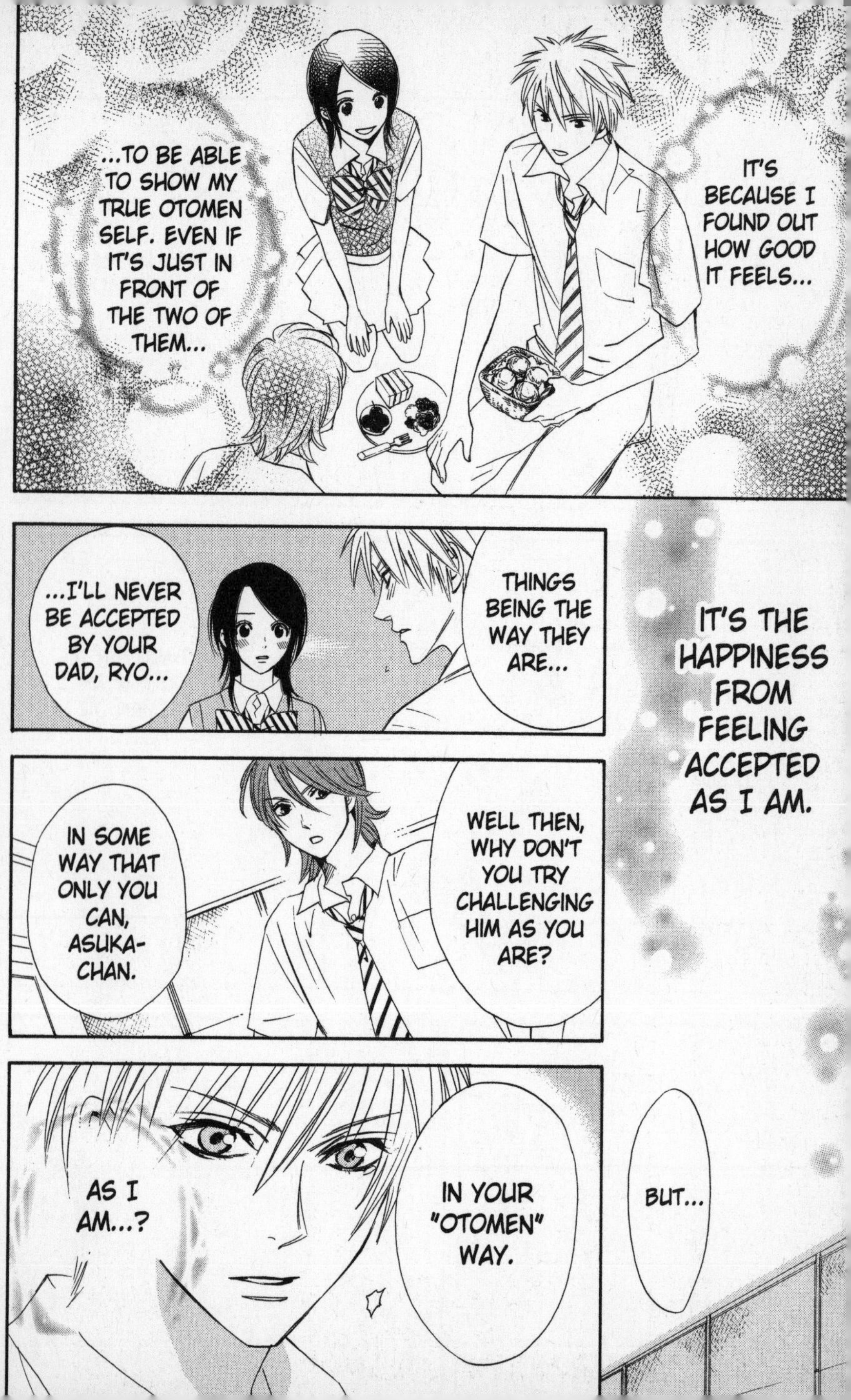
IT'S BECAUSE I FOUND OUT HOW GOOD IT FEELS...
...TO BE ABLE TO SHOW MY TRUE OTOMEN SELF. EVEN IF IT'S JUST IN FRONT OF THE TWO OF THEM...
IT'S THE HAPPINESS FROM FEELING ACCEPTED AS I AM.
THINGS BEING THE WAY THEY ARE...
...I'LL NEVER BE ACCEPTED BY YOUR DAD, RYO...
WELL THEN, WHY DON'T YOU TRY CHALLENGING HIM AS YOU ARE?
IN SOME WAY THAT ONLY YOU CAN, ASUKA-CHAN.
BUT...
IN YOUR "OTOMEN" WAY.
AS I AM...?

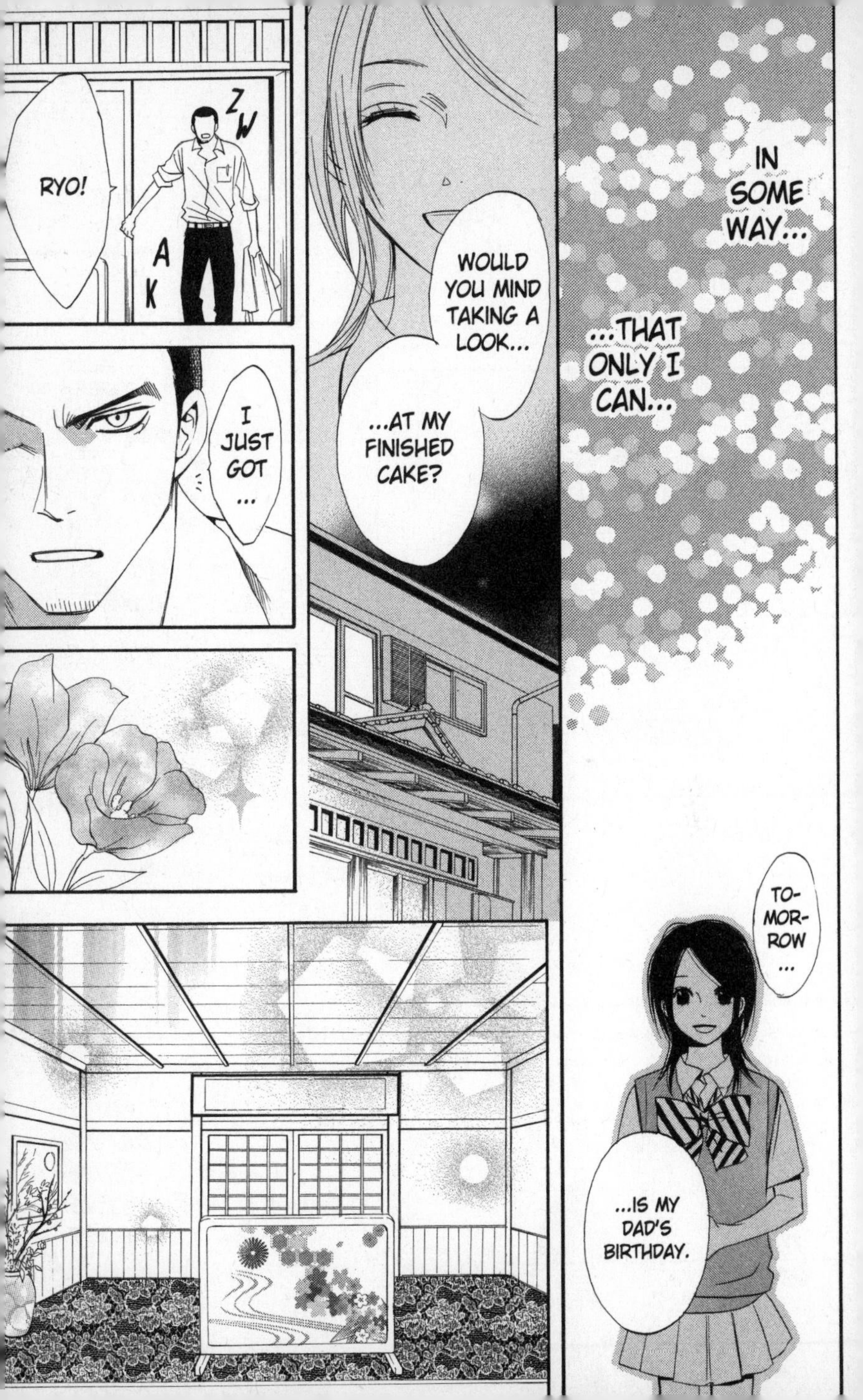
IN SOME WAY...
...THAT ONLY I CAN...
TO-MOR-ROW...
...IS MY DAD'S BIRTHDAY.
WOULD YOU MIND TAKING A LOOK...
...AT MY FINISHED CAKE?
RYO!
ZWAK
I JUST GOT...

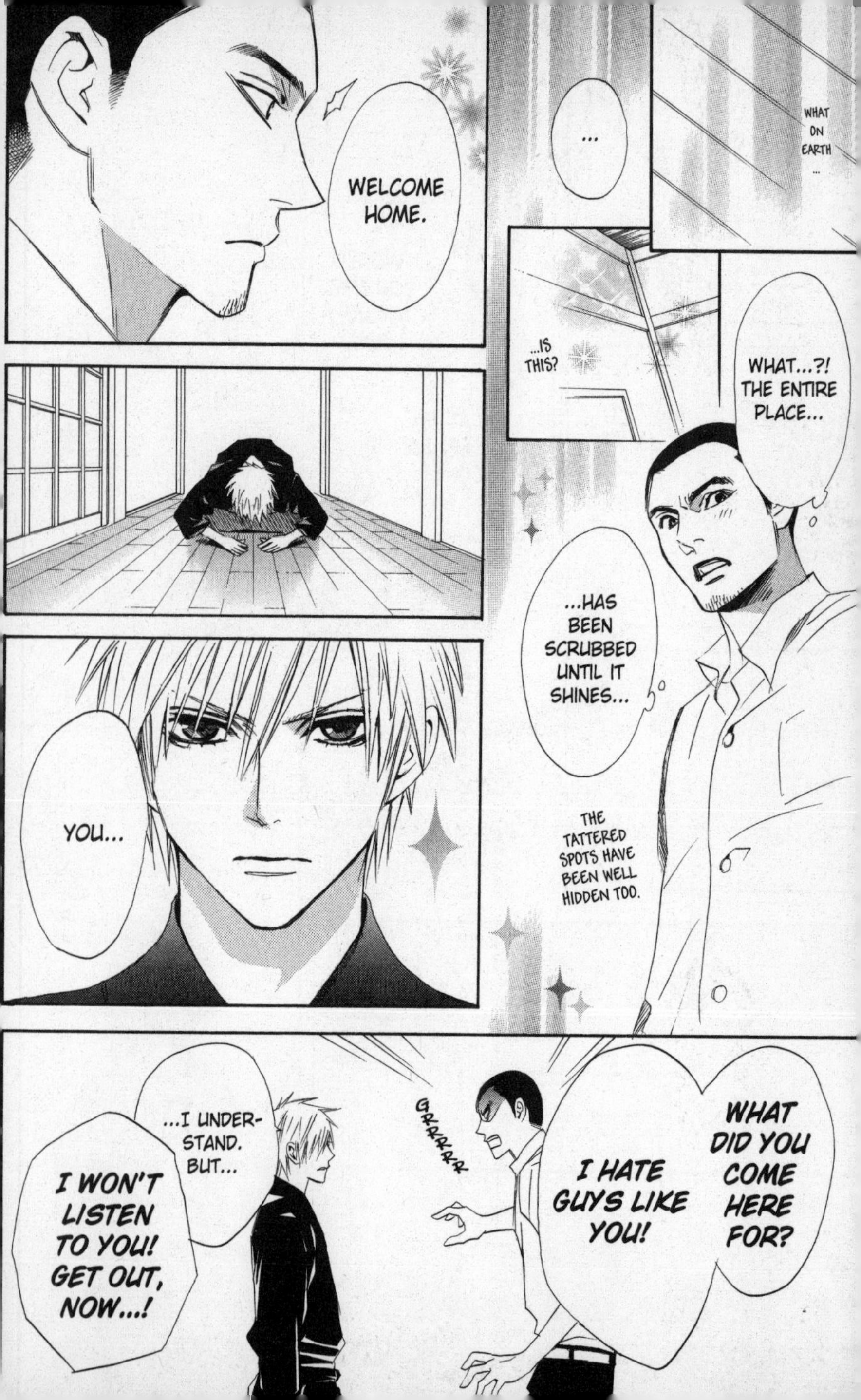
WHAT ON EARTH ...
...
...IS THIS?
WHAT...?! THE ENTIRE PLACE...
...HAS BEEN SCRUBBED UNTIL IT SHINES...
THE TATTERED SPOTS HAVE BEEN WELL HIDDEN TOO.
WELCOME HOME.
YOU...
WHAT DID YOU COME HERE FOR?
I HATE GUYS LIKE YOU!
GRRRRR
...I UNDER-STAND. BUT...
I WON'T LISTEN TO YOU! GET OUT, NOW...!

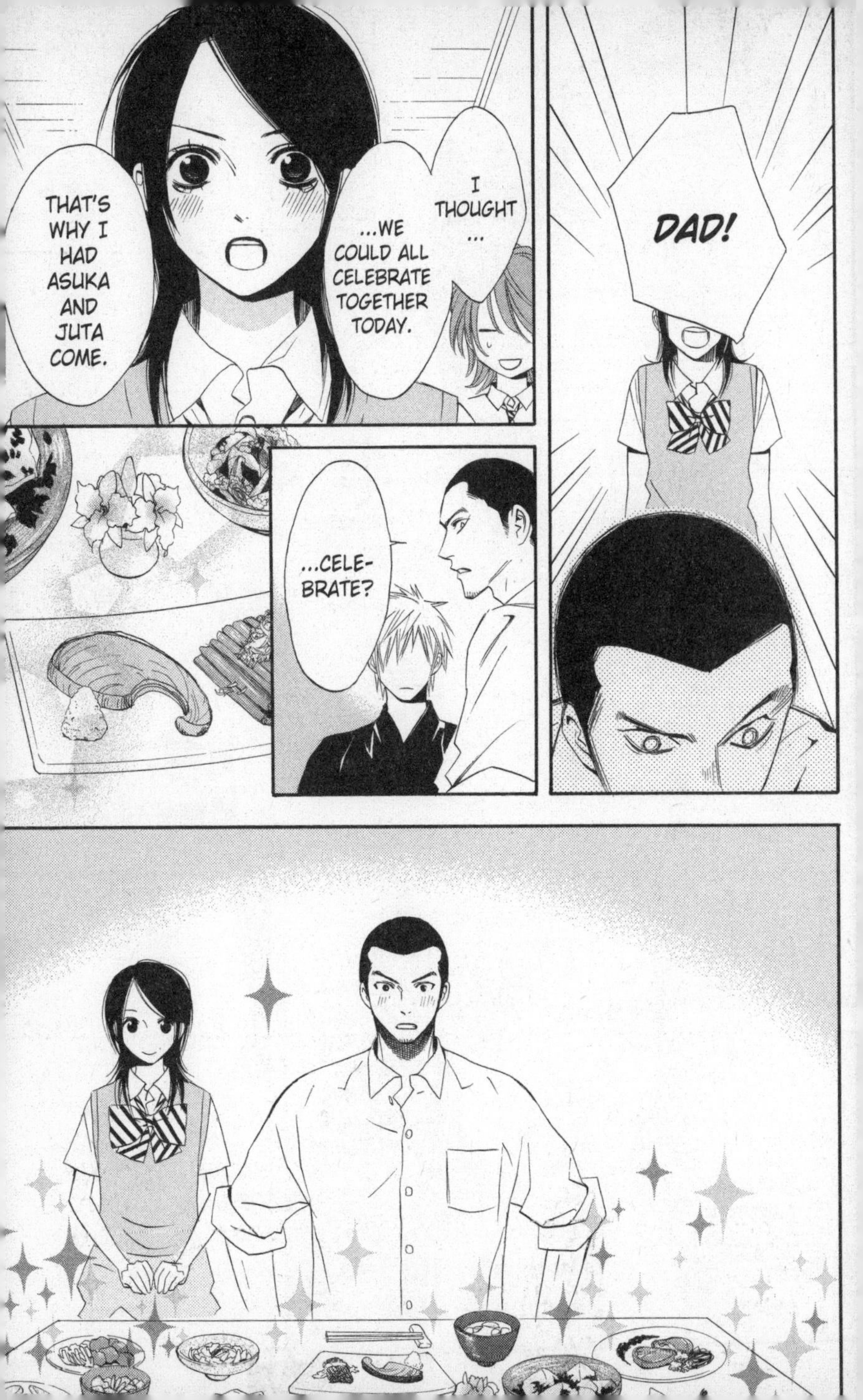
DAD!
I THOUGHT...
...WE COULD ALL CELEBRATE TOGETHER TODAY.
THAT'S WHY I HAD ASUKA AND JUTA COME.
...CELE-BRATE?

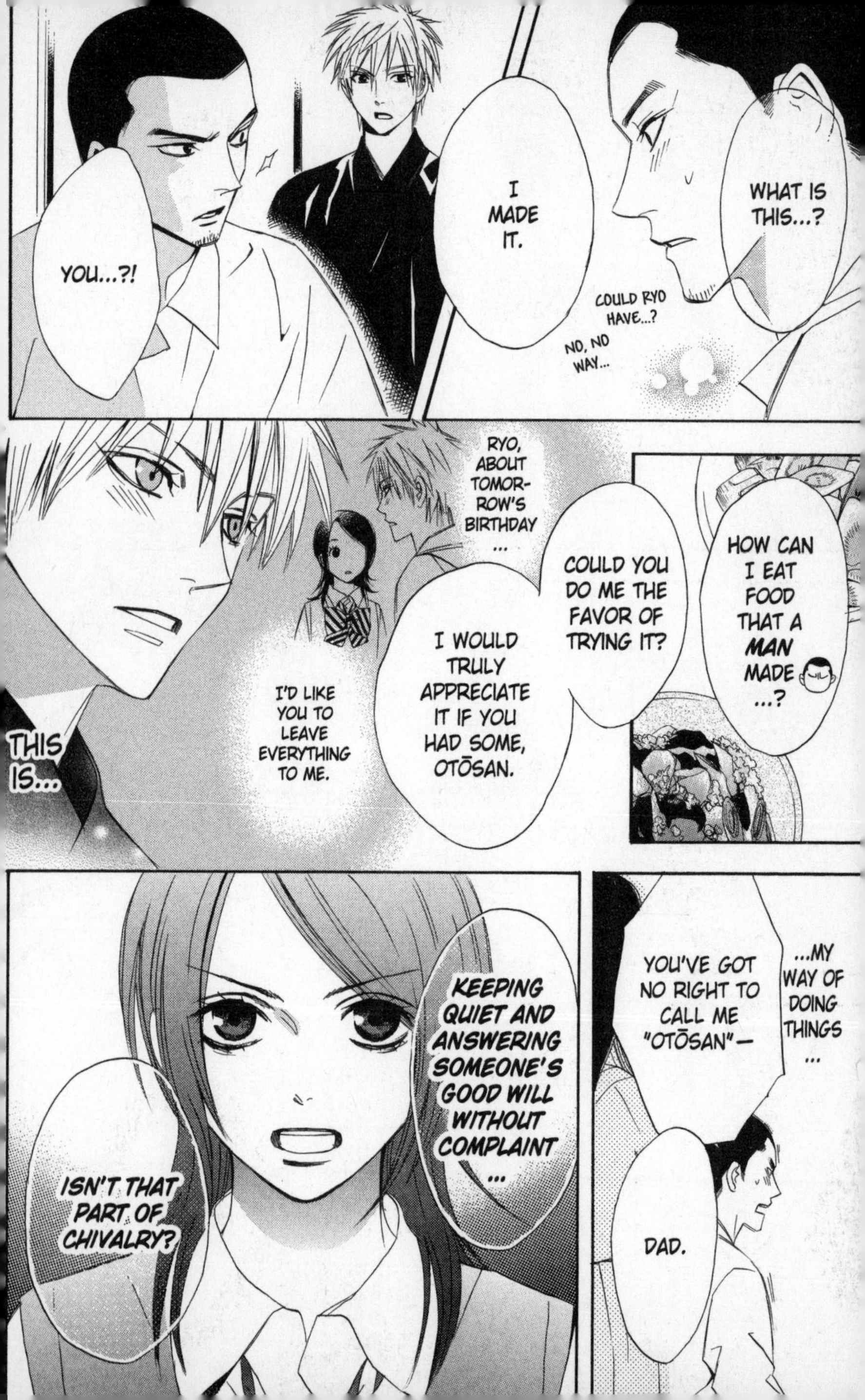
WHAT IS THIS...?
COULD RYO HAVE...?
NO, NO WAY...
I MADE IT.
YOU...?!
HOW CAN I EAT FOOD THAT A *MAN* MADE...?
COULD YOU DO ME THE FAVOR OF TRYING IT?
RYO, ABOUT TOMORROW'S BIRTHDAY...
I WOULD TRULY APPRECIATE IT IF YOU HAD SOME, OTŌSAN.
I'D LIKE YOU TO LEAVE EVERYTHING TO ME.
THIS IS...
...MY WAY OF DOING THINGS...
YOU'VE GOT NO RIGHT TO CALL ME "OTŌSAN"—
DAD.
KEEPING QUIET AND ANSWERING SOMEONE'S GOOD WILL WITHOUT COMPLAINT...
ISN'T THAT PART OF CHIVALRY?

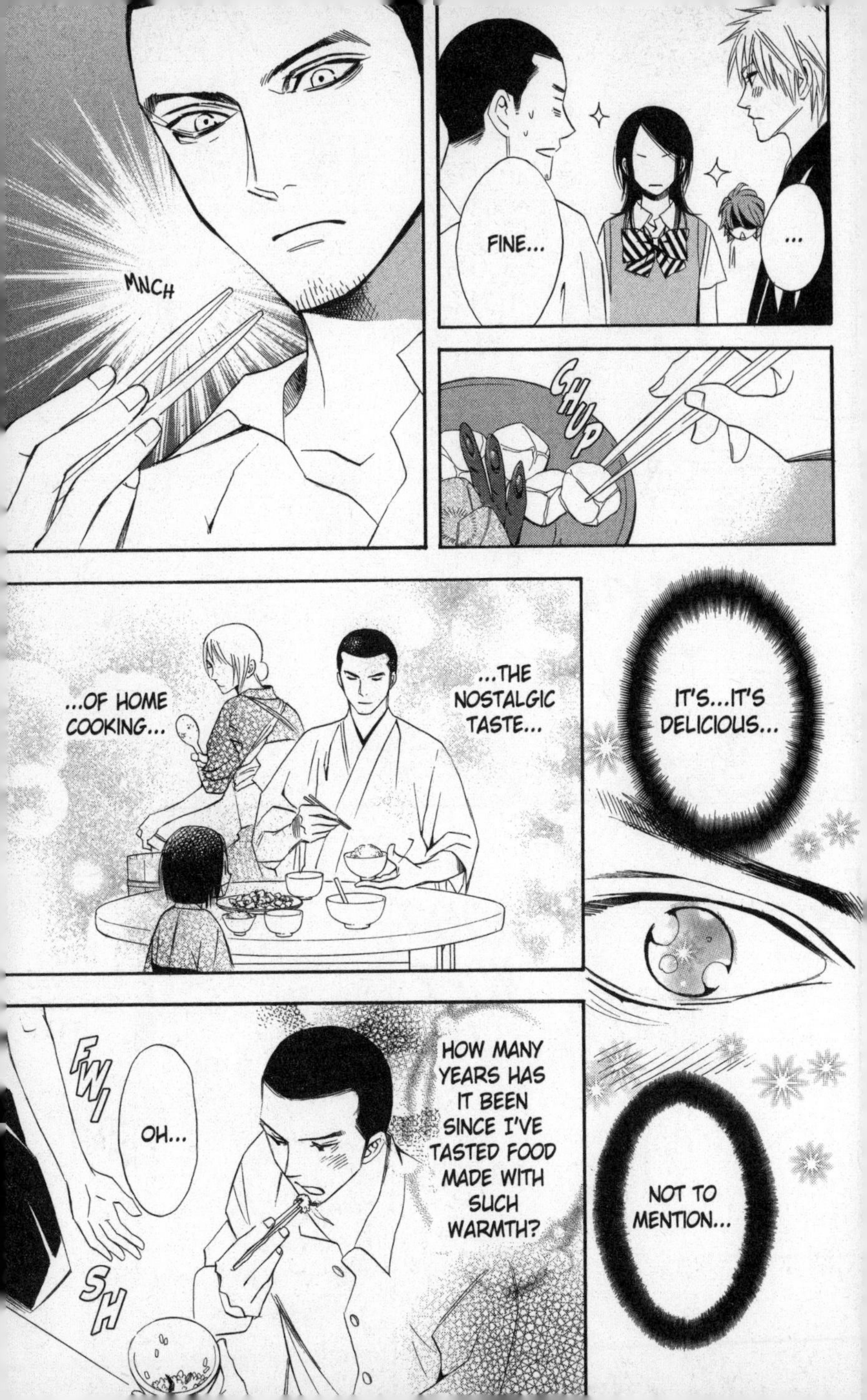
...
FINE...
CHUP
MNCH
IT'S...IT'S DELICIOUS...
...THE NOSTALGIC TASTE...
...OF HOME COOKING...
HOW MANY YEARS HAS IT BEEN SINCE I'VE TASTED FOOD MADE WITH SUCH WARMTH?
FWI
OH...
SH
NOT TO MENTION...

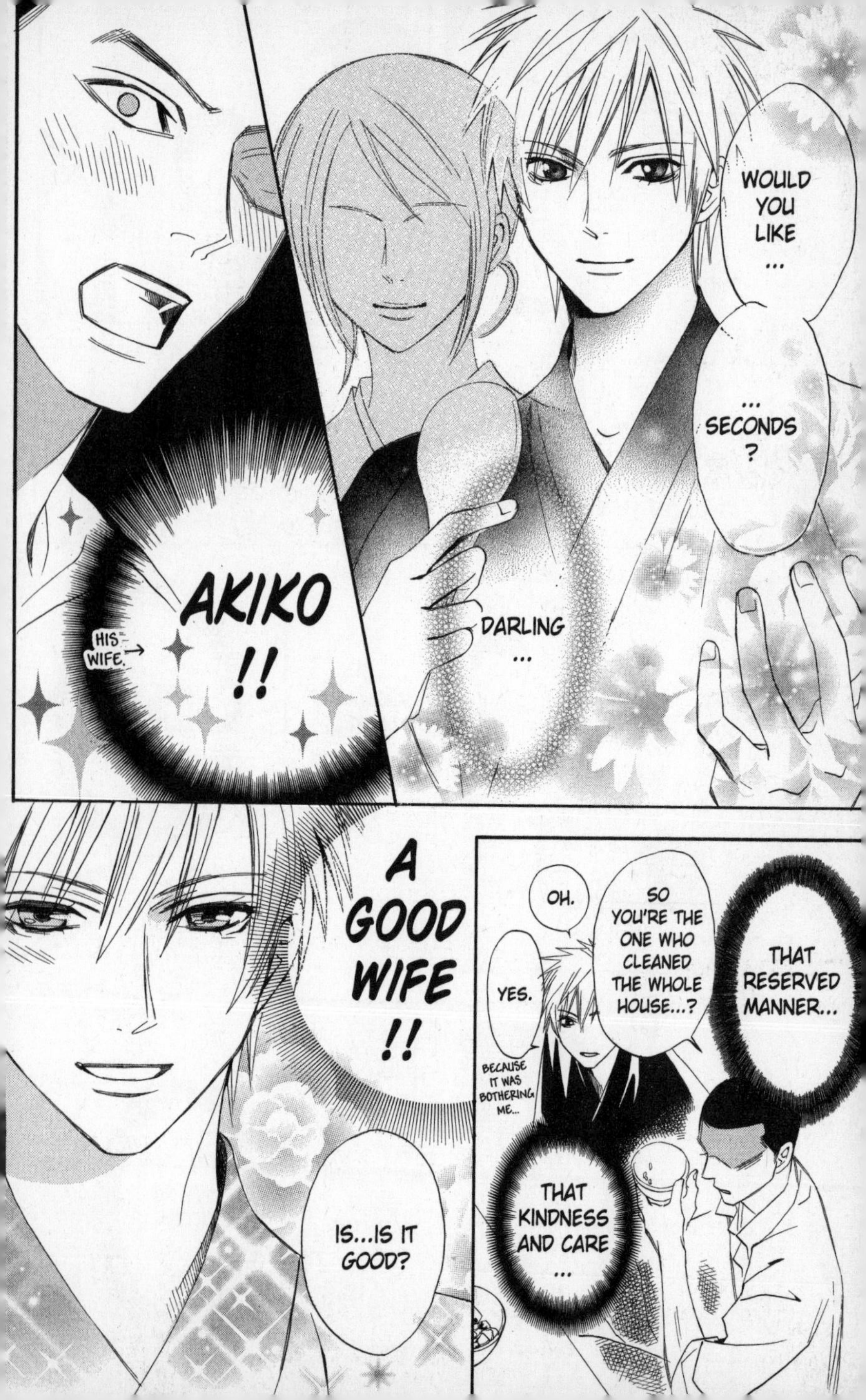
WOULD YOU LIKE ...
... SECONDS ?
DARLING ...
AKIKO !!
HIS WIFE.
THAT RESERVED MANNER...
SO YOU'RE THE ONE WHO CLEANED THE WHOLE HOUSE...?
OH.
YES.
BECAUSE IT WAS BOTHERING ME...
THAT KINDNESS AND CARE ...
A GOOD WIFE !!
IS...IS IT GOOD?

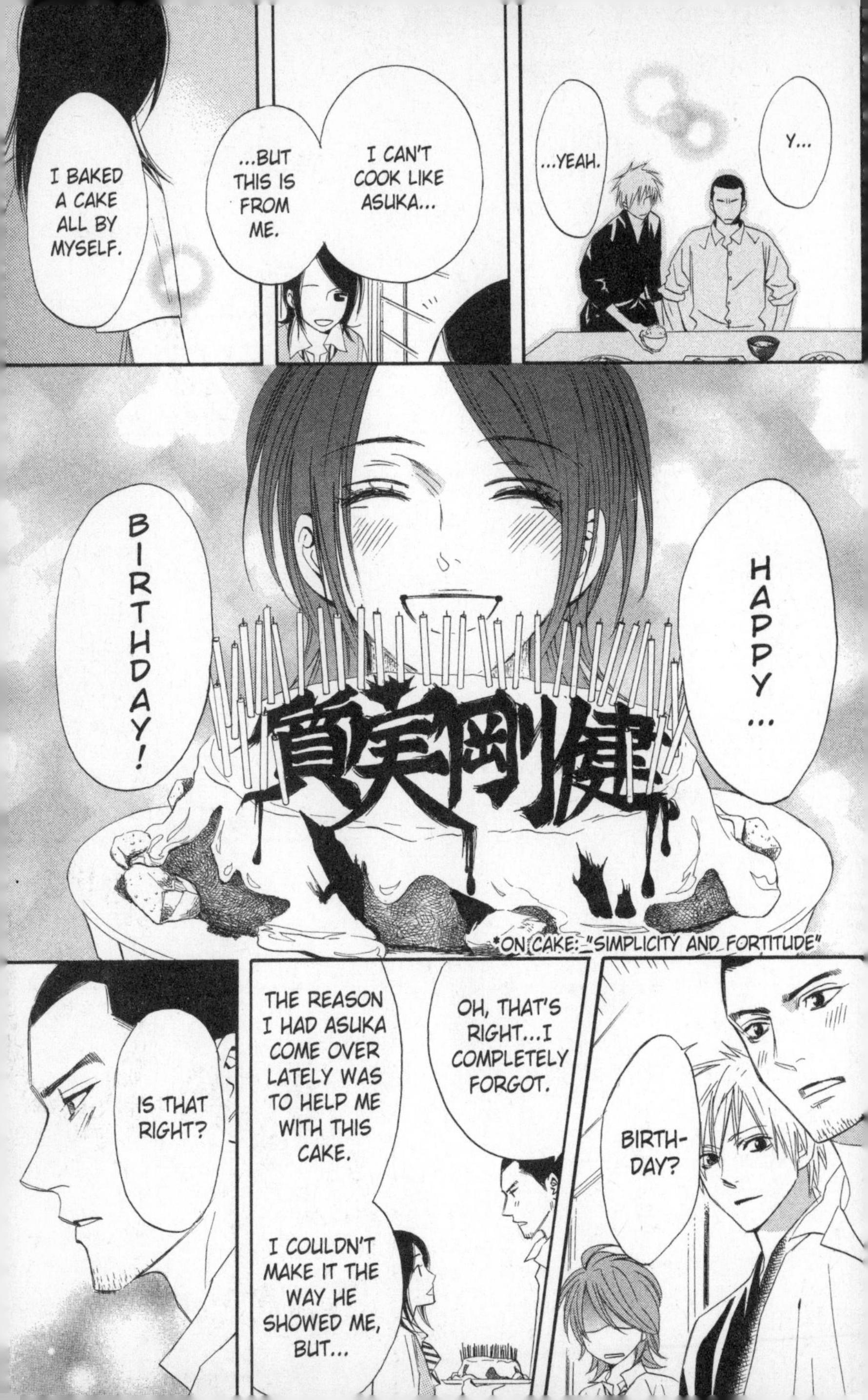
Y...
...YEAH.
I CAN'T COOK LIKE ASUKA...
...BUT THIS IS FROM ME.
I BAKED A CAKE ALL BY MYSELF.
HAPPY...
BIRTHDAY!
質実剛健
*ON CAKE: "SIMPLICITY AND FORTITUDE"
BIRTH-DAY?
OH, THAT'S RIGHT...I COMPLETELY FORGOT.
THE REASON I HAD ASUKA COME OVER LATELY WAS TO HELP ME WITH THIS CAKE.
I COULDN'T MAKE IT THE WAY HE SHOWED ME, BUT...
IS THAT RIGHT?

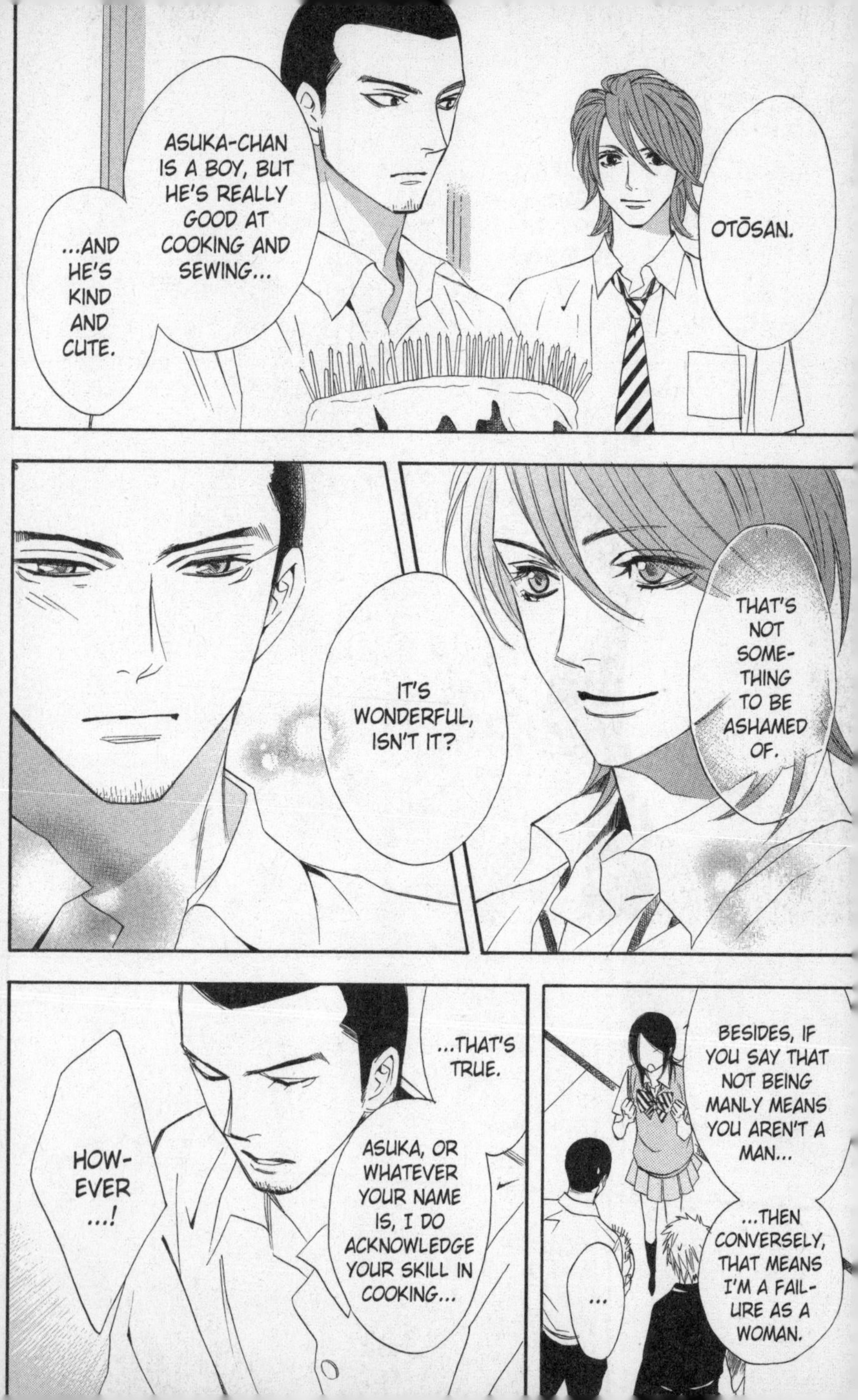
OTŌSAN.
ASUKA-CHAN IS A BOY, BUT HE'S REALLY GOOD AT COOKING AND SEWING...
...AND HE'S KIND AND CUTE.
THAT'S NOT SOME-THING TO BE ASHAMED OF.
IT'S WONDERFUL, ISN'T IT?
BESIDES, IF YOU SAY THAT NOT BEING MANLY MEANS YOU AREN'T A MAN...
...THEN CONVERSELY, THAT MEANS I'M A FAIL-URE AS A WOMAN.
...
...THAT'S TRUE.
ASUKA, OR WHATEVER YOUR NAME IS, I DO ACKNOWLEDGE YOUR SKILL IN COOKING...
HOW-EVER ...!

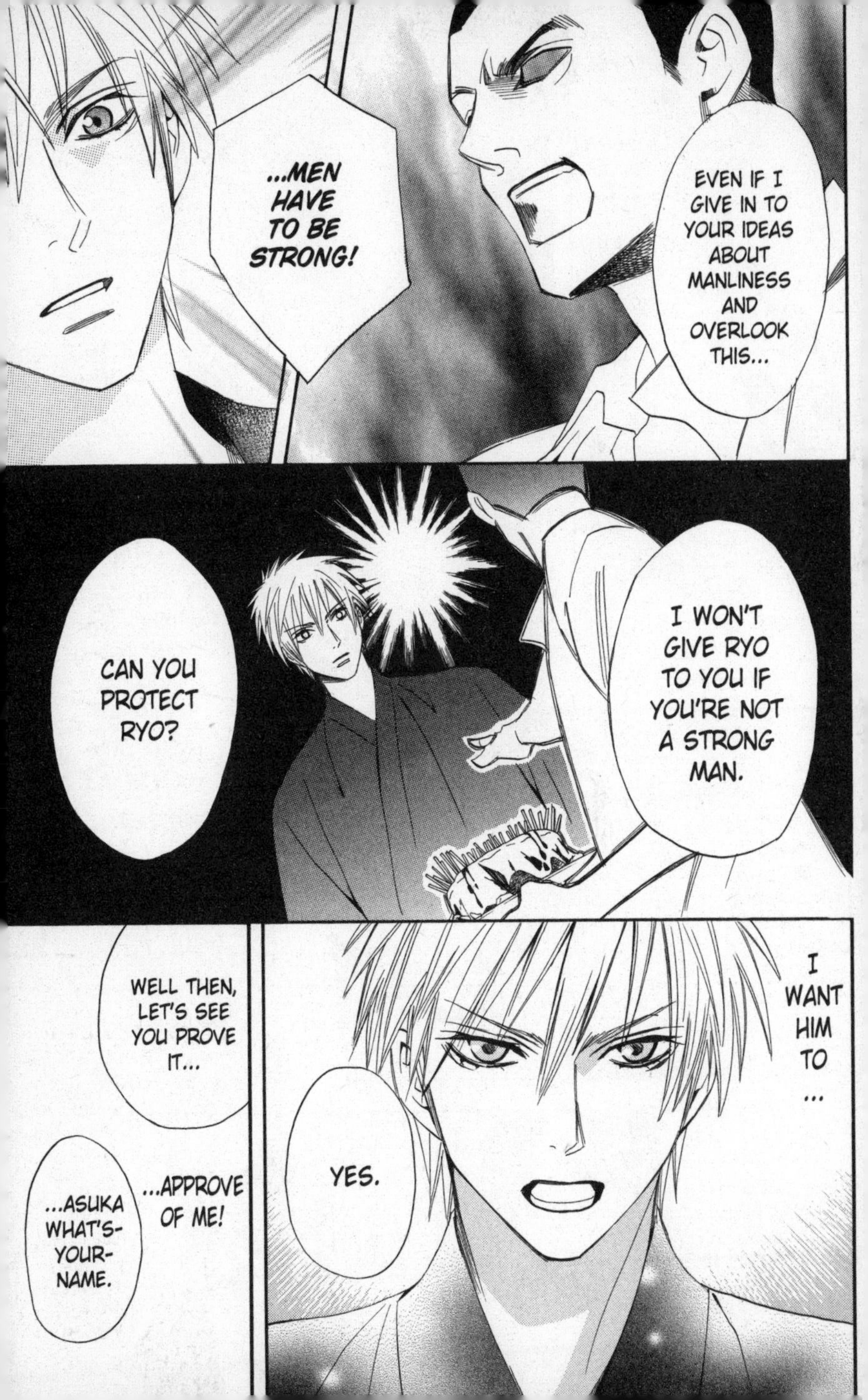
EVEN IF I GIVE IN TO YOUR IDEAS ABOUT MANLINESS AND OVERLOOK THIS...
...MEN HAVE TO BE STRONG!
I WON'T GIVE RYO TO YOU IF YOU'RE NOT A STRONG MAN.
CAN YOU PROTECT RYO?
I WANT HIM TO ...
YES.
WELL THEN, LET'S SEE YOU PROVE IT...
...APPROVE OF ME!
...ASUKA WHAT'S-YOUR-NAME.

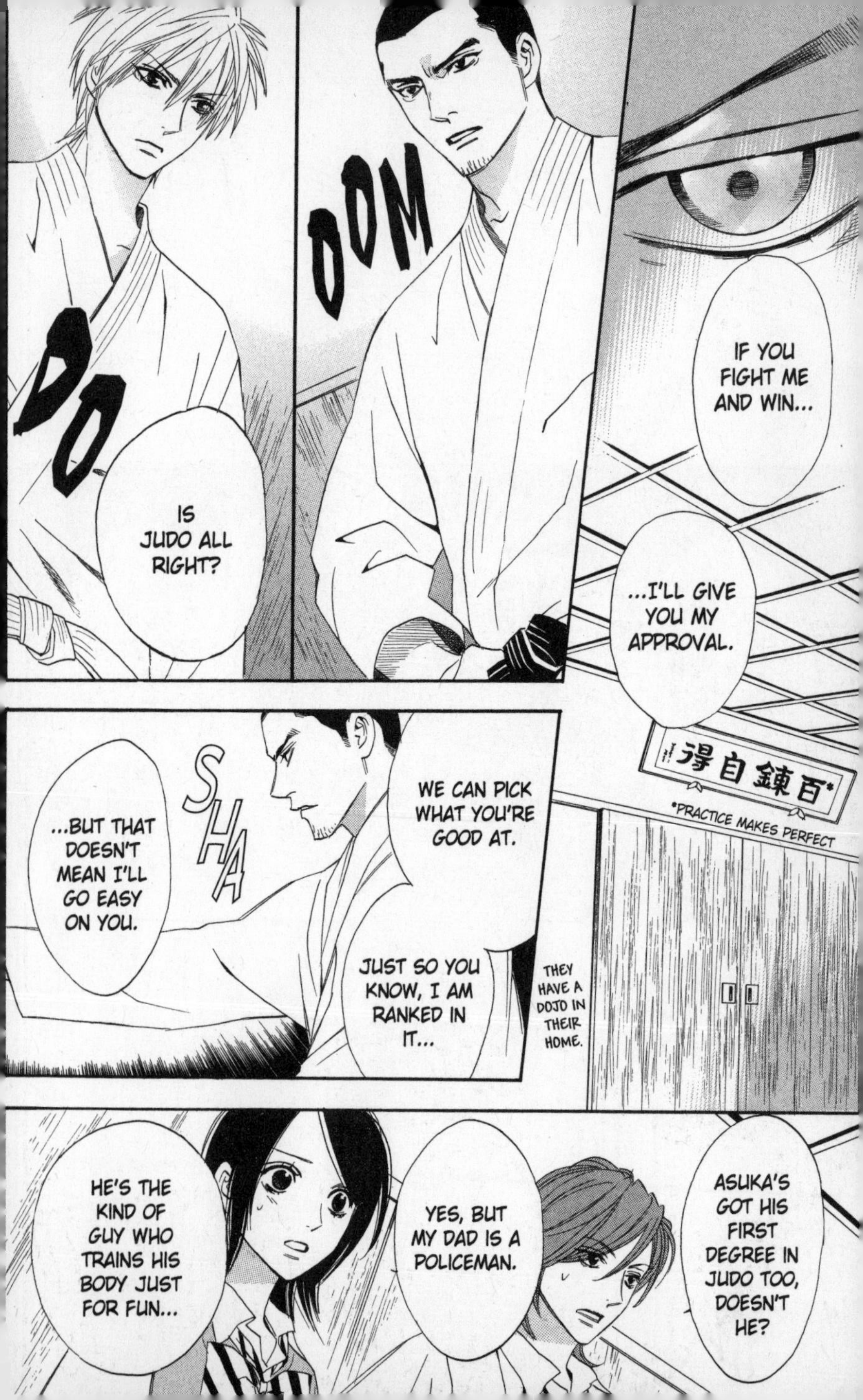
IF YOU FIGHT ME AND WIN...
...I'LL GIVE YOU MY APPROVAL.
DOM
DO
IS JUDO ALL RIGHT?
百錬自得*
*PRACTICE MAKES PERFECT
THEY HAVE A DOJO IN THEIR HOME.
WE CAN PICK WHAT YOU'RE GOOD AT.
JUST SO YOU KNOW, I AM RANKED IN IT...
SHA
...BUT THAT DOESN'T MEAN I'LL GO EASY ON YOU.
ASUKA'S GOT HIS FIRST DEGREE IN JUDO TOO, DOESN'T HE?
YES, BUT MY DAD IS A POLICEMAN.
HE'S THE KIND OF GUY WHO TRAINS HIS BODY JUST FOR FUN...

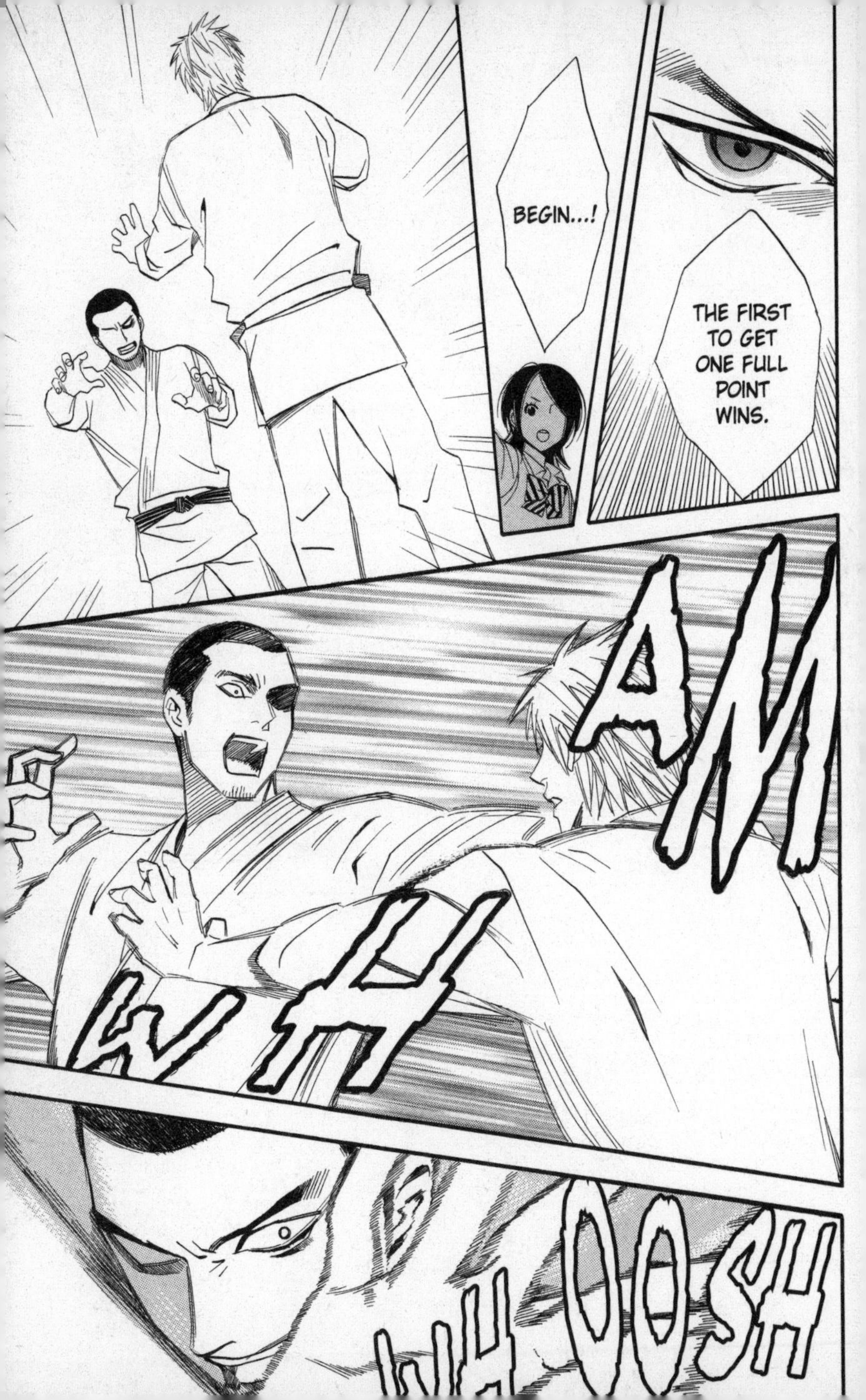
THE FIRST TO GET ONE FULL POINT WINS.
BEGIN...!
WHAM
WHOOSH

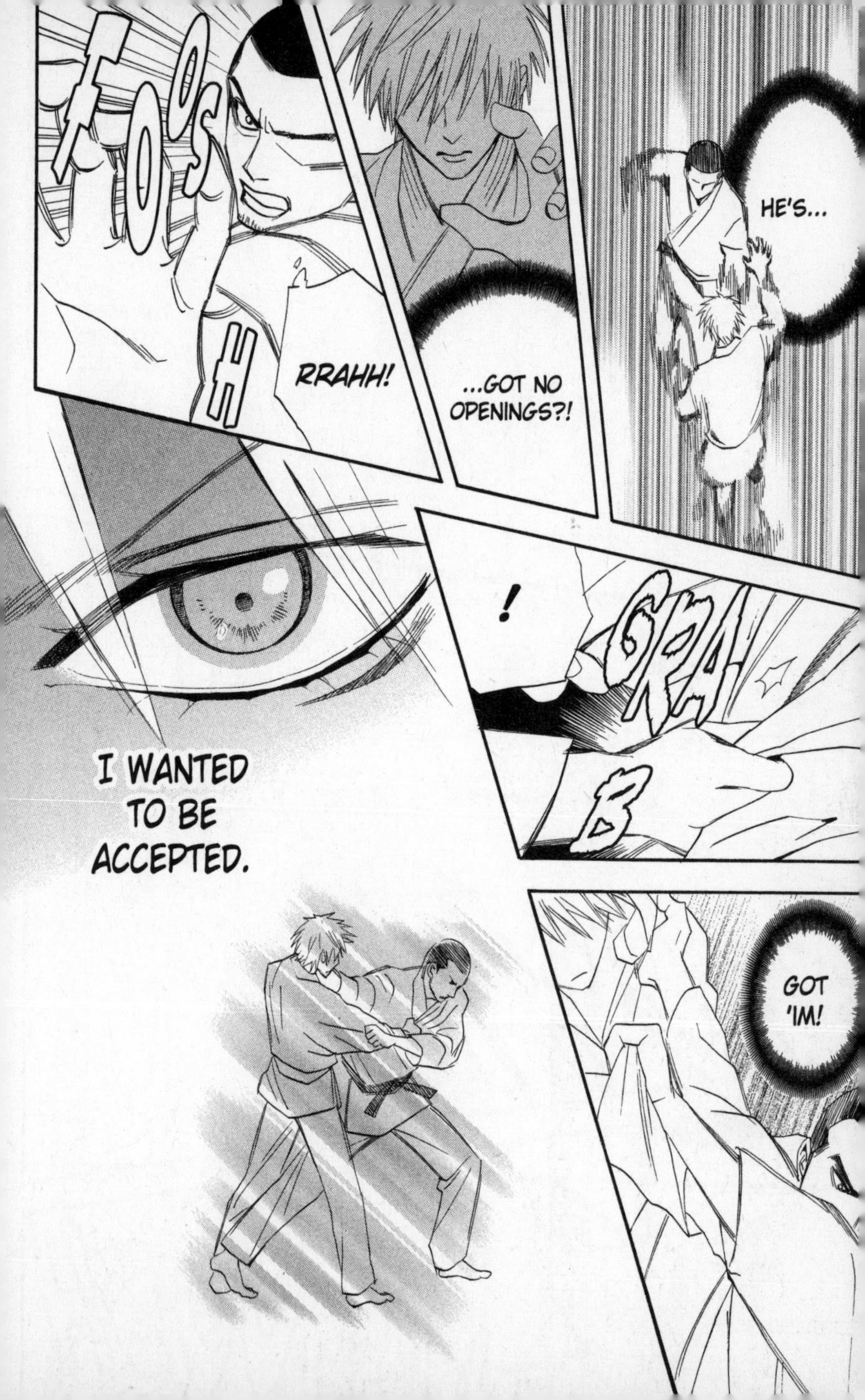
HE'S...
...GOT NO OPENINGS?!
RRAHH!
!
GRAB
I WANTED TO BE ACCEPTED.
GOT 'IM!

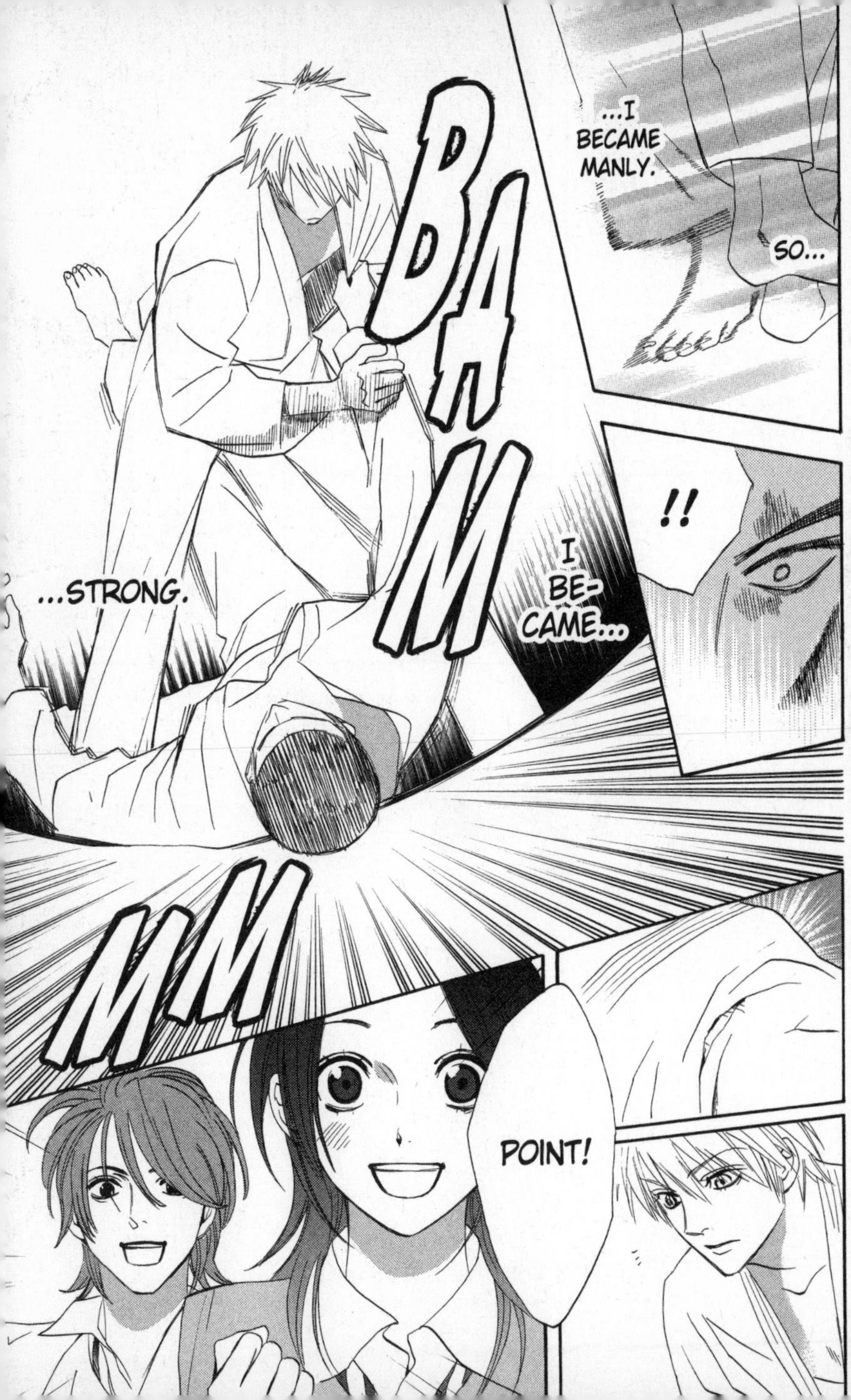
...I BECAME MANLY.
SO...
!!
I BE-CAME...
...STRONG.
BAMMM
POINT!

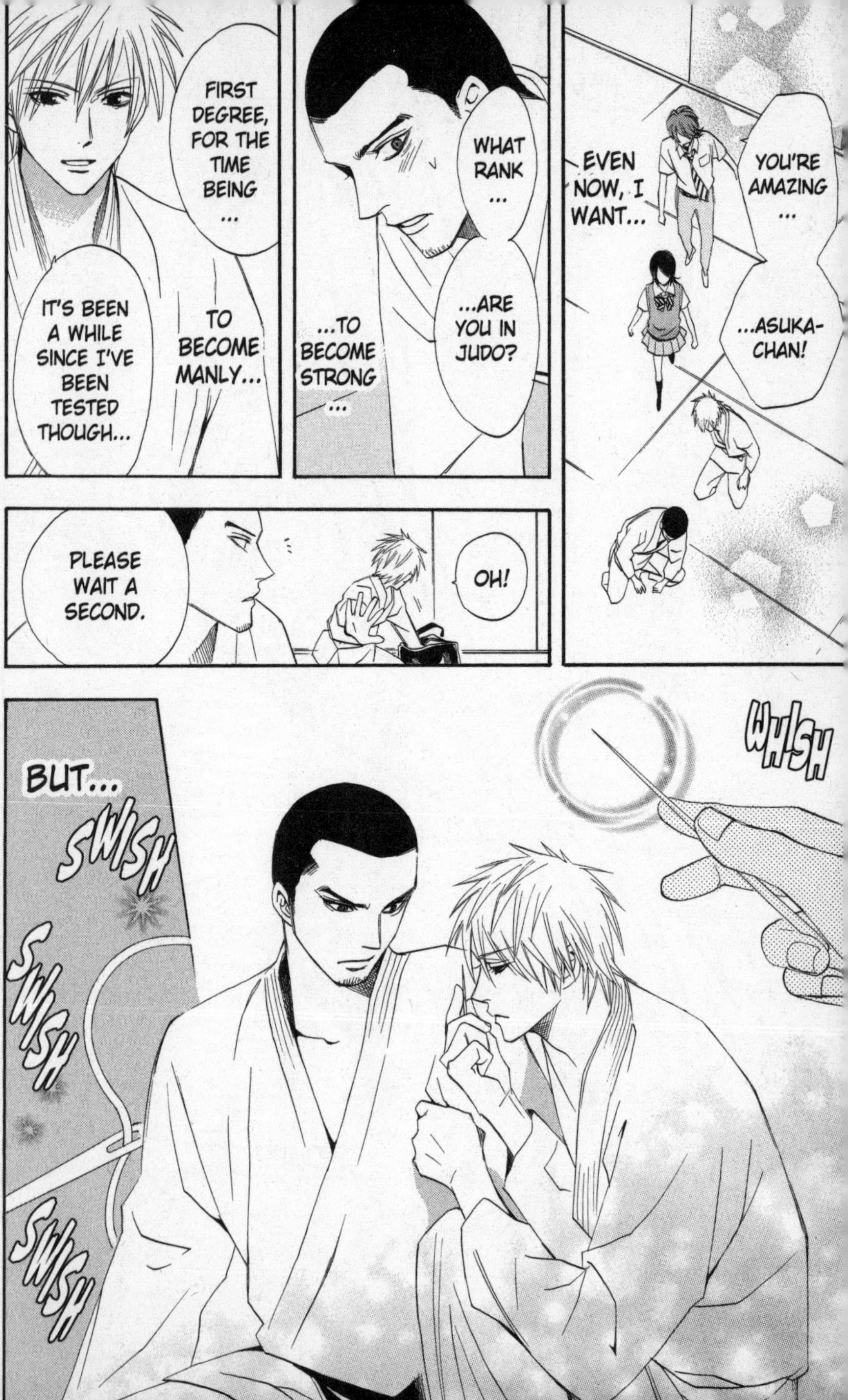
YOU'RE AMAZING ...
...ASUKA-CHAN!
EVEN NOW, I WANT...
WHAT RANK ...
...ARE YOU IN JUDO?
...TO BECOME STRONG ...
FIRST DEGREE, FOR THE TIME BEING ...
TO BECOME MANLY...
IT'S BEEN A WHILE SINCE I'VE BEEN TESTED THOUGH...
OH!
PLEASE WAIT A SECOND.
WHISH
BUT...
SWISH
SWISH
SWISH

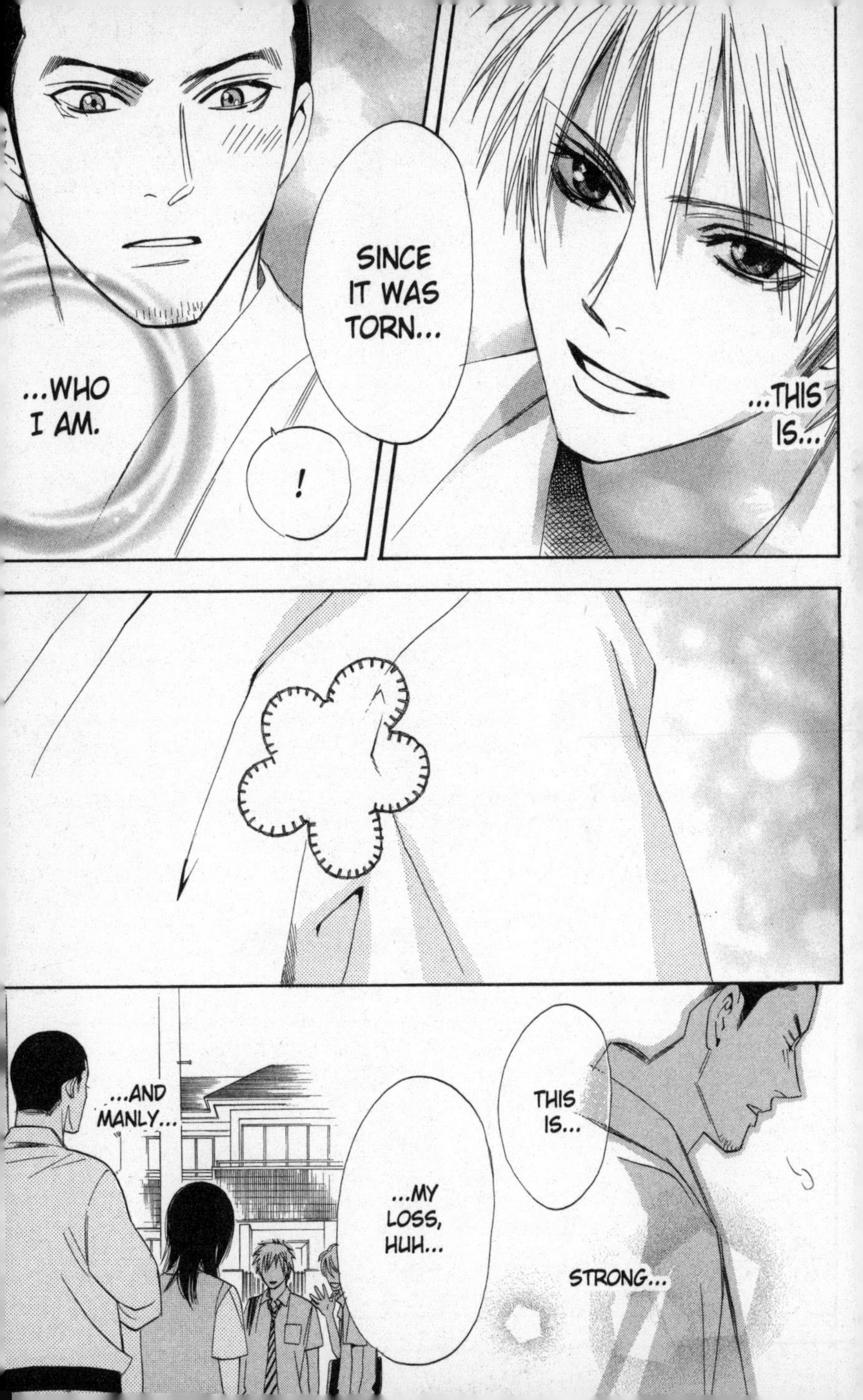
SINCE IT WAS TORN...
...THIS IS...
...WHO I AM.
!
THIS IS...
STRONG...
...AND MANLY...
...MY LOSS, HUH...

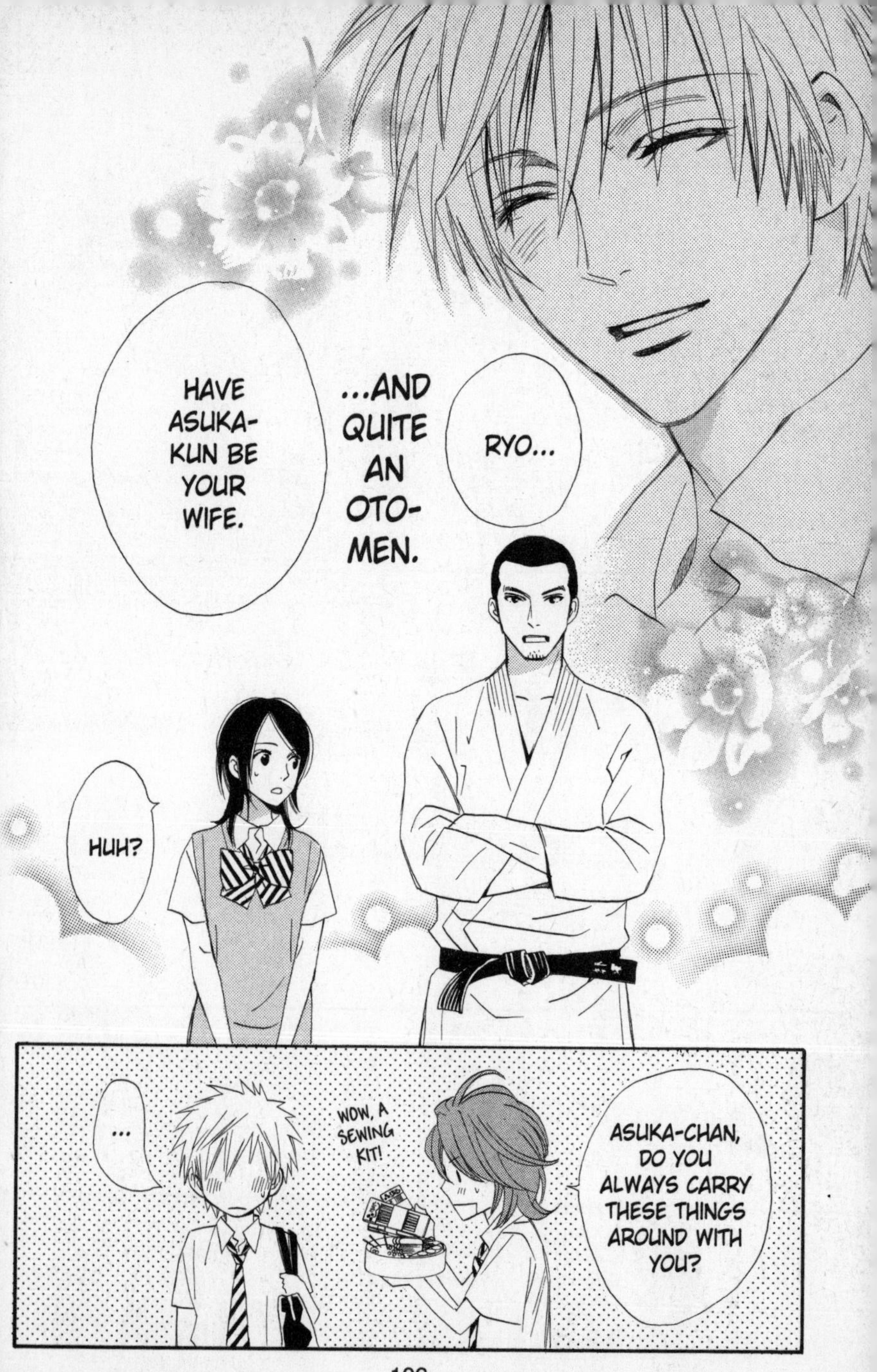
RYO...
...AND QUITE AN OTO-MEN.
HAVE ASUKA-KUN BE YOUR WIFE.
HUH?
ASUKA-CHAN, DO YOU ALWAYS CARRY THESE THINGS AROUND WITH YOU?
WOW, A SEWING KIT!
...

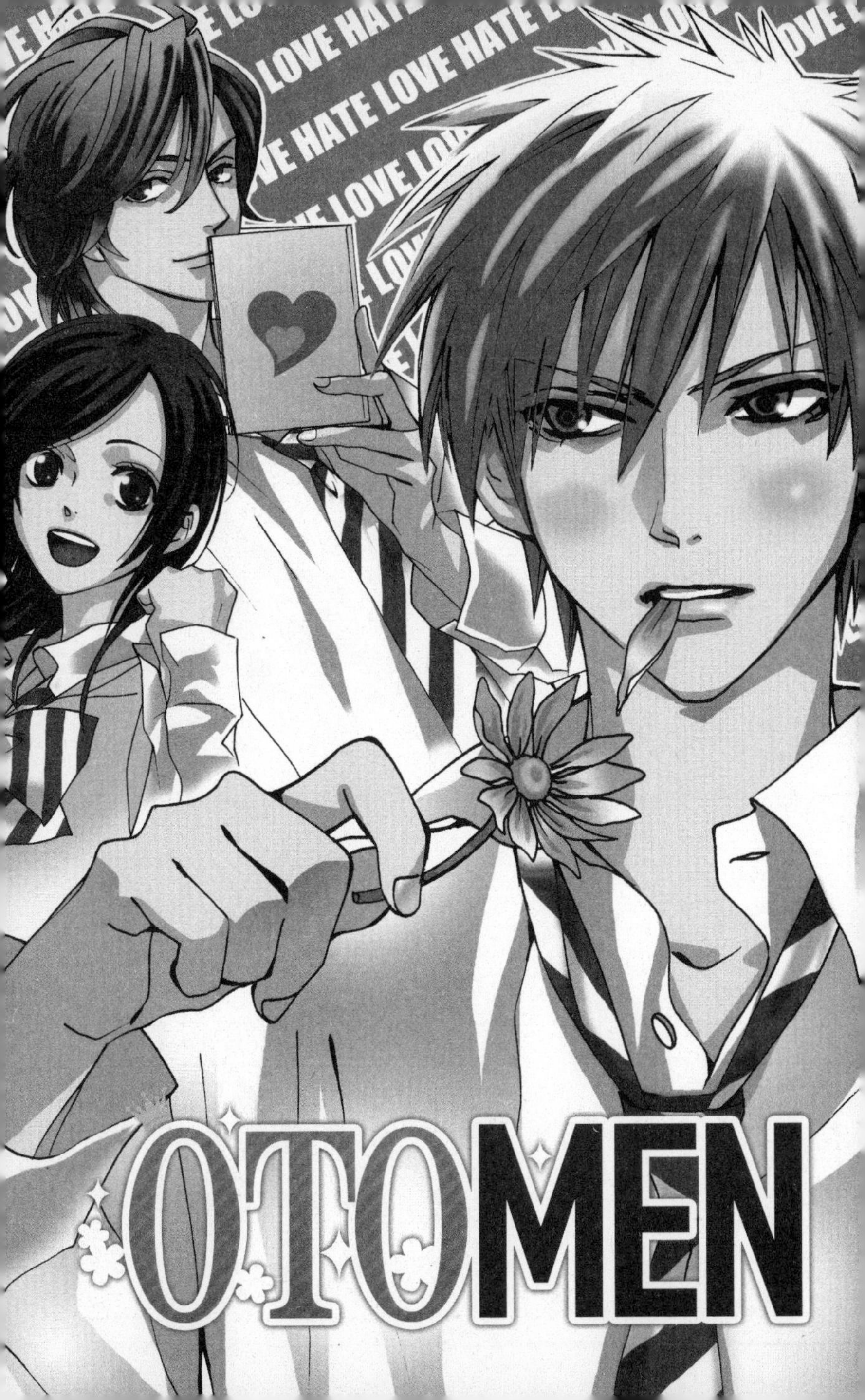

LOVE HATE LOVE HATE LOVE
OTOMEN

OTOMEN

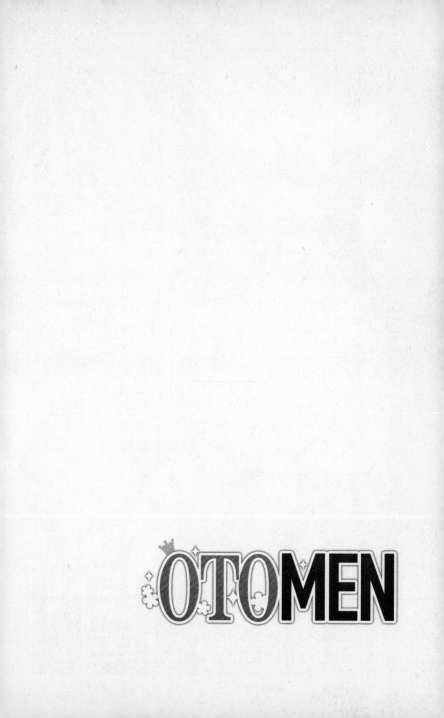

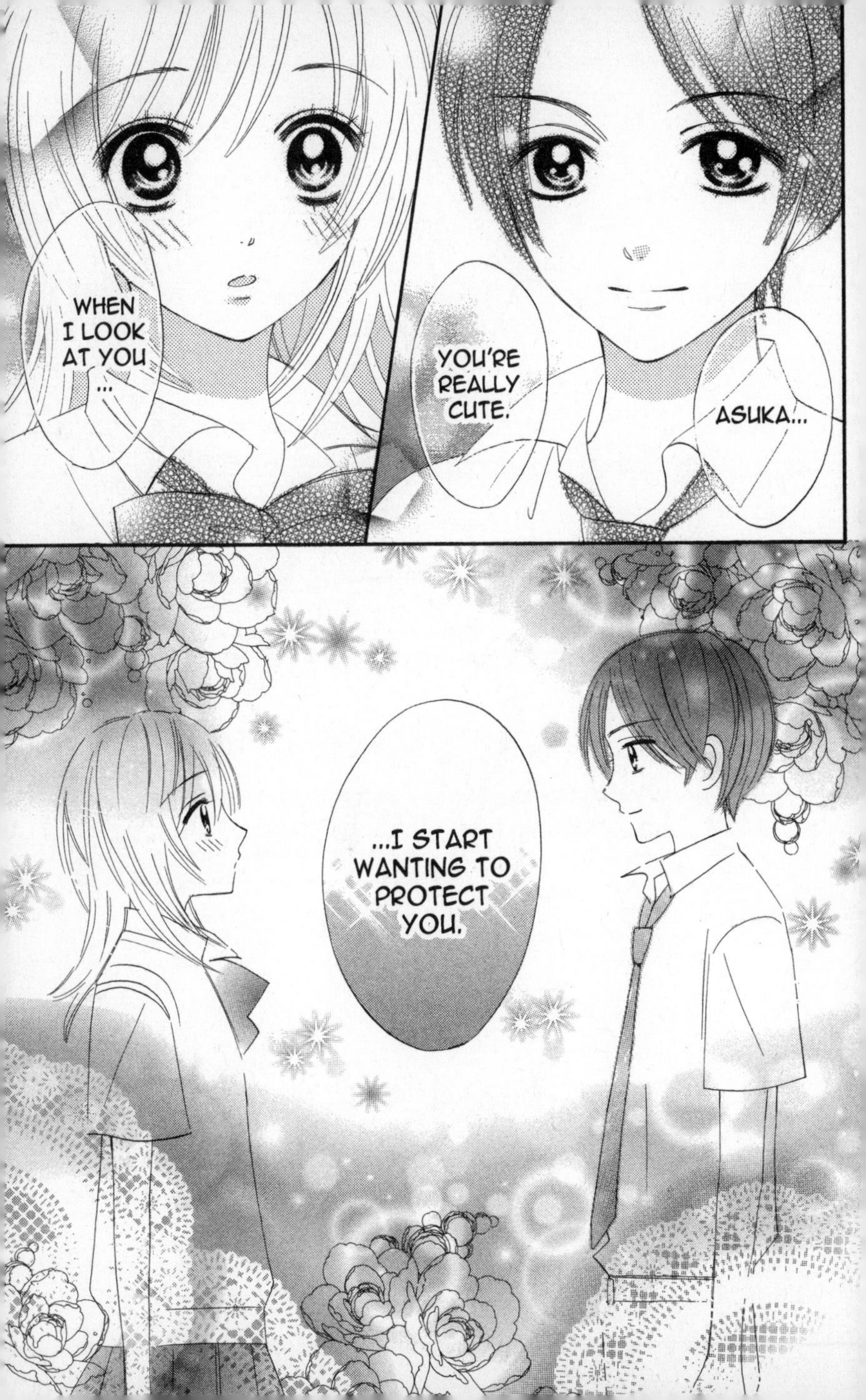
ASUKA...
YOU'RE REALLY CUTE.
WHEN I LOOK AT YOU ...
...I START WANTING TO PROTECT YOU.

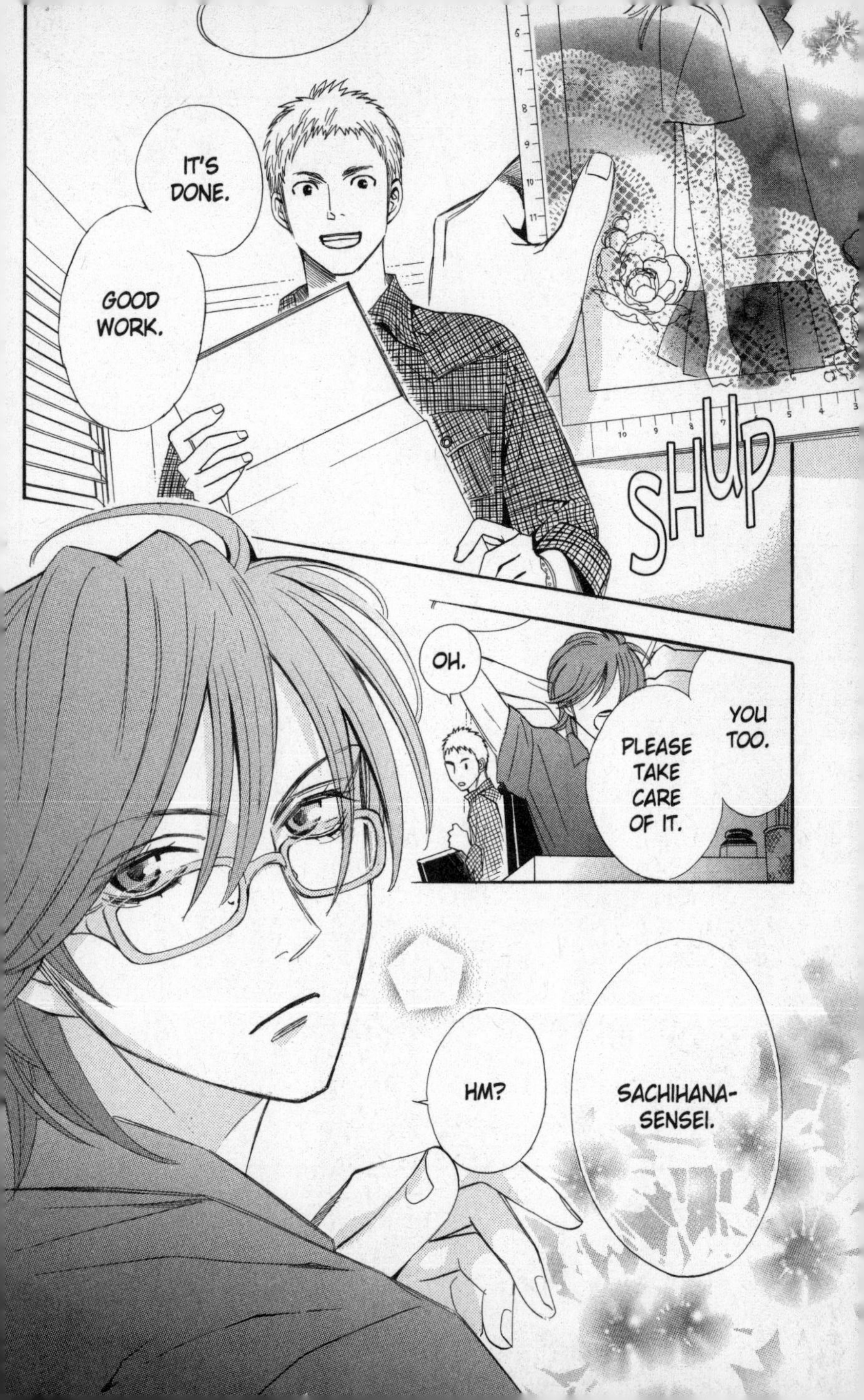
IT'S DONE.
GOOD WORK.
SHUP
YOU TOO.
PLEASE TAKE CARE OF IT.
OH.
SACHIHANA-SENSEI.
HM?

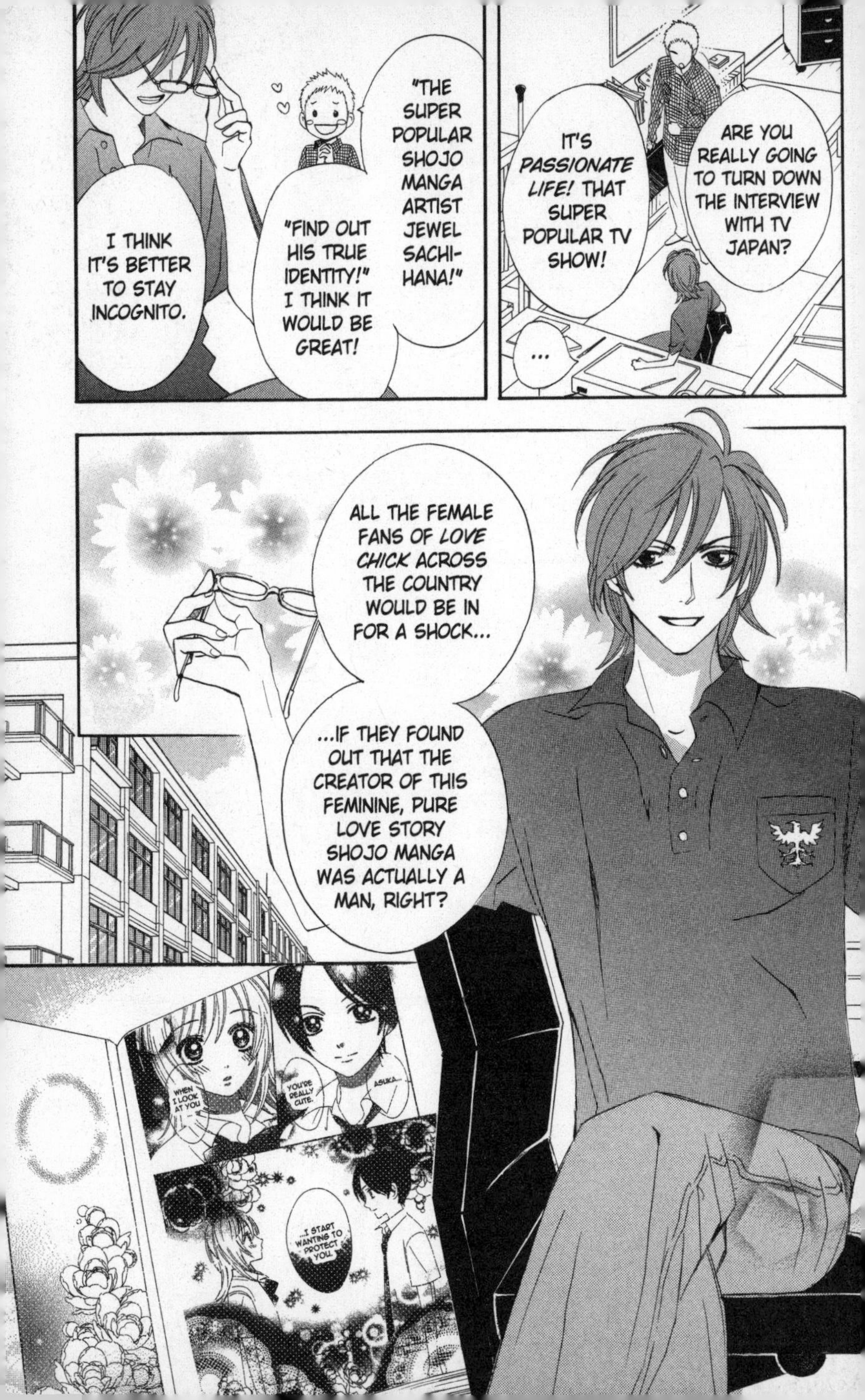
ARE YOU REALLY GOING TO TURN DOWN THE INTERVIEW WITH TV JAPAN?
IT'S *PASSIONATE LIFE!* THAT SUPER POPULAR TV SHOW!
...
"THE SUPER POPULAR SHOJO MANGA ARTIST JEWEL SACHI-HANA!"
"FIND OUT HIS TRUE IDENTITY!" I THINK IT WOULD BE GREAT!
I THINK IT'S BETTER TO STAY INCOGNITO.
ALL THE FEMALE FANS OF *LOVE CHICK* ACROSS THE COUNTRY WOULD BE IN FOR A SHOCK...
...IF THEY FOUND OUT THAT THE CREATOR OF THIS FEMININE, PURE LOVE STORY SHOJO MANGA WAS ACTUALLY A MAN, RIGHT?
ASUKA...
YOU'RE REALLY CUTE.
WHEN I LOOK AT YOU
...I START WANTING TO PROTECT YOU.

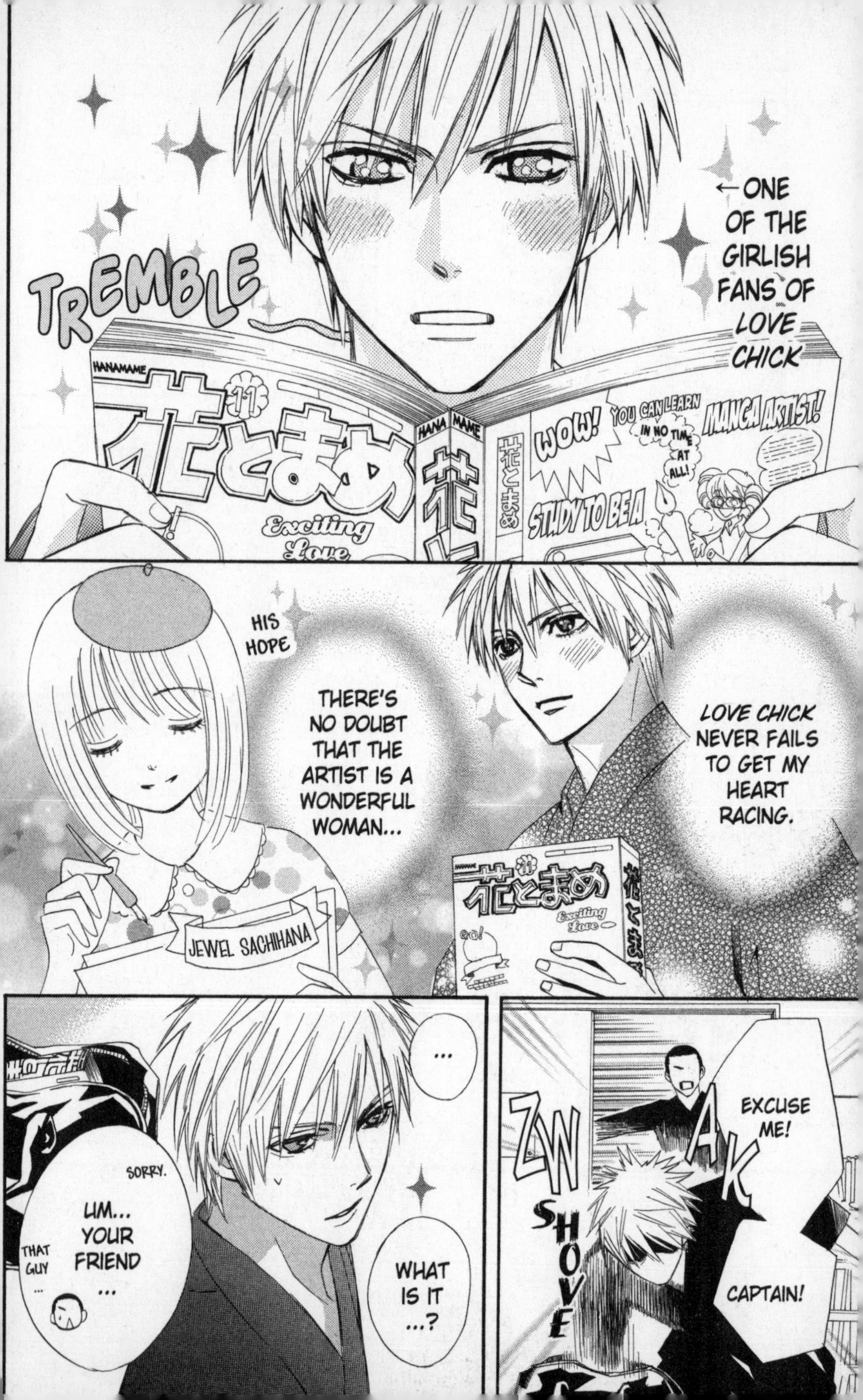
← ONE OF THE GIRLISH FANS OF LOVE CHICK
TREMBLE
HANAMAME
花とまめ
Exciting Love
HANA MAME
WOW!
YOU CAN LEARN IN NO TIME AT ALL!
STUDY TO BE A MANGA ARTIST!
LOVE CHICK NEVER FAILS TO GET MY HEART RACING.
THERE'S NO DOUBT THAT THE ARTIST IS A WONDERFUL WOMAN...
HIS HOPE
JEWEL SACHIHANA
EXCUSE ME!
ZWAK
SHOVE
CAPTAIN!
...
WHAT IS IT ...?
SORRY.
UM... YOUR FRIEND ...
THAT GUY ...

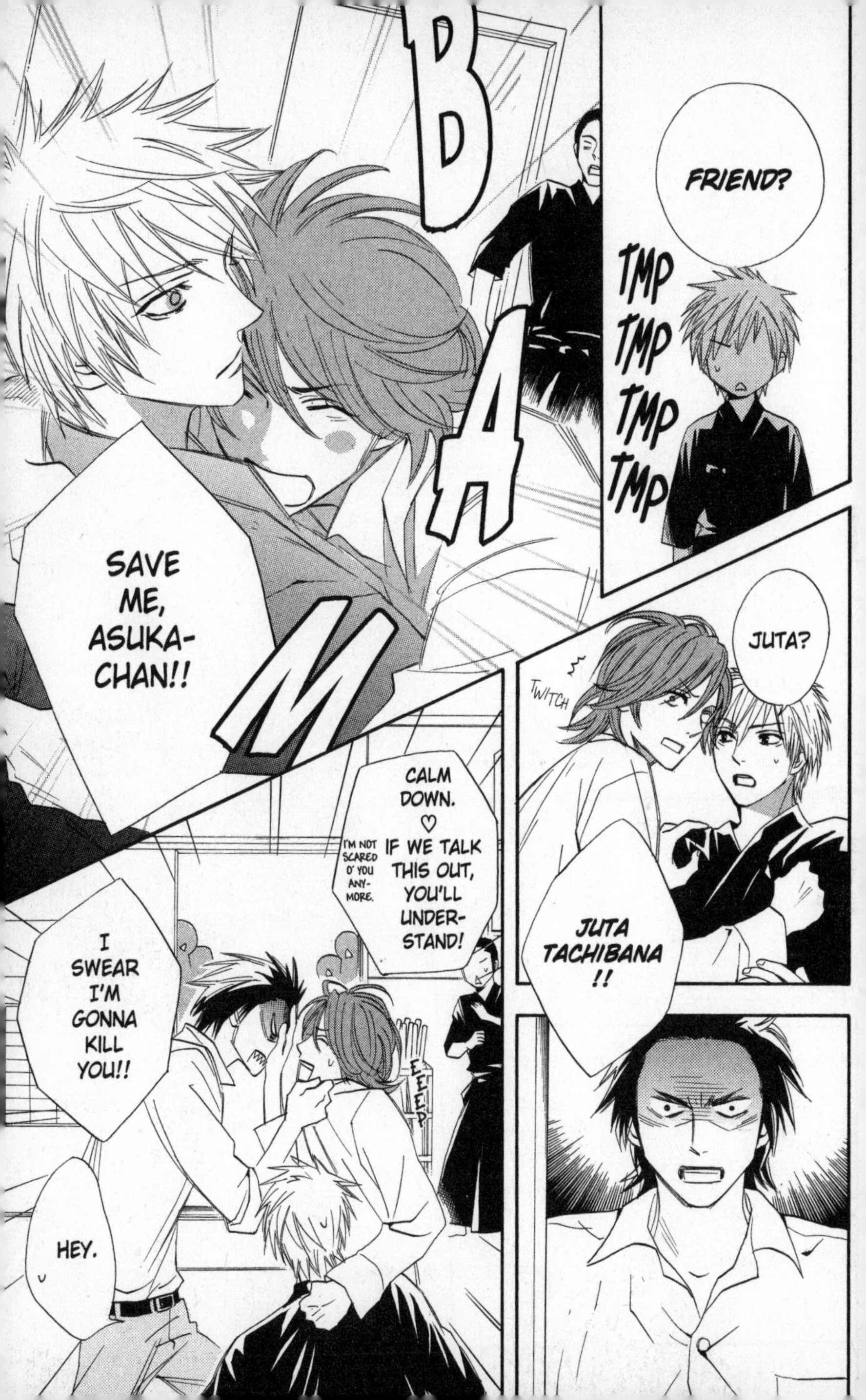
FRIEND?
TMP TMP TMP TMP
BAM
SAVE ME, ASUKA-CHAN!!
JUTA?
TWITCH
JUTA TACHIBANA!!
CALM DOWN. ♡ IF WE TALK THIS OUT, YOU'LL UNDERSTAND!
I'M NOT SCARED O' YOU ANYMORE.
I SWEAR I'M GONNA KILL YOU!!
WHAP
HEY.

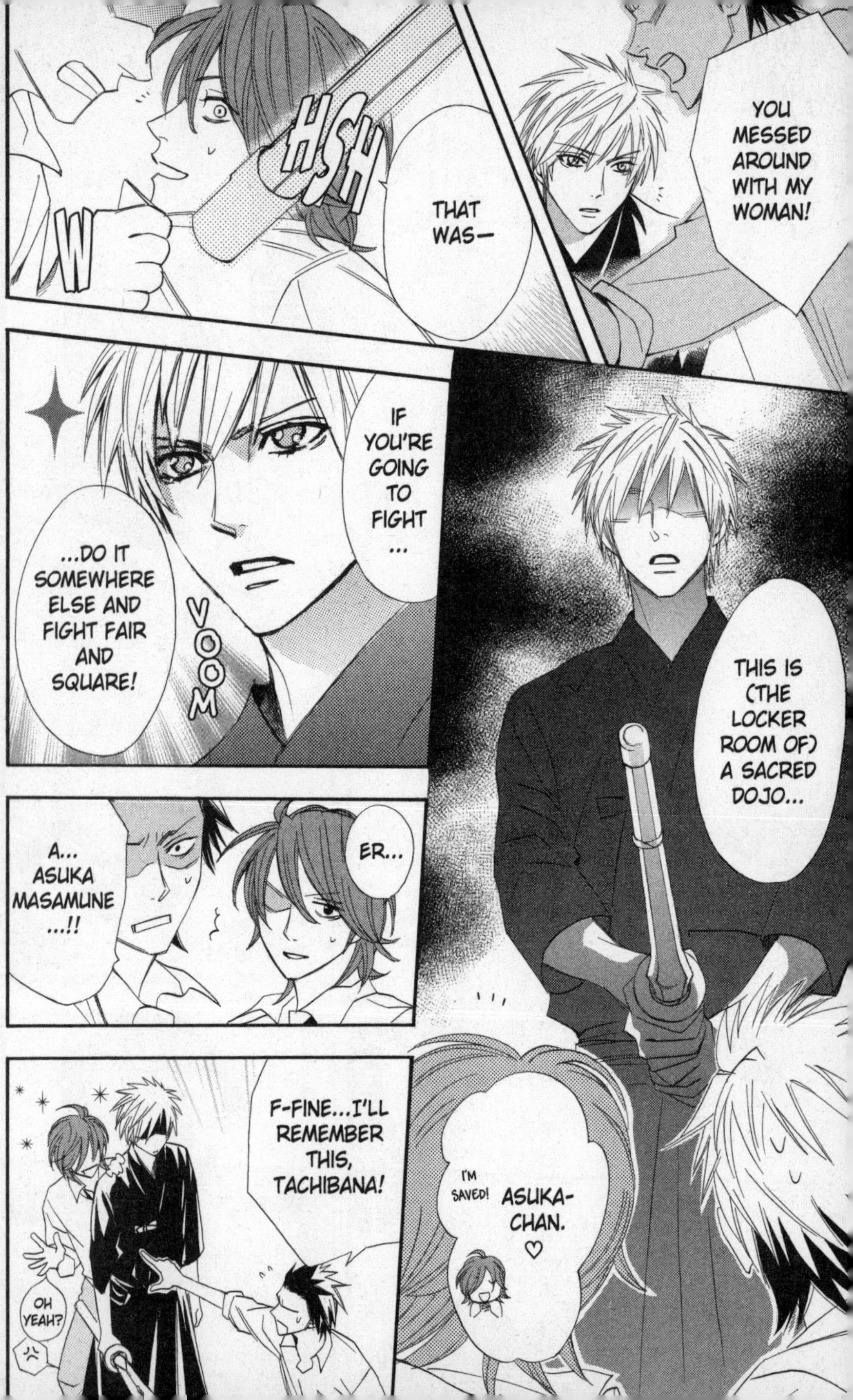
YOU MESSED AROUND WITH MY WOMAN!
THAT WAS—
WHSH
THIS IS (THE LOCKER ROOM OF) A SACRED DOJO...
I'M SAVED!
ASUKA-CHAN. ♡
IF YOU'RE GOING TO FIGHT...
...DO IT SOMEWHERE ELSE AND FIGHT FAIR AND SQUARE!
VOOM
ER...
A... ASUKA MASAMUNE ...!!
F-FINE...I'LL REMEMBER THIS, TACHIBANA!
OH YEAH?

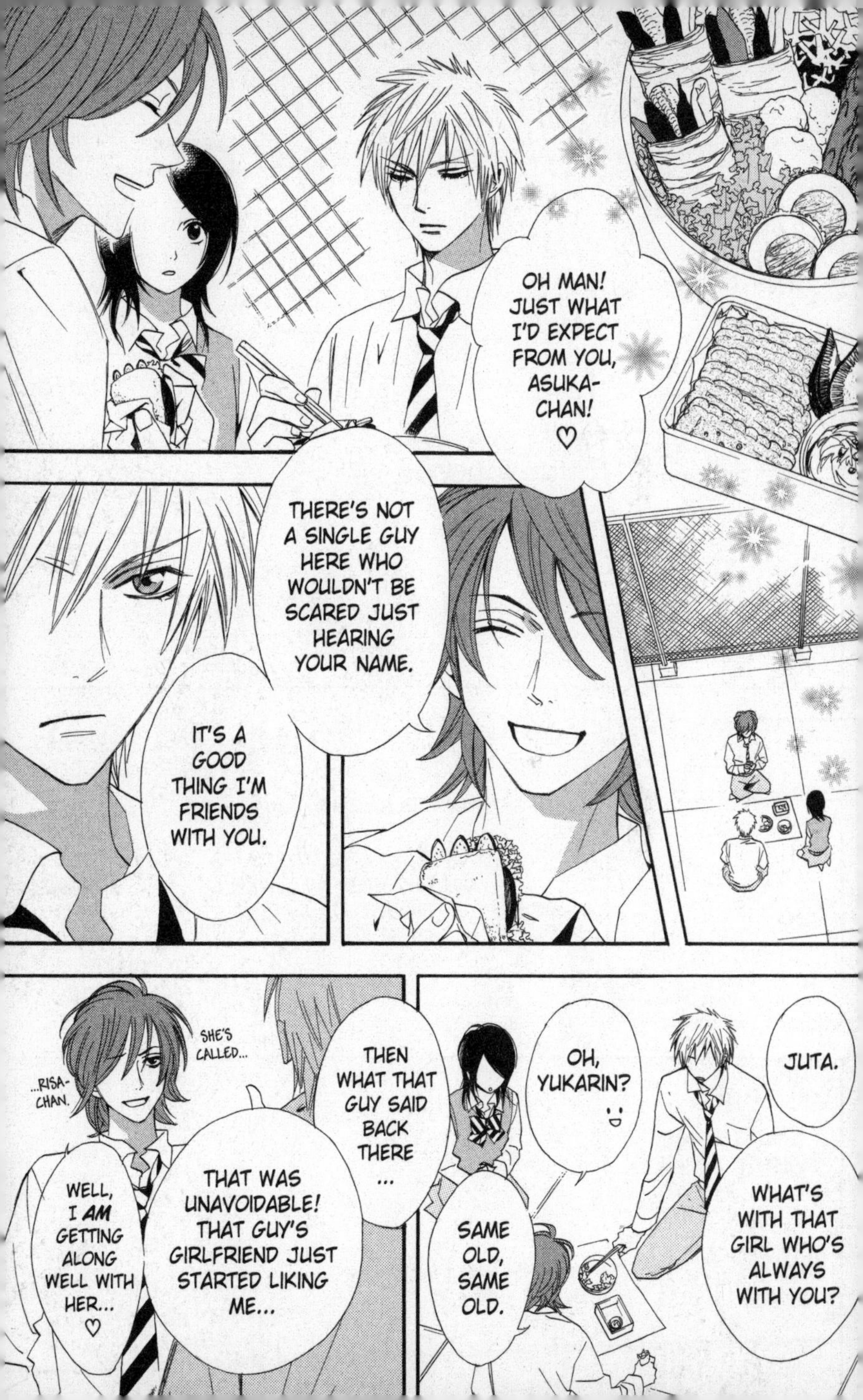
OH MAN! JUST WHAT I'D EXPECT FROM YOU, ASUKA-CHAN! ♡
THERE'S NOT A SINGLE GUY HERE WHO WOULDN'T BE SCARED JUST HEARING YOUR NAME.
IT'S A GOOD THING I'M FRIENDS WITH YOU.
JUTA.
OH, YUKARIN?
WHAT'S WITH THAT GIRL WHO'S ALWAYS WITH YOU?
SAME OLD, SAME OLD.
THEN WHAT THAT GUY SAID BACK THERE ...
THAT WAS UNAVOIDABLE! THAT GUY'S GIRLFRIEND JUST STARTED LIKING ME...
SHE'S CALLED...
...RISA-CHAN.
WELL, I *AM* GETTING ALONG WELL WITH HER... ♡

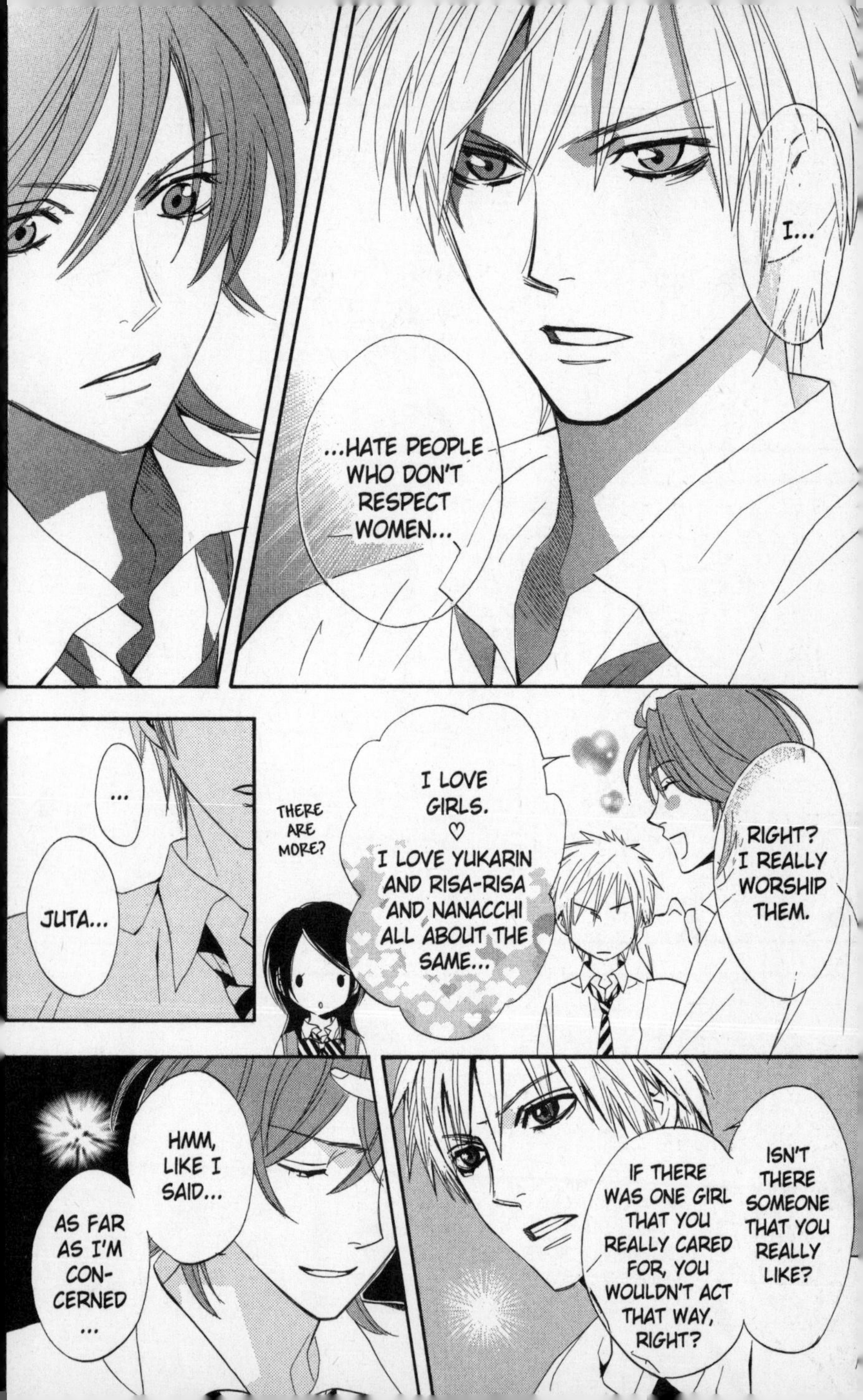
I...
...HATE PEOPLE WHO DON'T RESPECT WOMEN...
RIGHT? I REALLY WORSHIP THEM.
I LOVE GIRLS. ♡ I LOVE YUKARIN AND RISA-RISA AND NANACCHI ALL ABOUT THE SAME...
THERE ARE MORE?
...
JUTA...
ISN'T THERE SOMEONE THAT YOU REALLY LIKE?
IF THERE WAS ONE GIRL THAT YOU REALLY CARED FOR, YOU WOULDN'T ACT THAT WAY, RIGHT?
HMM, LIKE I SAID...
AS FAR AS I'M CON-CERNED ...

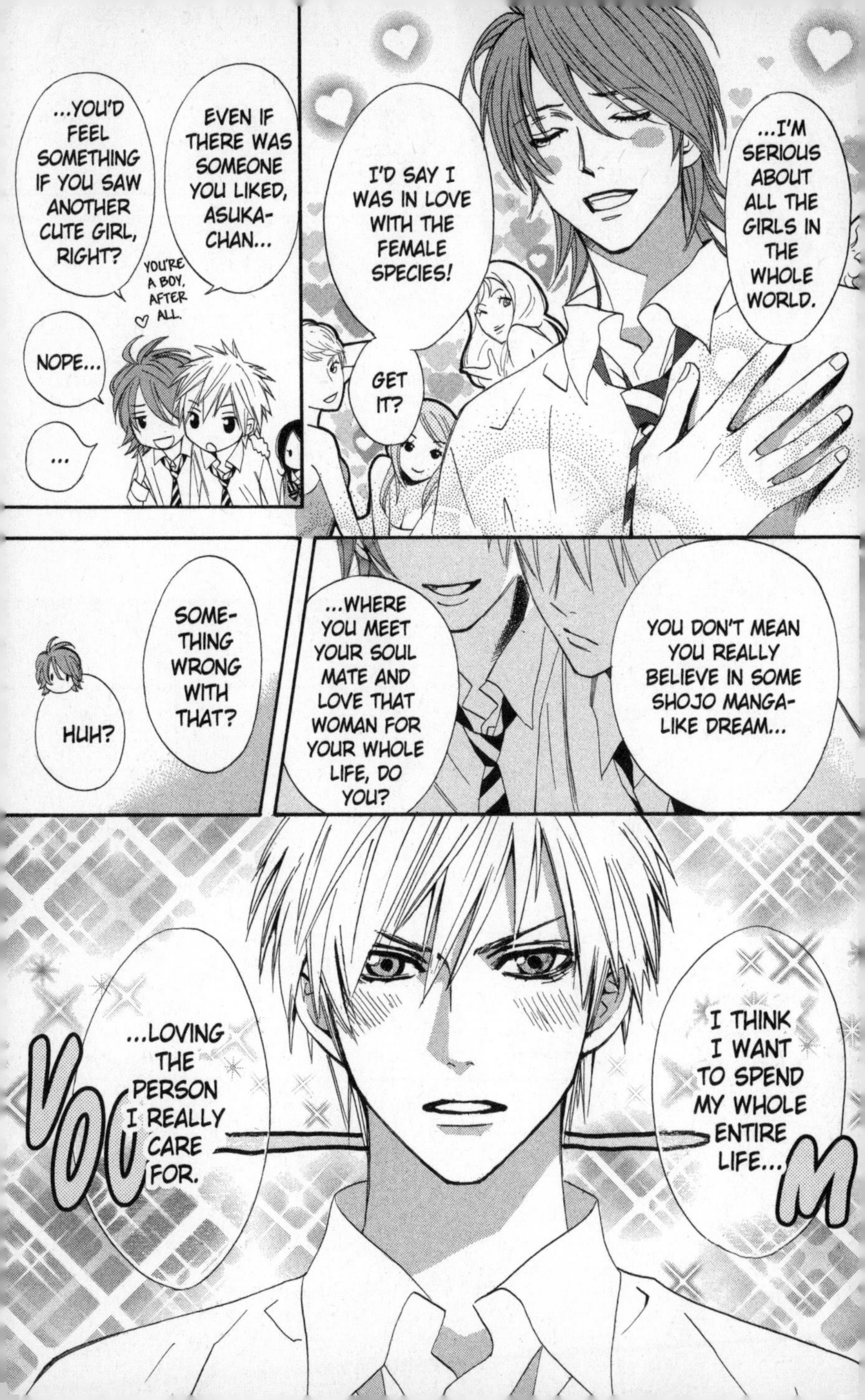
...I'M SERIOUS ABOUT ALL THE GIRLS IN THE WHOLE WORLD.
I'D SAY I WAS IN LOVE WITH THE FEMALE SPECIES!
GET IT?
EVEN IF THERE WAS SOMEONE YOU LIKED, ASUKA-CHAN...
...YOU'D FEEL SOMETHING IF YOU SAW ANOTHER CUTE GIRL, RIGHT?
YOU'RE A BOY, AFTER ALL. ♡
NOPE...
...
YOU DON'T MEAN YOU REALLY BELIEVE IN SOME SHOJO MANGA-LIKE DREAM...
...WHERE YOU MEET YOUR SOUL MATE AND LOVE THAT WOMAN FOR YOUR WHOLE LIFE, DO YOU?
SOME-THING WRONG WITH THAT?
HUH?
I THINK I WANT TO SPEND MY WHOLE ENTIRE LIFE...
...LOVING THE PERSON I REALLY CARE FOR.
VOOOM

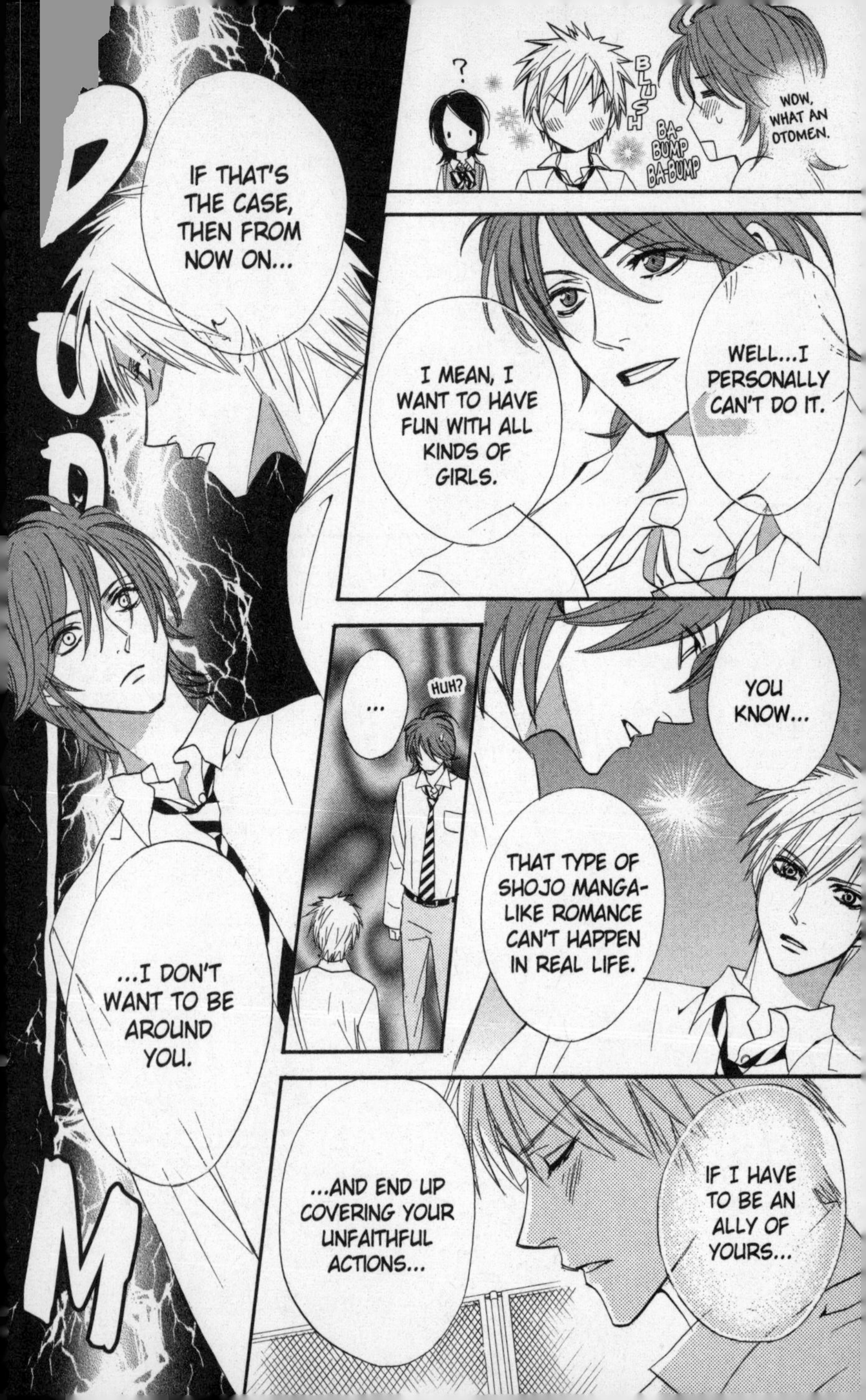
WOW, WHAT AN OTOMEN.
BA-BUMP BA-BUMP
BLUSH
?
WELL...I PERSONALLY CAN'T DO IT.
I MEAN, I WANT TO HAVE FUN WITH ALL KINDS OF GIRLS.
YOU KNOW...
THAT TYPE OF SHOJO MANGA-LIKE ROMANCE CAN'T HAPPEN IN REAL LIFE.
HUH?
...
IF I HAVE TO BE AN ALLY OF YOURS...
...AND END UP COVERING YOUR UNFAITHFUL ACTIONS...
IF THAT'S THE CASE, THEN FROM NOW ON...
...I DON'T WANT TO BE AROUND YOU.
DOOM

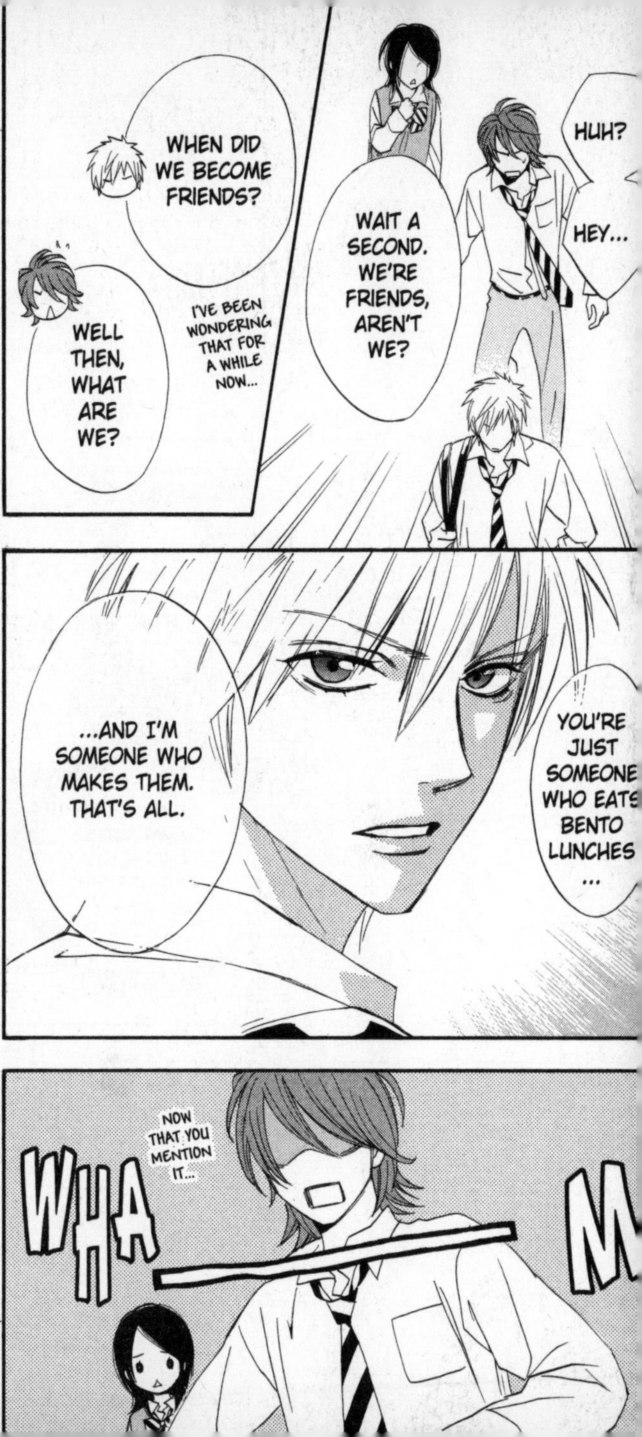
HUH?
HEY...
WAIT A SECOND. WE'RE FRIENDS, AREN'T WE?
WHEN DID WE BECOME FRIENDS?
I'VE BEEN WONDERING THAT FOR A WHILE NOW...
WELL THEN, WHAT ARE WE?
YOU'RE JUST SOMEONE WHO EATS BENTO LUNCHES...
...AND I'M SOMEONE WHO MAKES THEM. THAT'S ALL.
NOW THAT YOU MENTION IT...
WHA
M

In the beginning, Juta was supposed to be a relatively cool character. However, he becomes a comedic character in this third chapter and seems to get increasingly goofy from this point on... He's a shojo manga artist who's really passionate about his work (unlike me). He's a shojo manga artist through and through. It's amazing that he can enjoy his life as a student this much while living as a published (and very popular) artist. When does he sleep? Since he's the character who seems to be the most grounded, I can direct him easily.

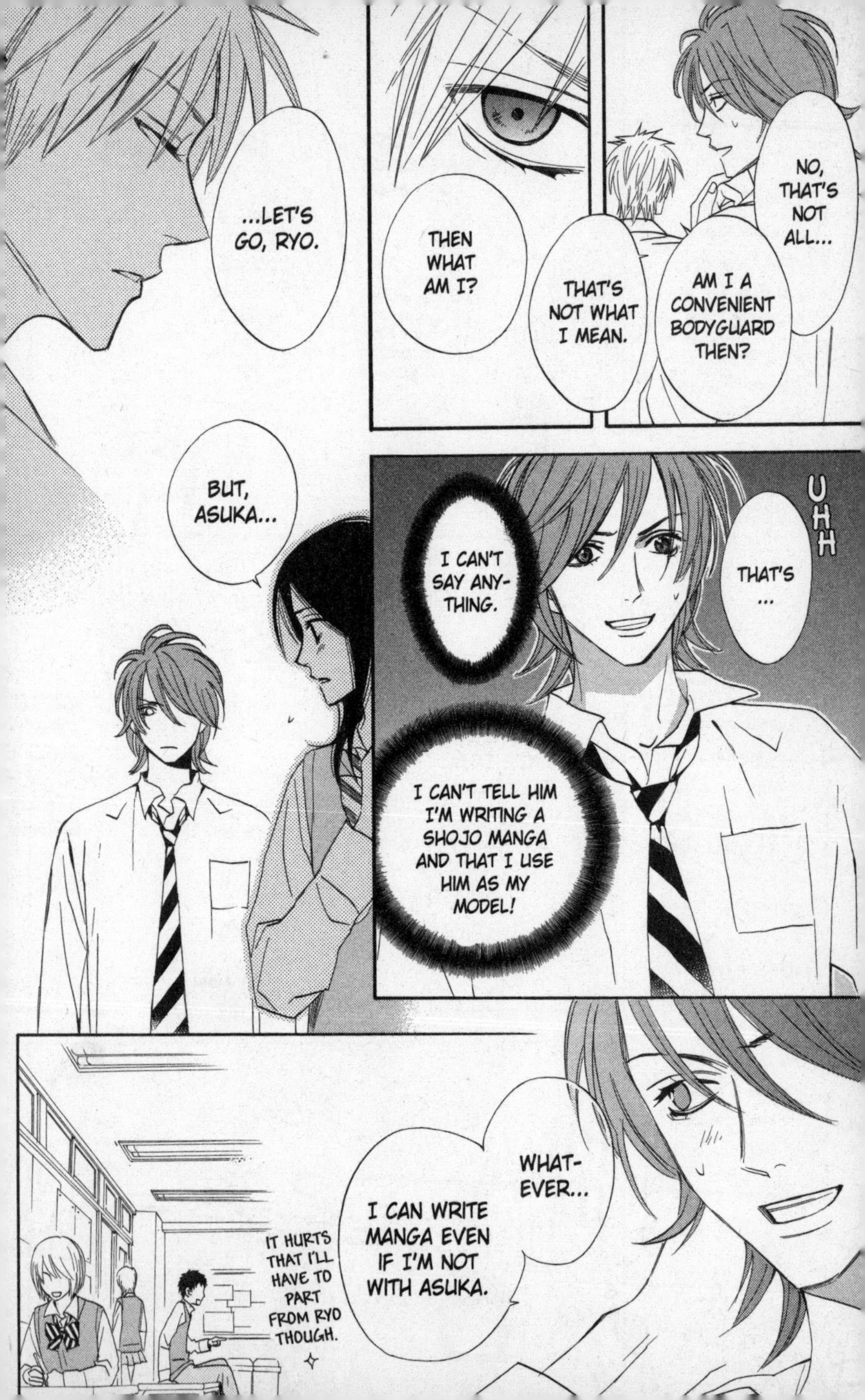
NO, THAT'S NOT ALL...
AM I A CONVENIENT BODYGUARD THEN?
THAT'S NOT WHAT I MEAN.
THEN WHAT AM I?
UHH
THAT'S ...
I CAN'T SAY ANY-THING.
I CAN'T TELL HIM I'M WRITING A SHOJO MANGA AND THAT I USE HIM AS MY MODEL!
...LET'S GO, RYO.
BUT, ASUKA...
WHAT-EVER...
I CAN WRITE MANGA EVEN IF I'M NOT WITH ASUKA.
IT HURTS THAT I'LL HAVE TO PART FROM RYO THOUGH.

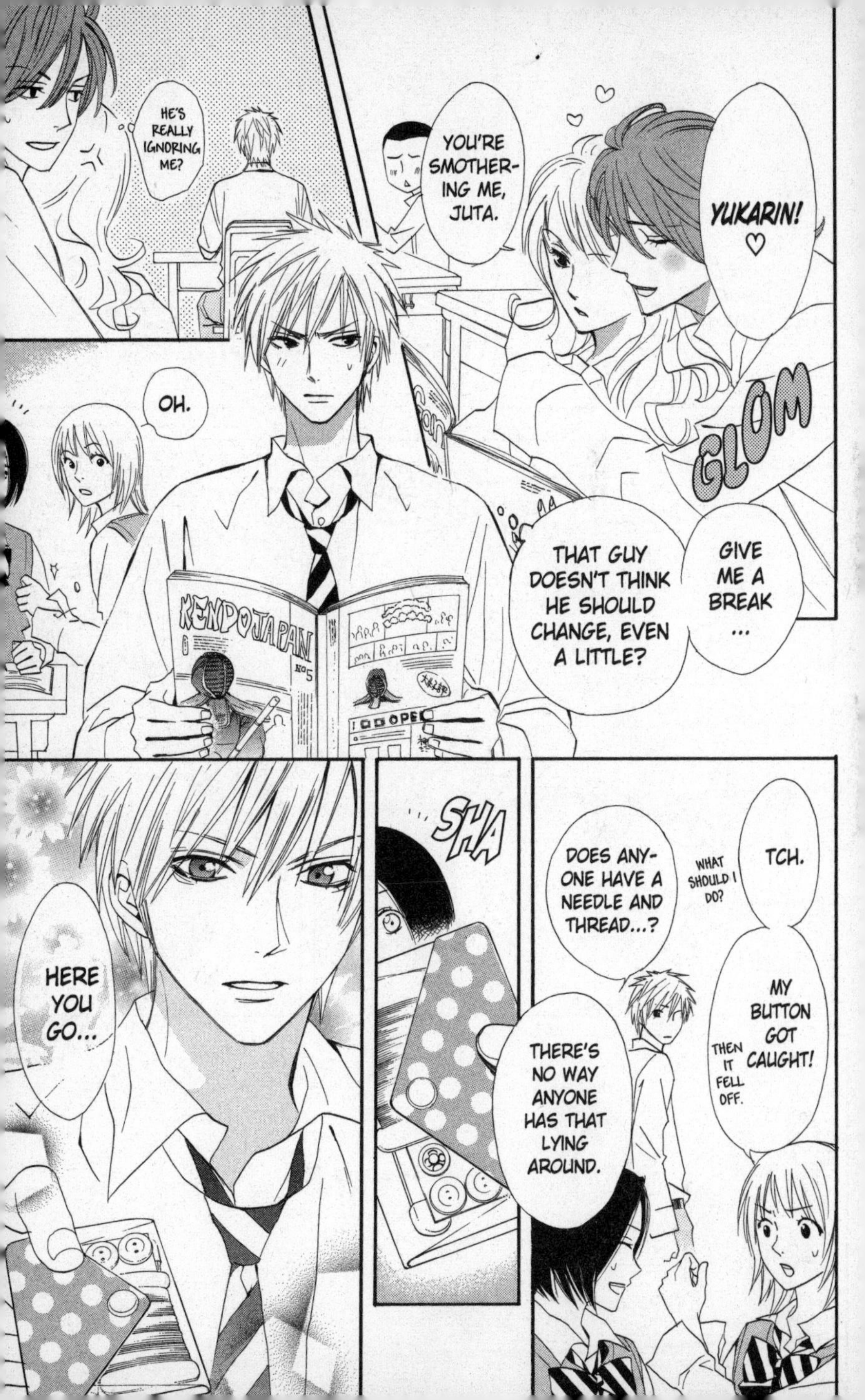
YUKARIN! ♡
YOU'RE SMOTHERING ME, JUTA.
GLOM
HE'S REALLY IGNORING ME?
GIVE ME A BREAK ...
THAT GUY DOESN'T THINK HE SHOULD CHANGE, EVEN A LITTLE?
OH.
KENDO JAPAN
TCH.
WHAT SHOULD I DO?
DOES ANYONE HAVE A NEEDLE AND THREAD...?
MY BUTTON GOT CAUGHT!
THEN IT FELL OFF.
THERE'S NO WAY ANYONE HAS THAT LYING AROUND.
SHA
HERE YOU GO...

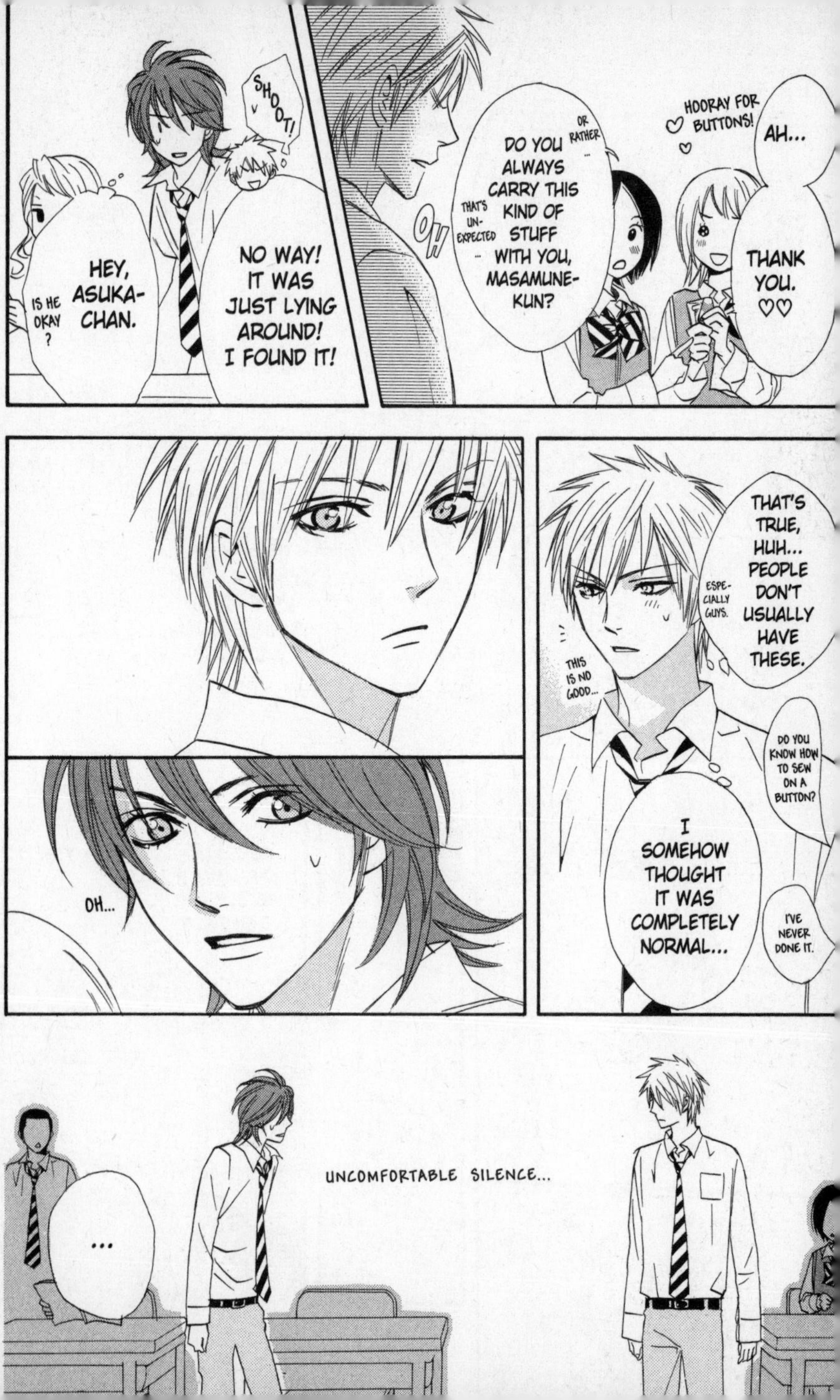
HOORAY FOR ♡ BUTTONS! ♡
AH...
THANK YOU. ♡♡
OR RATHER...
DO YOU ALWAYS CARRY THIS KIND OF STUFF WITH YOU, MASAMUNE-KUN?
THAT'S UN-EXPECTED...
OH
SHOOT!
NO WAY! IT WAS JUST LYING AROUND! I FOUND IT!
HEY, ASUKA-CHAN.
IS HE OKAY?
THAT'S TRUE, HUH... PEOPLE DON'T USUALLY HAVE THESE.
ESPE-CIALLY GUYS.
THIS IS NO GOOD...
DO YOU KNOW HOW TO SEW ON A BUTTON?
I'VE NEVER DONE IT.
I SOMEHOW THOUGHT IT WAS COMPLETELY NORMAL...
OH...
UNCOMFORTABLE SILENCE...
...

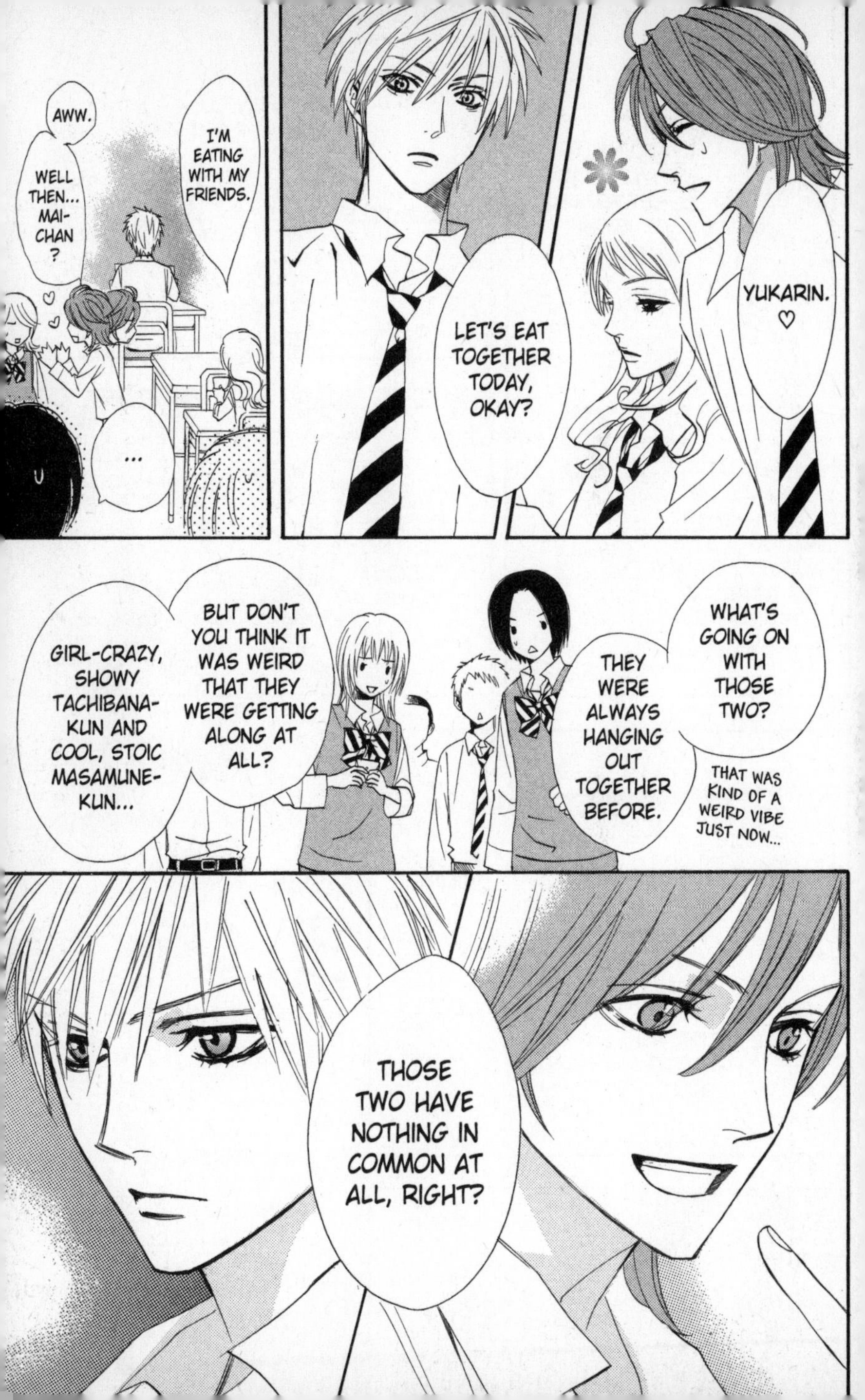
YUKARIN. ♡
LET'S EAT TOGETHER TODAY, OKAY?
I'M EATING WITH MY FRIENDS.
AWW.
WELL THEN... MAI-CHAN?
...
WHAT'S GOING ON WITH THOSE TWO?
THAT WAS KIND OF A WEIRD VIBE JUST NOW...
THEY WERE ALWAYS HANGING OUT TOGETHER BEFORE.
BUT DON'T YOU THINK IT WAS WEIRD THAT THEY WERE GETTING ALONG AT ALL?
GIRL-CRAZY, SHOWY TACHIBANA-KUN AND COOL, STOIC MASAMUNE-KUN...
THOSE TWO HAVE NOTHING IN COMMON AT ALL, RIGHT?

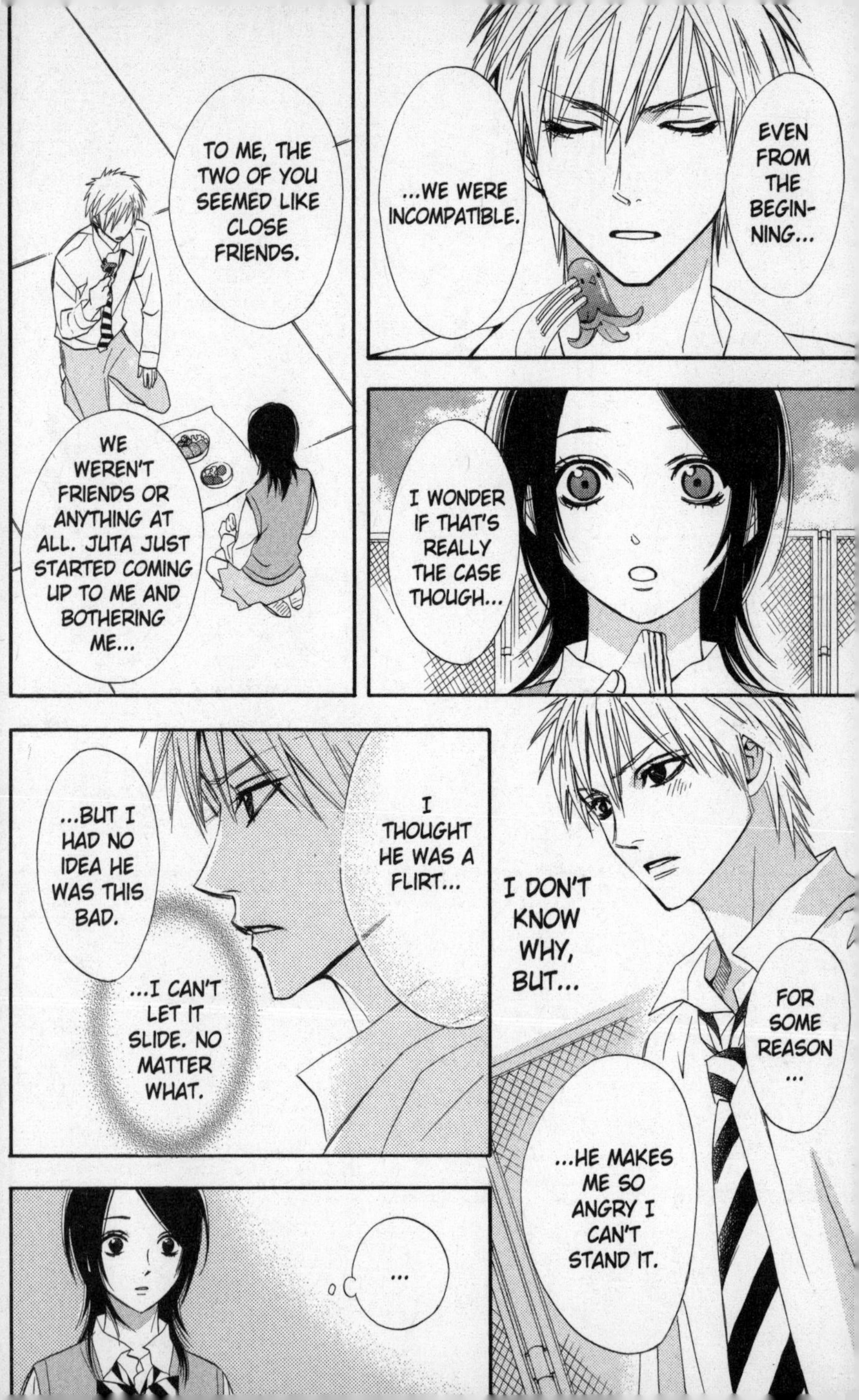
EVEN FROM THE BEGIN-NING...
...WE WERE INCOMPATIBLE.
I WONDER IF THAT'S REALLY THE CASE THOUGH...
TO ME, THE TWO OF YOU SEEMED LIKE CLOSE FRIENDS.
WE WEREN'T FRIENDS OR ANYTHING AT ALL. JUTA JUST STARTED COMING UP TO ME AND BOTHERING ME...
I DON'T KNOW WHY, BUT...
FOR SOME REASON...
...HE MAKES ME SO ANGRY I CAN'T STAND IT.
I THOUGHT HE WAS A FLIRT...
...BUT I HAD NO IDEA HE WAS THIS BAD.
...I CAN'T LET IT SLIDE. NO MATTER WHAT.
...

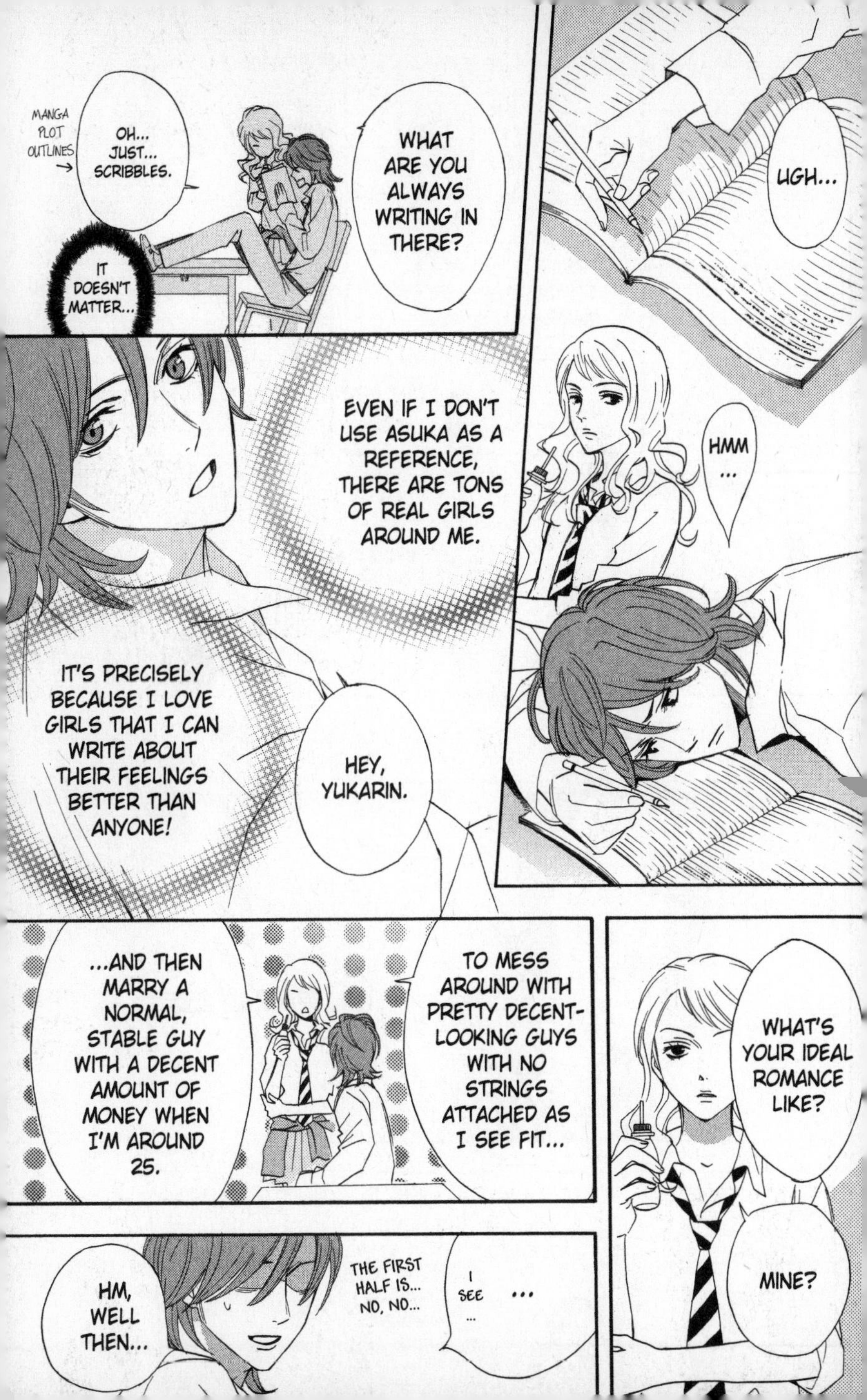
UGH...
HMM ...
WHAT ARE YOU ALWAYS WRITING IN THERE?
OH... JUST... SCRIBBLES.
MANGA PLOT OUTLINES
IT DOESN'T MATTER...
EVEN IF I DON'T USE ASUKA AS A REFERENCE, THERE ARE TONS OF REAL GIRLS AROUND ME.
IT'S PRECISELY BECAUSE I LOVE GIRLS THAT I CAN WRITE ABOUT THEIR FEELINGS BETTER THAN ANYONE!
HEY, YUKARIN.
WHAT'S YOUR IDEAL ROMANCE LIKE?
MINE?
TO MESS AROUND WITH PRETTY DECENT-LOOKING GUYS WITH NO STRINGS ATTACHED AS I SEE FIT...
...AND THEN MARRY A NORMAL, STABLE GUY WITH A DECENT AMOUNT OF MONEY WHEN I'M AROUND 25.
I SEE ...
...
THE FIRST HALF IS... NO, NO...
HM, WELL THEN...

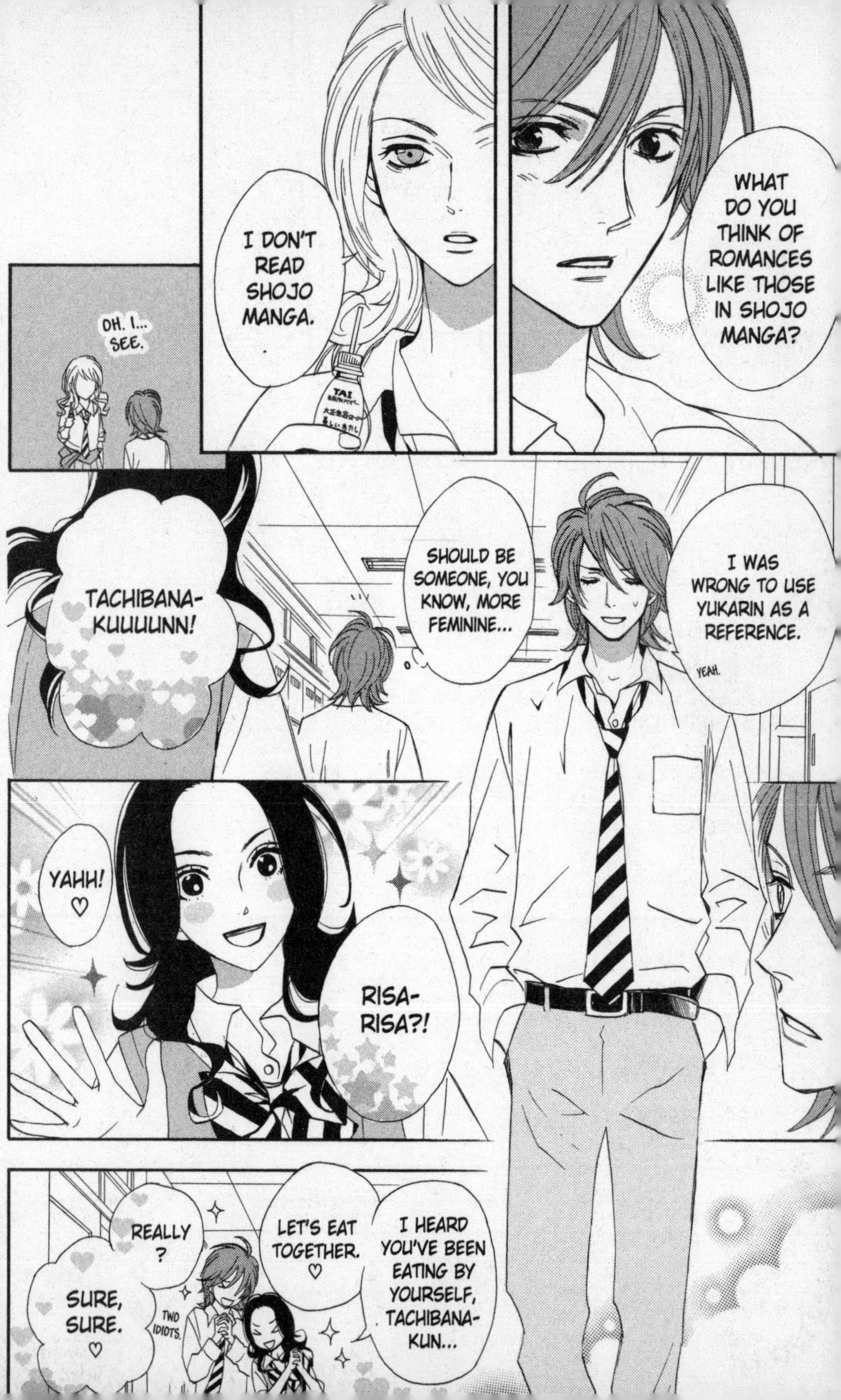
WHAT DO YOU THINK OF ROMANCES LIKE THOSE IN SHOJO MANGA?
I DON'T READ SHOJO MANGA.
OH. I... SEE.
I WAS WRONG TO USE YUKARIN AS A REFERENCE.
YEAH.
SHOULD BE SOMEONE, YOU KNOW, MORE FEMININE...
TACHIBANA-KUUUUNN!
RISA-RISA?!
YAHH! ♡
I HEARD YOU'VE BEEN EATING BY YOURSELF, TACHIBANA-KUN...
LET'S EAT TOGETHER. ♡
REALLY?
SURE, SURE. ♡
TWO IDIOTS.

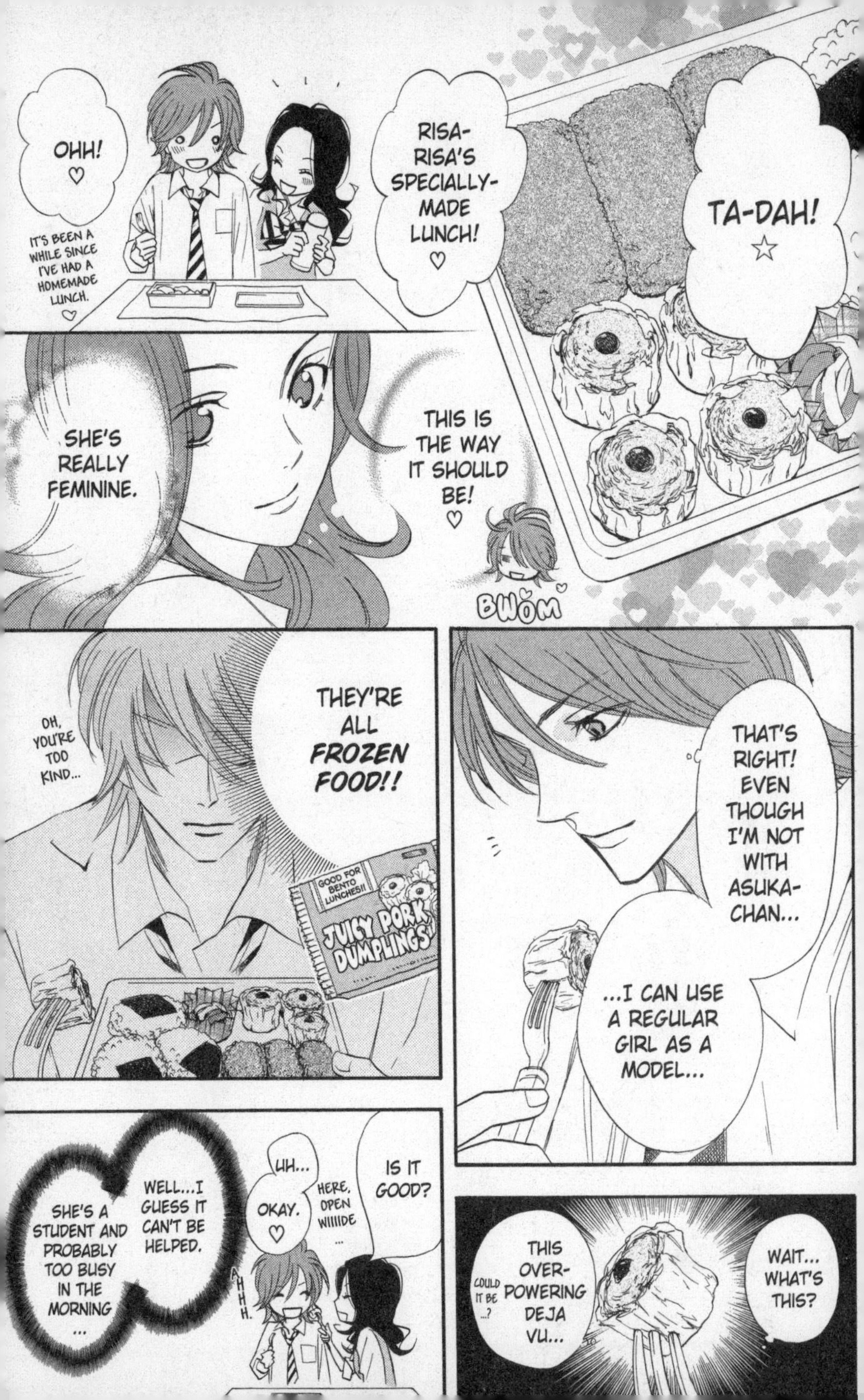

TA-DAH! ☆
RISA-RISA'S SPECIALLY-MADE LUNCH! ♡
OHH! ♡
IT'S BEEN A WHILE SINCE I'VE HAD A HOMEMADE LUNCH. ♡
THIS IS THE WAY IT SHOULD BE! ♡
BWOM
SHE'S REALLY FEMININE.
THAT'S RIGHT! EVEN THOUGH I'M NOT WITH ASUKA-CHAN...
...I CAN USE A REGULAR GIRL AS A MODEL...
THEY'RE ALL FROZEN FOOD!!
OH, YOU'RE TOO KIND...
GOOD FOR BENTO LUNCHES!!
JUICY PORK DUMPLINGS
WAIT... WHAT'S THIS?
THIS OVER-POWERING DEJA VU...
COULD IT BE ...?
IS IT GOOD?
HERE, OPEN WIIIIDE ...
UH...
OKAY. ♡
AHHH.
WELL...I GUESS IT CAN'T BE HELPED.
SHE'S A STUDENT AND PROBABLY TOO BUSY IN THE MORNING ...

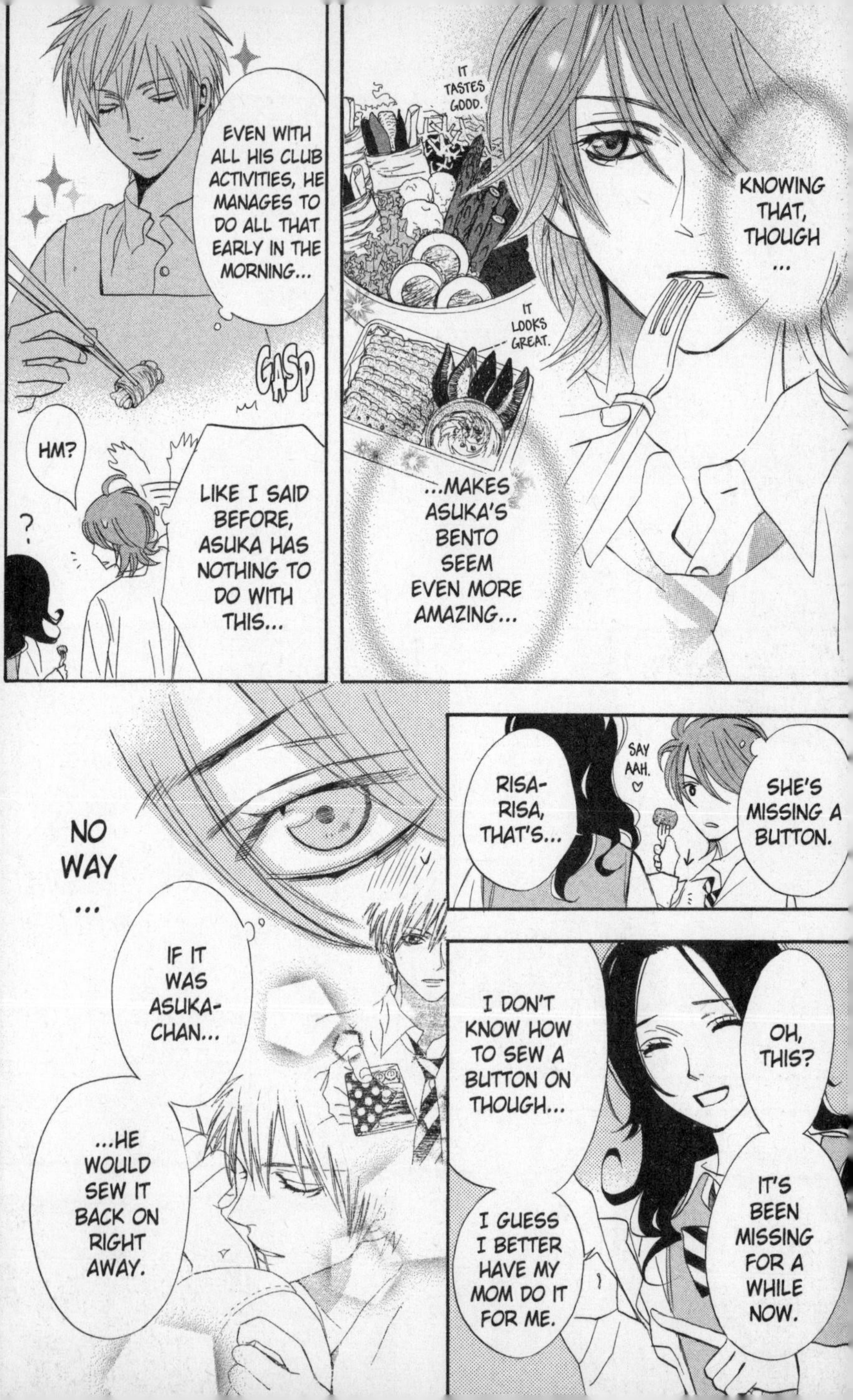
KNOWING THAT, THOUGH...
IT TASTES GOOD.
IT LOOKS GREAT.
...MAKES ASUKA'S BENTO SEEM EVEN MORE AMAZING...
EVEN WITH ALL HIS CLUB ACTIVITIES, HE MANAGES TO DO ALL THAT EARLY IN THE MORNING...
GASP
HM?
LIKE I SAID BEFORE, ASUKA HAS NOTHING TO DO WITH THIS...
?
SHE'S MISSING A BUTTON.
SAY AAH.
RISA-RISA, THAT'S...
OH, THIS?
IT'S BEEN MISSING FOR A WHILE NOW.
I DON'T KNOW HOW TO SEW A BUTTON ON THOUGH...
I GUESS I BETTER HAVE MY MOM DO IT FOR ME.
NO WAY...
IF IT WAS ASUKA-CHAN...
...HE WOULD SEW IT BACK ON RIGHT AWAY.

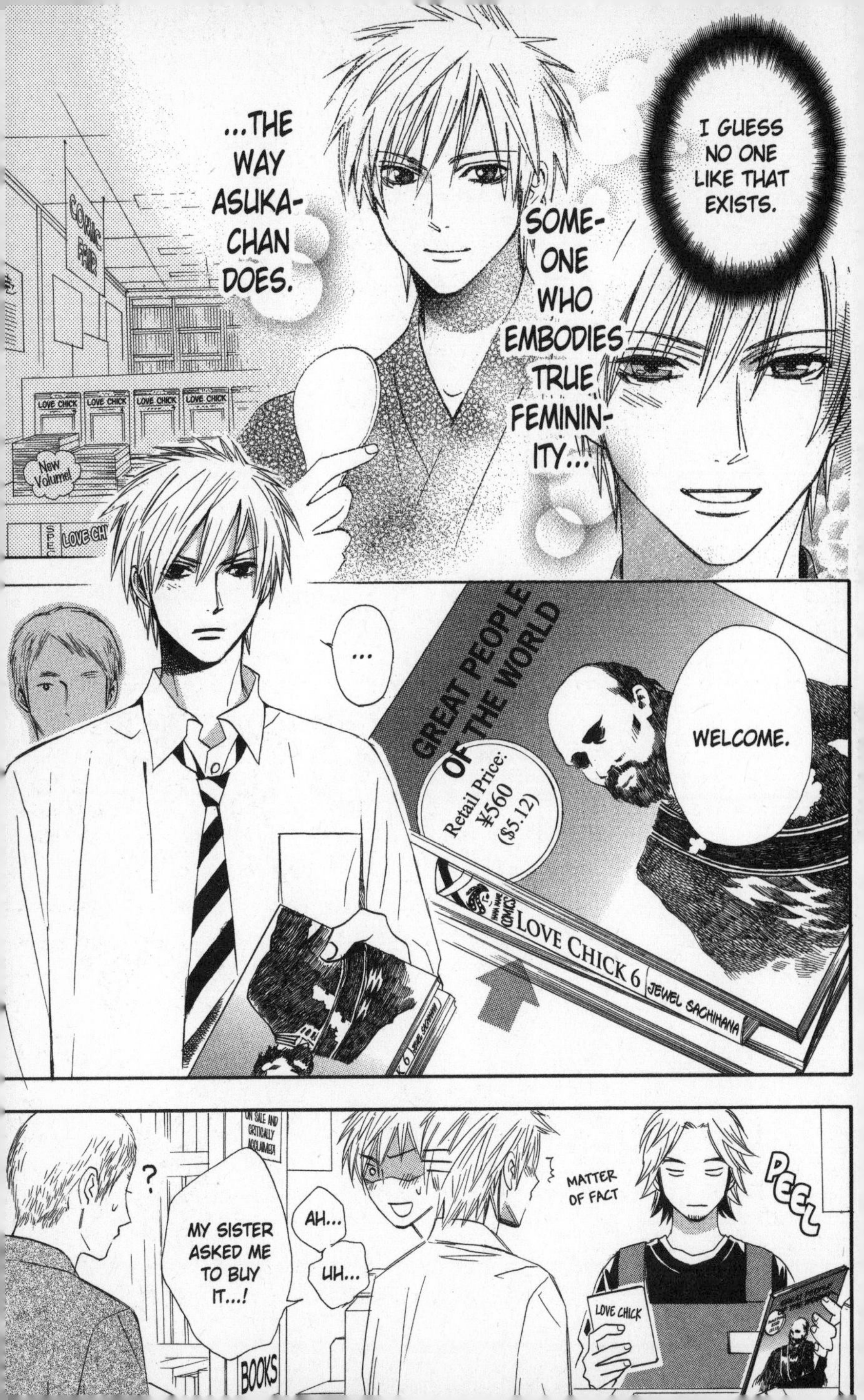
I GUESS NO ONE LIKE THAT EXISTS.
SOME-ONE WHO EMBODIES TRUE FEMININ-ITY...
...THE WAY ASUKA-CHAN DOES.
COMIC FAIR
LOVE CHICK
LOVE CHICK
LOVE CHICK
LOVE CHICK
New Volume!
LOVE CH
GREAT PEOPLE OF THE WORLD
Retail Price: ¥560 ($5.12)
LOVE CHICK 6
JEWEL SACHIHANA
WELCOME.
...
PEEL
MATTER OF FACT
LOVE CHICK
AH...
UH...
MY SISTER ASKED ME TO BUY IT...!
?
ON SALE AND CRITICALLY ACCLAIMED!
BOOKS

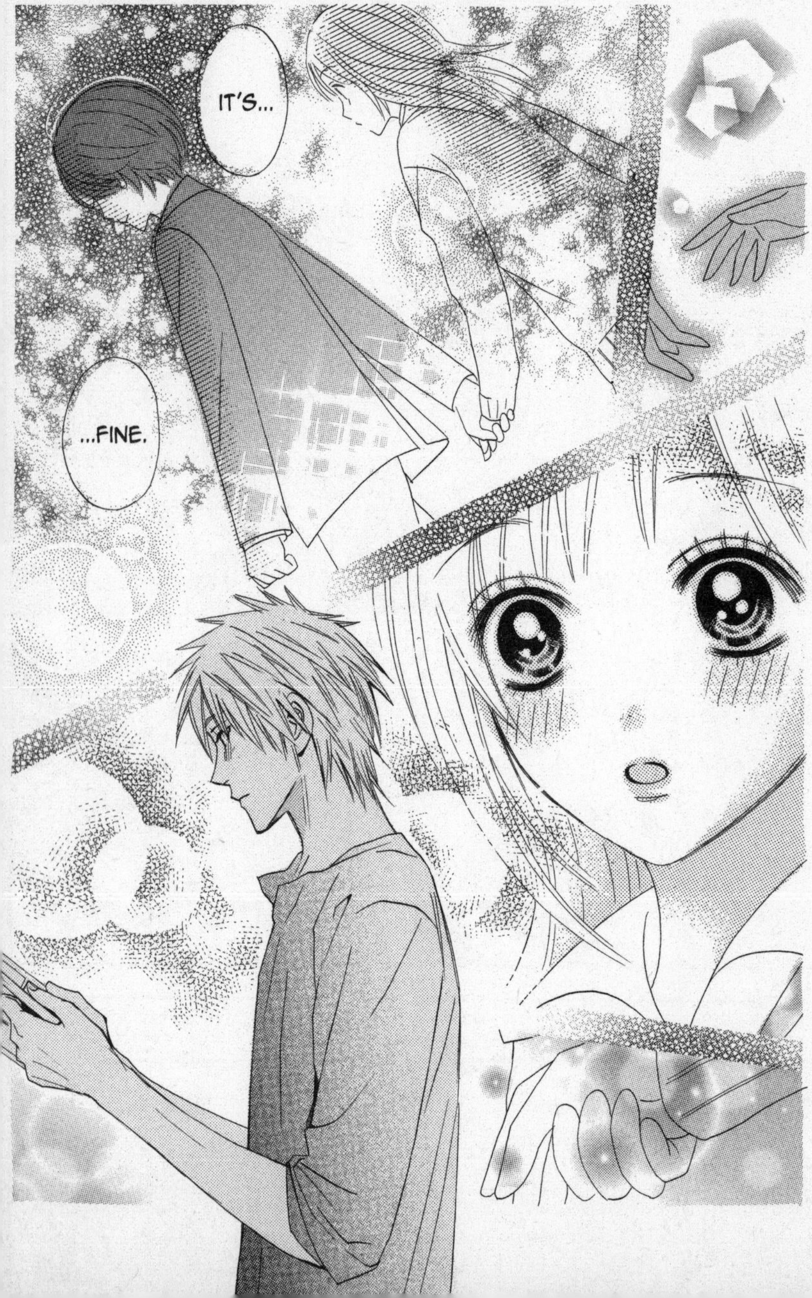
IT'S...
...FINE.

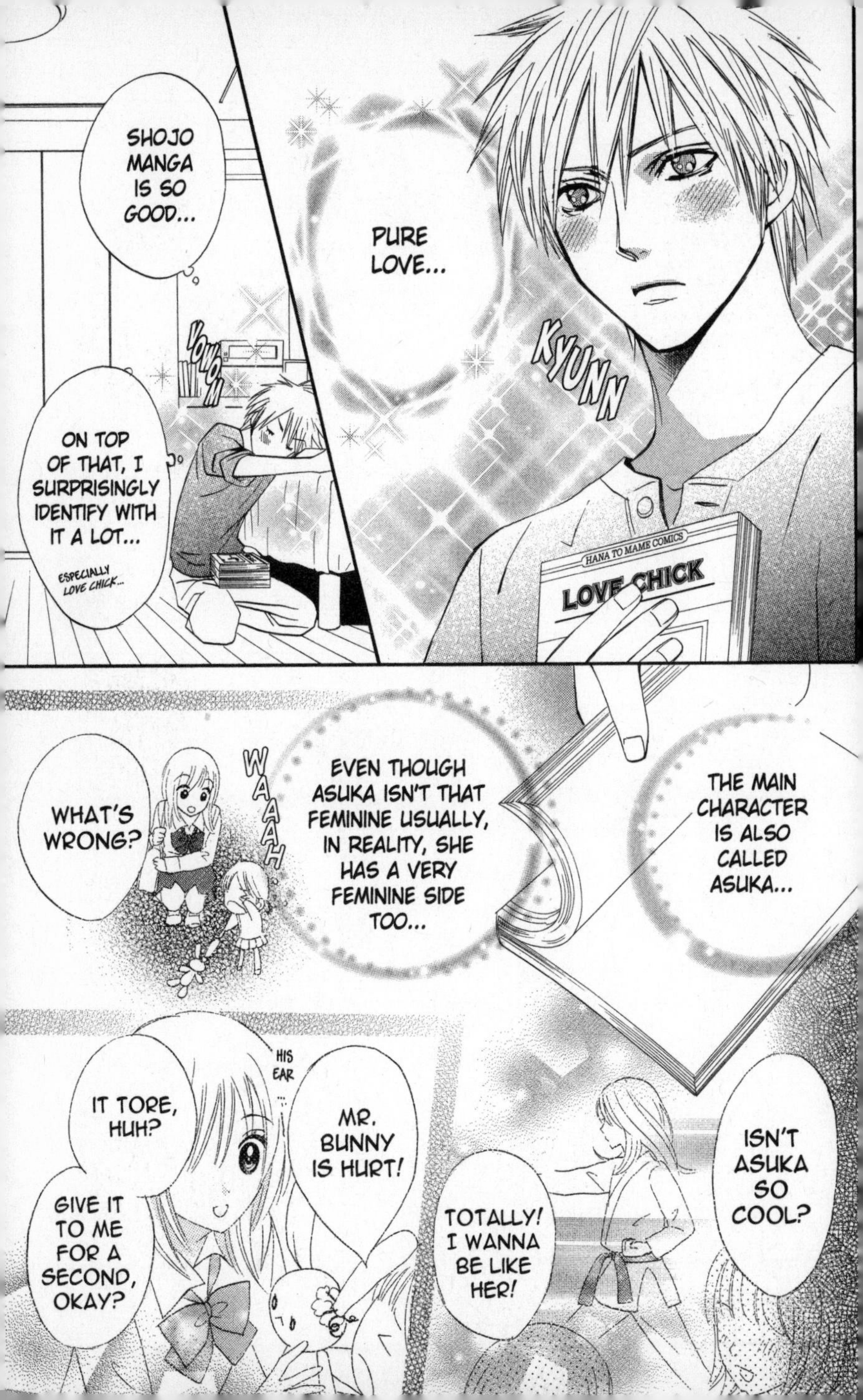
PURE LOVE...
KYUNN
HANA TO MAME COMICS
LOVE CHICK
SHOJO MANGA IS SO GOOD...
VOVON
ON TOP OF THAT, I SURPRISINGLY IDENTIFY WITH IT A LOT...
ESPECIALLY LOVE CHICK...
THE MAIN CHARACTER IS ALSO CALLED ASUKA...
EVEN THOUGH ASUKA ISN'T THAT FEMININE USUALLY, IN REALITY, SHE HAS A VERY FEMININE SIDE TOO...
WAAAH
WHAT'S WRONG?
ISN'T ASUKA SO COOL?
TOTALLY! I WANNA BE LIKE HER!
MR. BUNNY IS HURT!
HIS EAR...
IT TORE, HUH?
GIVE IT TO ME FOR A SECOND, OKAY?

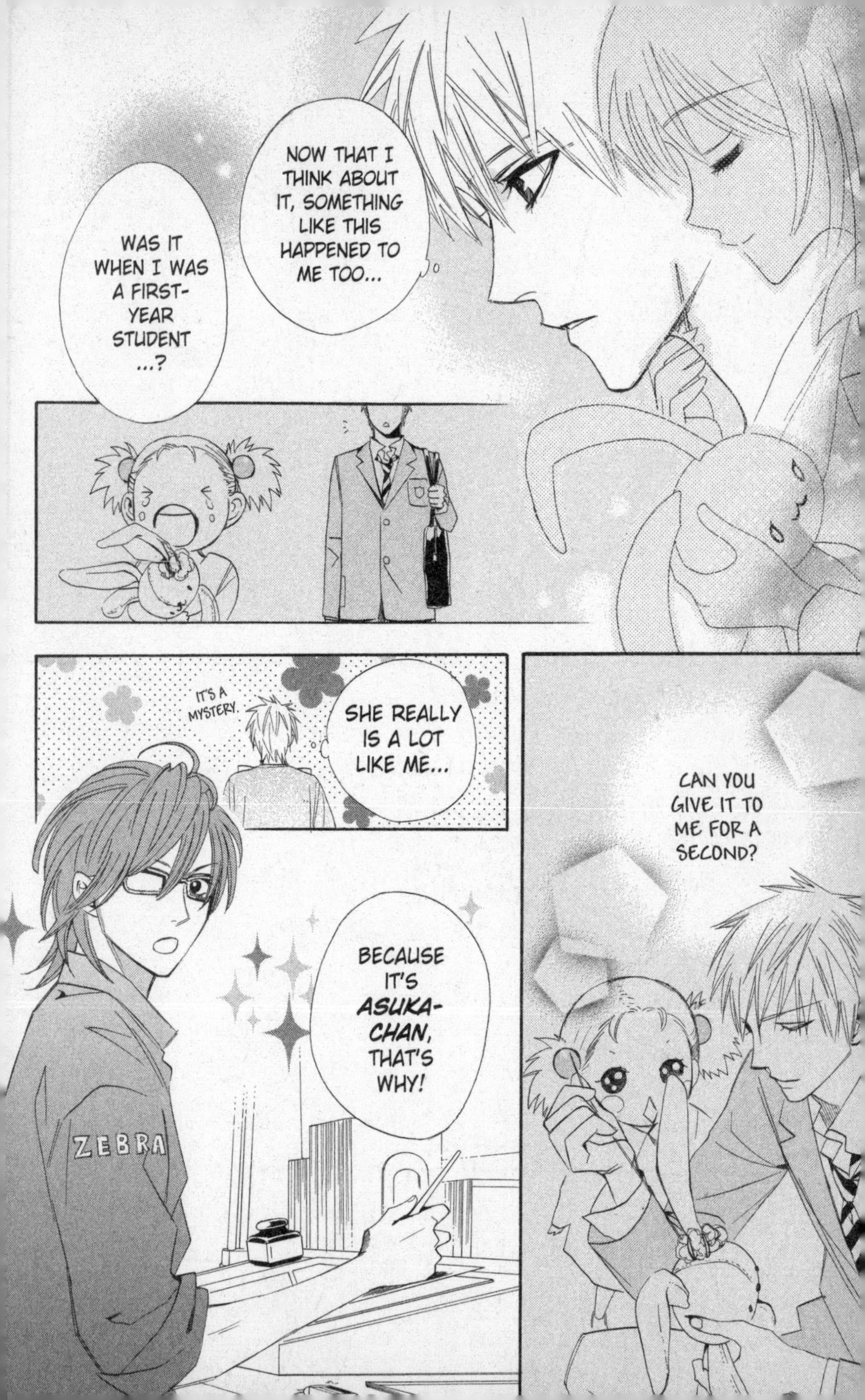
NOW THAT I THINK ABOUT IT, SOMETHING LIKE THIS HAPPENED TO ME TOO...
WAS IT WHEN I WAS A FIRST-YEAR STUDENT ...?
CAN YOU GIVE IT TO ME FOR A SECOND?
SHE REALLY IS A LOT LIKE ME...
IT'S A MYSTERY.
BECAUSE IT'S *ASUKA-CHAN*, THAT'S WHY!
ZEBRA

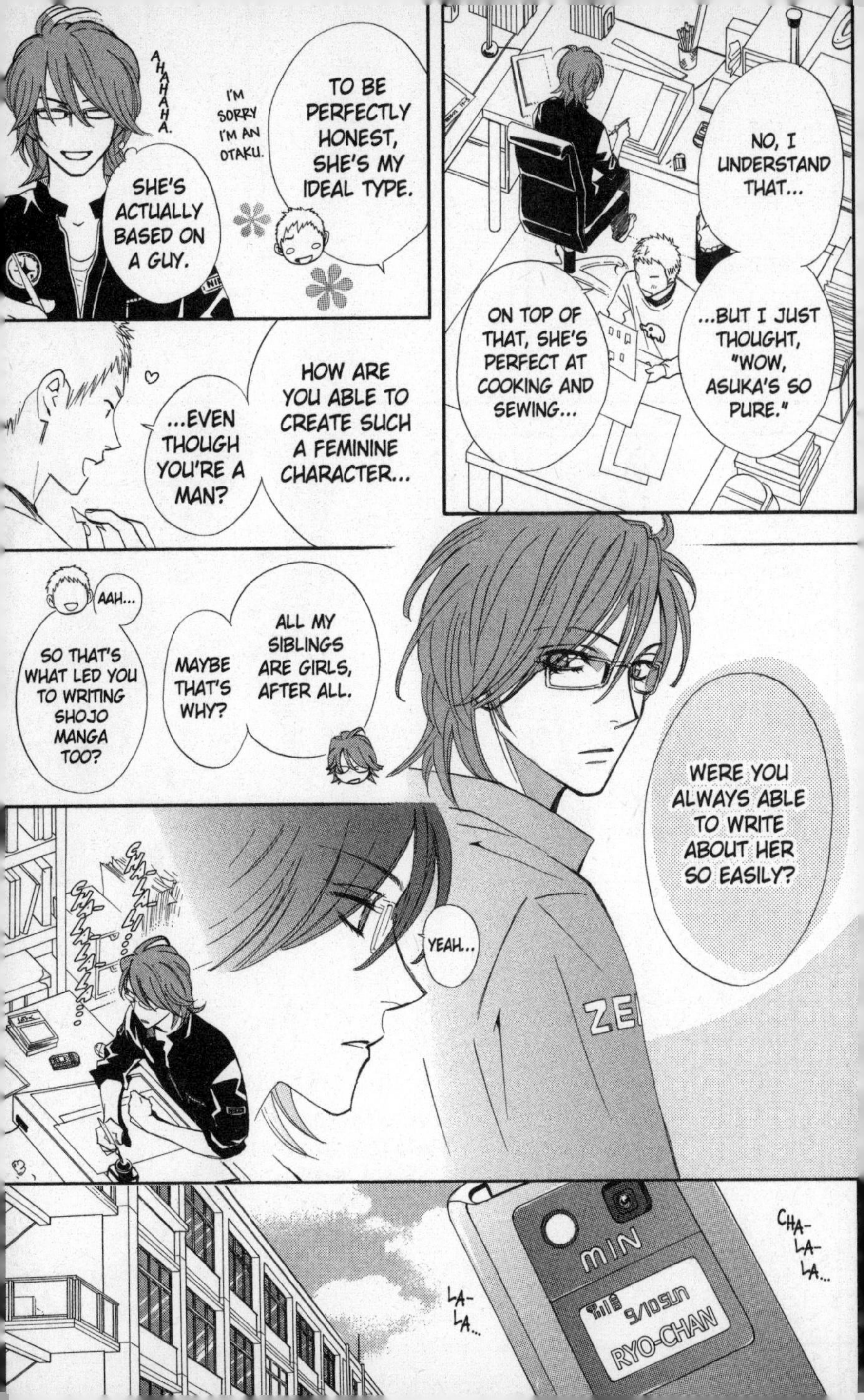
NO, I UNDERSTAND THAT...
...BUT I JUST THOUGHT, "WOW, ASUKA'S SO PURE."
ON TOP OF THAT, SHE'S PERFECT AT COOKING AND SEWING...
TO BE PERFECTLY HONEST, SHE'S MY IDEAL TYPE.
I'M SORRY I'M AN OTAKU.
AHAHAHA.
SHE'S ACTUALLY BASED ON A GUY.
HOW ARE YOU ABLE TO CREATE SUCH A FEMININE CHARACTER...
...EVEN THOUGH YOU'RE A MAN?
WERE YOU ALWAYS ABLE TO WRITE ABOUT HER SO EASILY?
YEAH...
ALL MY SIBLINGS ARE GIRLS, AFTER ALL.
MAYBE THAT'S WHY?
AAH...
SO THAT'S WHAT LED YOU TO WRITING SHOJO MANGA TOO?
CHA-LA-LA...
MIN
9/10 SUN
RYO-CHAN
LA-LA...

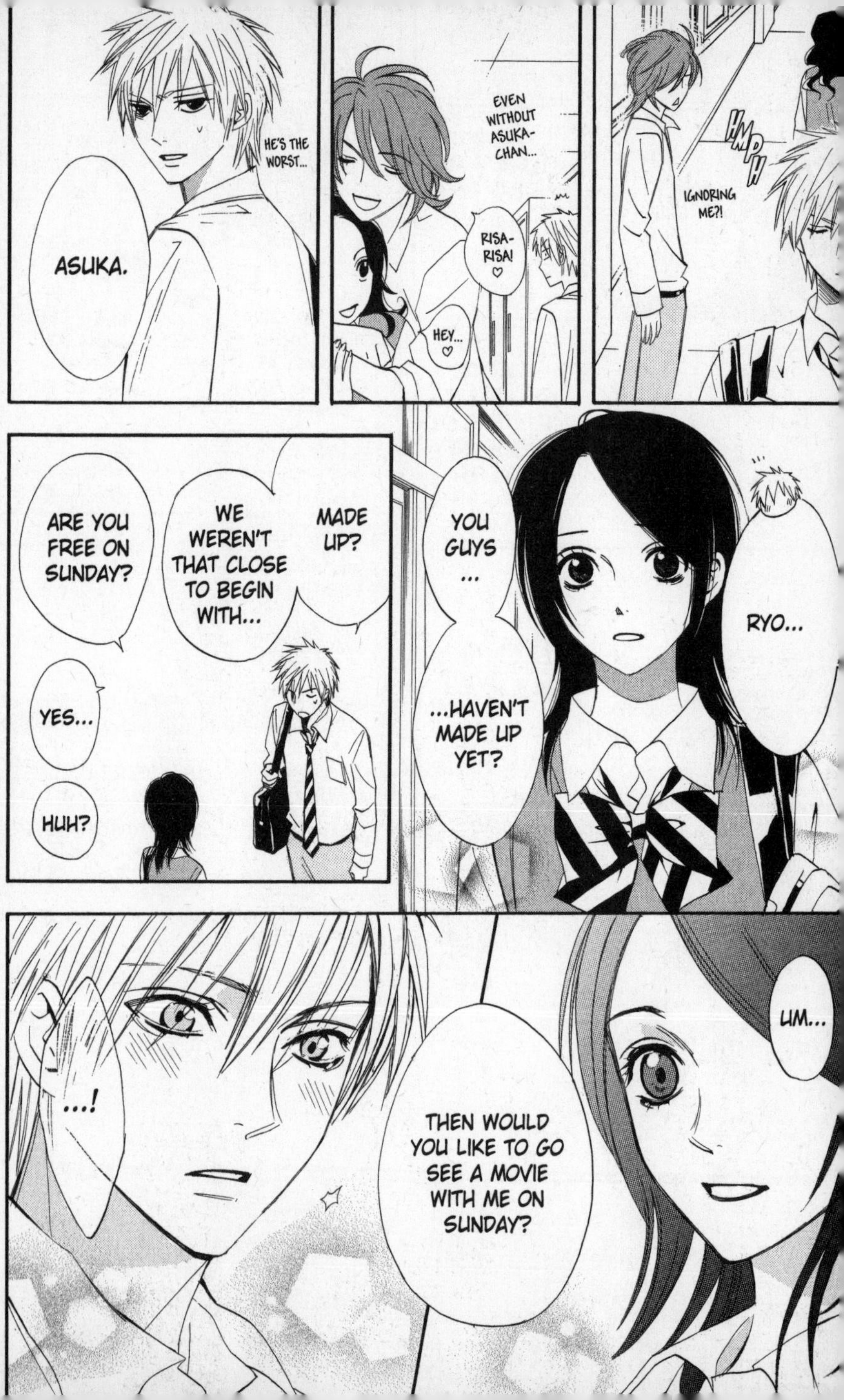
HMPH
IGNORING ME?!
EVEN WITHOUT ASUKA-CHAN...
RISA-RISA! ♡
HEY... ♡
HE'S THE WORST...
ASUKA.
RYO...
YOU GUYS ...
...HAVEN'T MADE UP YET?
MADE UP?
WE WEREN'T THAT CLOSE TO BEGIN WITH...
ARE YOU FREE ON SUNDAY?
YES...
HUH?
UM...
THEN WOULD YOU LIKE TO GO SEE A MOVIE WITH ME ON SUNDAY?
...!

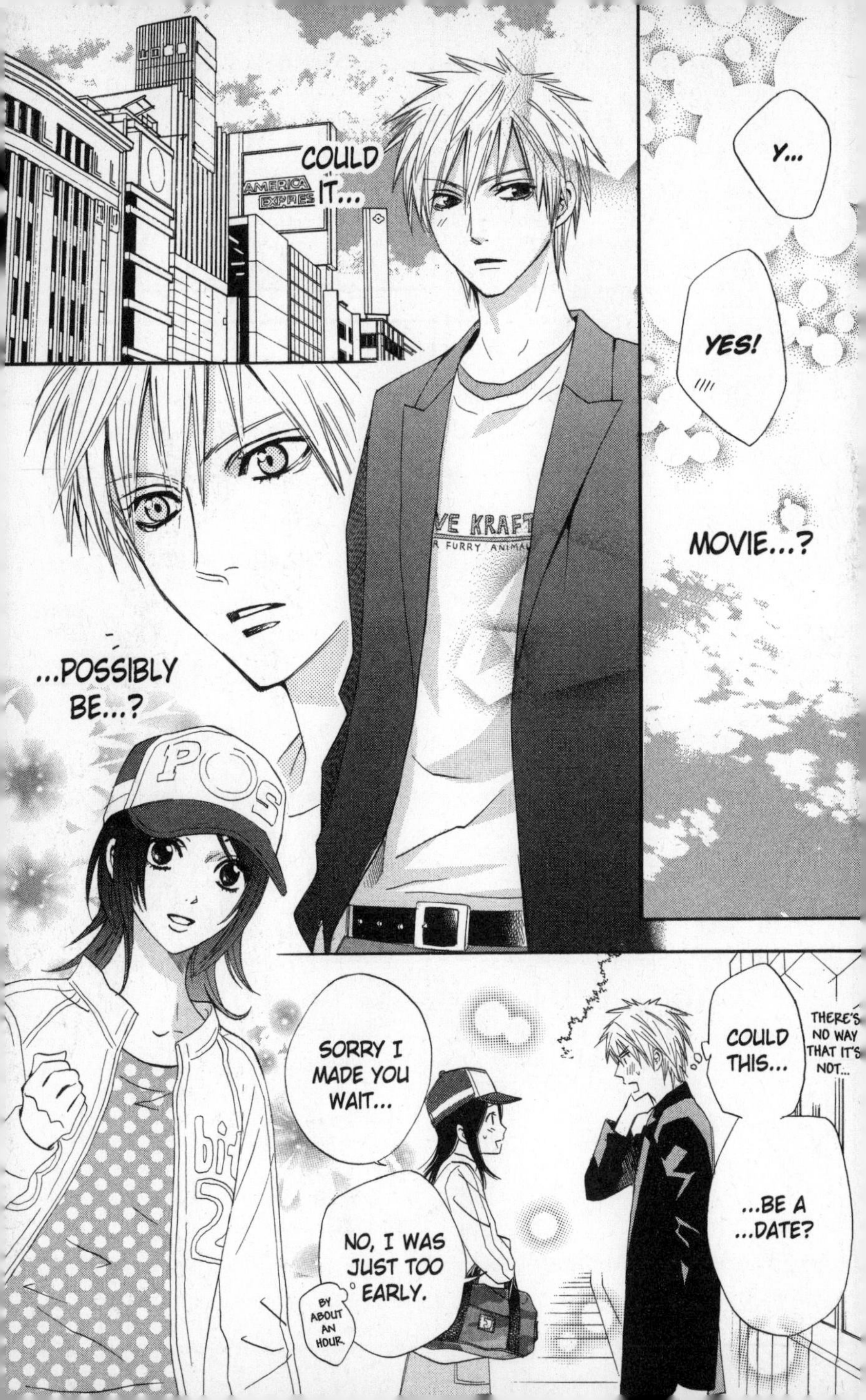
Y...
YES!
MOVIE...?
COULD IT...
...POSSIBLY BE...?
THERE'S NO WAY THAT IT'S NOT...
COULD THIS...
...BE A ...DATE?
SORRY I MADE YOU WAIT...
NO, I WAS JUST TOO EARLY.
BY ABOUT AN HOUR.

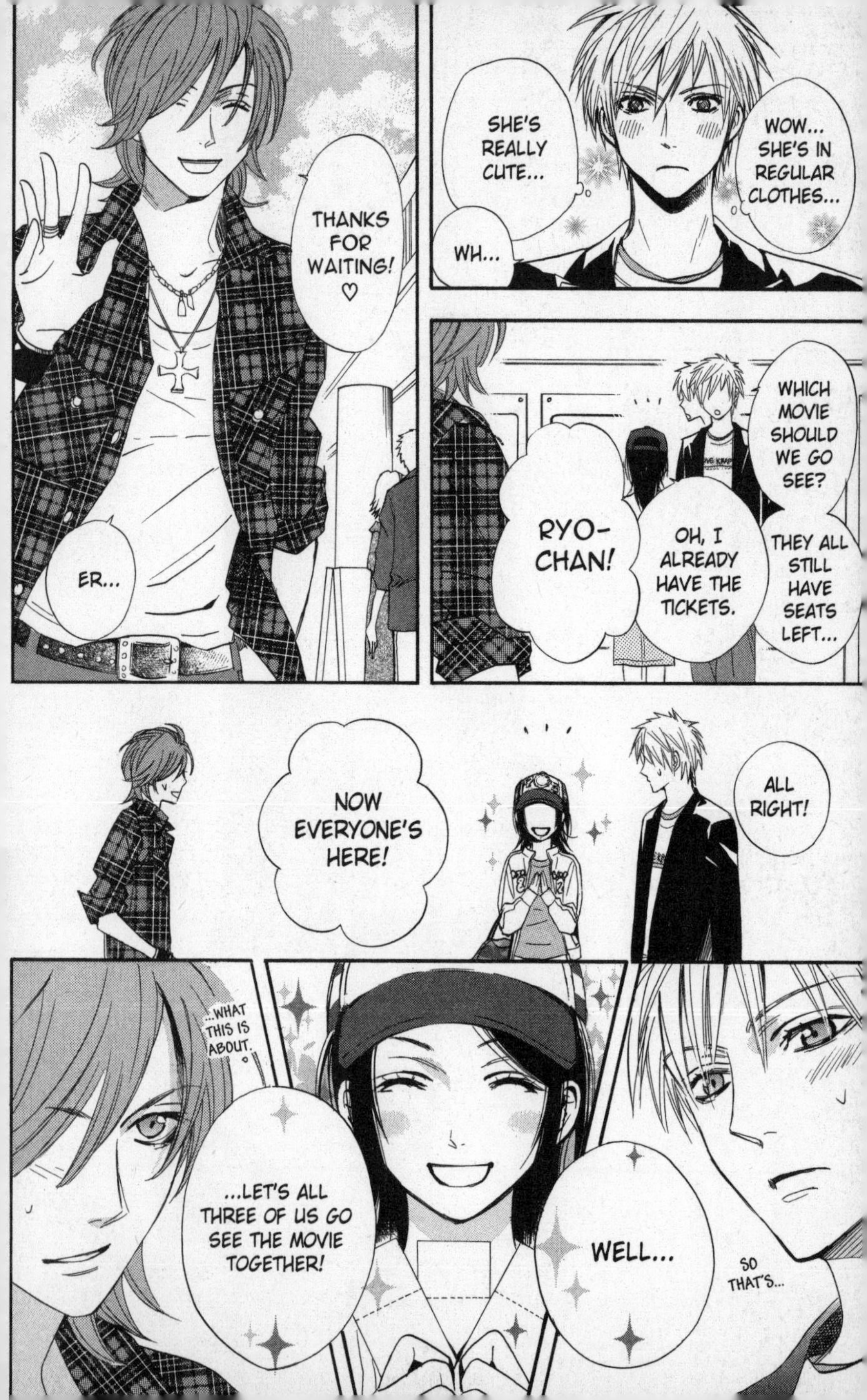
WOW... SHE'S IN REGULAR CLOTHES...
SHE'S REALLY CUTE...
WH...
WHICH MOVIE SHOULD WE GO SEE?
THEY ALL STILL HAVE SEATS LEFT...
OH, I ALREADY HAVE THE TICKETS.
RYO-CHAN!
THANKS FOR WAITING! ♡
ER...
ALL RIGHT!
NOW EVERYONE'S HERE!
SO THAT'S...
WELL...
...LET'S ALL THREE OF US GO SEE THE MOVIE TOGETHER!
...WHAT THIS IS ABOUT.

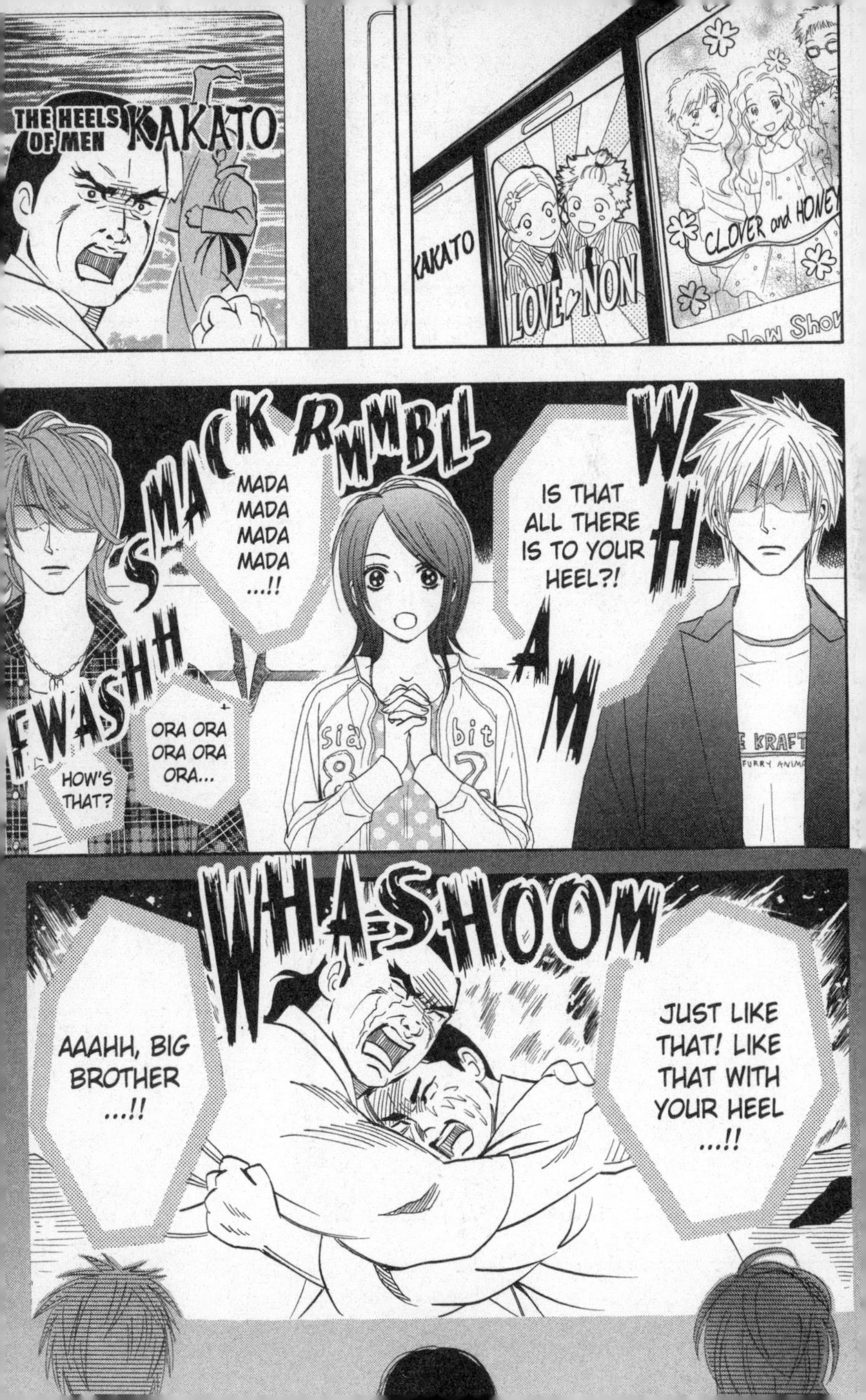
KAKATO
LOVE NON
CLOVER and HONEY
THE HEELS OF MEN
KAKATO
WHAM
IS THAT ALL THERE IS TO YOUR HEEL?!
RMMBLL
MADA MADA MADA MADA ...!!
SMACK
FWASHH
ORA ORA ORA ORA ORA...
HOW'S THAT?
WHASHOOM
JUST LIKE THAT! LIKE THAT WITH YOUR HEEL ...!!
AAAHH, BIG BROTHER ...!!

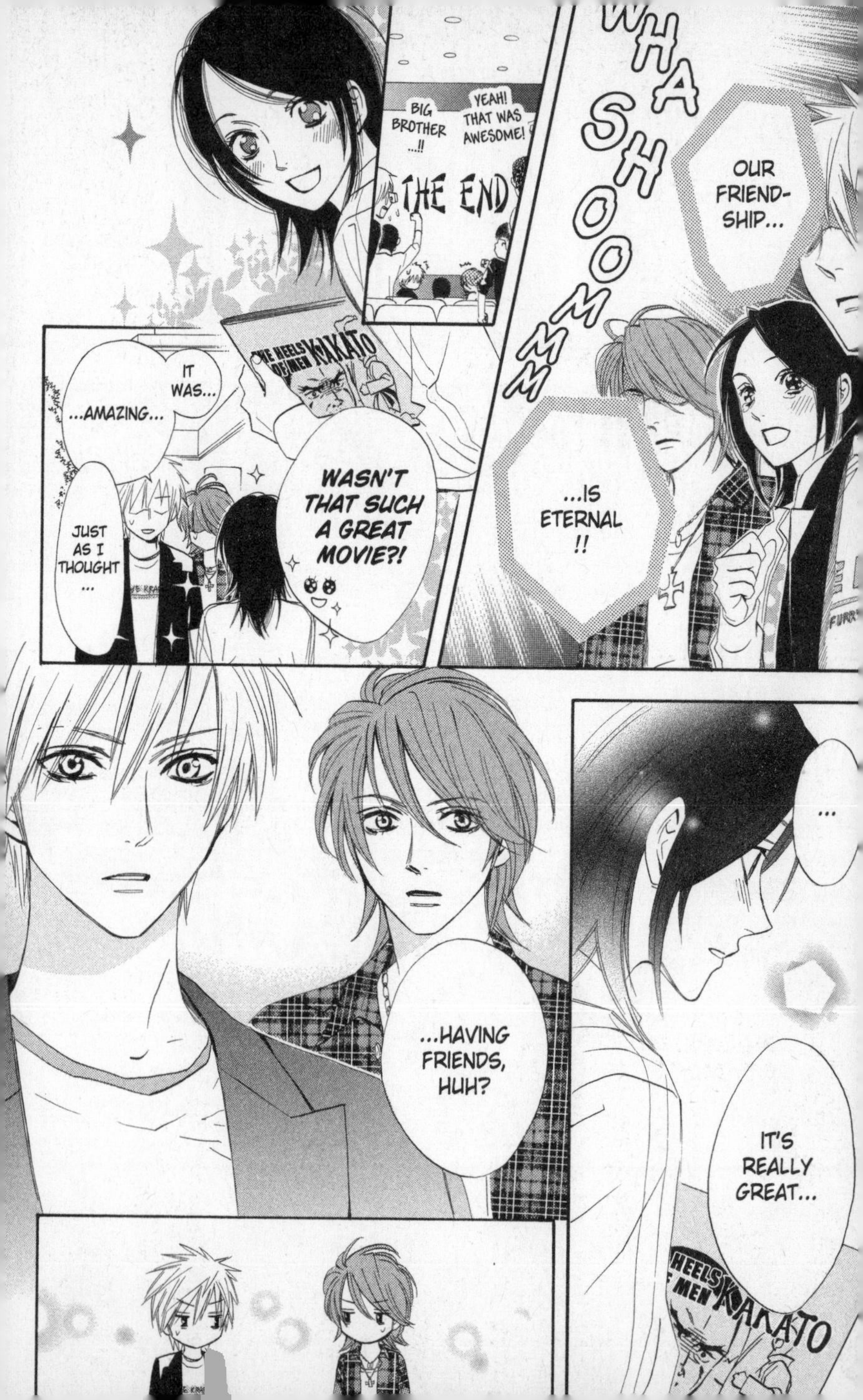
WHA SHOOMMM
OUR FRIEND-SHIP...
...IS ETERNAL!!
YEAH! THAT WAS AWESOME!
BIG BROTHER ...!!
THE END
THE HEELS OF MEN KAKATO
WASN'T THAT SUCH A GREAT MOVIE?!
IT WAS...
...AMAZING...
JUST AS I THOUGHT...
...
IT'S REALLY GREAT...
HEELS OF MEN KAKATO
...HAVING FRIENDS, HUH?

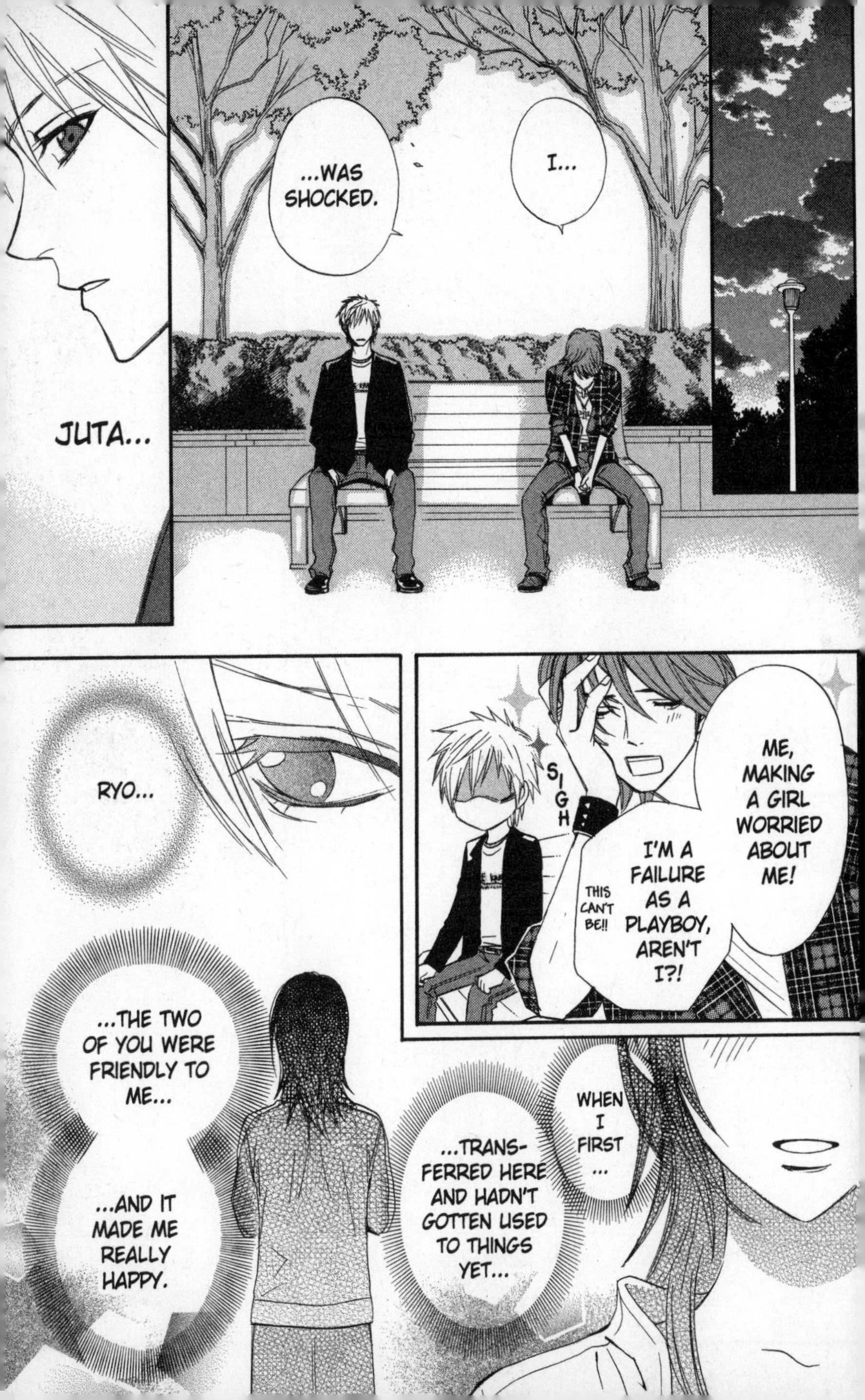
I...
...WAS SHOCKED.
JUTA...
ME, MAKING A GIRL WORRIED ABOUT ME!
I'M A FAILURE AS A PLAYBOY, AREN'T I?!
THIS CAN'T BE!!
SIGH
RYO...
WHEN I FIRST ...
...TRANSFERRED HERE AND HADN'T GOTTEN USED TO THINGS YET...
...THE TWO OF YOU WERE FRIENDLY TO ME...
...AND IT MADE ME REALLY HAPPY.

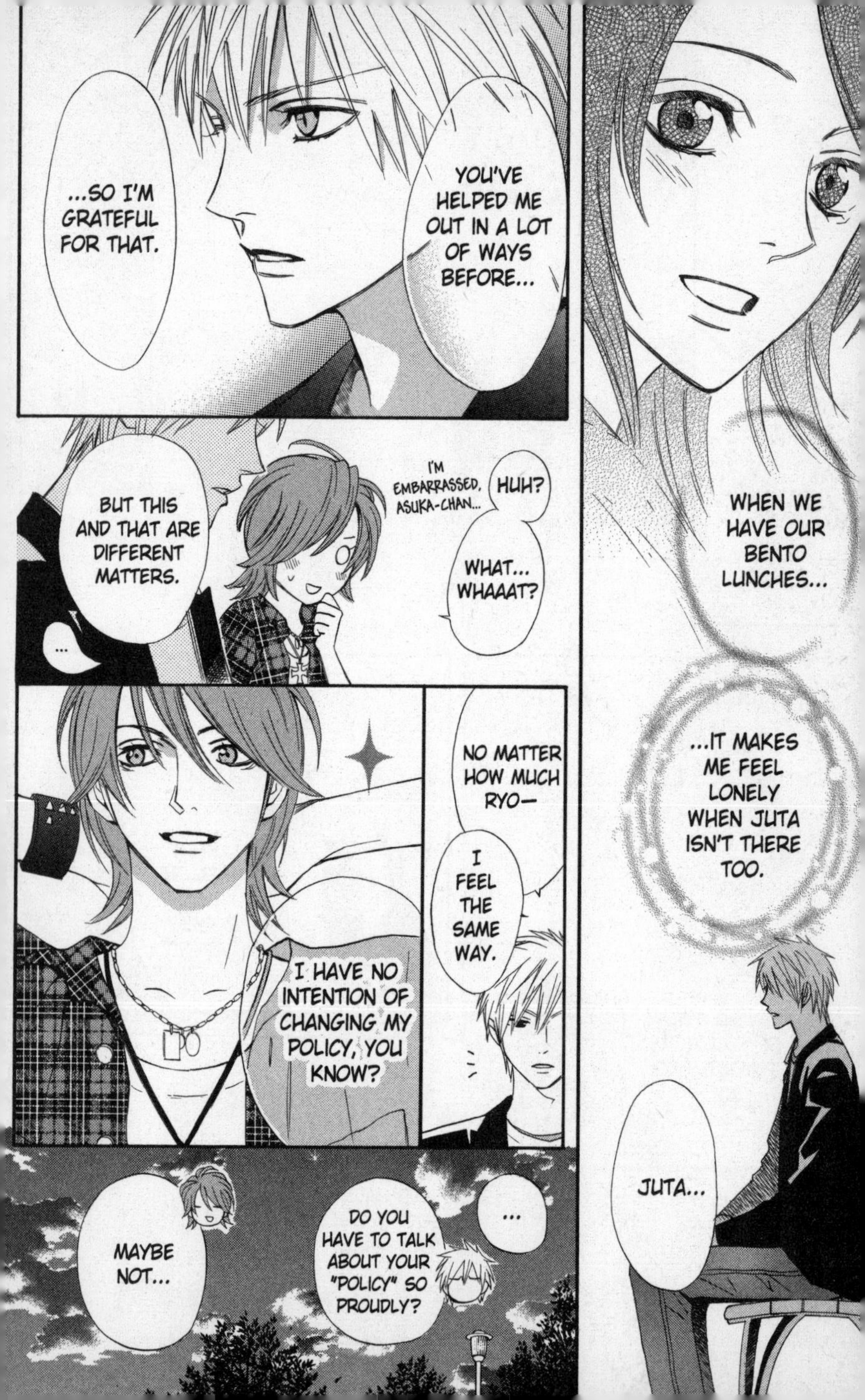
WHEN WE HAVE OUR BENTO LUNCHES...
...IT MAKES ME FEEL LONELY WHEN JUTA ISN'T THERE TOO.
JUTA...
YOU'VE HELPED ME OUT IN A LOT OF WAYS BEFORE...
...SO I'M GRATEFUL FOR THAT.
HUH?
I'M EMBARRASSED, ASUKA-CHAN...
WHAT... WHAAAT?
BUT THIS AND THAT ARE DIFFERENT MATTERS.
...
NO MATTER HOW MUCH RYO—
I FEEL THE SAME WAY.
I HAVE NO INTENTION OF CHANGING MY POLICY, YOU KNOW?
...
DO YOU HAVE TO TALK ABOUT YOUR "POLICY" SO PROUDLY?
MAYBE NOT...

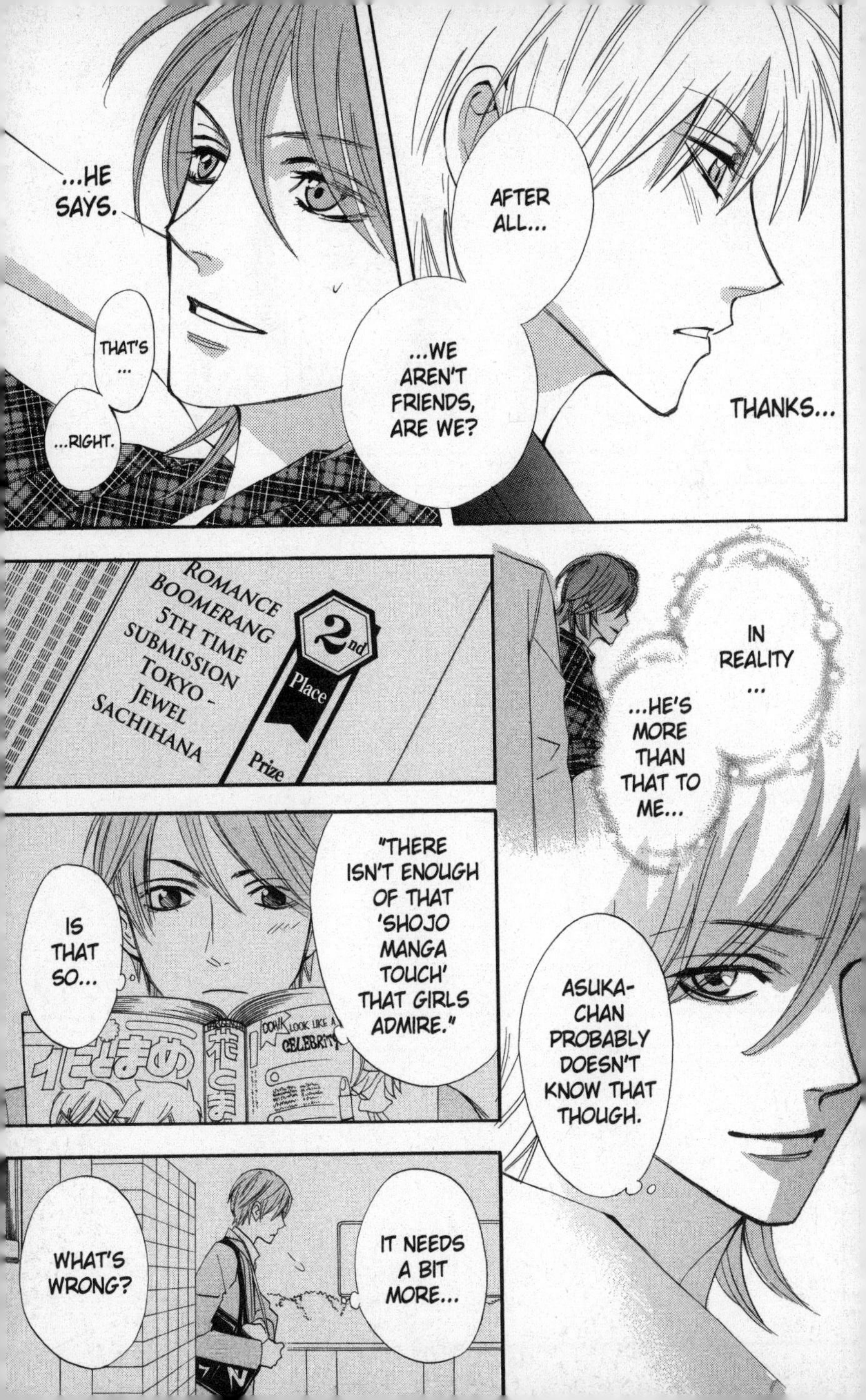
THANKS...
AFTER ALL...
...WE AREN'T FRIENDS, ARE WE?
...HE SAYS.
THAT'S ...
...RIGHT.
IN REALITY ...
...HE'S MORE THAN THAT TO ME...
ASUKA-CHAN PROBABLY DOESN'T KNOW THAT THOUGH.
ROMANCE BOOMERANG 5TH TIME SUBMISSION TOKYO - JEWEL SACHIHANA
2nd Place Prize
"THERE ISN'T ENOUGH OF THAT 'SHOJO MANGA TOUCH' THAT GIRLS ADMIRE."
IS THAT SO...
LOOK LIKE A CELEBRITY
IT NEEDS A BIT MORE...
WHAT'S WRONG?

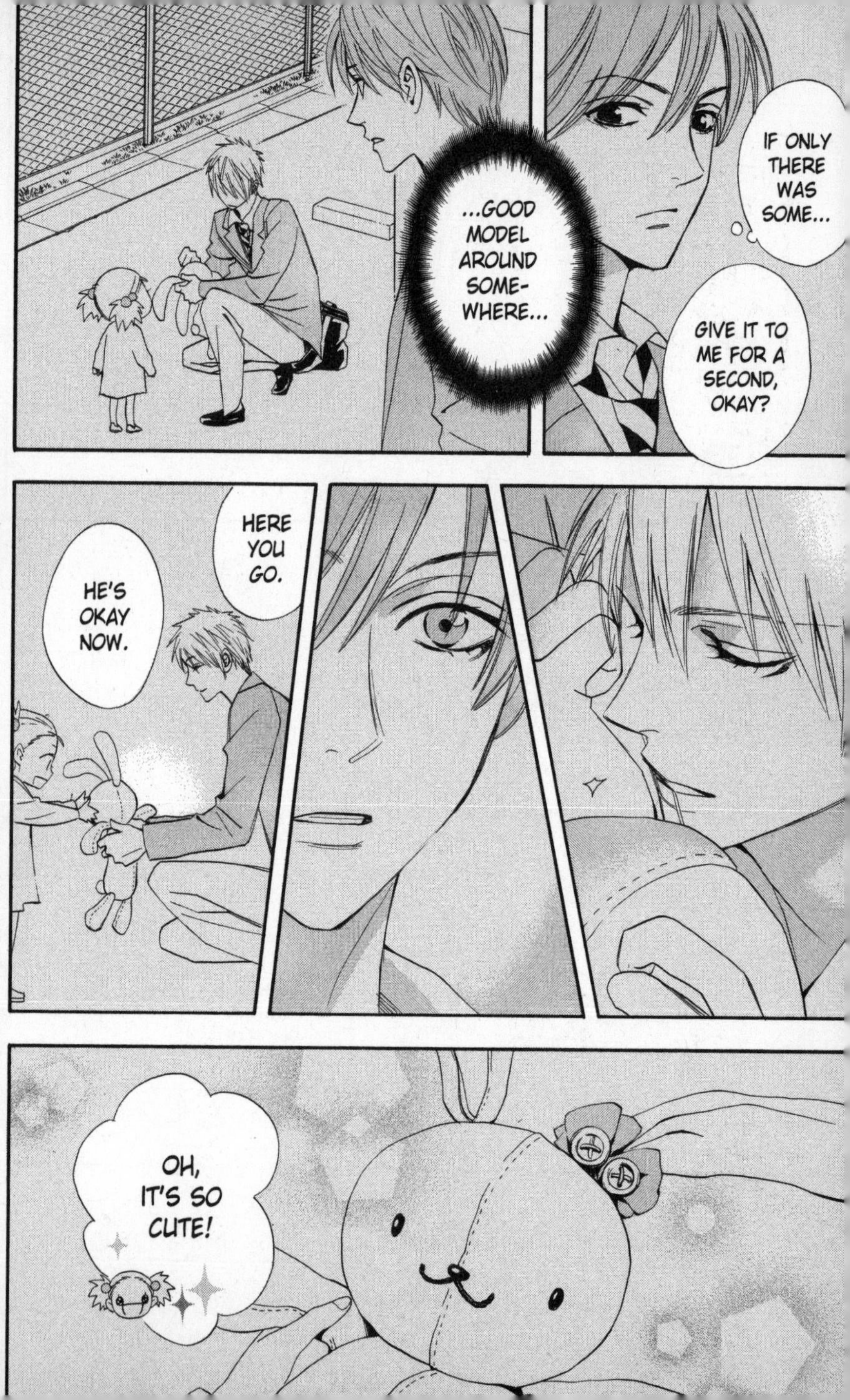
IF ONLY THERE WAS SOME...
...GOOD MODEL AROUND SOME-WHERE...
GIVE IT TO ME FOR A SECOND, OKAY?
HERE YOU GO.
HE'S OKAY NOW.
OH, IT'S SO CUTE!

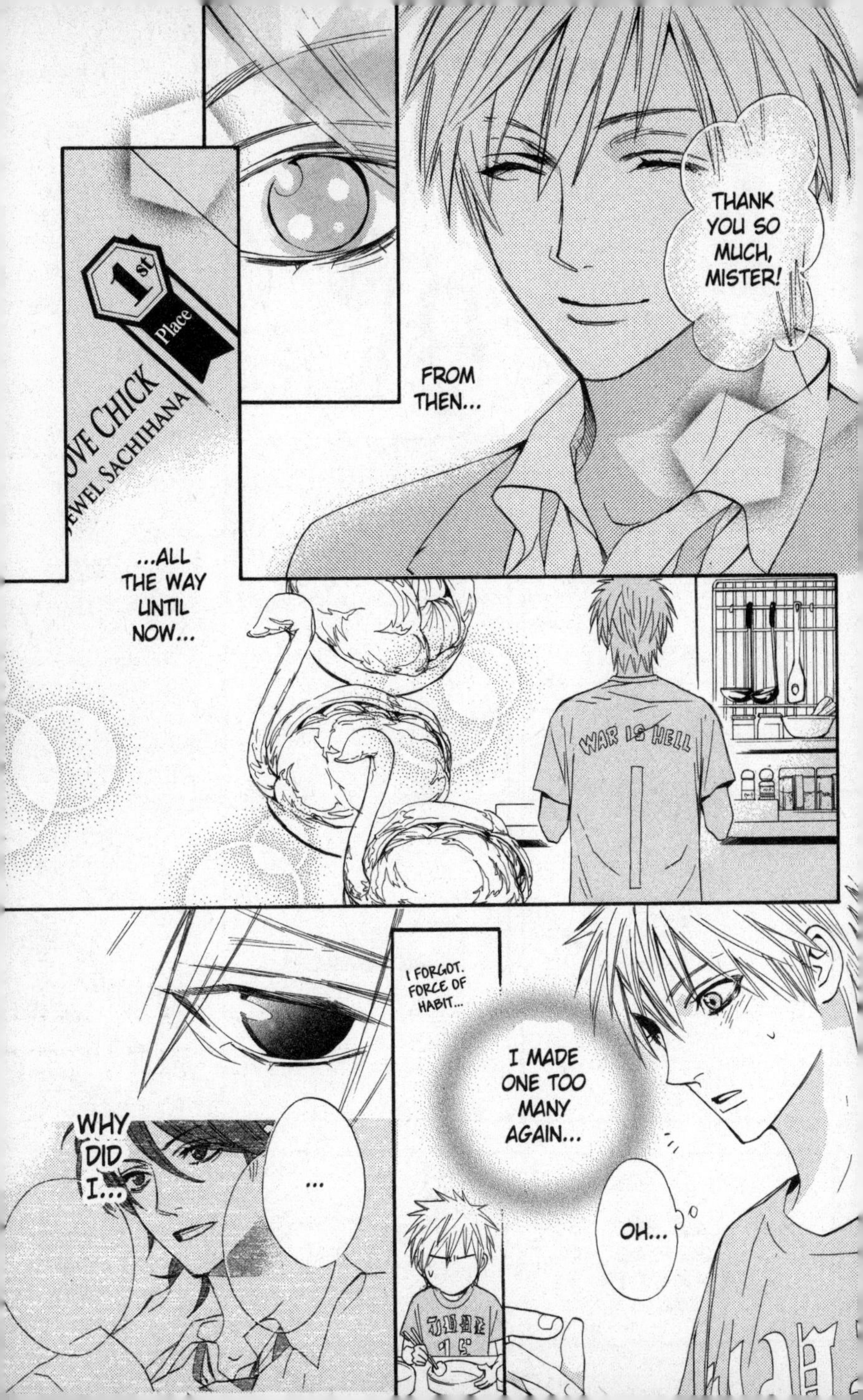
THANK YOU SO MUCH, MISTER!
FROM THEN...
1st Place
OVE CHICK
EWEL SACHIHANA
...ALL THE WAY UNTIL NOW...
WAR IS HELL
OH...
I MADE ONE TOO MANY AGAIN...
I FORGOT. FORCE OF HABIT...
...
WHY DID I...

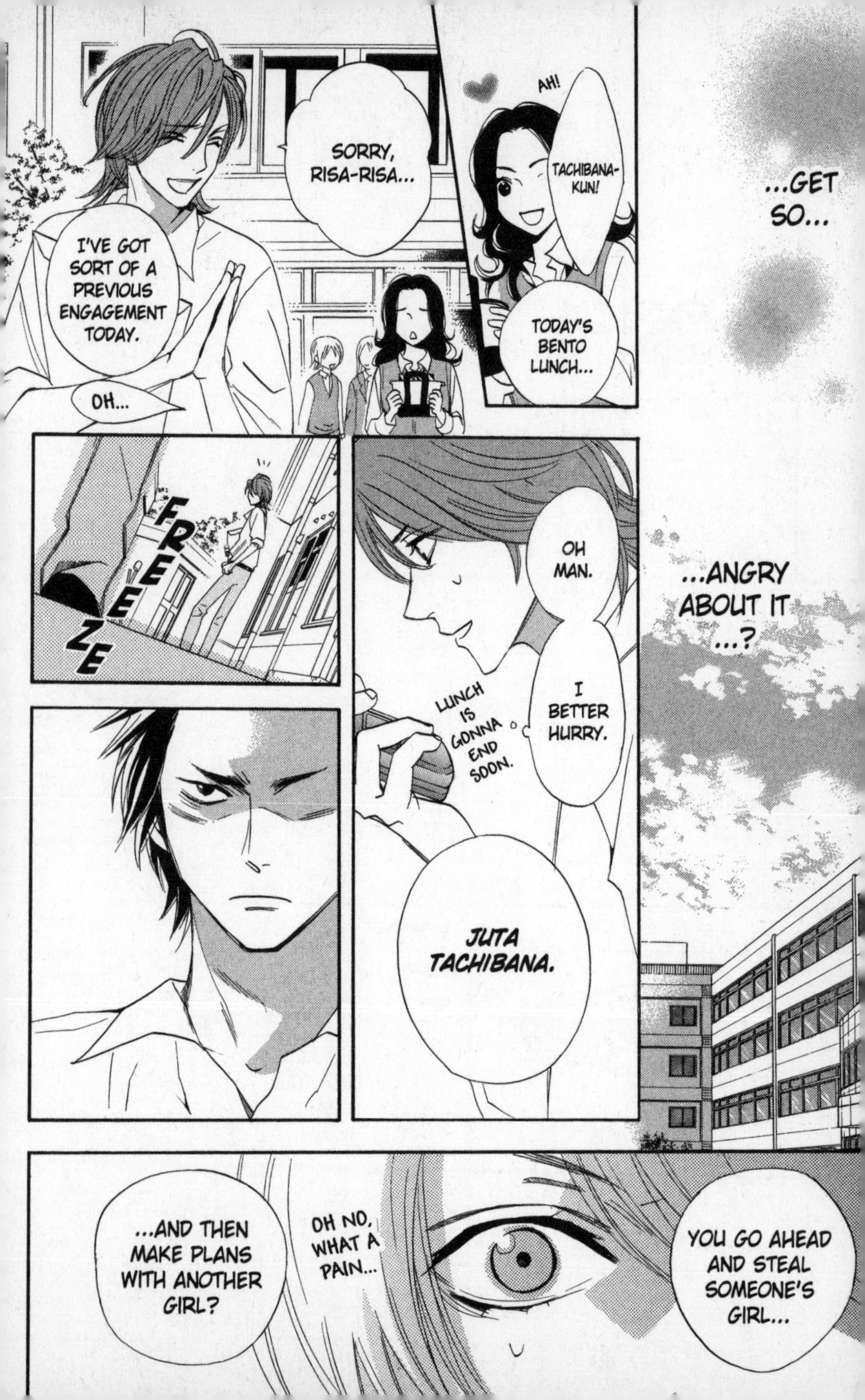
...GET SO...
AH!
TACHIBANA-KUN!
TODAY'S BENTO LUNCH...
SORRY, RISA-RISA...
I'VE GOT SORT OF A PREVIOUS ENGAGEMENT TODAY.
OH...
...ANGRY ABOUT IT ...?
OH MAN.
I BETTER HURRY.
LUNCH IS GONNA END SOON.
JUTA TACHIBANA.
FREEZE
YOU GO AHEAD AND STEAL SOMEONE'S GIRL...
OH NO, WHAT A PAIN...
...AND THEN MAKE PLANS WITH ANOTHER GIRL?

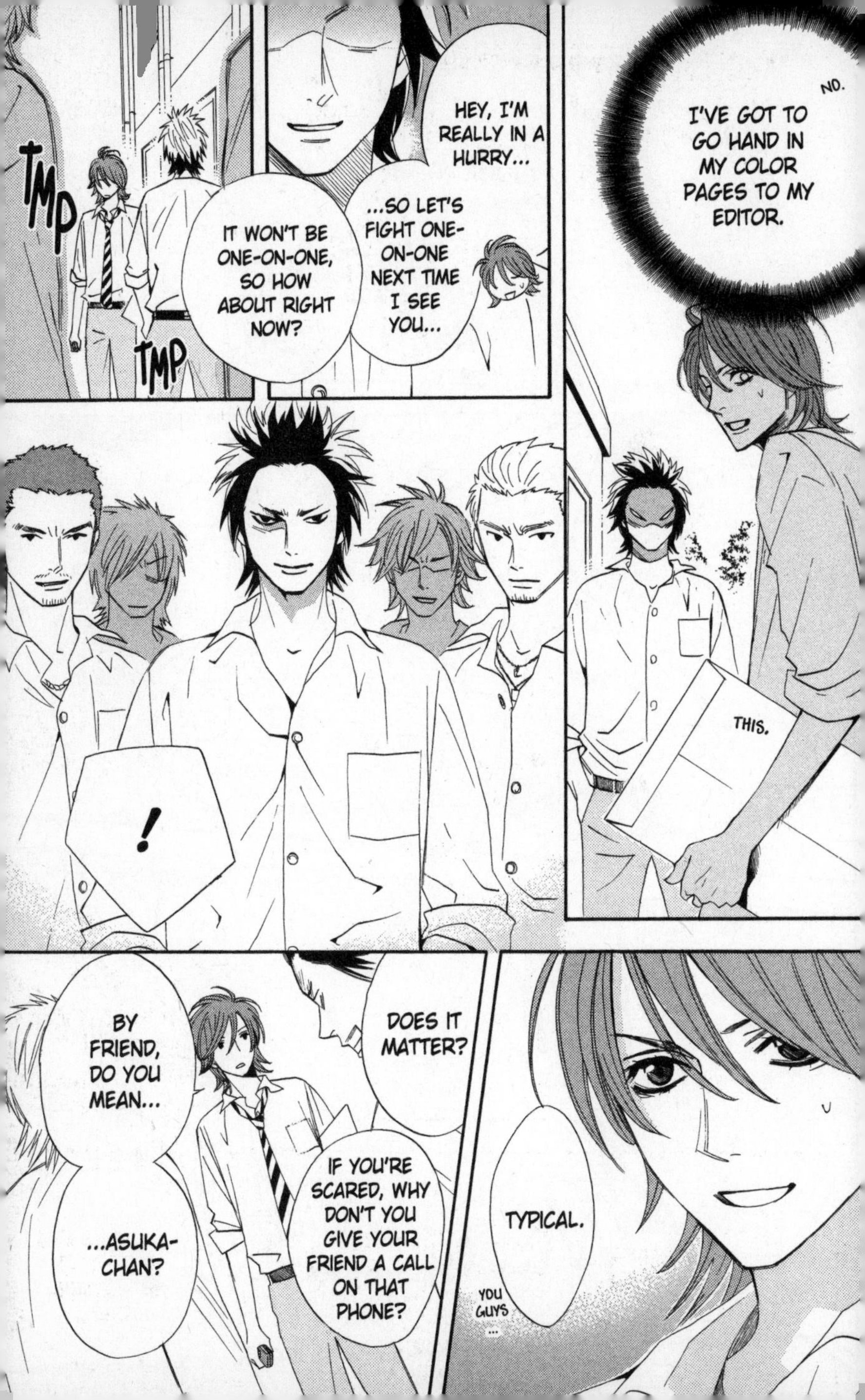
NO.
I'VE GOT TO GO HAND IN MY COLOR PAGES TO MY EDITOR.
THIS.
HEY, I'M REALLY IN A HURRY...
...SO LET'S FIGHT ONE-ON-ONE NEXT TIME I SEE YOU...
IT WON'T BE ONE-ON-ONE, SO HOW ABOUT RIGHT NOW?
TMP
TMP
!
TYPICAL.
YOU GUYS...
DOES IT MATTER?
IF YOU'RE SCARED, WHY DON'T YOU GIVE YOUR FRIEND A CALL ON THAT PHONE?
BY FRIEND, DO YOU MEAN...
...ASUKA-CHAN?

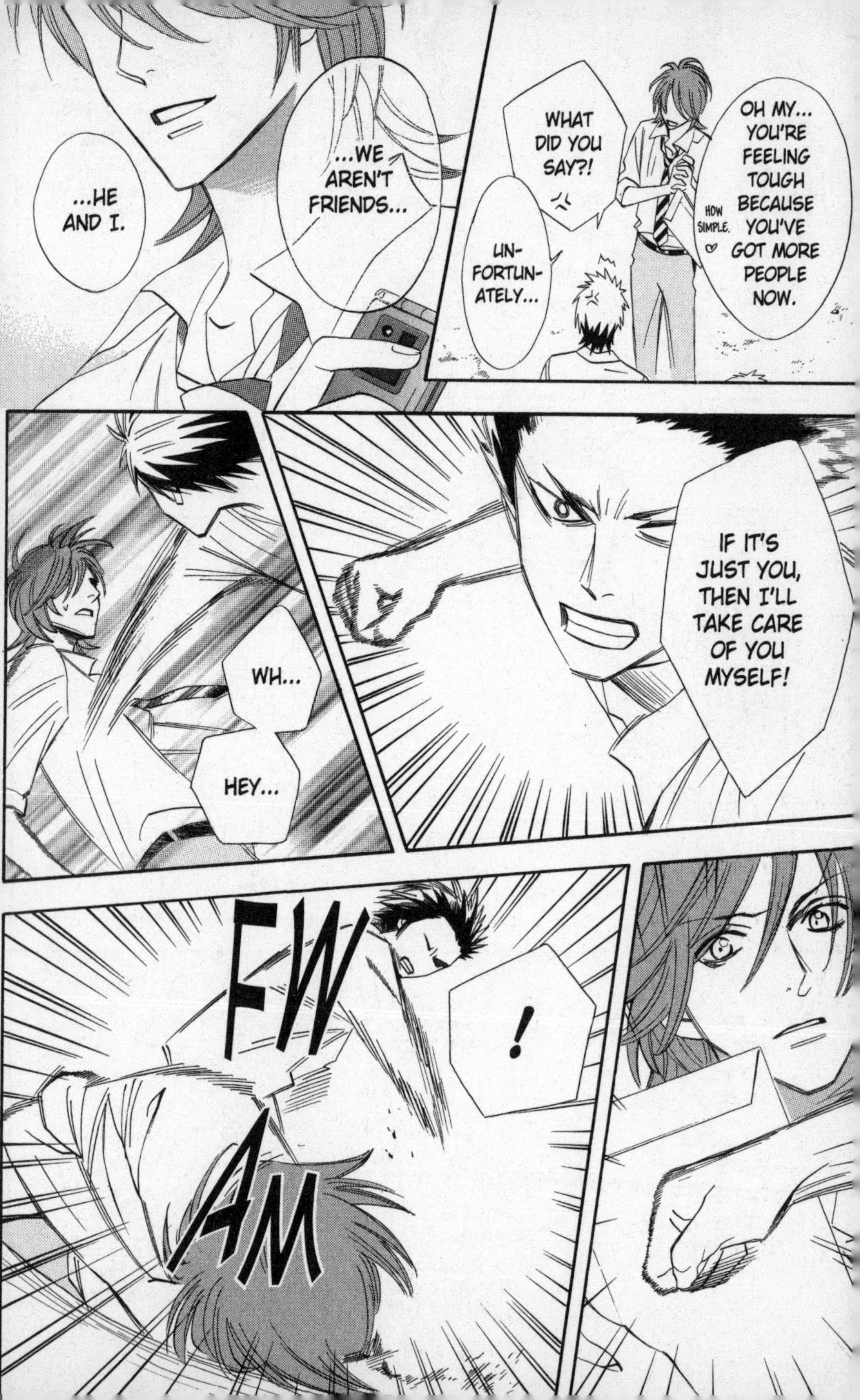
OH MY... YOU'RE FEELING TOUGH BECAUSE YOU'VE GOT MORE PEOPLE NOW.
HOW SIMPLE. ♡
WHAT DID YOU SAY?!
UN-FORTUN-ATELY...
...WE AREN'T FRIENDS...
...HE AND I.
IF IT'S JUST YOU, THEN I'LL TAKE CARE OF YOU MYSELF!
WH...
HEY...
!
FWAM

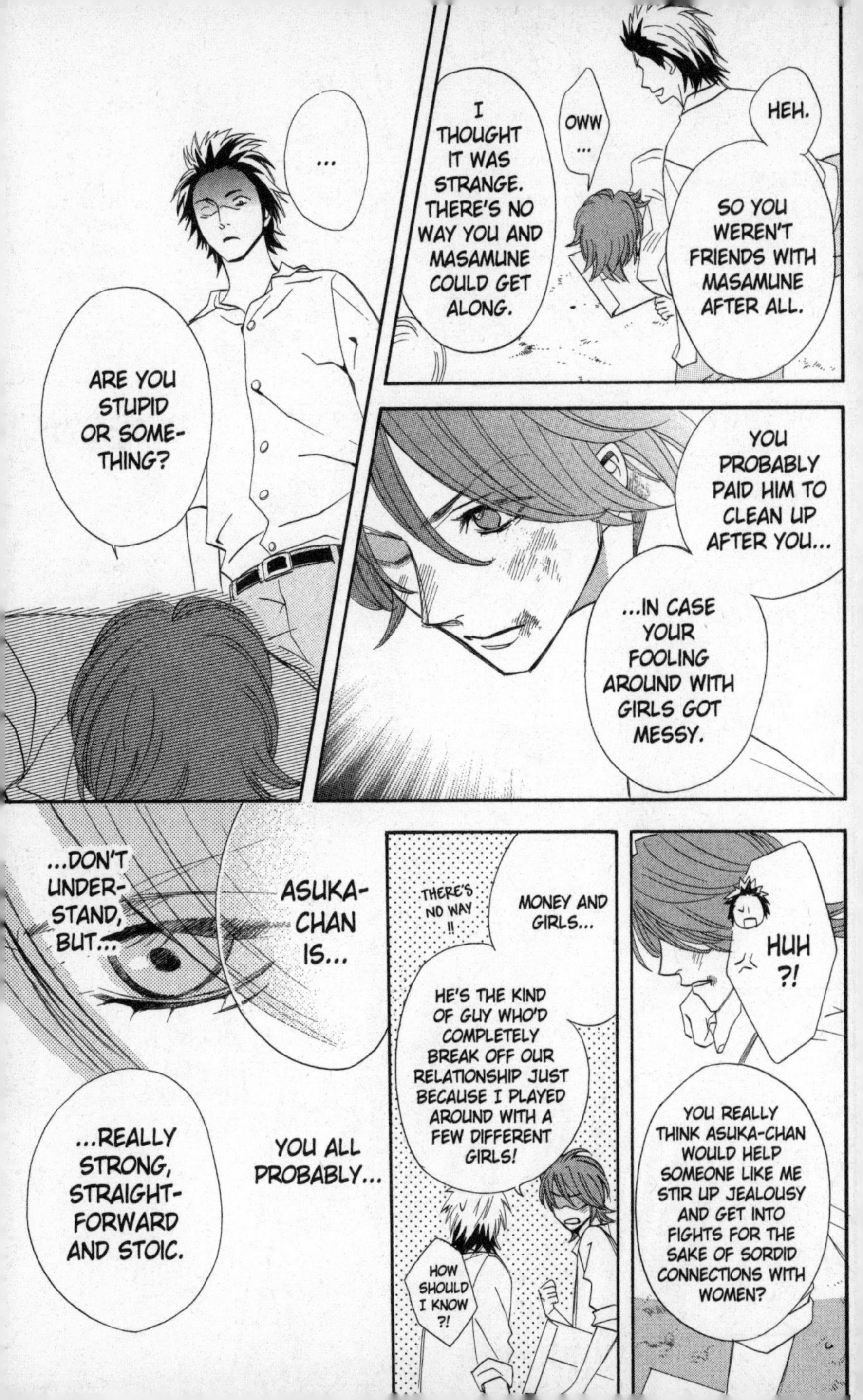
HEH.
SO YOU WEREN'T FRIENDS WITH MASAMUNE AFTER ALL.
OWW...
I THOUGHT IT WAS STRANGE. THERE'S NO WAY YOU AND MASAMUNE COULD GET ALONG.
YOU PROBABLY PAID HIM TO CLEAN UP AFTER YOU...
...IN CASE YOUR FOOLING AROUND WITH GIRLS GOT MESSY.
...
ARE YOU STUPID OR SOME-THING?
HUH ?!
YOU REALLY THINK ASUKA-CHAN WOULD HELP SOMEONE LIKE ME STIR UP JEALOUSY AND GET INTO FIGHTS FOR THE SAKE OF SORDID CONNECTIONS WITH WOMEN?
MONEY AND GIRLS...
THERE'S NO WAY !!
HE'S THE KIND OF GUY WHO'D COMPLETELY BREAK OFF OUR RELATIONSHIP JUST BECAUSE I PLAYED AROUND WITH A FEW DIFFERENT GIRLS!
HOW SHOULD I KNOW ?!
ASUKA-CHAN IS...
...DON'T UNDER-STAND, BUT...
YOU ALL PROBABLY...
...REALLY STRONG, STRAIGHT-FORWARD AND STOIC.

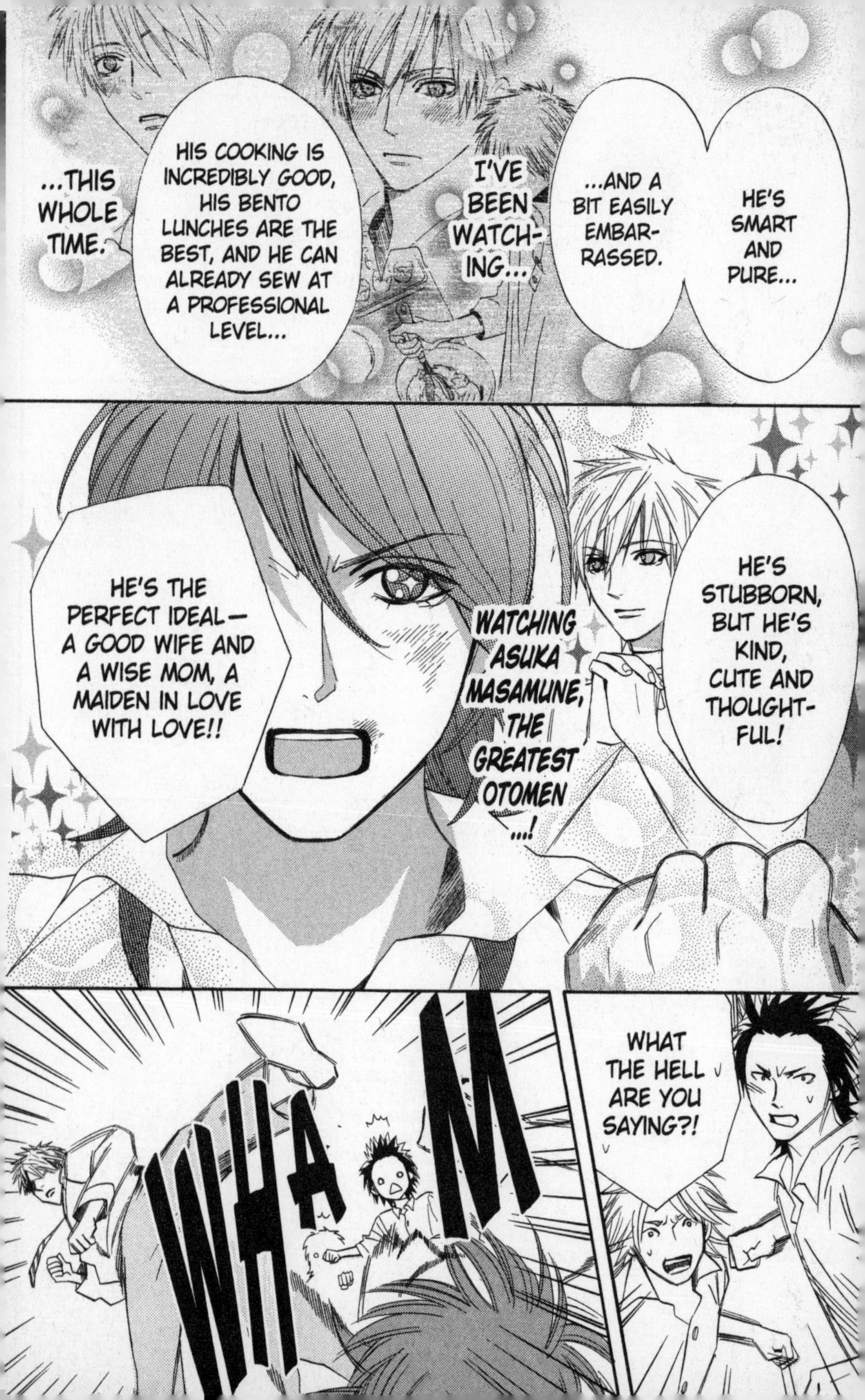
HE'S SMART AND PURE...
...AND A BIT EASILY EMBARRASSED.
I'VE BEEN WATCHING...
HIS COOKING IS INCREDIBLY GOOD, HIS BENTO LUNCHES ARE THE BEST, AND HE CAN ALREADY SEW AT A PROFESSIONAL LEVEL...
...THIS WHOLE TIME.
HE'S STUBBORN, BUT HE'S KIND, CUTE AND THOUGHTFUL!
WATCHING ASUKA MASAMUNE, THE GREATEST OTOMEN...!
HE'S THE PERFECT IDEAL—A GOOD WIFE AND A WISE MOM, A MAIDEN IN LOVE WITH LOVE!!
WHAT THE HELL ARE YOU SAYING?!
WHAM

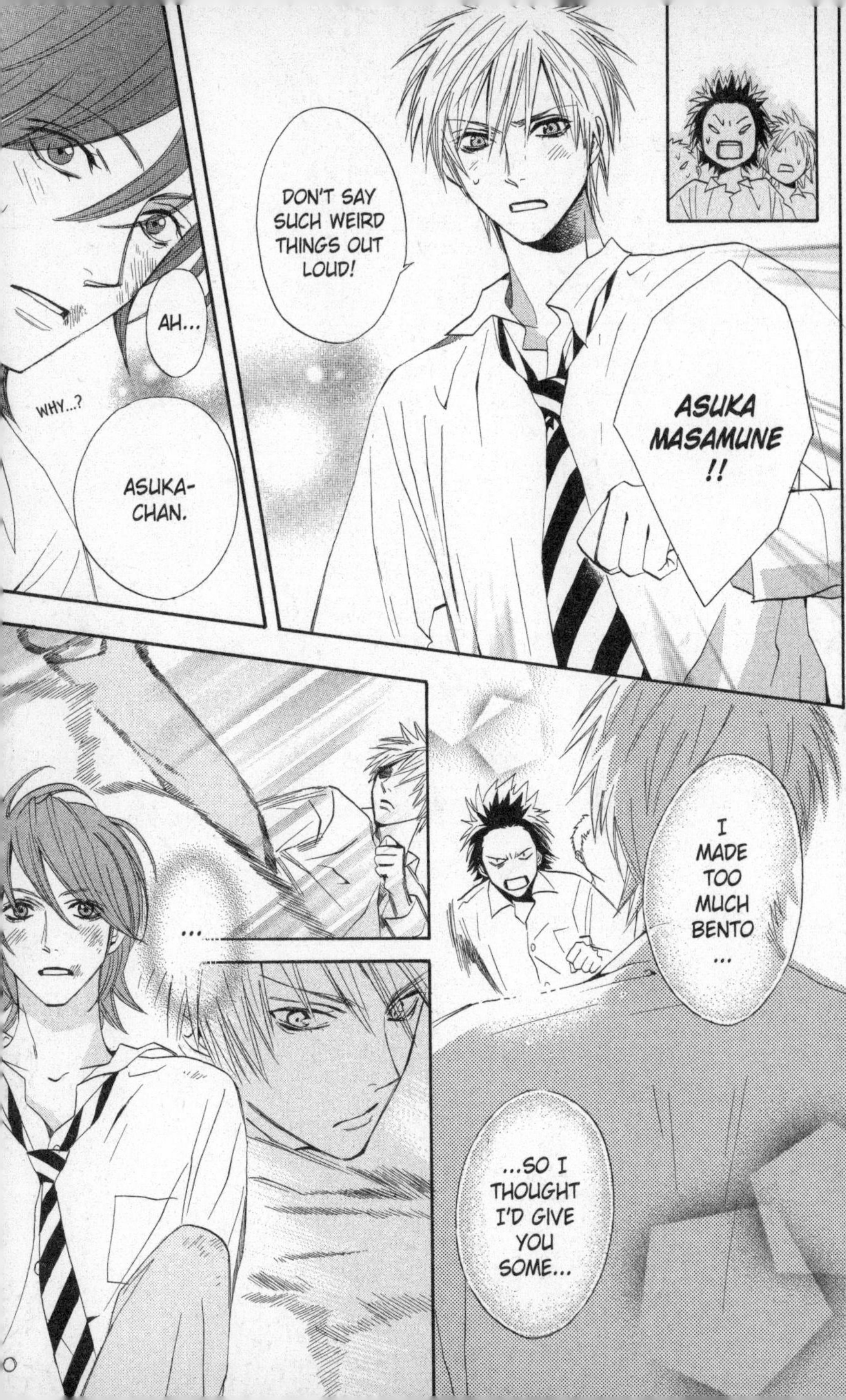
ASUKA MASAMUNE!!
DON'T SAY SUCH WEIRD THINGS OUT LOUD!
AH...
WHY...?
ASUKA-CHAN.
I MADE TOO MUCH BENTO...
...SO I THOUGHT I'D GIVE YOU SOME...
...

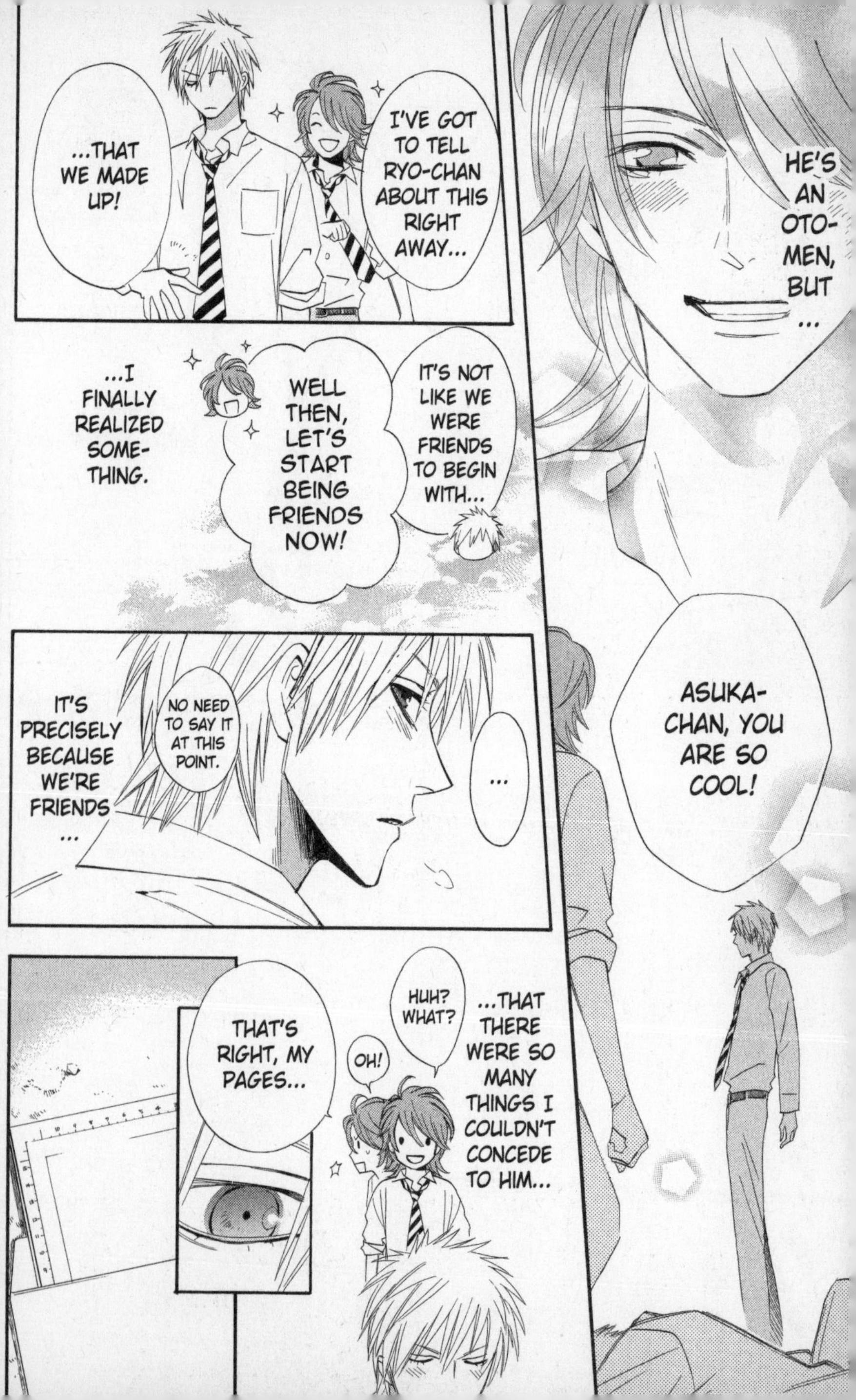
HE'S AN OTOMEN, BUT ...
ASUKA-CHAN, YOU ARE SO COOL!
I'VE GOT TO TELL RYO-CHAN ABOUT THIS RIGHT AWAY...
...THAT WE MADE UP!
IT'S NOT LIKE WE WERE FRIENDS TO BEGIN WITH...
WELL THEN, LET'S START BEING FRIENDS NOW!
...I FINALLY REALIZED SOME-THING.
...
NO NEED TO SAY IT AT THIS POINT.
IT'S PRECISELY BECAUSE WE'RE FRIENDS ...
...THAT THERE WERE SO MANY THINGS I COULDN'T CONCEDE TO HIM...
HUH? WHAT?
OH!
THAT'S RIGHT, MY PAGES...

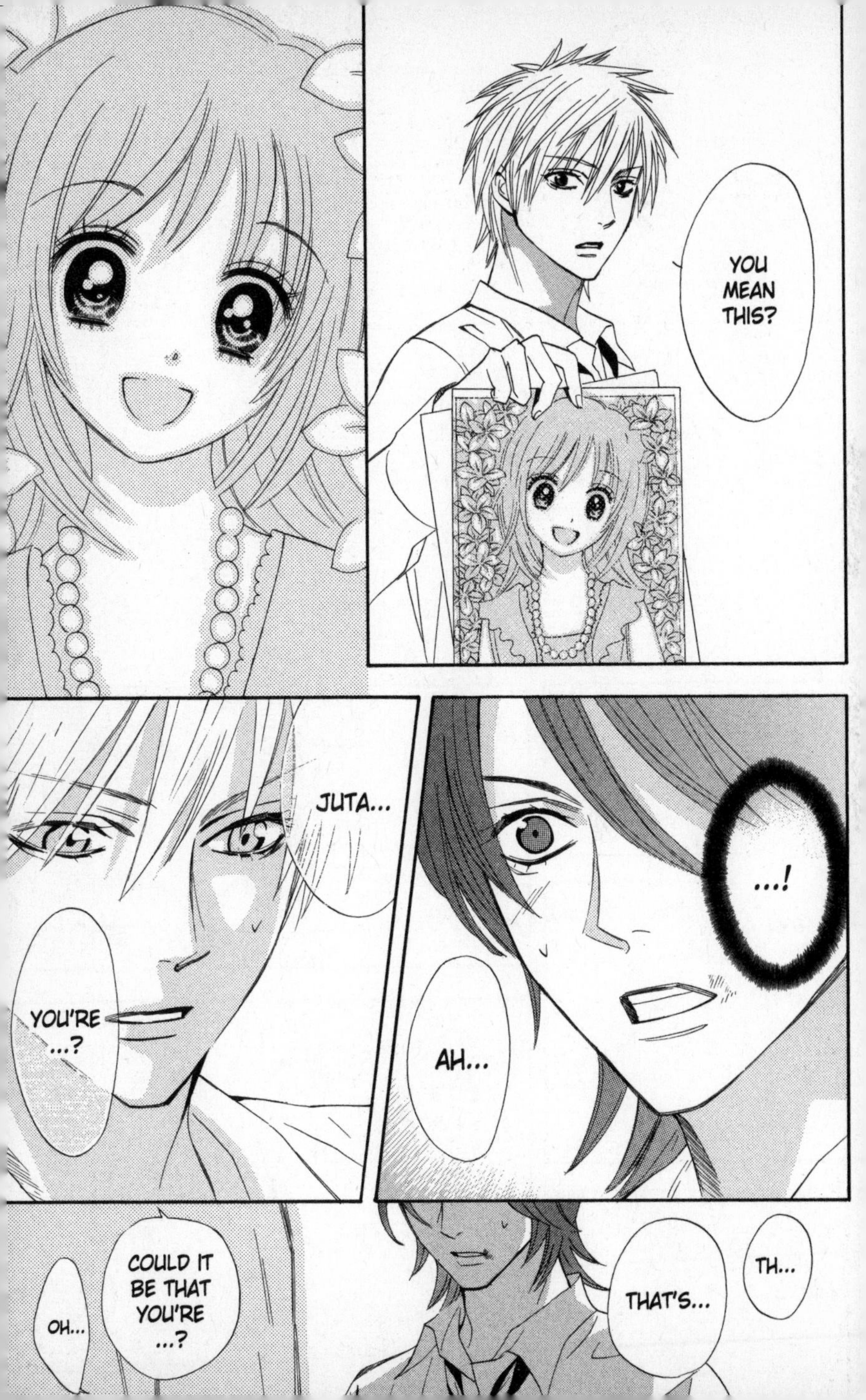
YOU MEAN THIS?
...!
AH...
JUTA...
YOU'RE ...?
TH...
THAT'S...
COULD IT BE THAT YOU'RE ...?
OH...

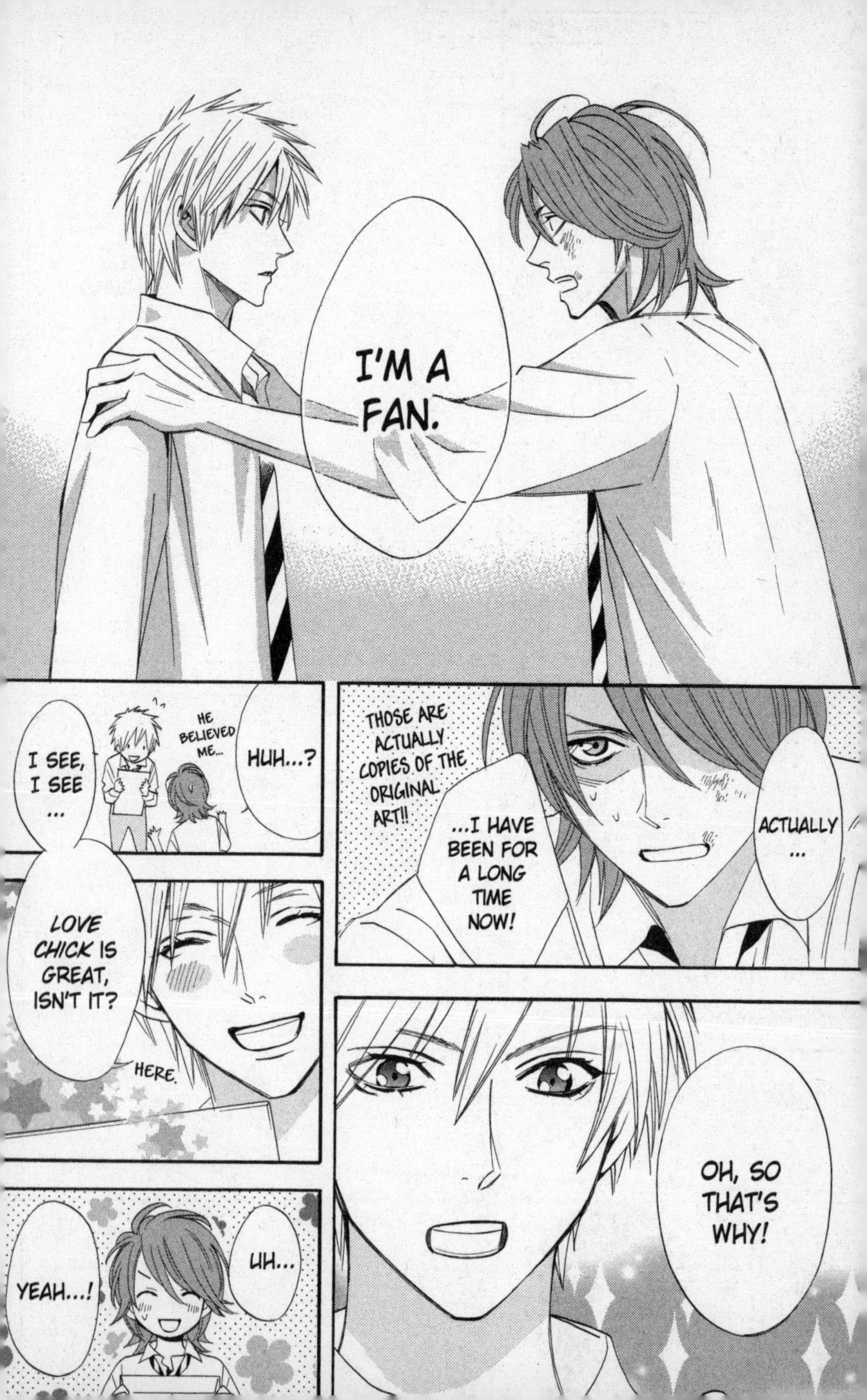
I'M A FAN.
ACTUALLY ...
...I HAVE BEEN FOR A LONG TIME NOW!
THOSE ARE ACTUALLY COPIES OF THE ORIGINAL ART!!
OH, SO THAT'S WHY!
HUH...?
HE BELIEVED ME...
I SEE, I SEE ...
LOVE CHICK IS GREAT, ISN'T IT?
HERE.
UH...
YEAH...!

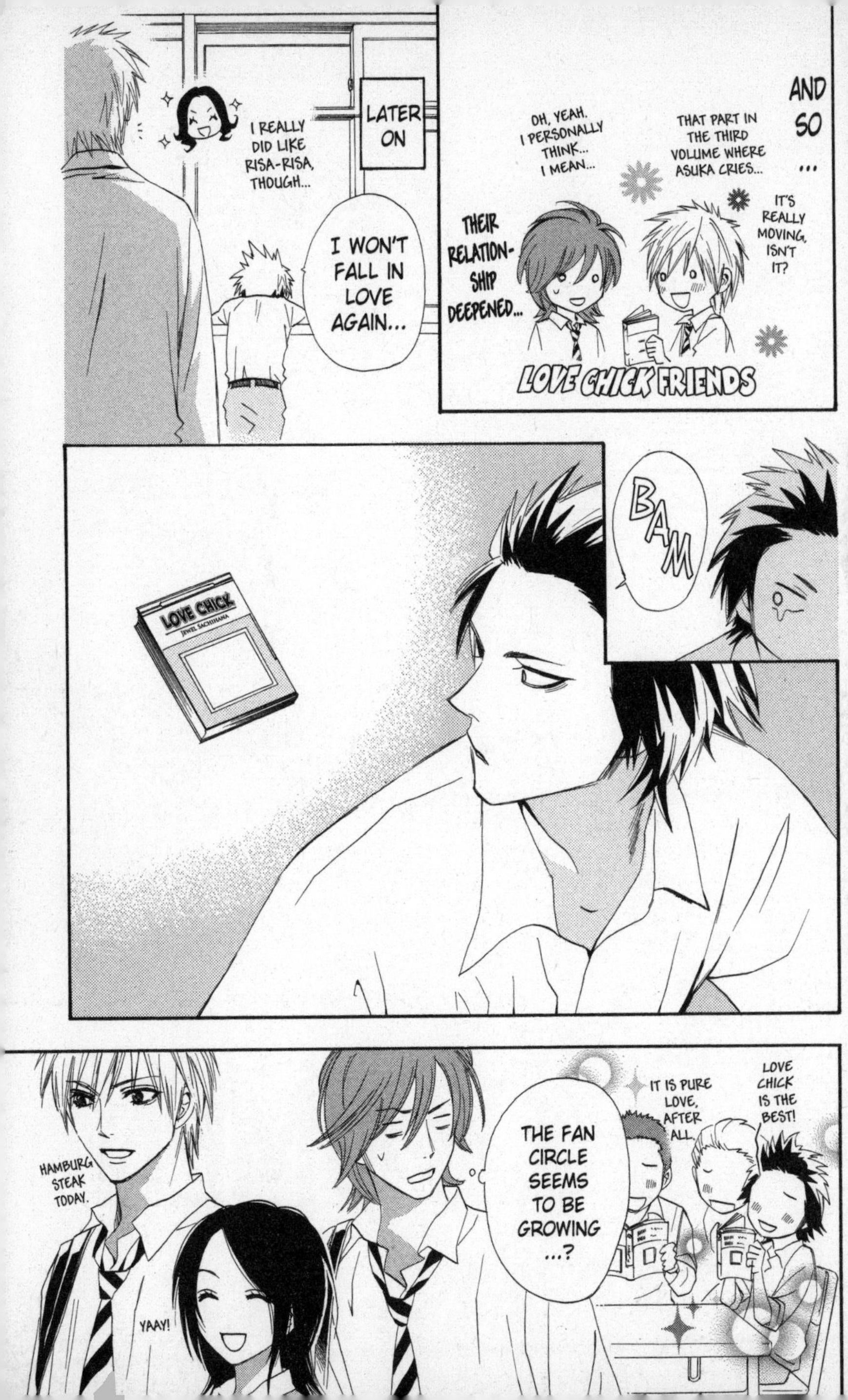
AND SO ...
THAT PART IN THE THIRD VOLUME WHERE ASUKA CRIES...
IT'S REALLY MOVING, ISN'T IT?
OH, YEAH. I PERSONALLY THINK... I MEAN...
THEIR RELATIONSHIP DEEPENED...
LOVE CHICK FRIENDS
LATER ON
I REALLY DID LIKE RISA-RISA, THOUGH...
I WON'T FALL IN LOVE AGAIN...
BAM
LOVE CHICK
JEWEL SACHIHANA
LOVE CHICK IS THE BEST!
IT IS PURE LOVE, AFTER ALL.
THE FAN CIRCLE SEEMS TO BE GROWING ...?
HAMBURG STEAK TODAY.
YAAY!

OTOMEN

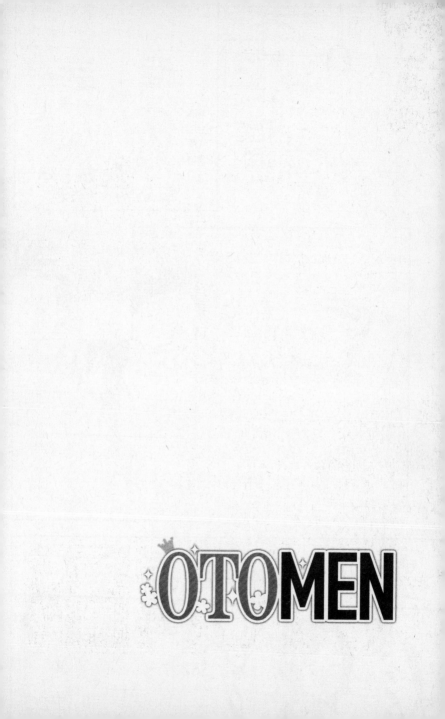

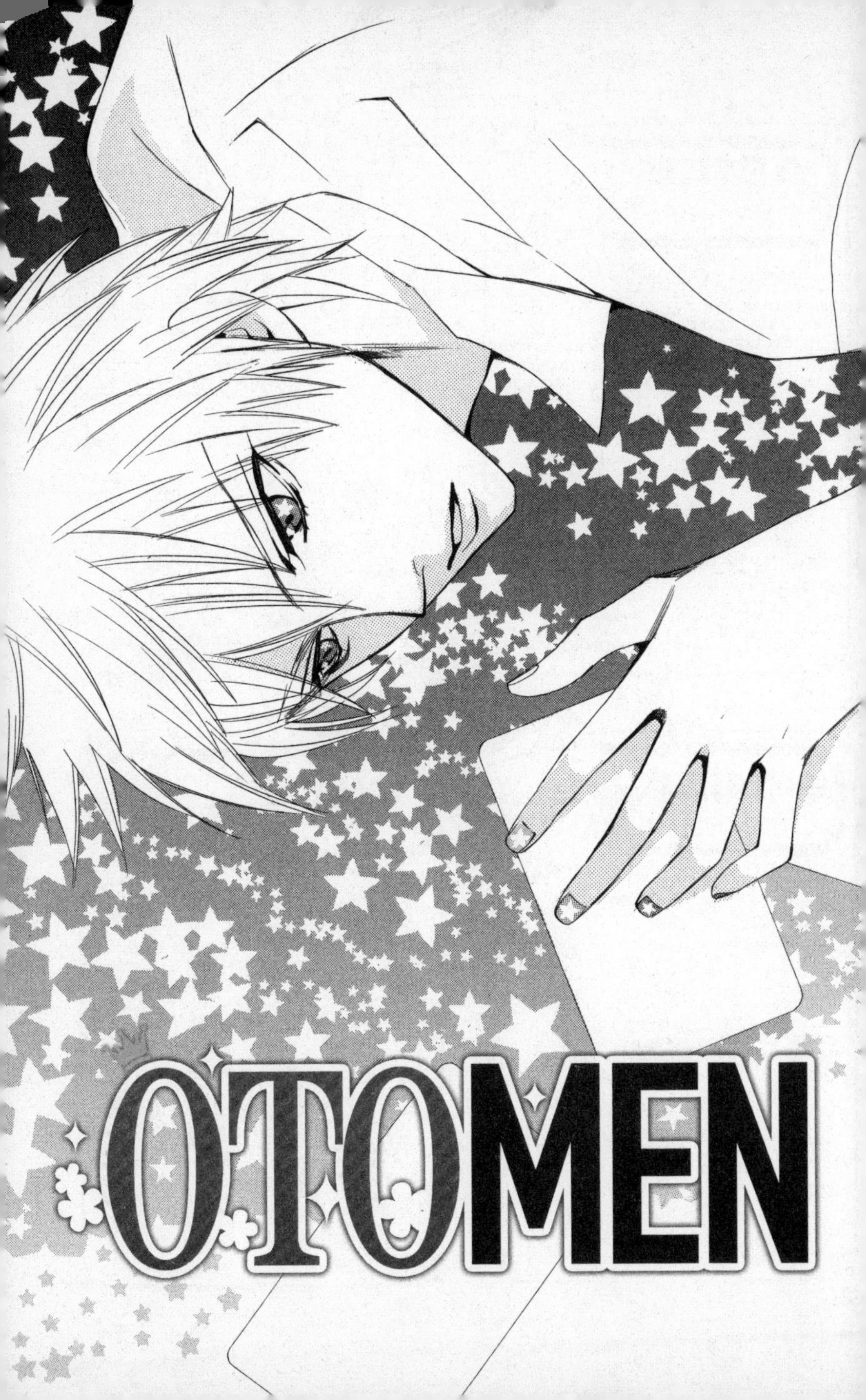
OTOMEN

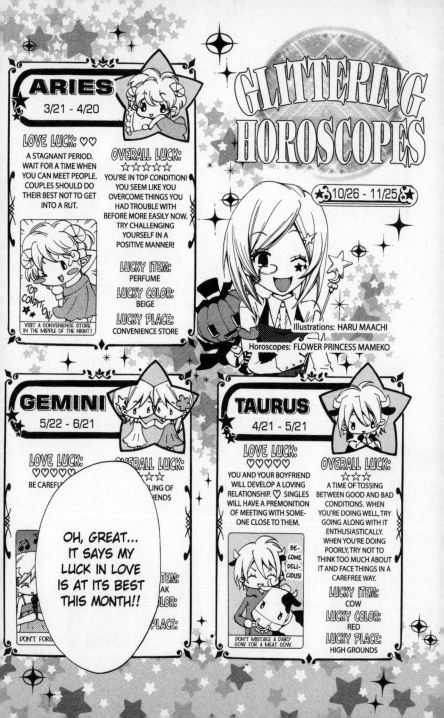

GLITTERING HOROSCOPES

10/26 - 11/25

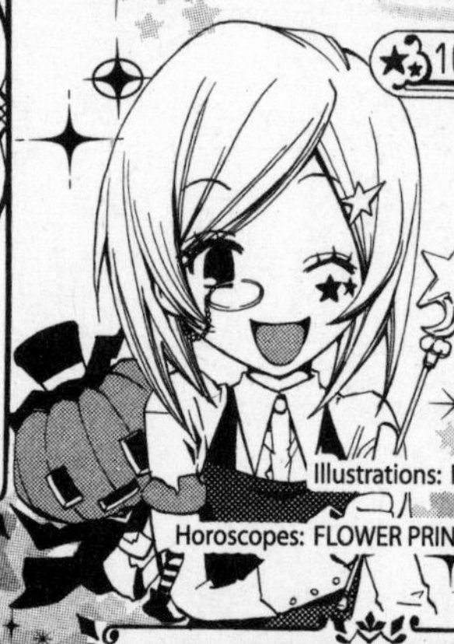

Illustrations: HARU MAACHI

Horoscopes: FLOWER PRINCESS MAMEKO

ARIES

3/21 - 4/20

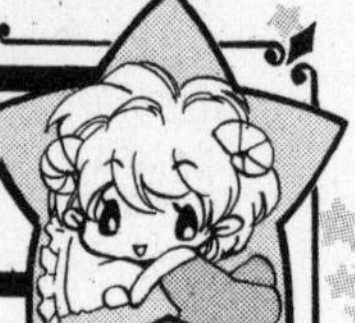

LOVE LUCK: ♡♡

A STAGNANT PERIOD. WAIT FOR A TIME WHEN YOU CAN MEET PEOPLE. COUPLES SHOULD DO THEIR BEST NOT TO GET INTO A RUT.

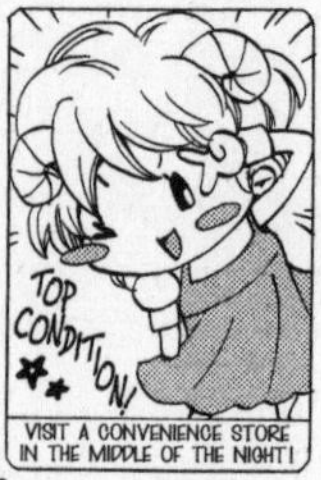
TOP CONDITION!
VISIT A CONVENIENCE STORE IN THE MIDDLE OF THE NIGHT!

OVERALL LUCK: ☆☆☆☆☆

YOU'RE IN TOP CONDITION! YOU SEEM LIKE YOU OVERCOME THINGS YOU HAD TROUBLE WITH BEFORE MORE EASILY NOW. TRY CHALLENGING YOURSELF IN A POSITIVE MANNER!

LUCKY ITEM: PERFUME

LUCKY COLOR: BEIGE

LUCKY PLACE: CONVENIENCE STORE

TAURUS

4/21 - 5/21

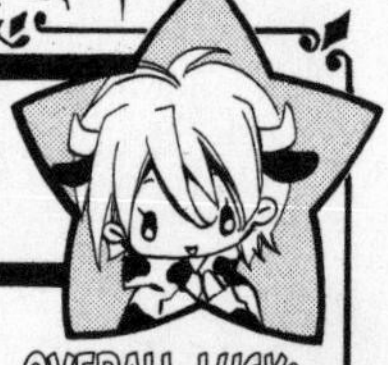

LOVE LUCK: ♡♡♡♡♡

YOU AND YOUR BOYFRIEND WILL DEVELOP A LOVING RELATIONSHIP. ♡ SINGLES WILL HAVE A PREMONITION OF MEETING WITH SOME-ONE CLOSE TO THEM.

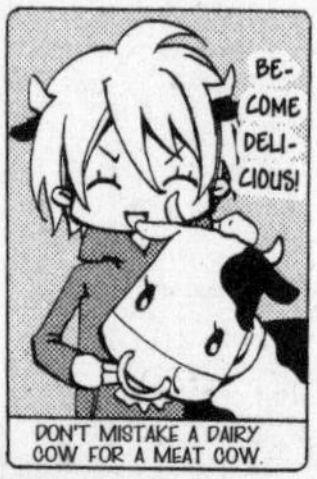
BE-COME DELI-CIOUS!
DON'T MISTAKE A DAIRY COW FOR A MEAT COW.

OVERALL LUCK: ☆☆☆

A TIME OF TOSSING BETWEEN GOOD AND BAD CONDITIONS. WHEN YOU'RE DOING WELL, TRY GOING ALONG WITH IT ENTHUSIASTICALLY. WHEN YOU'RE DOING POORLY, TRY NOT TO THINK TOO MUCH ABOUT IT AND FACE THINGS IN A CAREFREE WAY.

LUCKY ITEM: COW

LUCKY COLOR: RED

LUCKY PLACE: HIGH GROUNDS

GEMINI

5/22 - 6/21

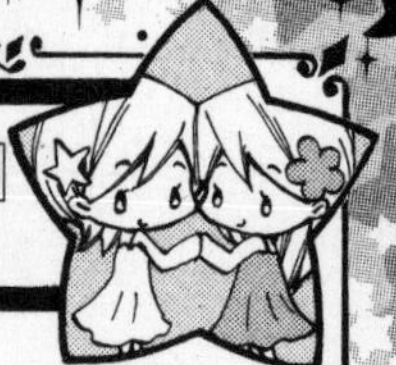

LOVE LUCK: ♡♡♡♡♡

BE CAREFU...

OVERALL LUCK: ☆☆☆

...LING OF ...IENDS

...ITEM: ...AK

...OLOR:

...PLACE:

DON'T FORG...

OH, GREAT... IT SAYS MY LUCK IN LOVE IS AT ITS BEST THIS MONTH!!

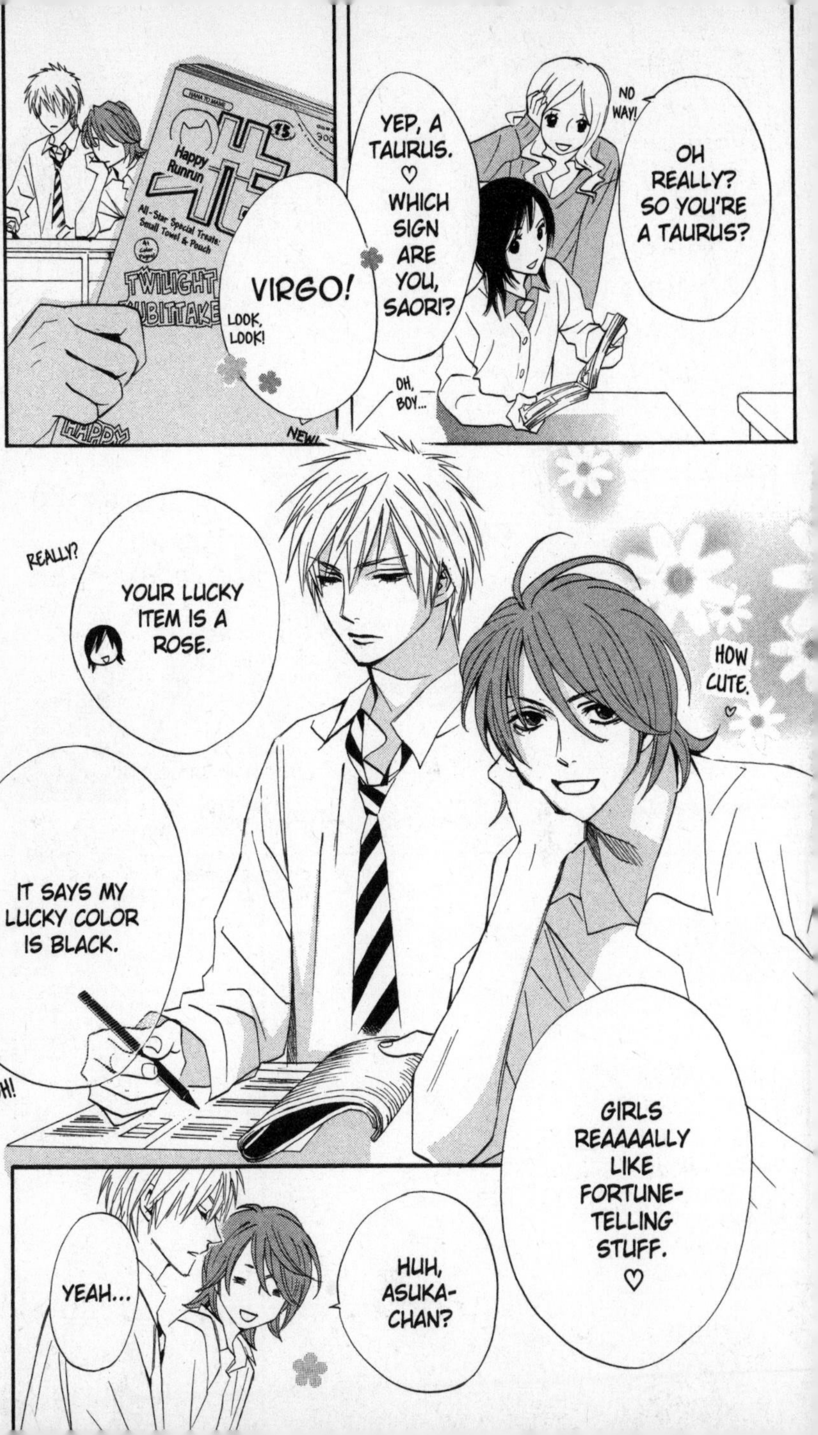
NO WAY!
OH REALLY? SO YOU'RE A TAURUS?
YEP, A TAURUS. ♡ WHICH SIGN ARE YOU, SAORI?
OH, BOY...
VIRGO!
LOOK, LOOK!
Happy Runrun
All-Star Special Treats: Small Towel & Pouch
TWILIGHT
NEW!
HOW CUTE. ♡
REALLY?
YOUR LUCKY ITEM IS A ROSE.
IT SAYS MY LUCKY COLOR IS BLACK.
OH!
GIRLS REAAAALLY LIKE FORTUNE-TELLING STUFF. ♡
HUH, ASUKA-CHAN?
YEAH...

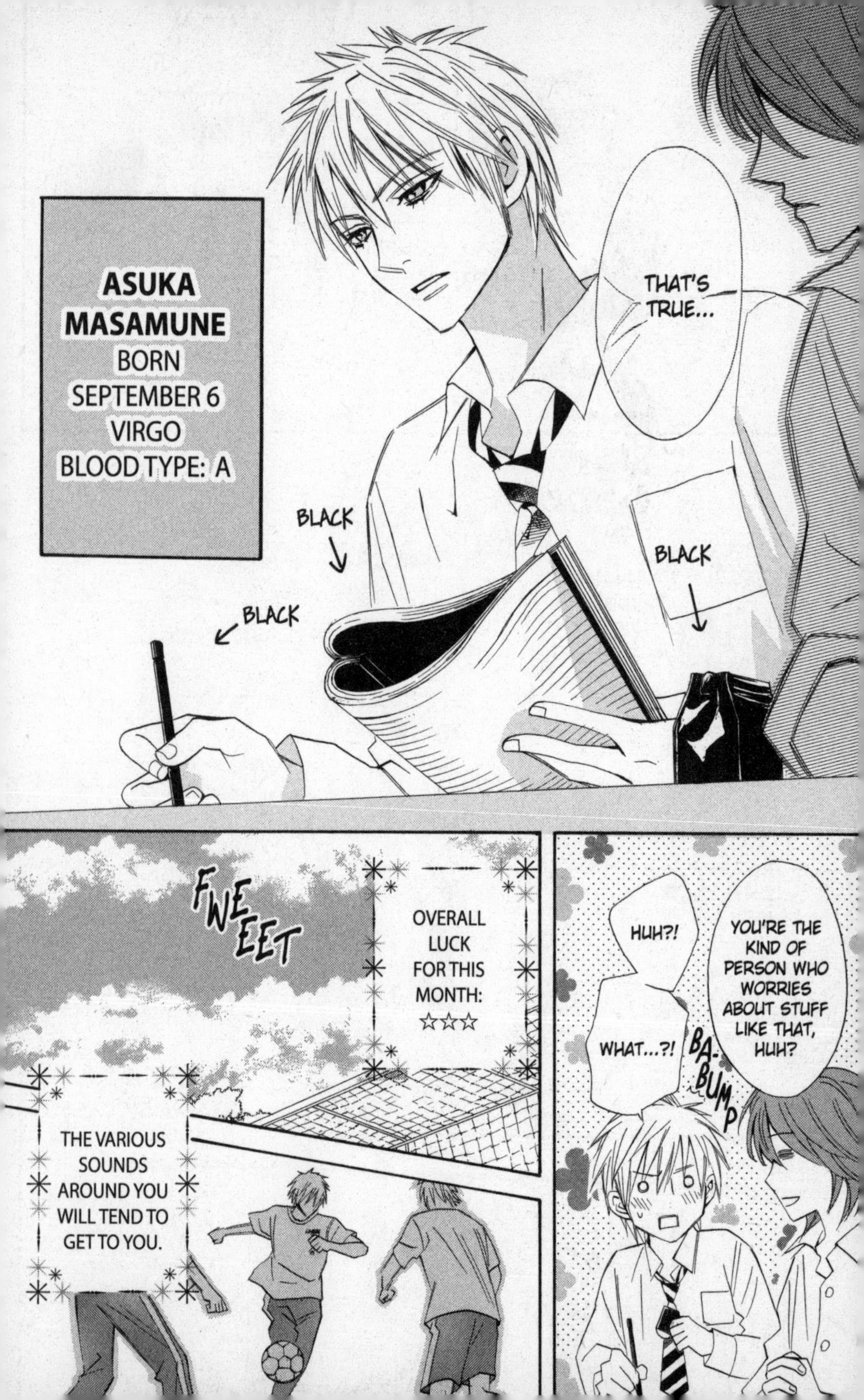
THAT'S TRUE...
ASUKA MASAMUNE
BORN SEPTEMBER 6
VIRGO
BLOOD TYPE: A
BLACK
BLACK
BLACK
YOU'RE THE KIND OF PERSON WHO WORRIES ABOUT STUFF LIKE THAT, HUH?
HUH?!
WHAT...?!
BA-BUMP
OVERALL LUCK FOR THIS MONTH: ☆☆☆
FWEEET
THE VARIOUS SOUNDS AROUND YOU WILL TEND TO GET TO YOU.

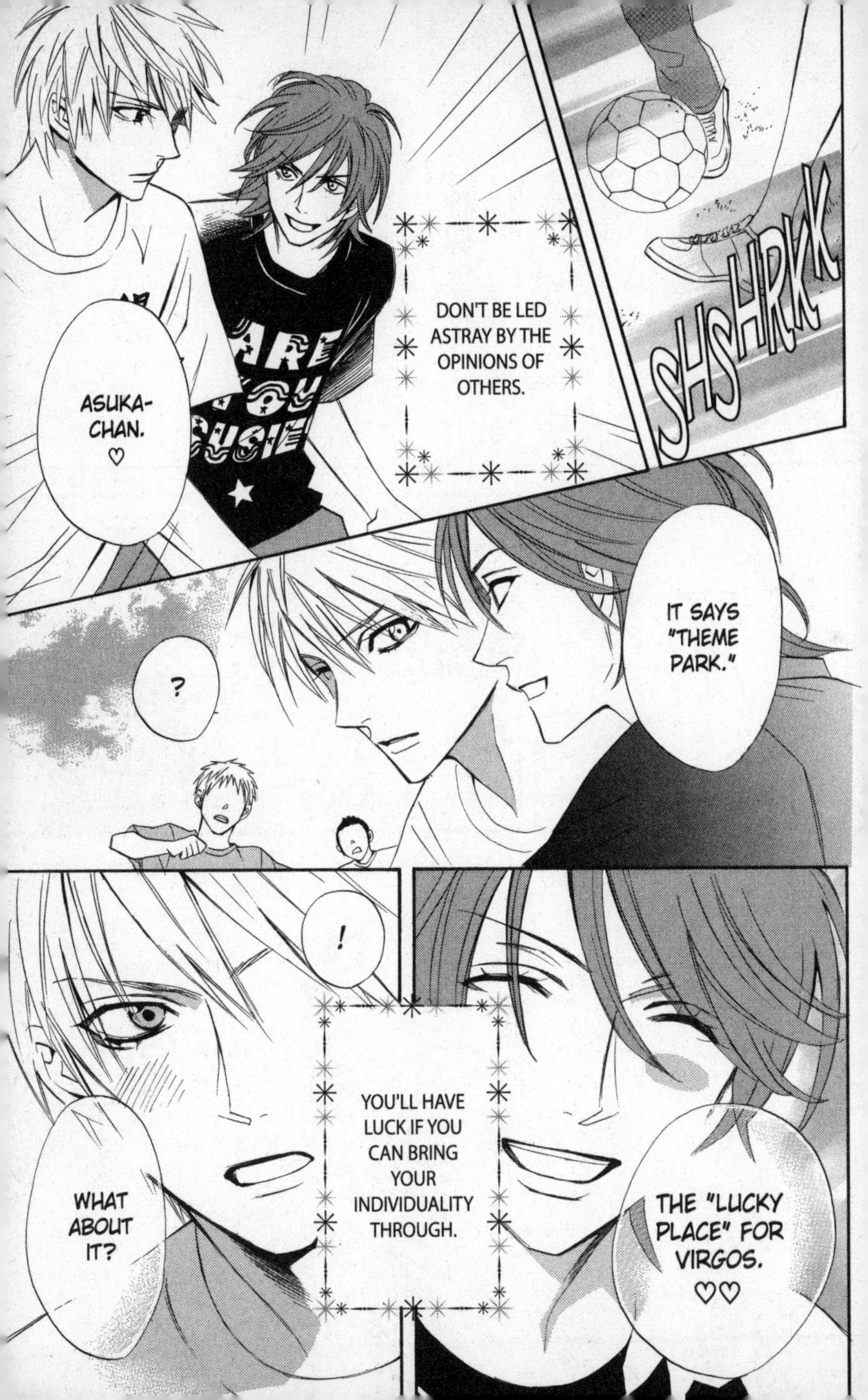
SHSHRKK
DON'T BE LED ASTRAY BY THE OPINIONS OF OTHERS.
ASUKA-CHAN. ♡
IT SAYS "THEME PARK."
?
THE "LUCKY PLACE" FOR VIRGOS. ♡♡
!
YOU'LL HAVE LUCK IF YOU CAN BRING YOUR INDIVIDUALITY THROUGH.
WHAT ABOUT IT?

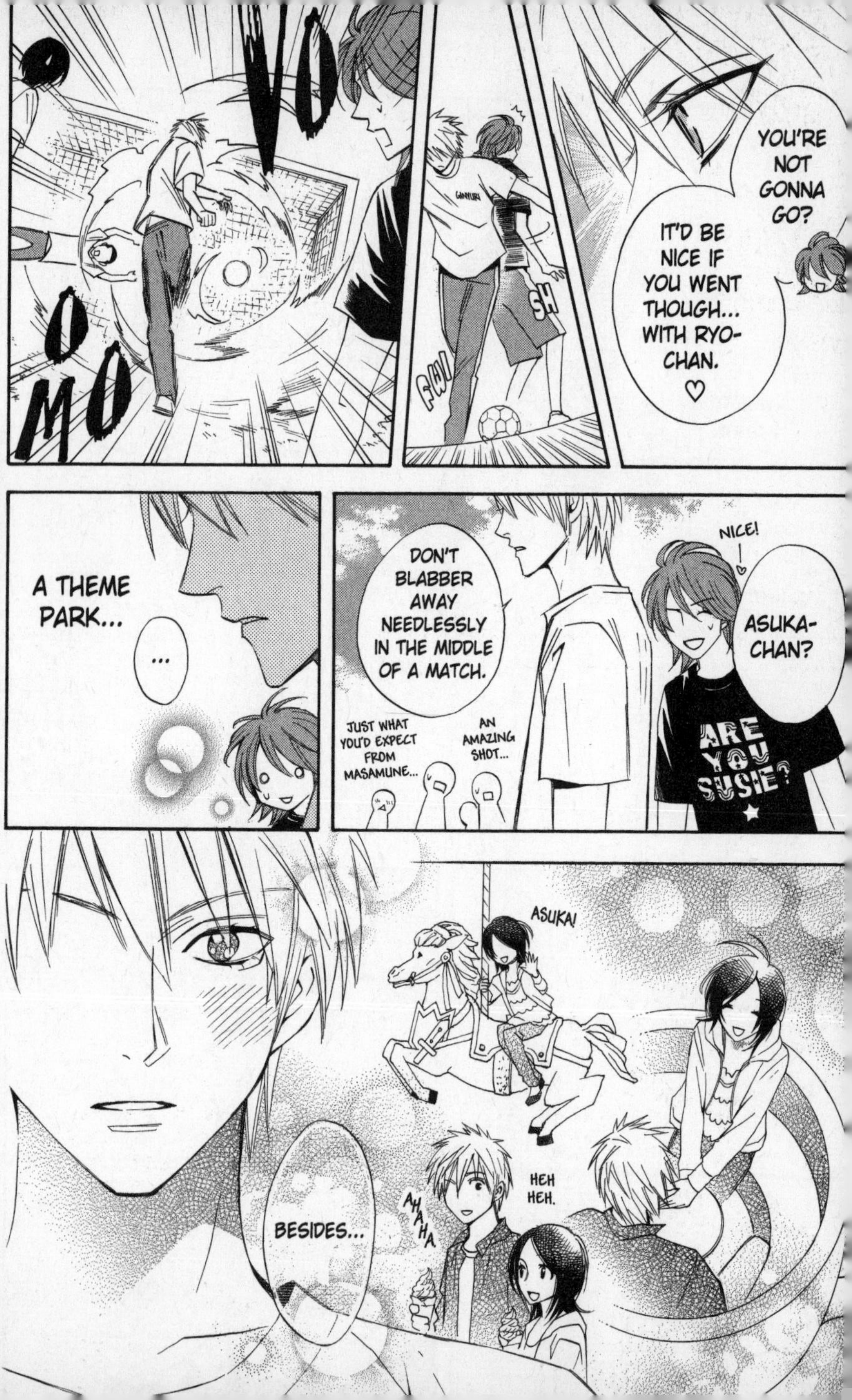
YOU'RE NOT GONNA GO?
IT'D BE NICE IF YOU WENT THOUGH... WITH RYO-CHAN. ♡
SH
FWI
VO
O
MO
NICE!
ASUKA-CHAN?
DON'T BLABBER AWAY NEEDLESSLY IN THE MIDDLE OF A MATCH.
ARE YOU SUSIE?
AN AMAZING SHOT...
JUST WHAT YOU'D EXPECT FROM MASAMUNE...
A THEME PARK...
...
ASUKA!
HEH HEH.
AHAHA
BESIDES...

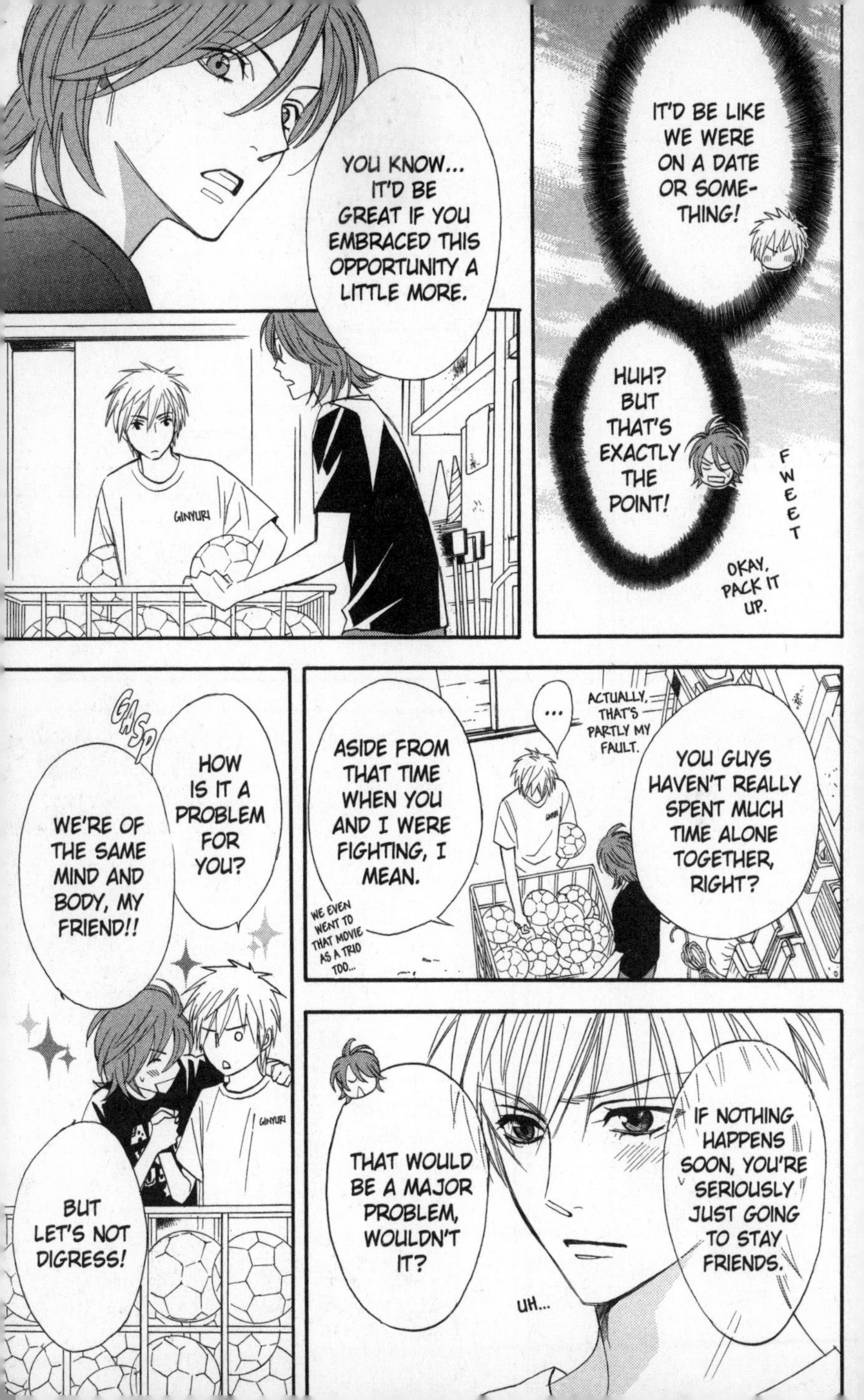
IT'D BE LIKE WE WERE ON A DATE OR SOME-THING!
HUH? BUT THAT'S EXACTLY THE POINT!
FWEET
OKAY, PACK IT UP.
YOU KNOW... IT'D BE GREAT IF YOU EMBRACED THIS OPPORTUNITY A LITTLE MORE.
GINYURI
YOU GUYS HAVEN'T REALLY SPENT MUCH TIME ALONE TOGETHER, RIGHT?
ACTUALLY, THAT'S PARTLY MY FAULT.
...
ASIDE FROM THAT TIME WHEN YOU AND I WERE FIGHTING, I MEAN.
WE EVEN WENT TO THAT MOVIE AS A TRIO TOO...
IF NOTHING HAPPENS SOON, YOU'RE SERIOUSLY JUST GOING TO STAY FRIENDS.
THAT WOULD BE A MAJOR PROBLEM, WOULDN'T IT?
UH...
HOW IS IT A PROBLEM FOR YOU?
GASP
WE'RE OF THE SAME MIND AND BODY, MY FRIEND!!
GINYURI
BUT LET'S NOT DIGRESS!

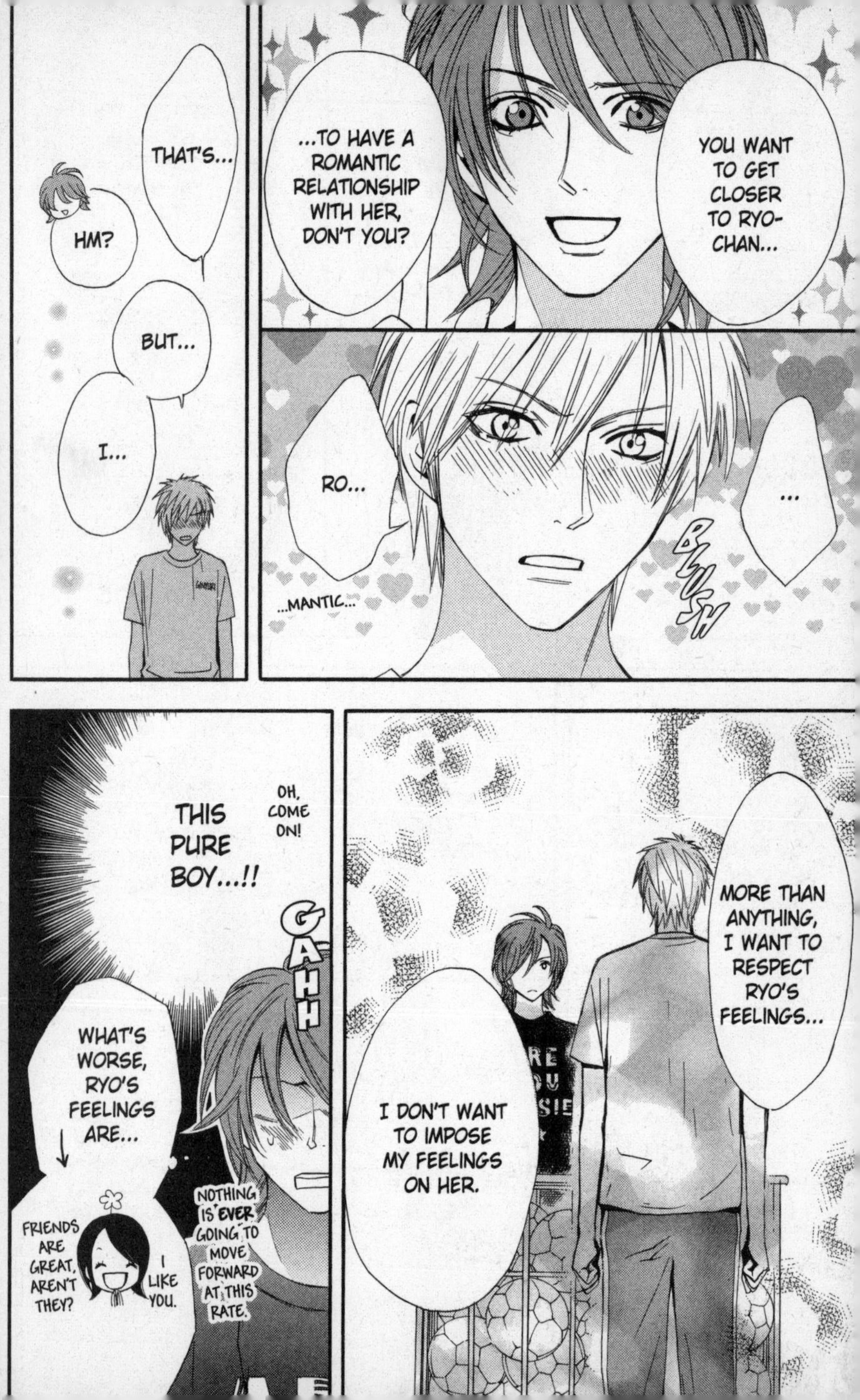
YOU WANT TO GET CLOSER TO RYO-CHAN...
...TO HAVE A ROMANTIC RELATIONSHIP WITH HER, DON'T YOU?
...
BLUSH
RO...
...MANTIC...
THAT'S...
HM?
BUT...
I...
MORE THAN ANYTHING, I WANT TO RESPECT RYO'S FEELINGS...
I DON'T WANT TO IMPOSE MY FEELINGS ON HER.
OH, COME ON!
THIS PURE BOY...!!
GAHH
WHAT'S WORSE, RYO'S FEELINGS ARE...
NOTHING IS **EVER** GOING TO MOVE FORWARD AT THIS RATE.
I LIKE YOU.
FRIENDS ARE GREAT, AREN'T THEY?

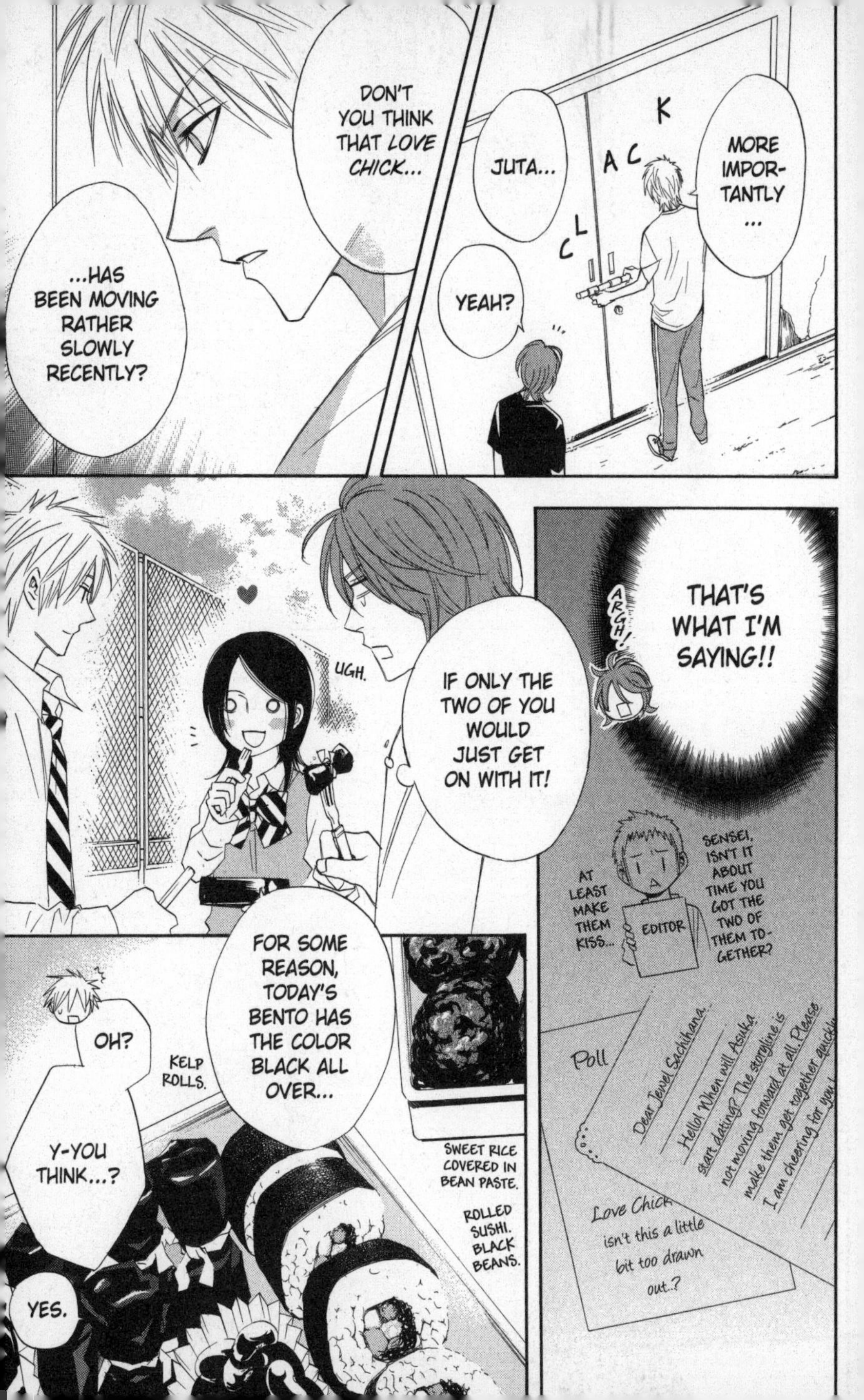
MORE IMPORTANTLY...
CLACK
JUTA...
YEAH?
DON'T YOU THINK THAT LOVE CHICK...
...HAS BEEN MOVING RATHER SLOWLY RECENTLY?
ARGH!
THAT'S WHAT I'M SAYING!!
SENSEI, ISN'T IT ABOUT TIME YOU GOT THE TWO OF THEM TOGETHER?
AT LEAST MAKE THEM KISS...
EDITOR
Poll
Dear Jewel Sachihana,
Hello! When will Asuka start dating? The storyline is not moving forward at all. Please make them get together quickly! I am cheering for you!
Love Chick isn't this a little bit too drawn out..?
IF ONLY THE TWO OF YOU WOULD JUST GET ON WITH IT!
UGH.
FOR SOME REASON, TODAY'S BENTO HAS THE COLOR BLACK ALL OVER...
OH?
KELP ROLLS.
SWEET RICE COVERED IN BEAN PASTE.
ROLLED SUSHI. BLACK BEANS.
Y-YOU THINK...?
YES.

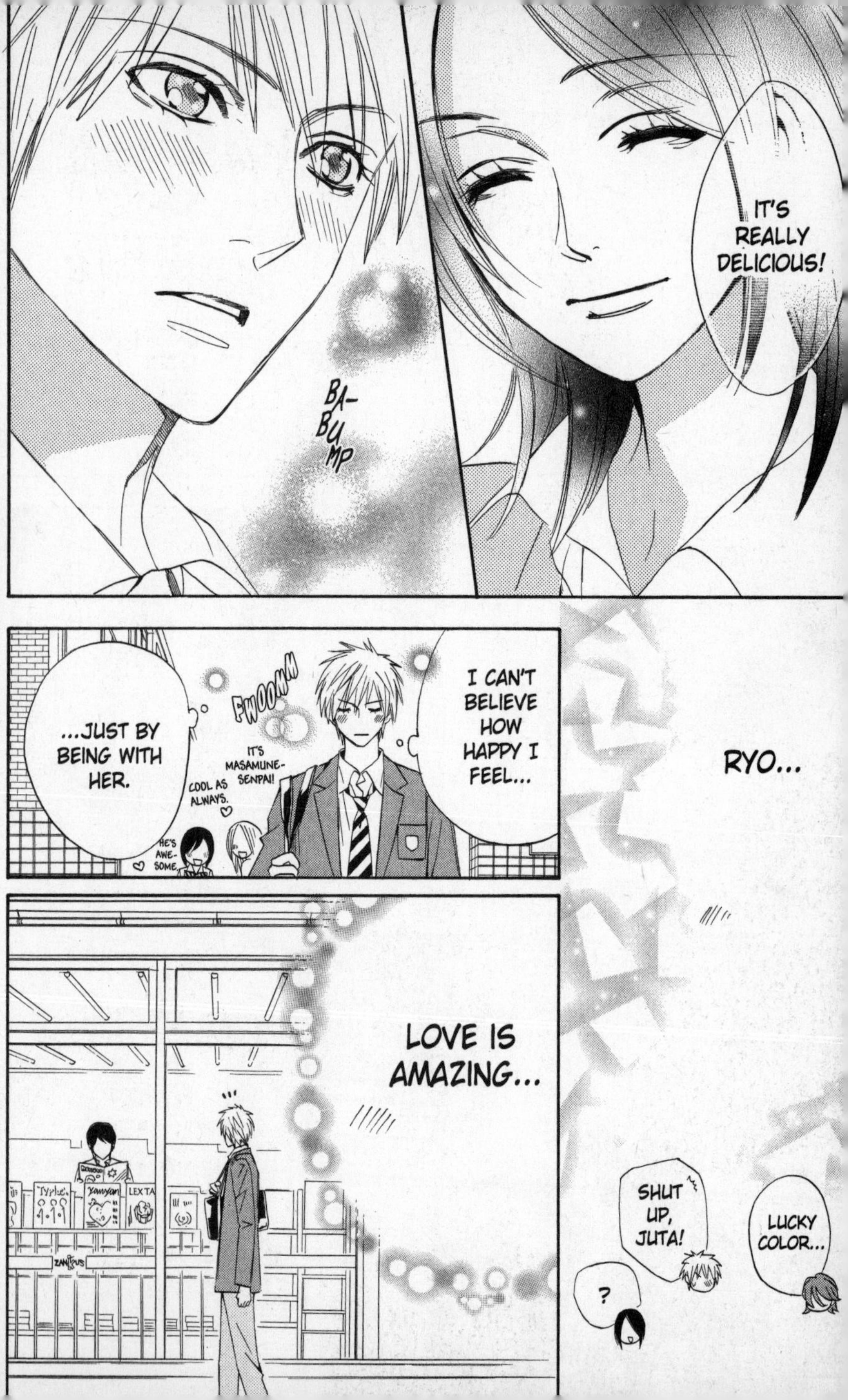
IT'S REALLY DELICIOUS!
BA-BUMP
RYO...
LUCKY COLOR...
SHUT UP, JUTA!
?
I CAN'T BELIEVE HOW HAPPY I FEEL...
FWOOMM
IT'S MASAMUNE-SENPAI!
COOL AS ALWAYS.
HE'S AWE-SOME.
...JUST BY BEING WITH HER.
LOVE IS AMAZING...

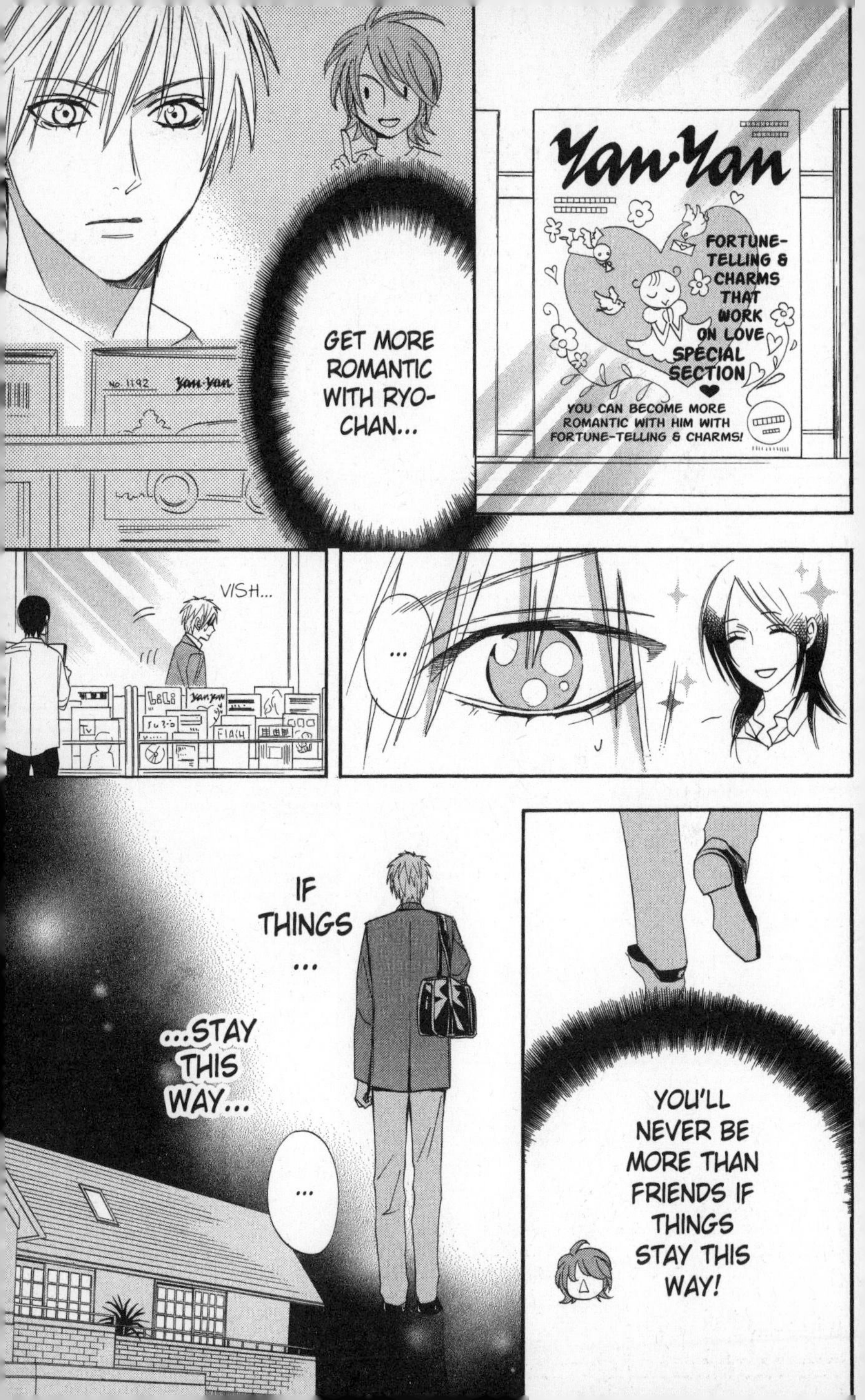
Yan-Yan
FORTUNE-TELLING & CHARMS THAT WORK ON LOVE SPECIAL SECTION
YOU CAN BECOME MORE ROMANTIC WITH HIM WITH FORTUNE-TELLING & CHARMS!
GET MORE ROMANTIC WITH RYO-CHAN...
...
VISH...
YOU'LL NEVER BE MORE THAN FRIENDS IF THINGS STAY THIS WAY!
IF THINGS ...
...STAY THIS WAY...
...

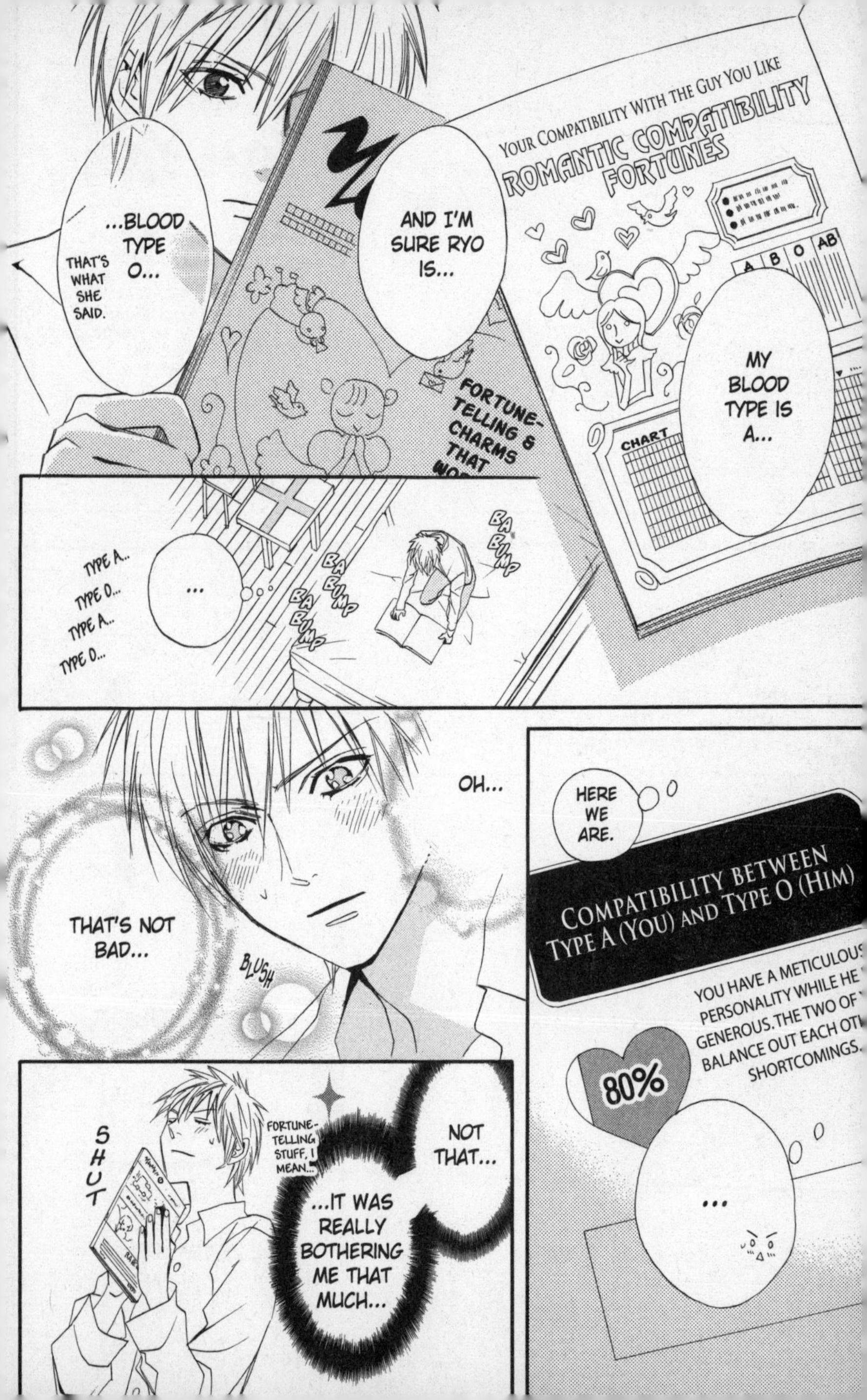
YOUR COMPATIBILITY WITH THE GUY YOU LIKE
ROMANTIC COMPATIBILITY FORTUNES
A B O AB
CHART
MY BLOOD TYPE IS A...
AND I'M SURE RYO IS...
...BLOOD TYPE O...
THAT'S WHAT SHE SAID.
FORTUNE-TELLING & CHARMS THAT WO...
BA BUMP
BA BUMP
BA BUMP
...
TYPE A...
TYPE O...
TYPE A...
TYPE O...
HERE WE ARE.
COMPATIBILITY BETWEEN TYPE A (YOU) AND TYPE O (HIM)
YOU HAVE A METICULOUS PERSONALITY WHILE HE GENEROUS. THE TWO OF BALANCE OUT EACH OT SHORTCOMINGS.
80%
...
OH...
THAT'S NOT BAD...
BLUSH
NOT THAT...
FORTUNE-TELLING STUFF, I MEAN...
...IT WAS REALLY BOTHERING ME THAT MUCH...
SHUT

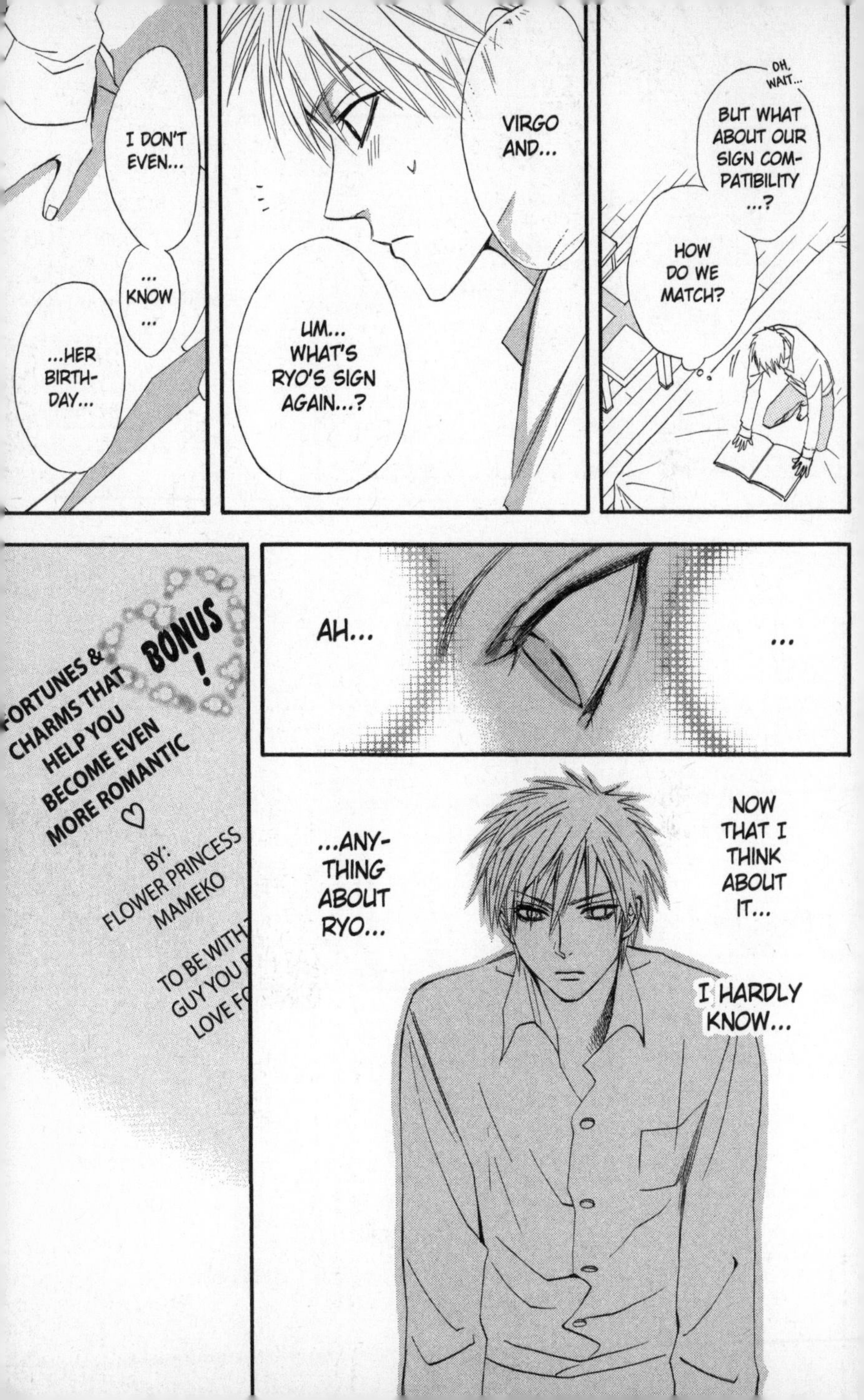

OH, WAIT...
BUT WHAT ABOUT OUR SIGN COMPATIBILITY ...?
HOW DO WE MATCH?
VIRGO AND...
UM... WHAT'S RYO'S SIGN AGAIN...?
I DON'T EVEN...
... KNOW ...
...HER BIRTHDAY...
...
AH...
NOW THAT I THINK ABOUT IT...
I HARDLY KNOW...
...ANYTHING ABOUT RYO...
BONUS!
FORTUNES & CHARMS THAT HELP YOU BECOME EVEN MORE ROMANTIC ♡
BY: FLOWER PRINCESS MAMEKO
TO BE WITH
GUY YOU

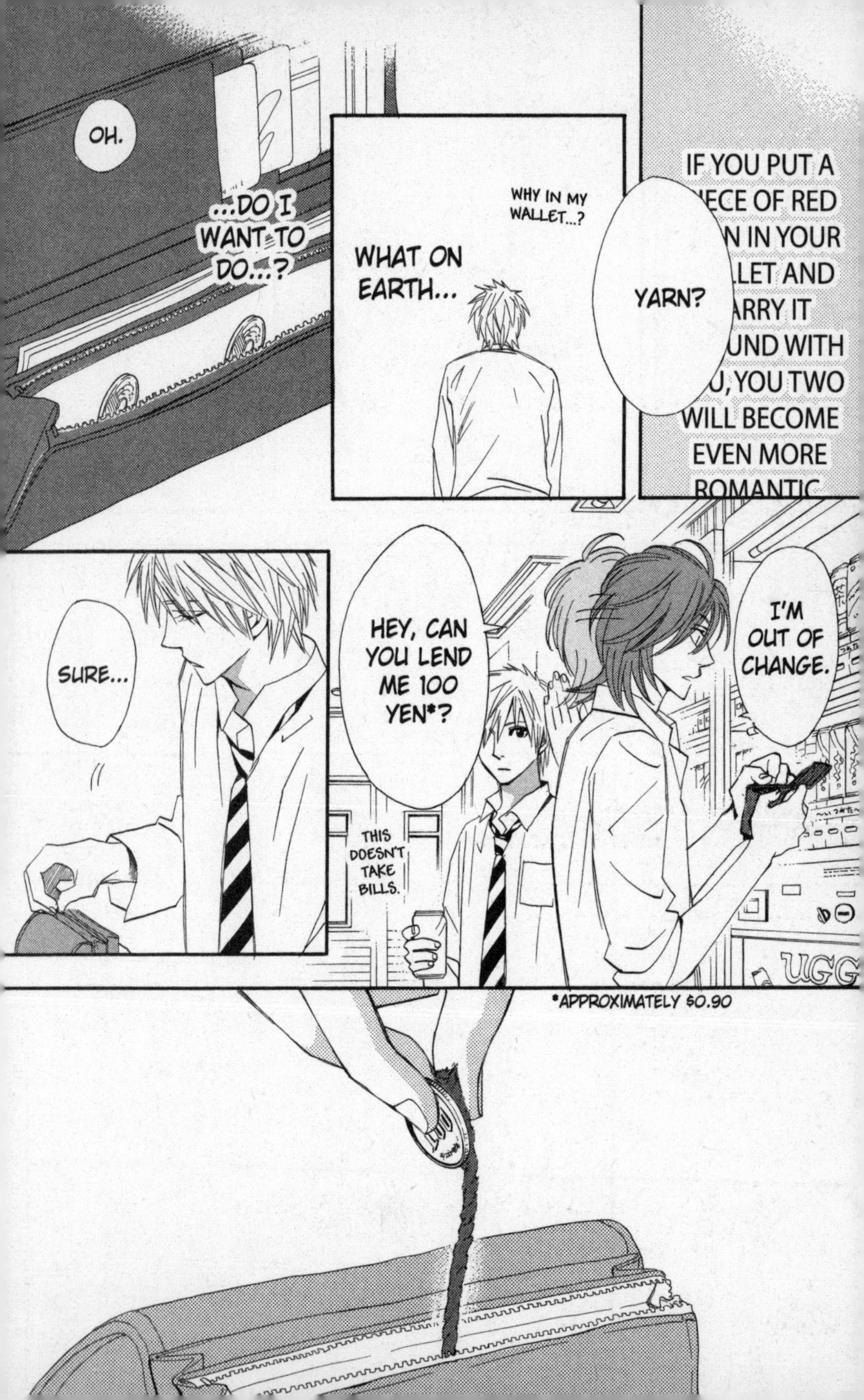
IF YOU PUT A
IECE OF RED
N IN YOUR
LLET AND
ARRY IT
UND WITH
U, YOU TWO
WILL BECOME
EVEN MORE
ROMANTIC
YARN?
WHY IN MY WALLET...?
WHAT ON EARTH...
...DO I WANT TO DO...?
OH.
I'M OUT OF CHANGE.
HEY, CAN YOU LEND ME 100 YEN*?
THIS DOESN'T TAKE BILLS.
UGG
SURE...
*APPROXIMATELY $0.90

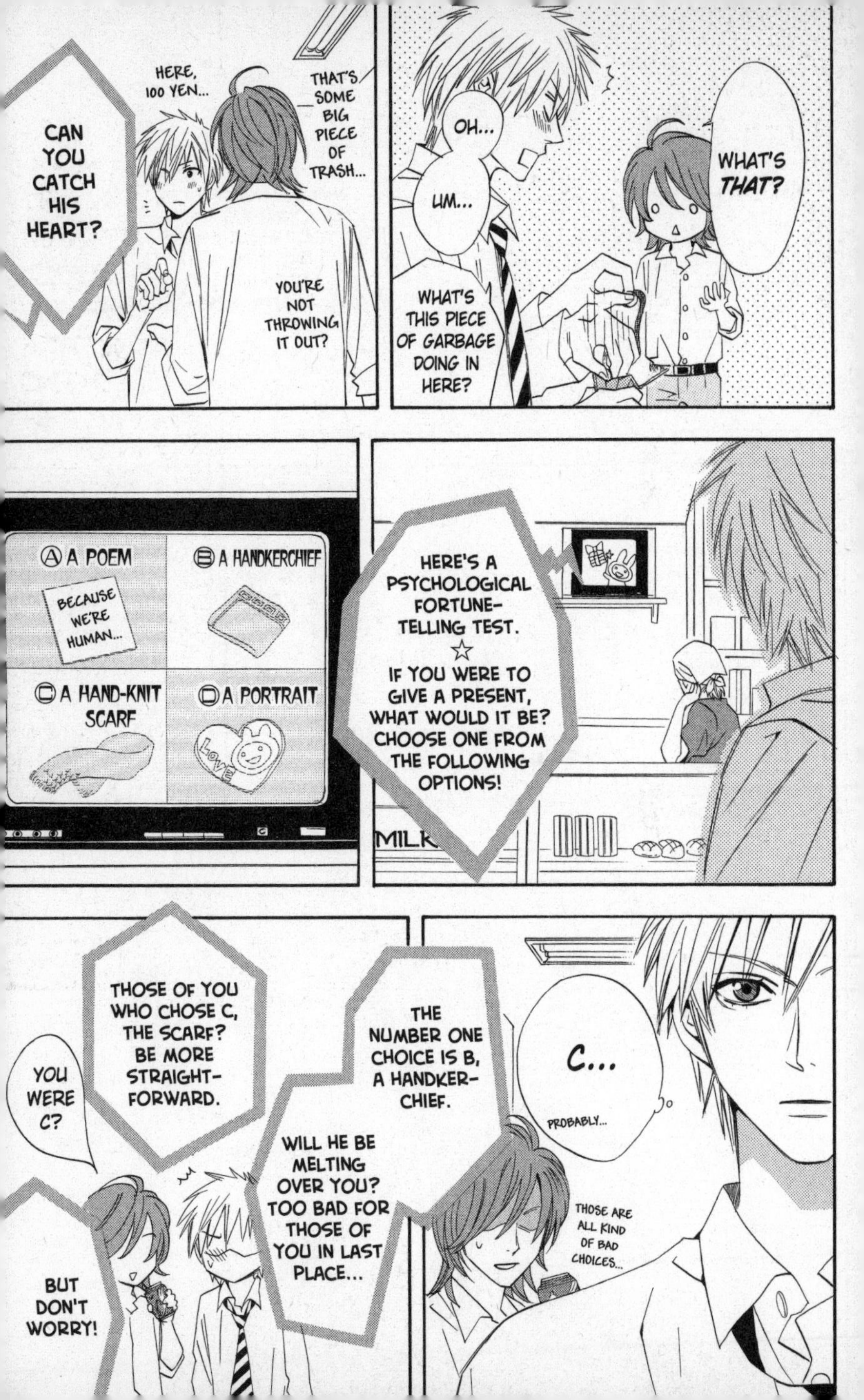
WHAT'S *THAT?*
OH...
UM...
WHAT'S THIS PIECE OF GARBAGE DOING IN HERE?
THAT'S SOME BIG PIECE OF TRASH...
HERE, 100 YEN...
CAN YOU CATCH HIS HEART?
YOU'RE NOT THROWING IT OUT?
HERE'S A PSYCHOLOGICAL FORTUNE-TELLING TEST. ☆ IF YOU WERE TO GIVE A PRESENT, WHAT WOULD IT BE? CHOOSE ONE FROM THE FOLLOWING OPTIONS!
MILK
Ⓐ A POEM
BECAUSE WE'RE HUMAN...
Ⓑ A HANDKERCHIEF
Ⓒ A HAND-KNIT SCARF
Ⓓ A PORTRAIT
LOVE
C...
PROBABLY...
THE NUMBER ONE CHOICE IS B, A HANDKER-CHIEF.
THOSE ARE ALL KIND OF BAD CHOICES...
THOSE OF YOU WHO CHOSE C, THE SCARF? BE MORE STRAIGHT-FORWARD.
YOU WERE C?
WILL HE BE MELTING OVER YOU? TOO BAD FOR THOSE OF YOU IN LAST PLACE...
BUT DON'T WORRY!

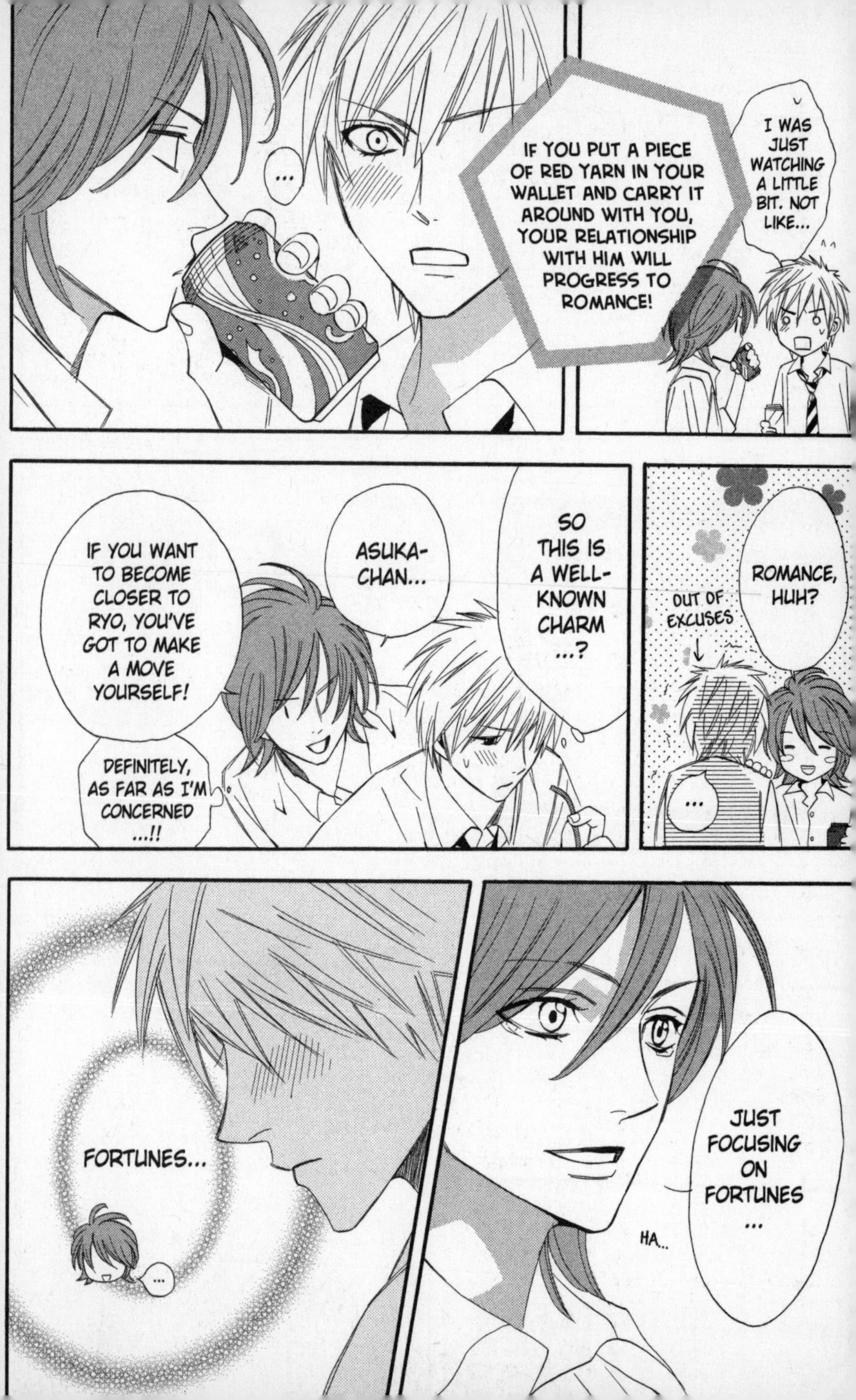
I WAS JUST WATCHING A LITTLE BIT. NOT LIKE...
IF YOU PUT A PIECE OF RED YARN IN YOUR WALLET AND CARRY IT AROUND WITH YOU, YOUR RELATIONSHIP WITH HIM WILL PROGRESS TO ROMANCE!
...
ROMANCE, HUH?
OUT OF EXCUSES
...
SO THIS IS A WELL-KNOWN CHARM ...?
ASUKA-CHAN...
IF YOU WANT TO BECOME CLOSER TO RYO, YOU'VE GOT TO MAKE A MOVE YOURSELF!
DEFINITELY, AS FAR AS I'M CONCERNED ...!!
JUST FOCUSING ON FORTUNES ...
HA...
FORTUNES...
...

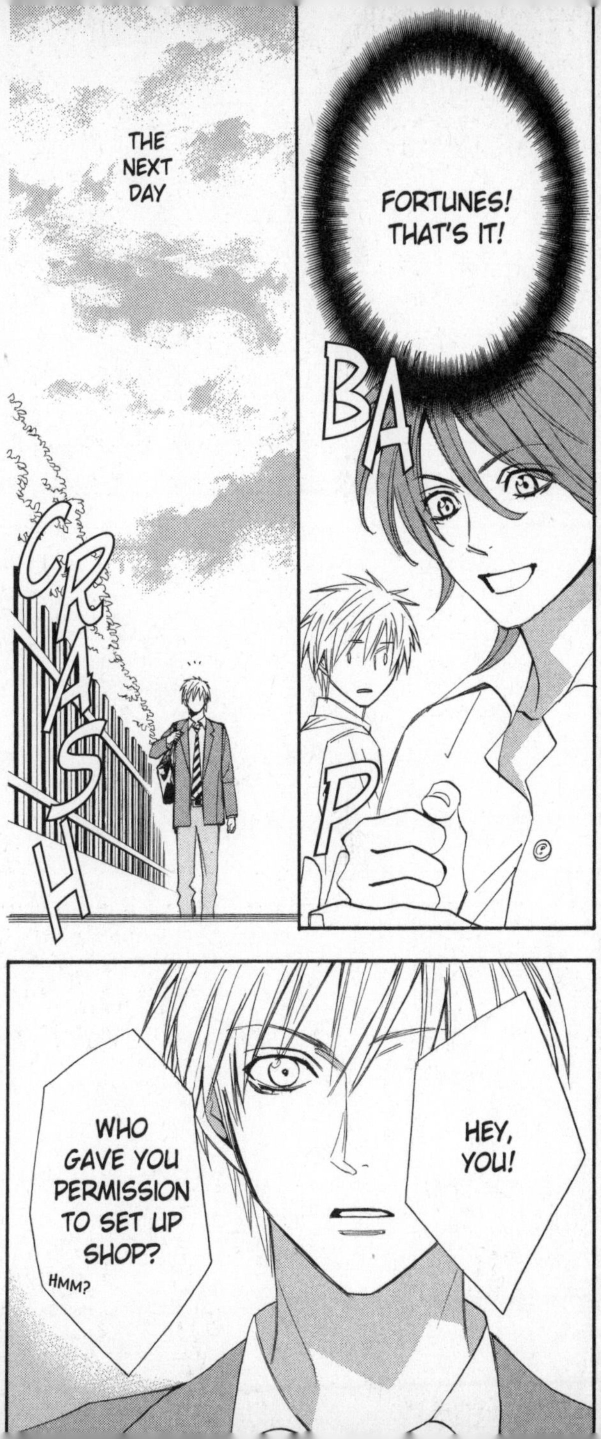
FORTUNES! THAT'S IT!
BAP
THE NEXT DAY
CRASH
HEY, YOU!
WHO GAVE YOU PERMISSION TO SET UP SHOP?
HMM?

Production Assistance:
Shimada-san
Koinuma-san
Kawashima-san
Sayaka-san
Kuwana-san
Tanaka-san
Nishizawa-san
Kaneko-san
Suzuki-san
Fujimoto-san

Special Thanks:
Yutaka-san
Abe-san
Abewo
My Readers

Thank you for reading. I'd be happy if we can meet again.

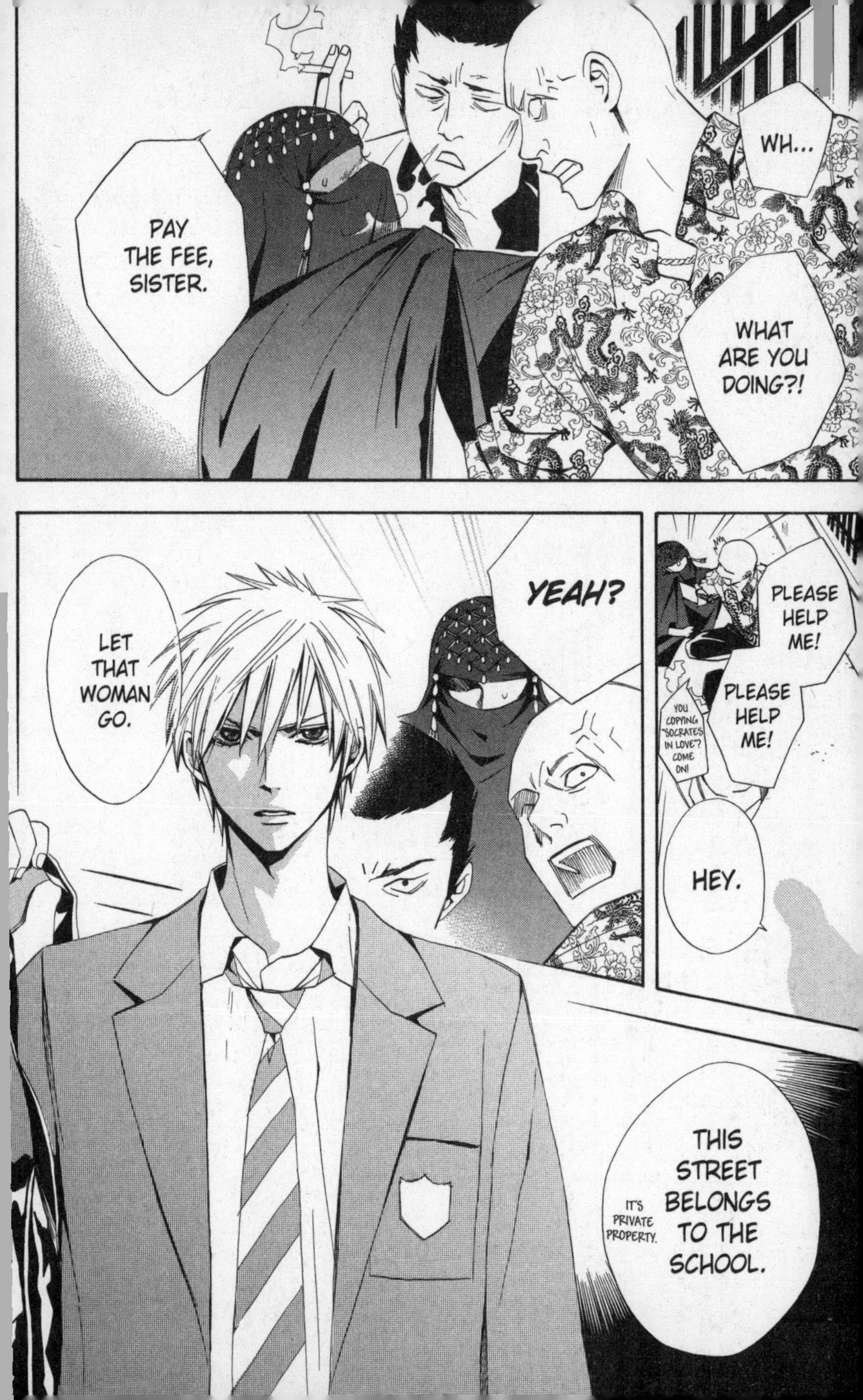

WH...
WHAT ARE YOU DOING?!
PAY THE FEE, SISTER.
PLEASE HELP ME!
PLEASE HELP ME!
YOU COPYING "SOCRATES IN LOVE"? COME ON!
HEY.
YEAH?
LET THAT WOMAN GO.
THIS STREET BELONGS TO THE SCHOOL.
IT'S PRIVATE PROPERTY.

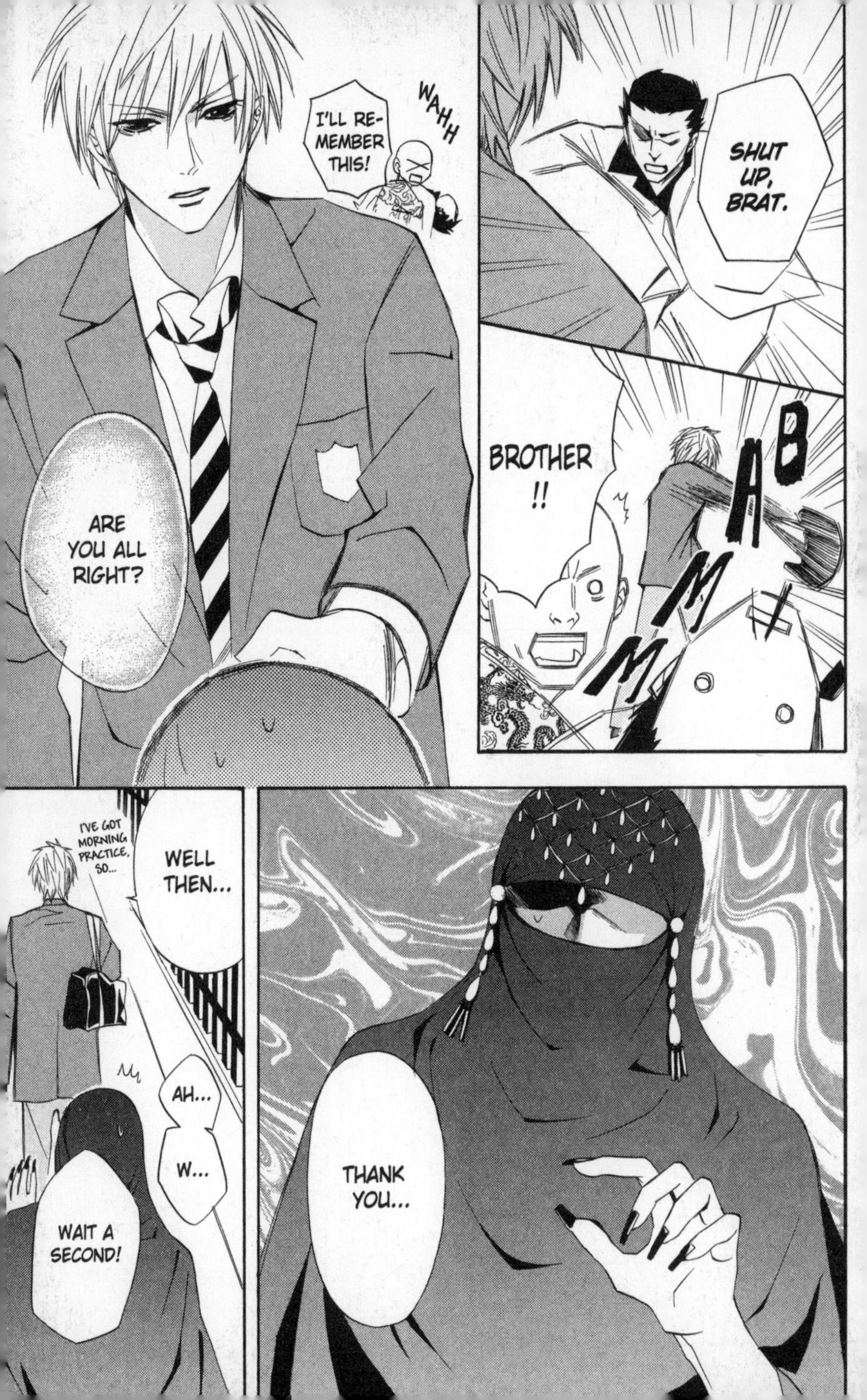
SHUT UP, BRAT.
BROTHER !!
BAMM
I'LL RE-MEMBER THIS!
WAHH
ARE YOU ALL RIGHT?
THANK YOU...
WELL THEN...
I'VE GOT MORNING PRACTICE, SO...
AH...
W...
WAIT A SECOND!

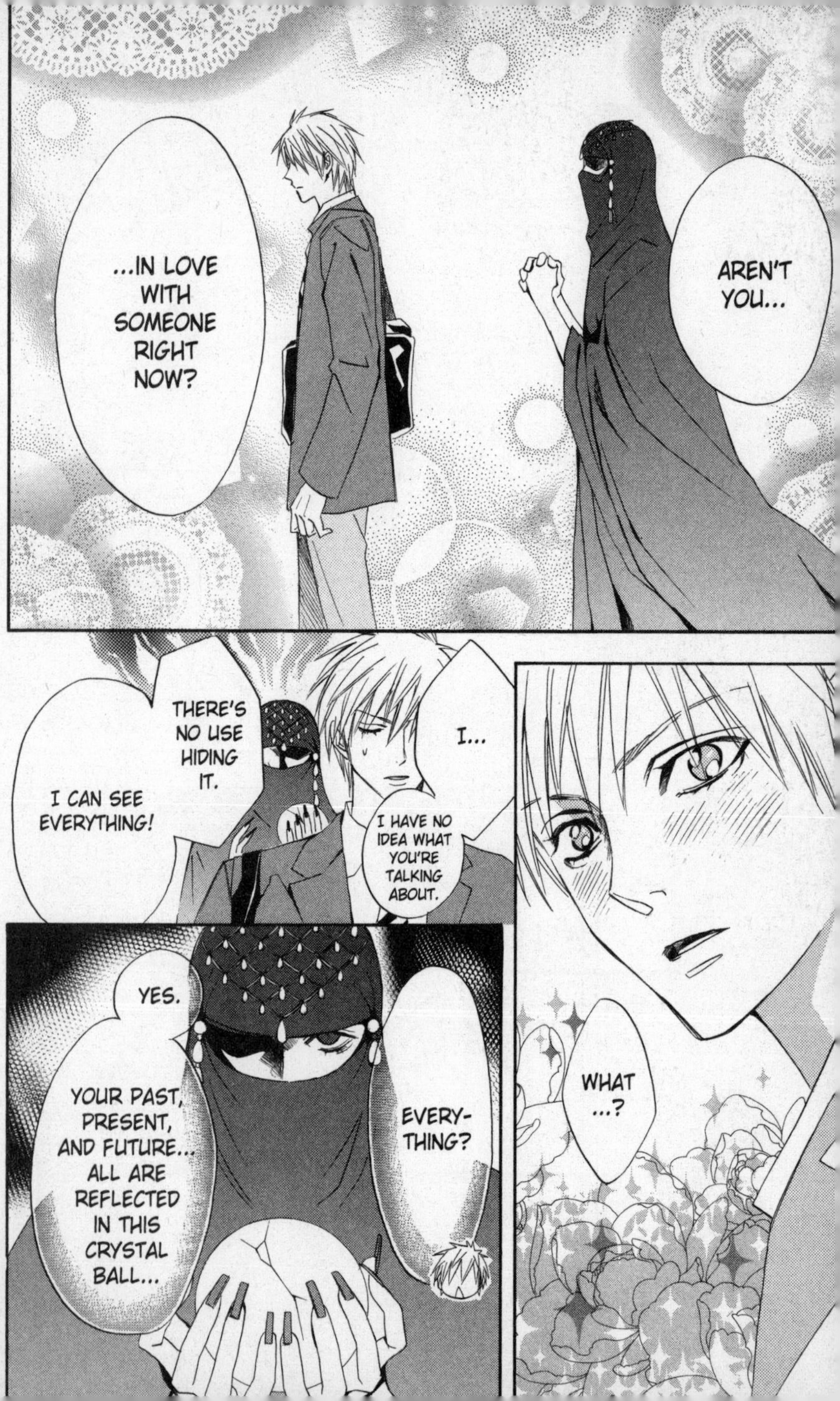
AREN'T YOU...
...IN LOVE WITH SOMEONE RIGHT NOW?
I...
I HAVE NO IDEA WHAT YOU'RE TALKING ABOUT.
THERE'S NO USE HIDING IT.
I CAN SEE EVERYTHING!
WHAT ...?
EVERY-THING?
YES.
YOUR PAST, PRESENT, AND FUTURE... ALL ARE REFLECTED IN THIS CRYSTAL BALL...

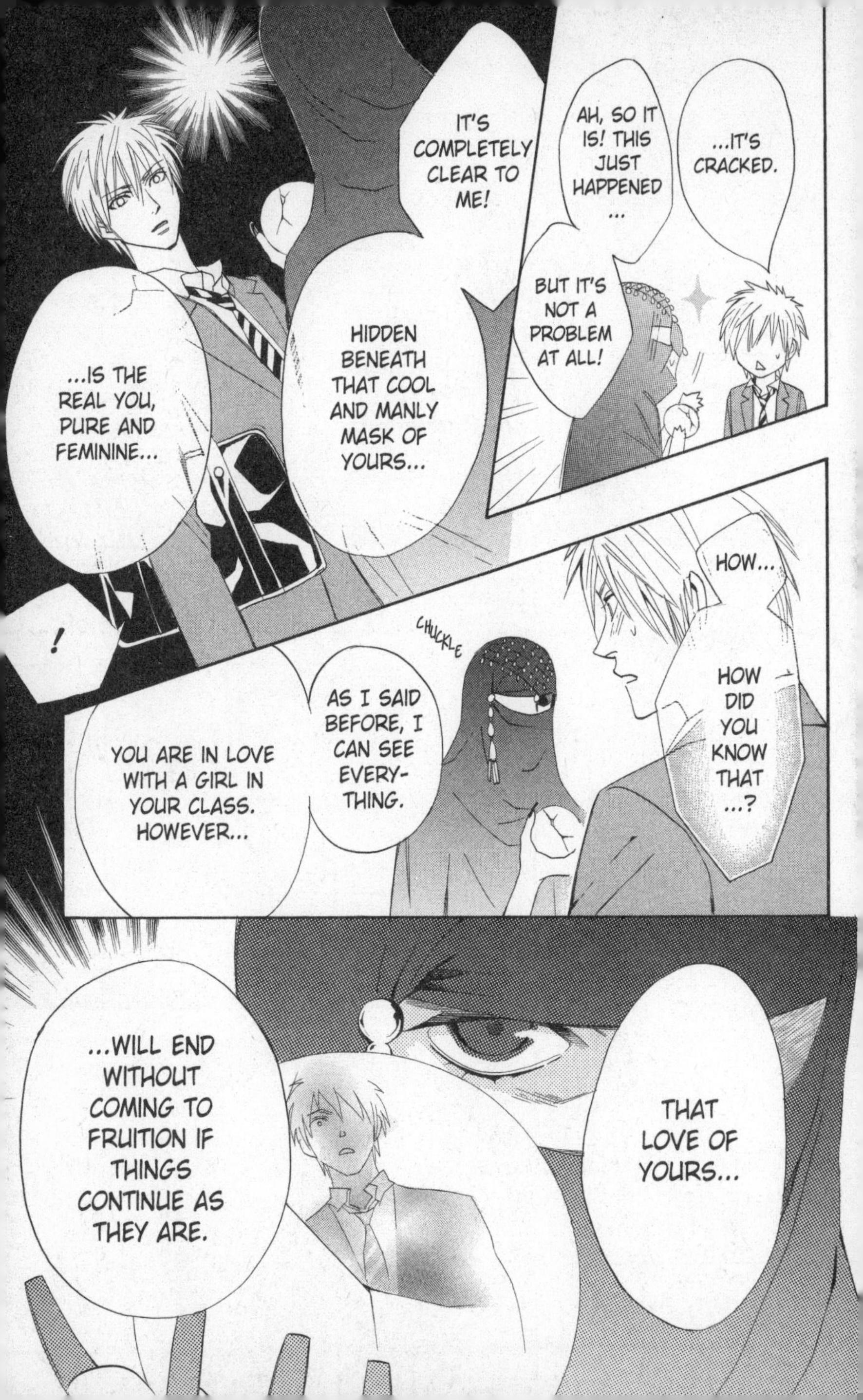
...IT'S CRACKED.
AH, SO IT IS! THIS JUST HAPPENED...
BUT IT'S NOT A PROBLEM AT ALL!
IT'S COMPLETELY CLEAR TO ME!
HIDDEN BENEATH THAT COOL AND MANLY MASK OF YOURS...
...IS THE REAL YOU, PURE AND FEMININE...
!
HOW...
HOW DID YOU KNOW THAT...?
CHUCKLE
AS I SAID BEFORE, I CAN SEE EVERY-THING.
YOU ARE IN LOVE WITH A GIRL IN YOUR CLASS. HOWEVER...
THAT LOVE OF YOURS...
...WILL END WITHOUT COMING TO FRUITION IF THINGS CONTINUE AS THEY ARE.

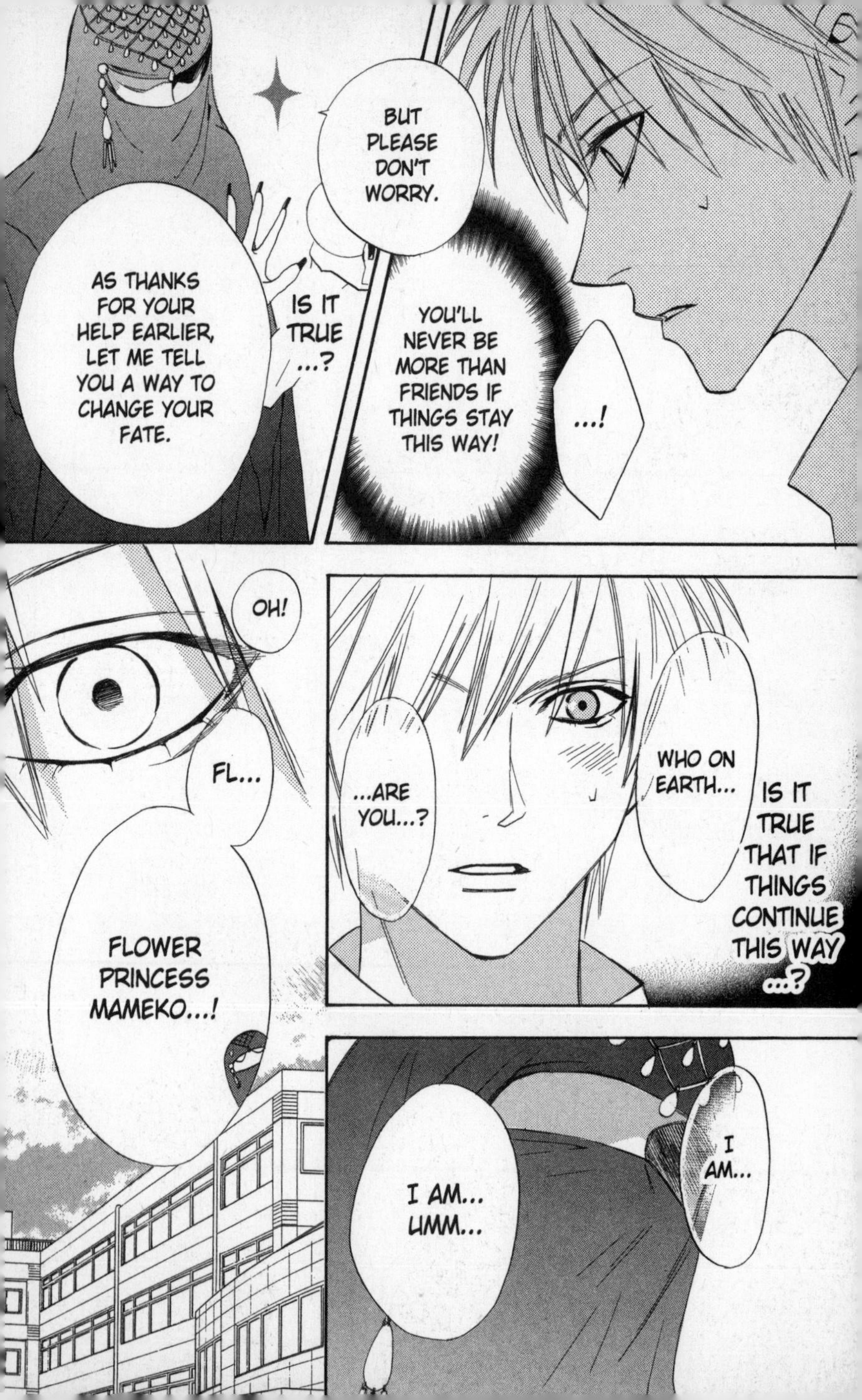
BUT PLEASE DON'T WORRY.
YOU'LL NEVER BE MORE THAN FRIENDS IF THINGS STAY THIS WAY!
...!
IS IT TRUE ...?
AS THANKS FOR YOUR HELP EARLIER, LET ME TELL YOU A WAY TO CHANGE YOUR FATE.
IS IT TRUE THAT IF THINGS CONTINUE THIS WAY ...?
WHO ON EARTH...
...ARE YOU...?
OH!
FL...
FLOWER PRINCESS MAMEKO...!
I AM...
I AM... UMM...

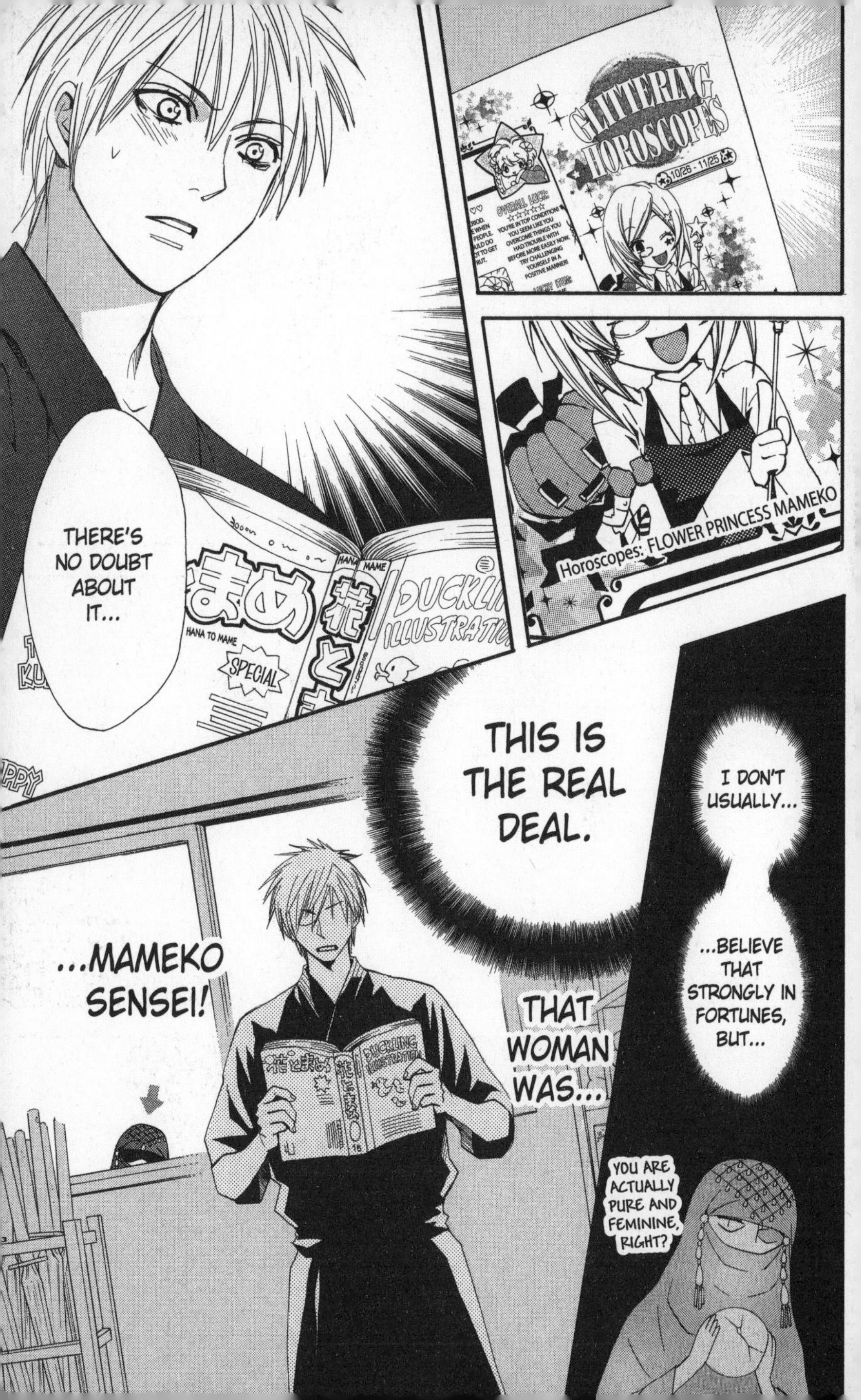
GLITTERING HOROSCOPES
10/26 - 11/25
OVERALL LUCK:
YOU'RE IN TOP CONDITION! YOU SEEM LIKE YOU OVERCOME THINGS YOU HAD TROUBLE WITH BEFORE MORE EASILY NOW. TRY CHALLENGING YOURSELF IN A POSITIVE MANNER!
Horoscopes: FLOWER PRINCESS MAMEKO
THERE'S NO DOUBT ABOUT IT...
HANA MAME
HANA TO MAME
SPECIAL
I DON'T USUALLY...
...BELIEVE THAT STRONGLY IN FORTUNES, BUT...
YOU ARE ACTUALLY PURE AND FEMININE, RIGHT?
THIS IS THE REAL DEAL.
THAT WOMAN WAS...
...MAMEKO SENSEI!
DUCKLING ILLUSTRATION

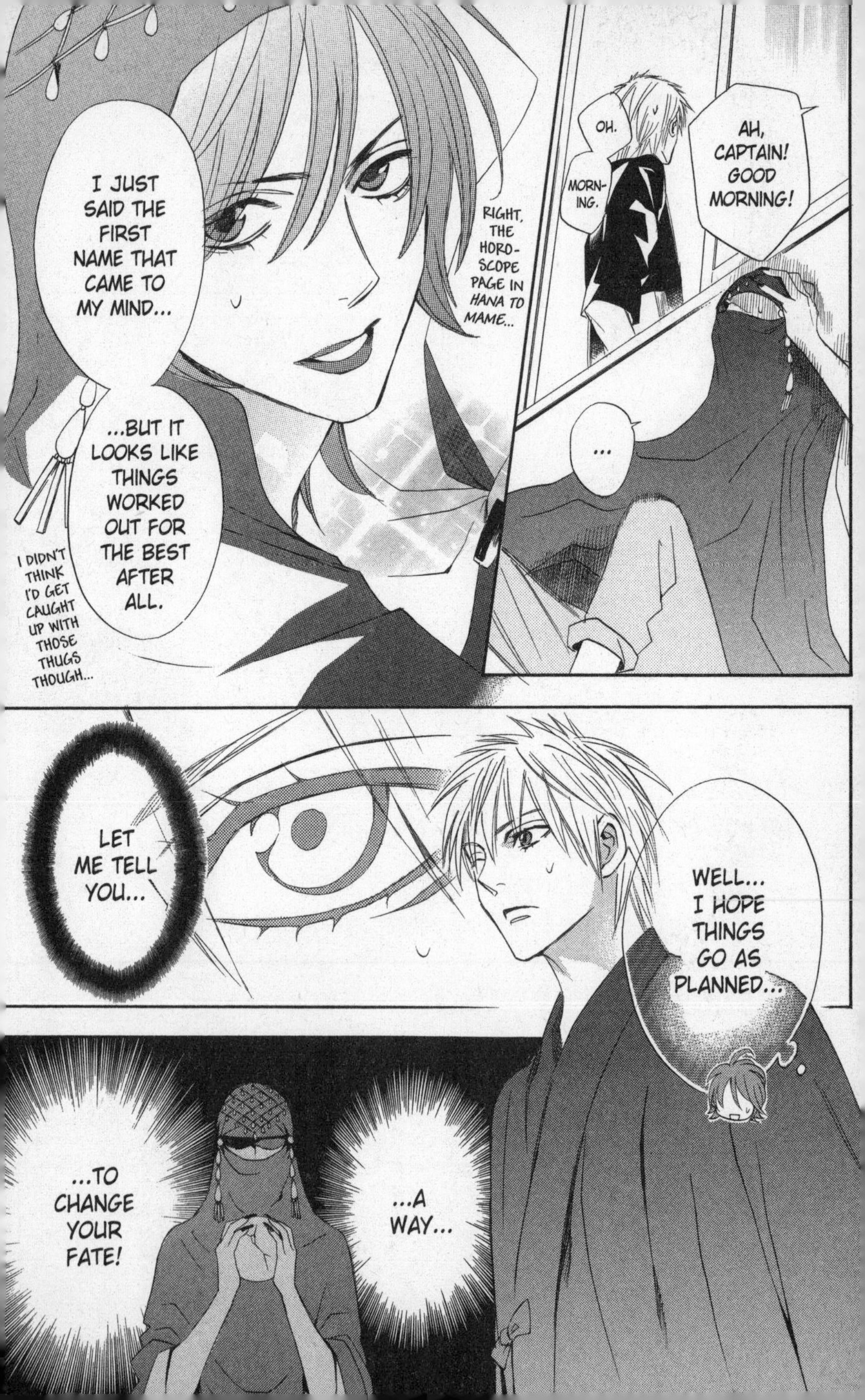
AH, CAPTAIN! GOOD MORNING!
OH.
MORNING.
...
RIGHT, THE HOROSCOPE PAGE IN HANA TO MAME...
I JUST SAID THE FIRST NAME THAT CAME TO MY MIND...
...BUT IT LOOKS LIKE THINGS WORKED OUT FOR THE BEST AFTER ALL.
I DIDN'T THINK I'D GET CAUGHT UP WITH THOSE THUGS THOUGH...
WELL... I HOPE THINGS GO AS PLANNED...
LET ME TELL YOU...
...A WAY...
...TO CHANGE YOUR FATE!

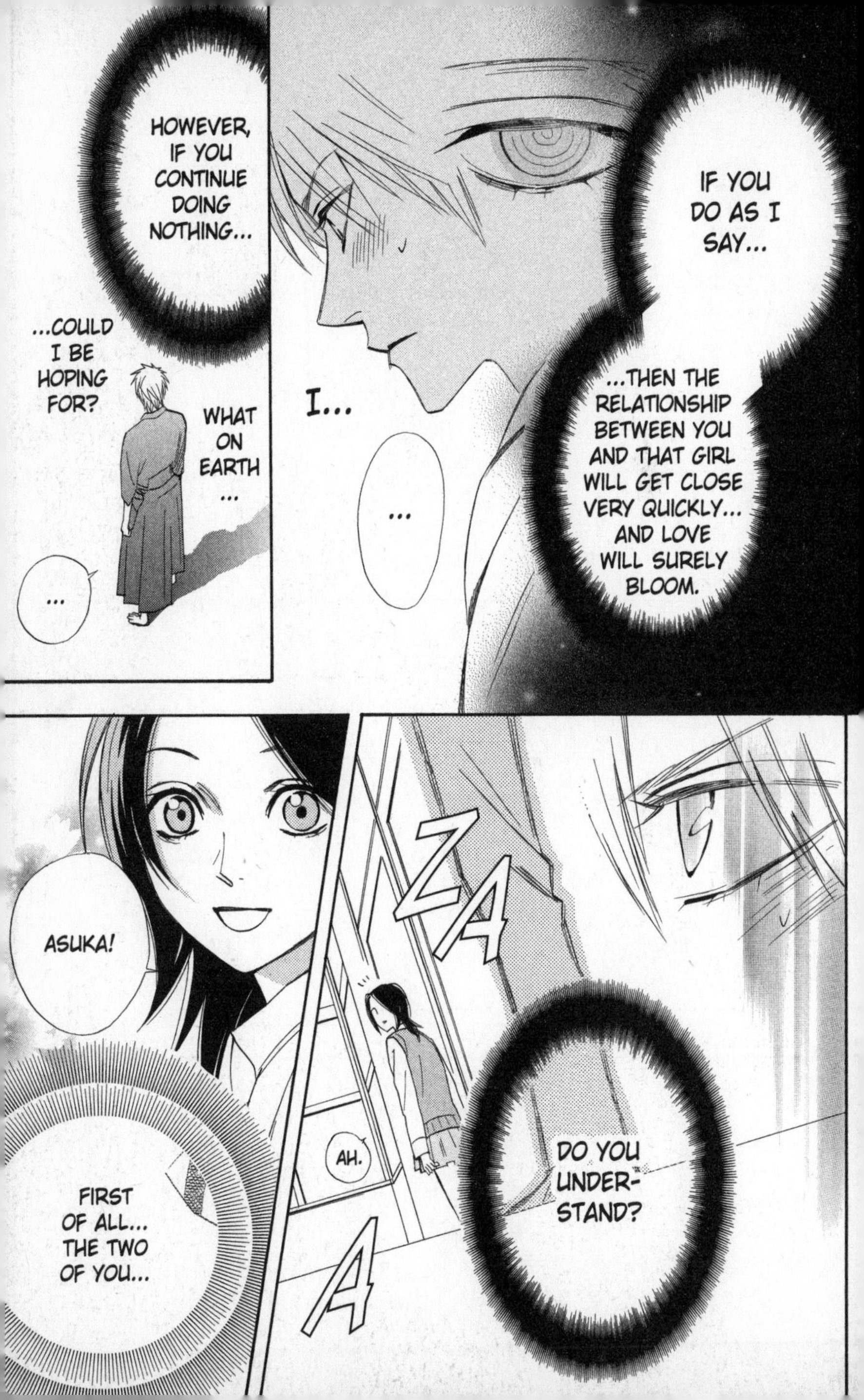
IF YOU DO AS I SAY...
...THEN THE RELATIONSHIP BETWEEN YOU AND THAT GIRL WILL GET CLOSE VERY QUICKLY... AND LOVE WILL SURELY BLOOM.
I...
...
HOWEVER, IF YOU CONTINUE DOING NOTHING...
WHAT ON EARTH ...
...COULD I BE HOPING FOR?
...
ZA
DO YOU UNDER-STAND?
A
AH.
ASUKA!
FIRST OF ALL... THE TWO OF YOU...

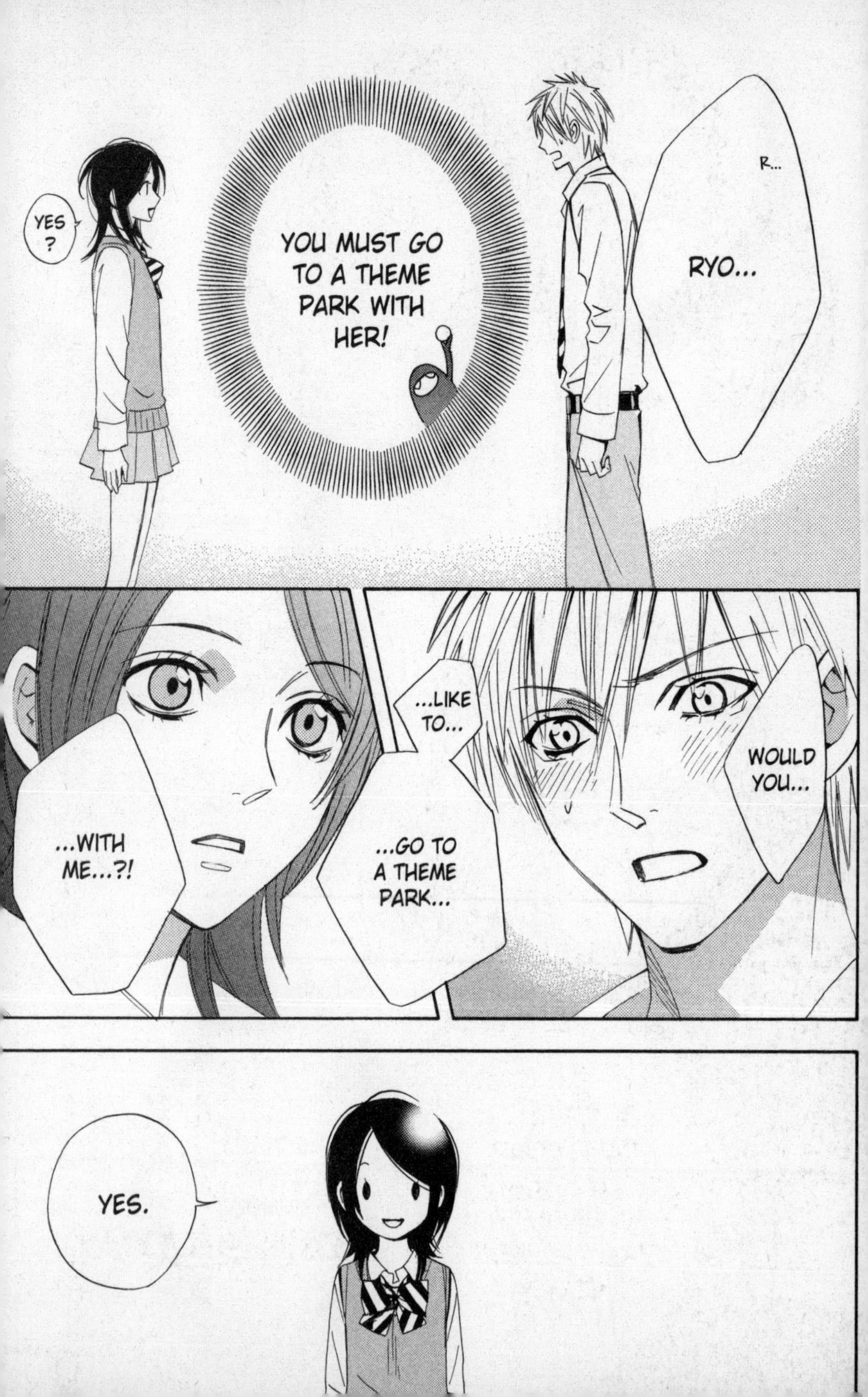
R...
RYO...
YOU MUST GO TO A THEME PARK WITH HER!
YES ?
WOULD YOU...
...LIKE TO...
...GO TO A THEME PARK...
...WITH ME...?!
YES.

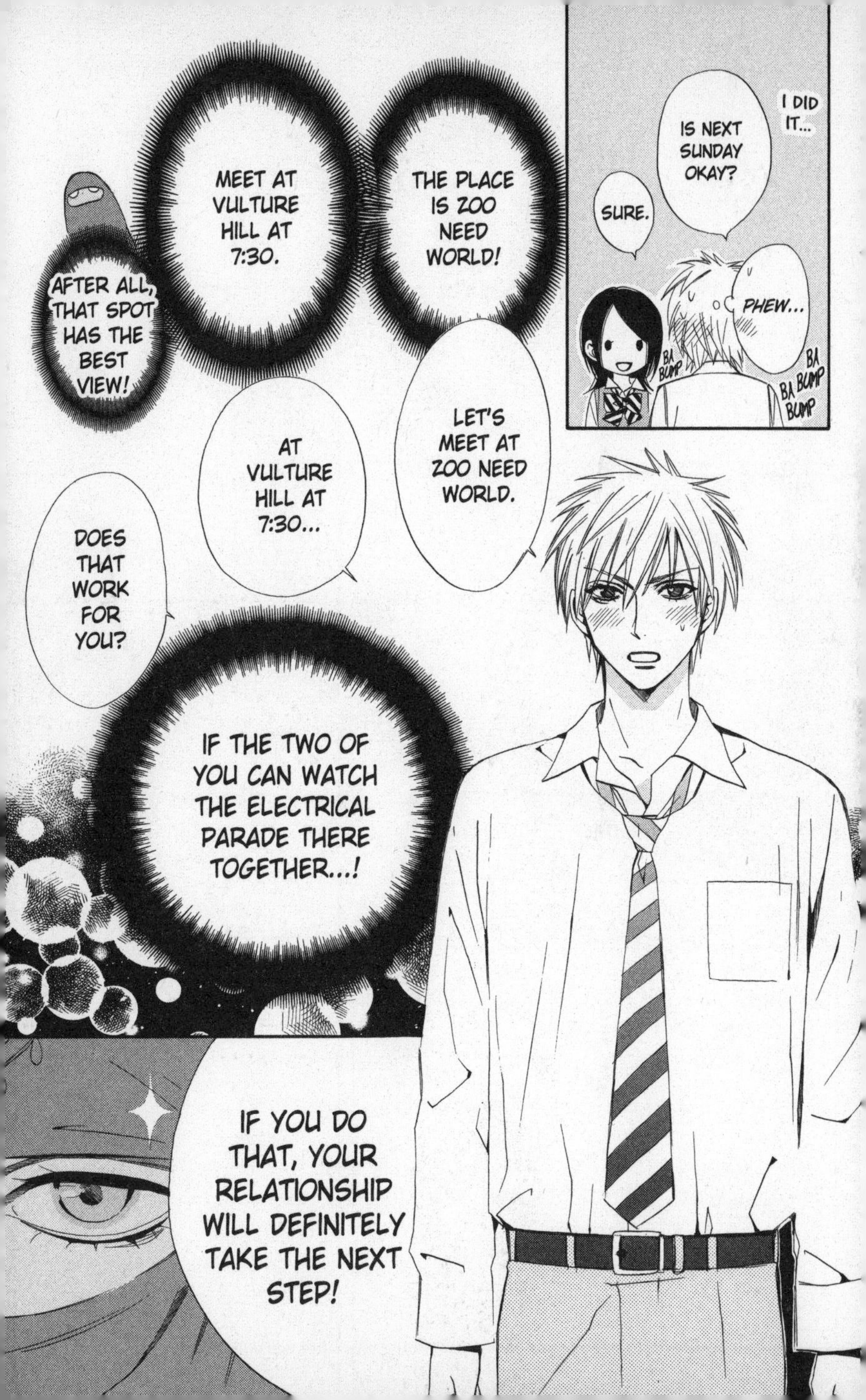
I DID IT...
IS NEXT SUNDAY OKAY?
SURE.
PHEW...
BA BUMP
BA BUMP
BA BUMP
BA BUMP
THE PLACE IS ZOO NEED WORLD!
MEET AT VULTURE HILL AT 7:30.
AFTER ALL, THAT SPOT HAS THE BEST VIEW!
LET'S MEET AT ZOO NEED WORLD.
AT VULTURE HILL AT 7:30...
DOES THAT WORK FOR YOU?
IF THE TWO OF YOU CAN WATCH THE ELECTRICAL PARADE THERE TOGETHER...!
IF YOU DO THAT, YOUR RELATIONSHIP WILL DEFINITELY TAKE THE NEXT STEP!

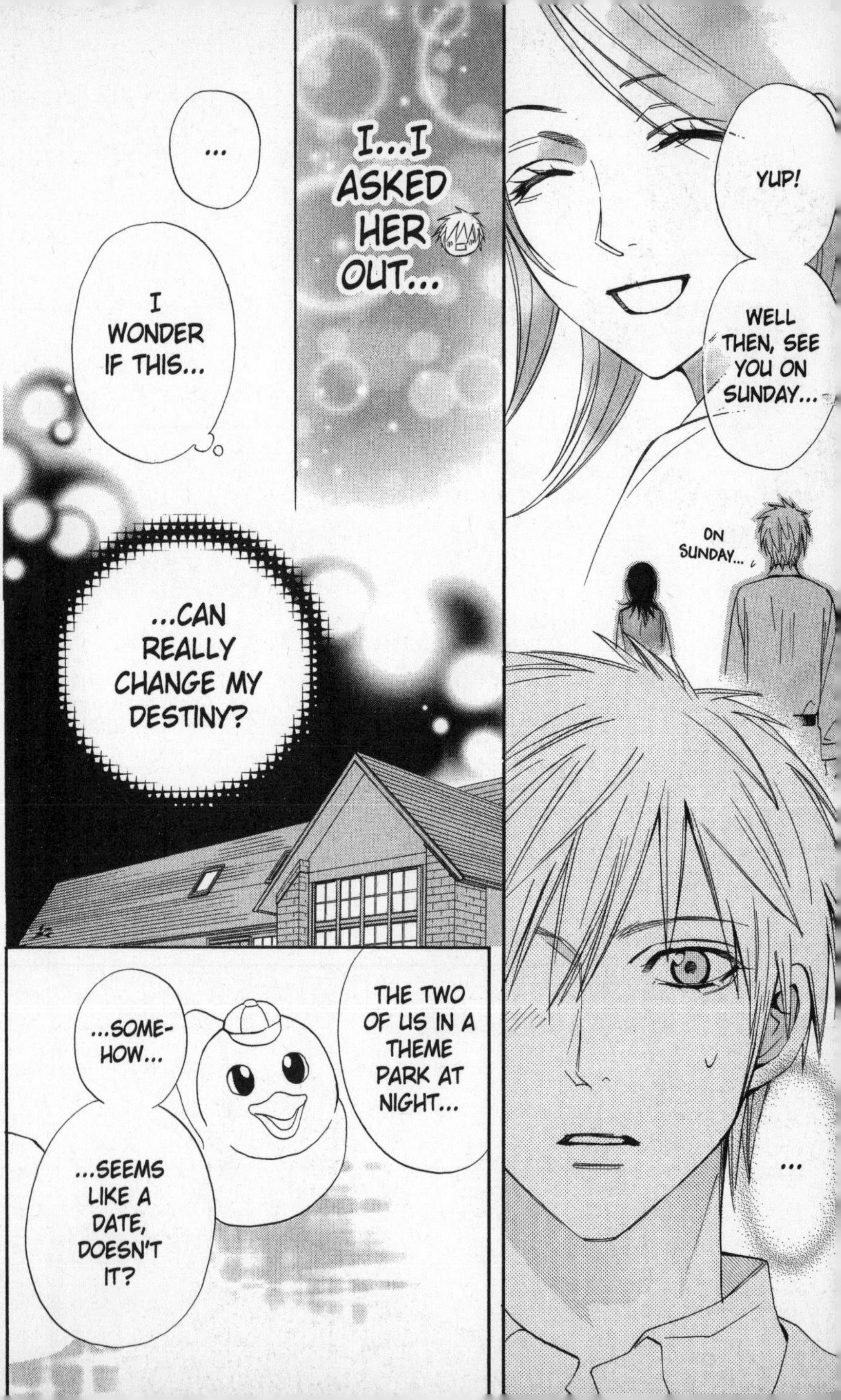
YUP!
WELL THEN, SEE YOU ON SUNDAY...
ON SUNDAY...
...
I...I ASKED HER OUT...
...
I WONDER IF THIS...
...CAN REALLY CHANGE MY DESTINY?
THE TWO OF US IN A THEME PARK AT NIGHT...
...SOME-HOW...
...SEEMS LIKE A DATE, DOESN'T IT?

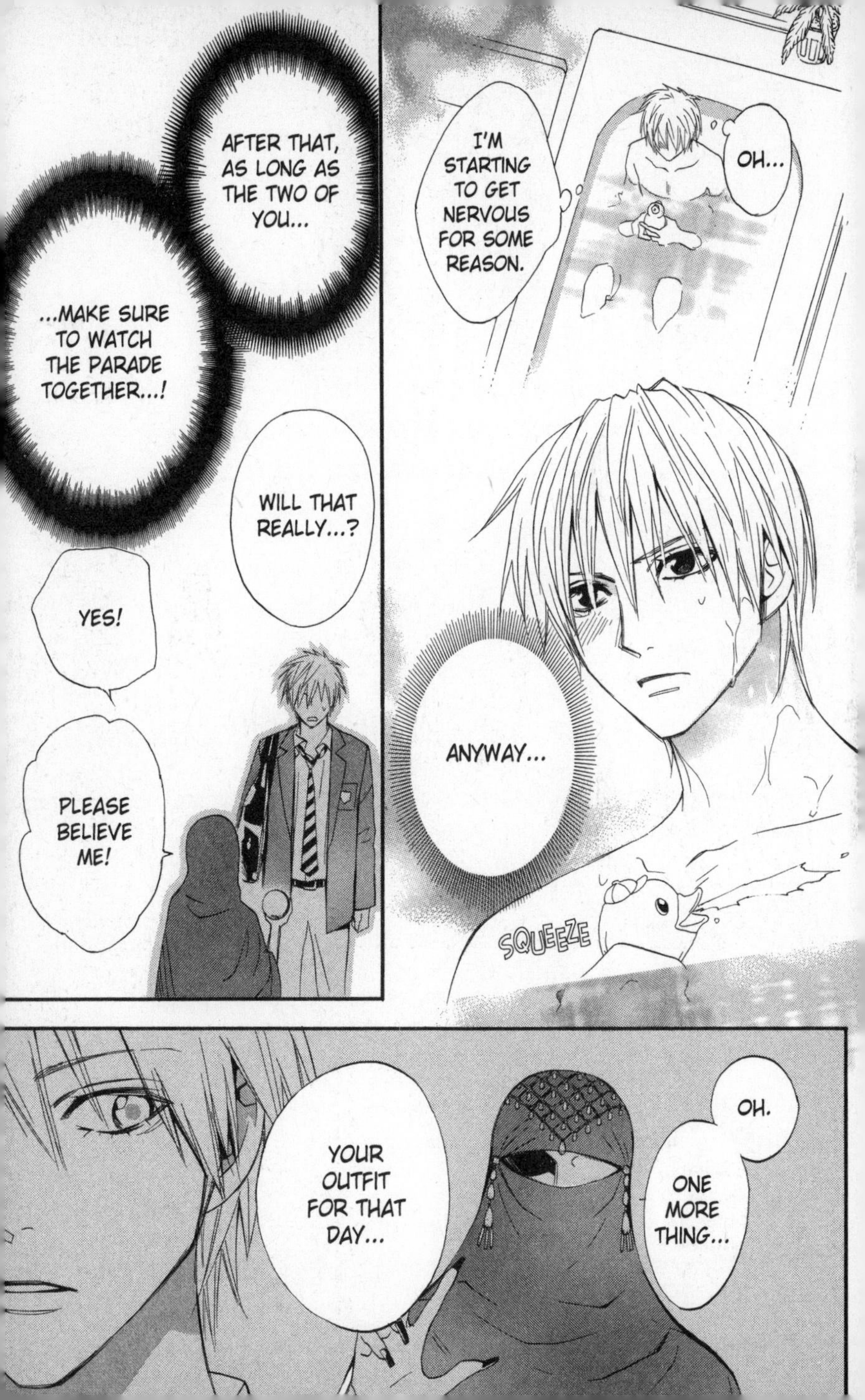
OH...
I'M STARTING TO GET NERVOUS FOR SOME REASON.
ANYWAY...
SQUEEZE
AFTER THAT, AS LONG AS THE TWO OF YOU...
...MAKE SURE TO WATCH THE PARADE TOGETHER...!
WILL THAT REALLY...?
YES!
PLEASE BELIEVE ME!
OH.
ONE MORE THING...
YOUR OUTFIT FOR THAT DAY...

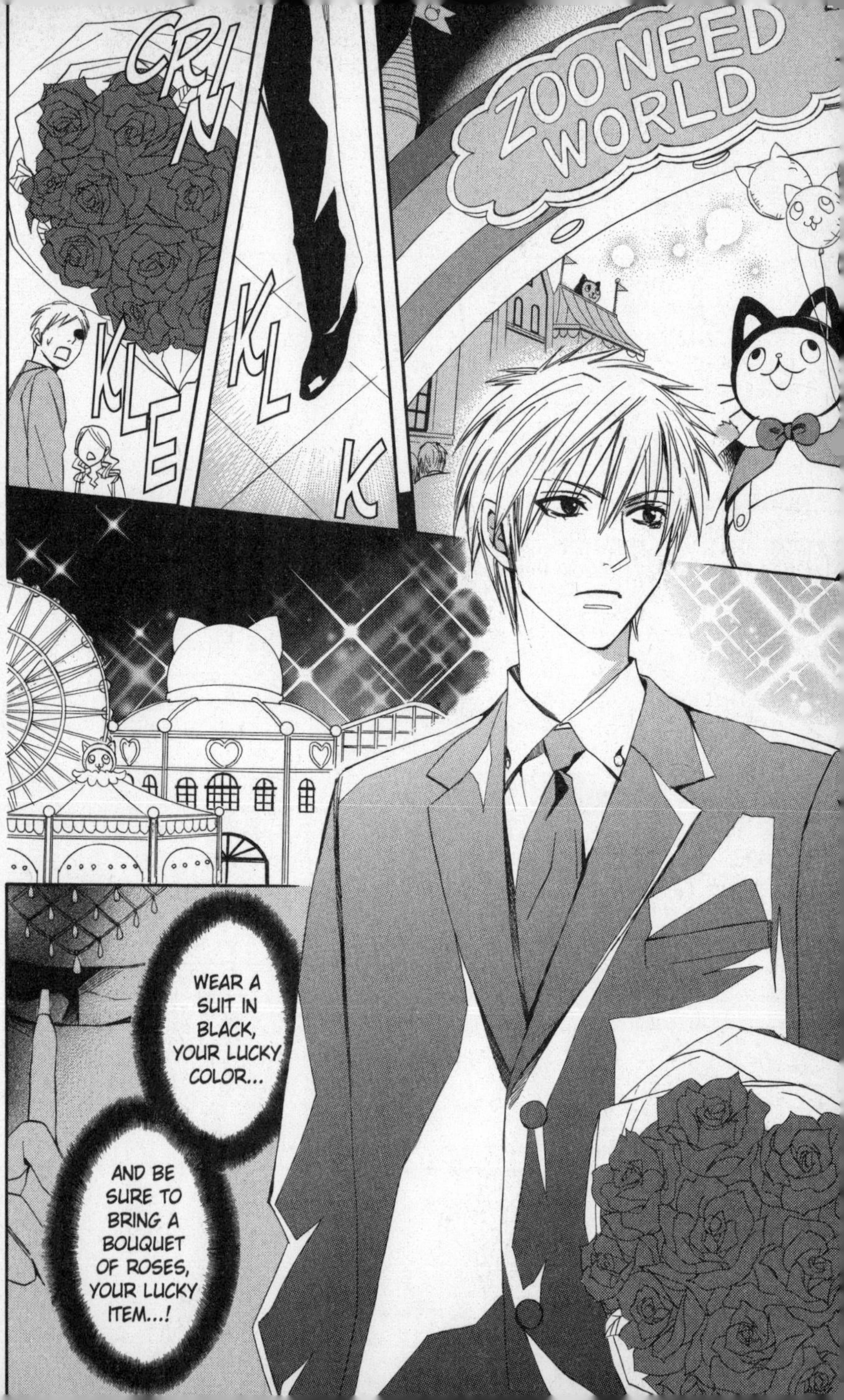
ZOO NEED WORLD
KLK
CRINKLE
WEAR A SUIT IN BLACK, YOUR LUCKY COLOR...
AND BE SURE TO BRING A BOUQUET OF ROSES, YOUR LUCKY ITEM...!

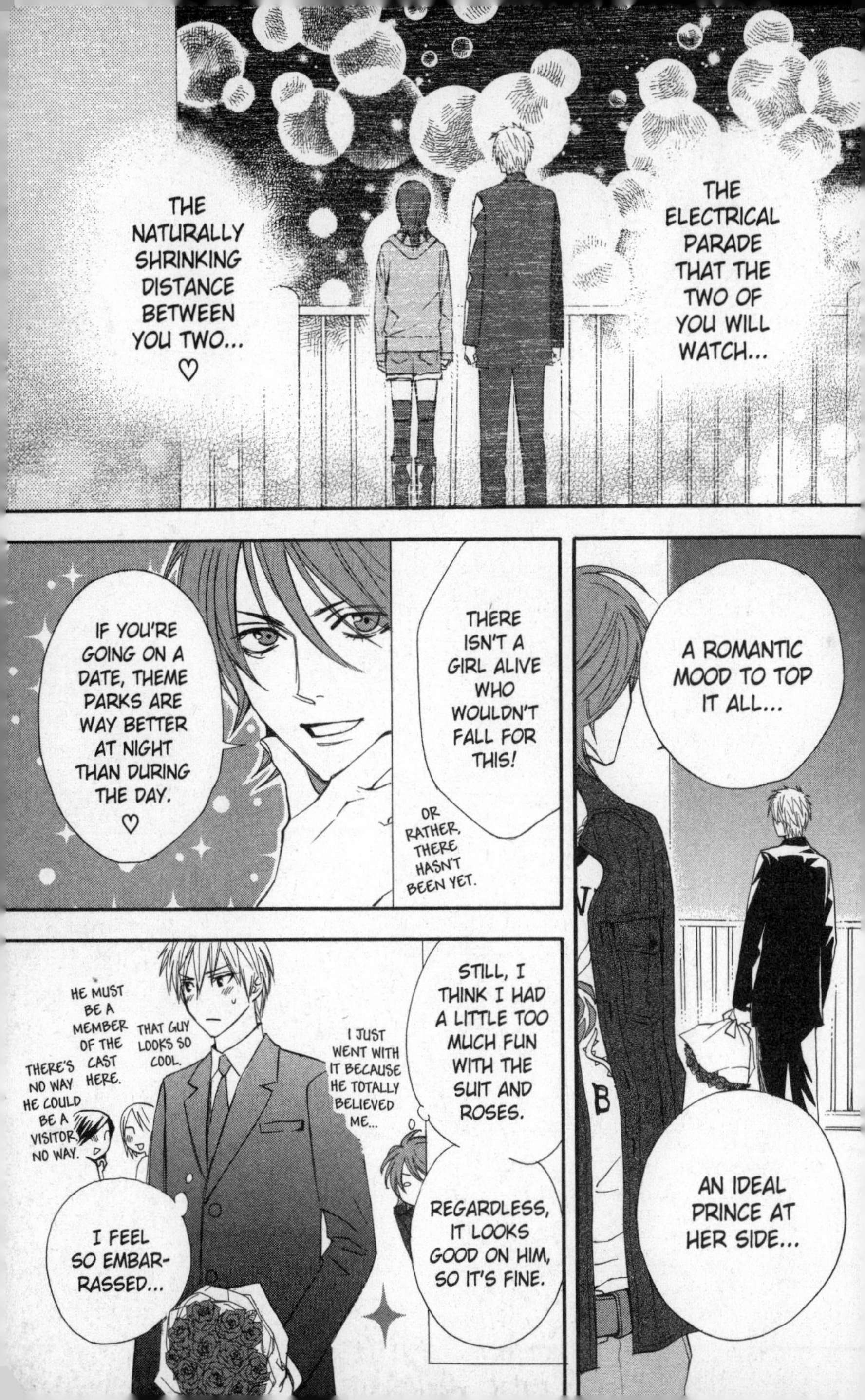
THE ELECTRICAL PARADE THAT THE TWO OF YOU WILL WATCH...
THE NATURALLY SHRINKING DISTANCE BETWEEN YOU TWO... ♡
A ROMANTIC MOOD TO TOP IT ALL...
AN IDEAL PRINCE AT HER SIDE...
THERE ISN'T A GIRL ALIVE WHO WOULDN'T FALL FOR THIS!
OR RATHER, THERE HASN'T BEEN YET.
IF YOU'RE GOING ON A DATE, THEME PARKS ARE WAY BETTER AT NIGHT THAN DURING THE DAY. ♡
STILL, I THINK I HAD A LITTLE TOO MUCH FUN WITH THE SUIT AND ROSES.
REGARDLESS, IT LOOKS GOOD ON HIM, SO IT'S FINE.
I JUST WENT WITH IT BECAUSE HE TOTALLY BELIEVED ME...
THAT GUY LOOKS SO COOL.
HE MUST BE A MEMBER OF THE CAST HERE.
THERE'S NO WAY HE COULD BE A VISITOR, NO WAY.
I FEEL SO EMBARRASSED...

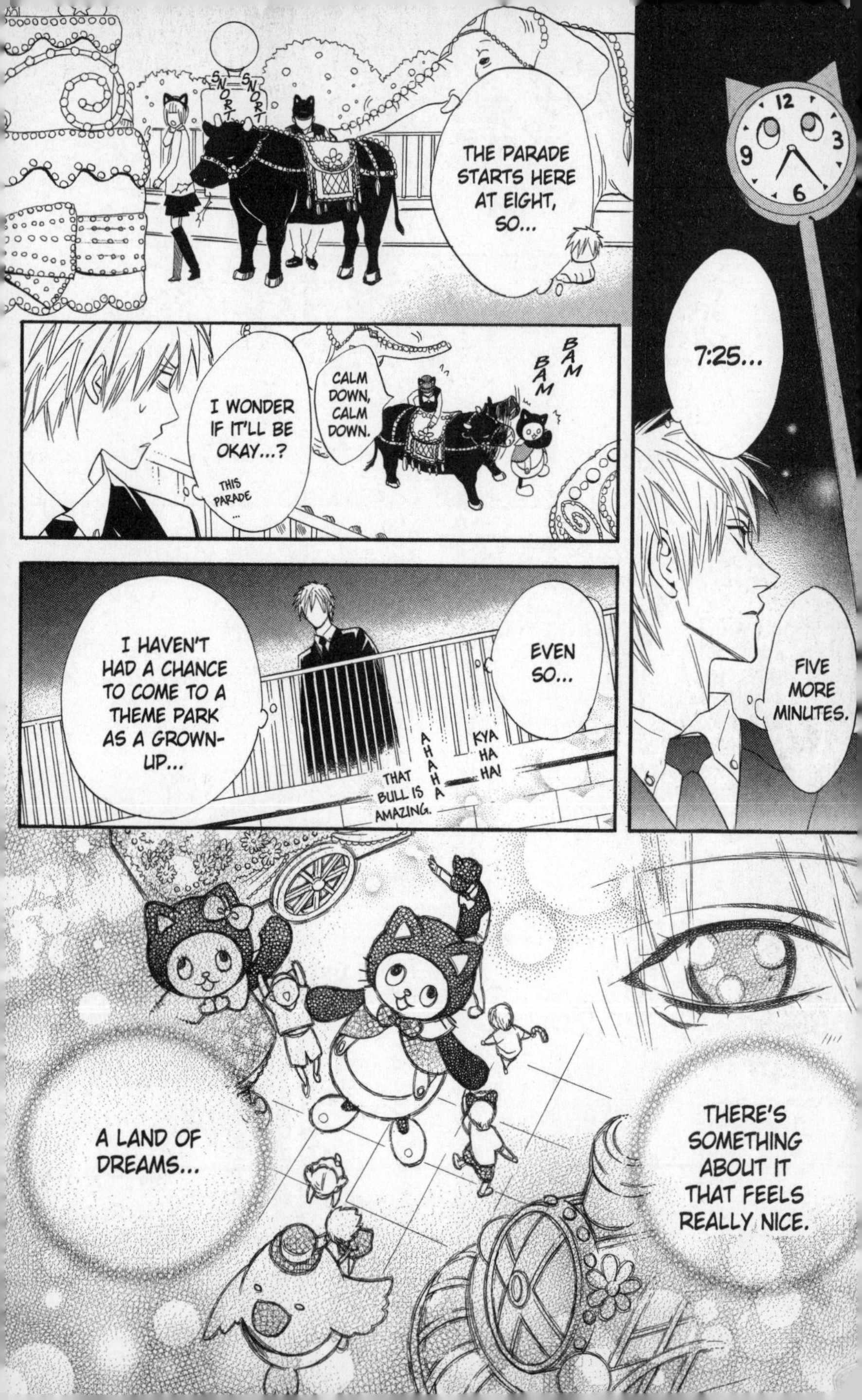
7:25...
FIVE MORE MINUTES.
THE PARADE STARTS HERE AT EIGHT, SO...
SNORT
SNORT
BAM BAM
CALM DOWN, CALM DOWN.
I WONDER IF IT'LL BE OKAY...?
THIS PARADE ...
EVEN SO...
KYA HA HA!
AHAHAHA
THAT BULL IS AMAZING.
I HAVEN'T HAD A CHANCE TO COME TO A THEME PARK AS A GROWN-UP...
THERE'S SOMETHING ABOUT IT THAT FEELS REALLY NICE.
A LAND OF DREAMS...

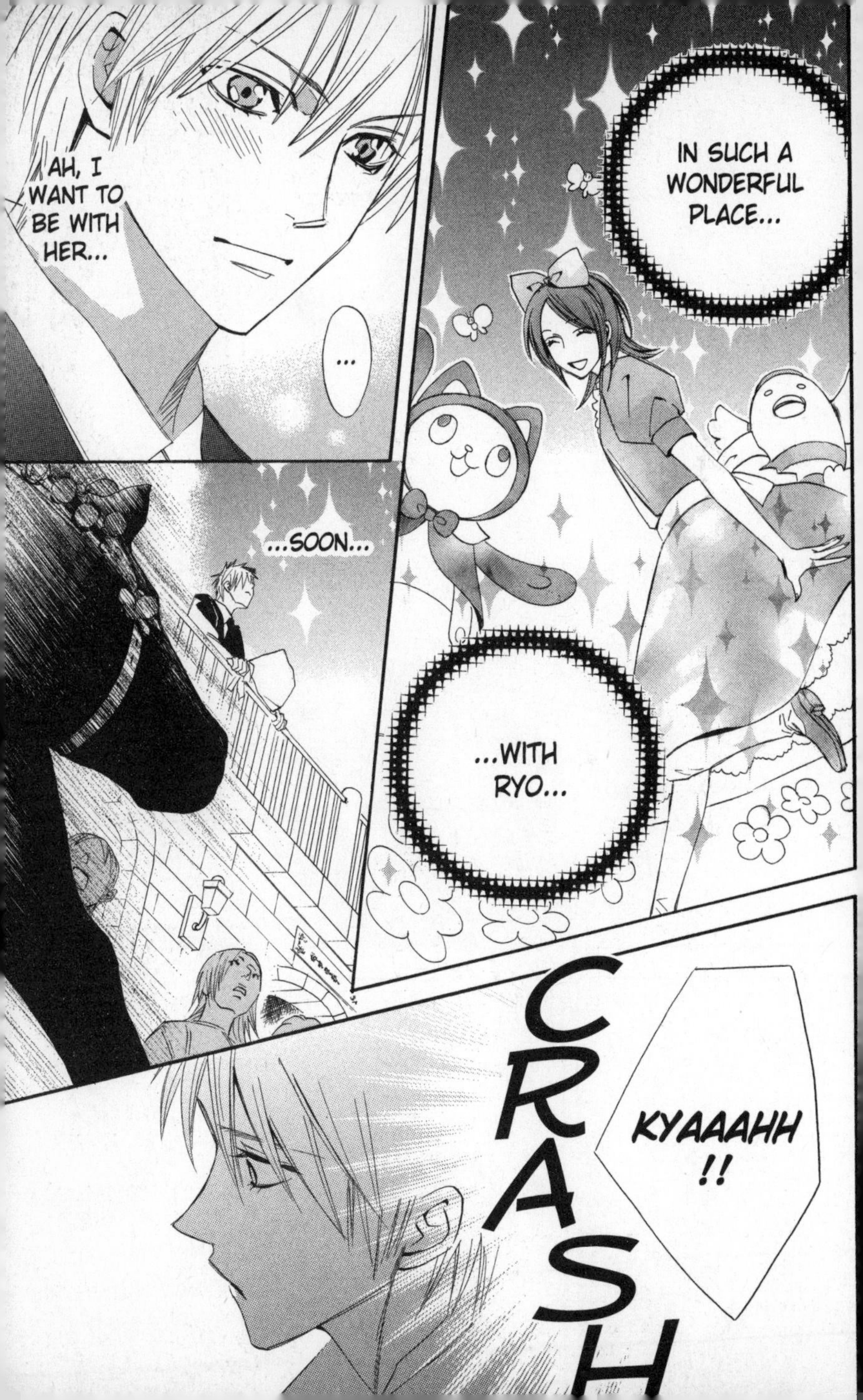
IN SUCH A WONDERFUL PLACE...
...WITH RYO...
AH, I WANT TO BE WITH HER...
...
...SOON...
KYAAAHH !!
CRASH

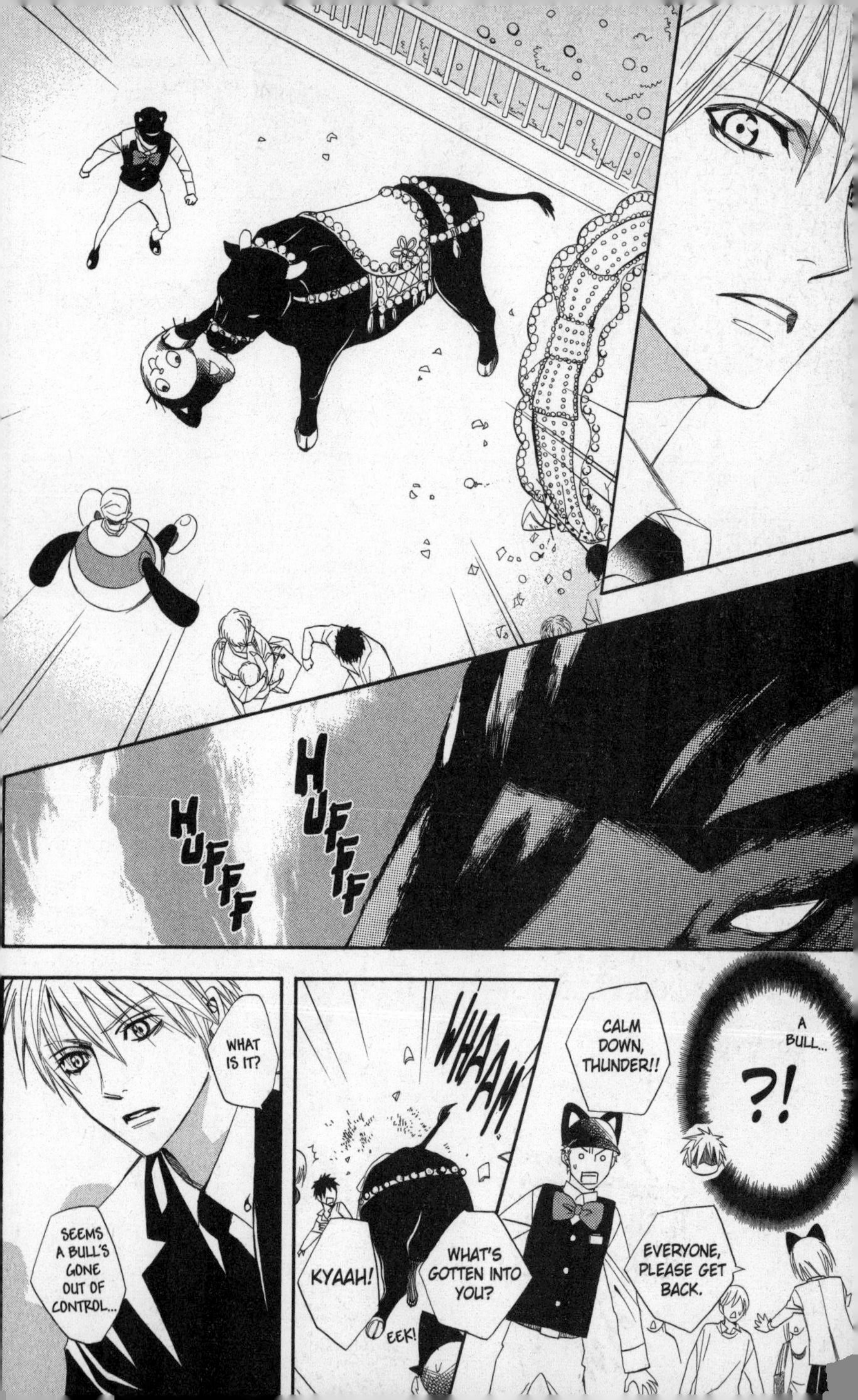
HUFFF
HUFFF
A BULL...
?!
CALM DOWN, THUNDER!!
EVERYONE, PLEASE GET BACK.
WHAT'S GOTTEN INTO YOU?
WHAAM
KYAAH!
EEK!
WHAT IS IT?
SEEMS A BULL'S GONE OUT OF CONTROL...

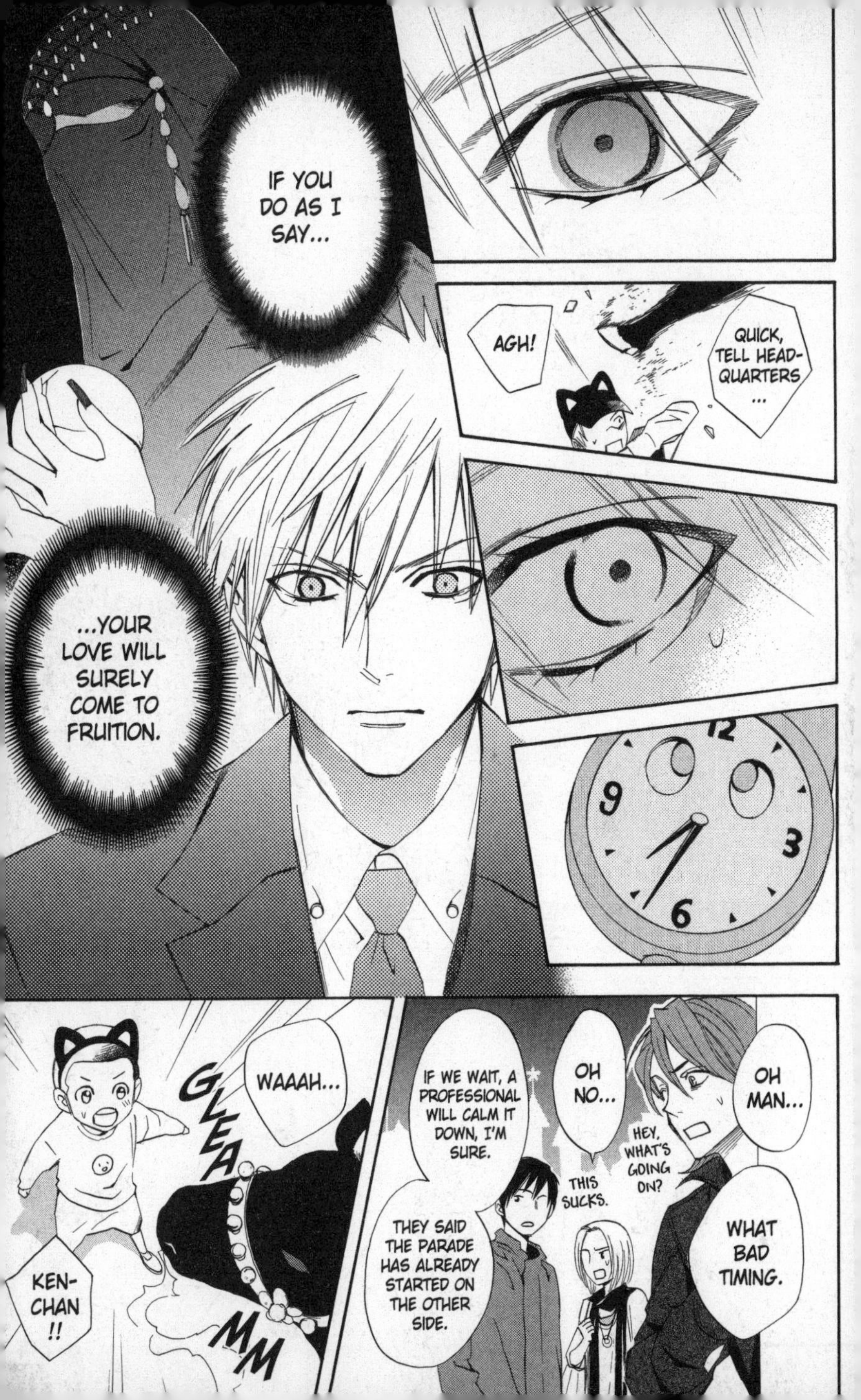
QUICK, TELL HEAD-QUARTERS...
AGH!
IF YOU DO AS I SAY...
...YOUR LOVE WILL SURELY COME TO FRUITION.
OH MAN...
OH NO...
IF WE WAIT, A PROFESSIONAL WILL CALM IT DOWN, I'M SURE.
HEY, WHAT'S GOING ON?
WHAT BAD TIMING.
THIS SUCKS.
THEY SAID THE PARADE HAS ALREADY STARTED ON THE OTHER SIDE.
WAAAH...
GLEAMM
KEN-CHAN!!

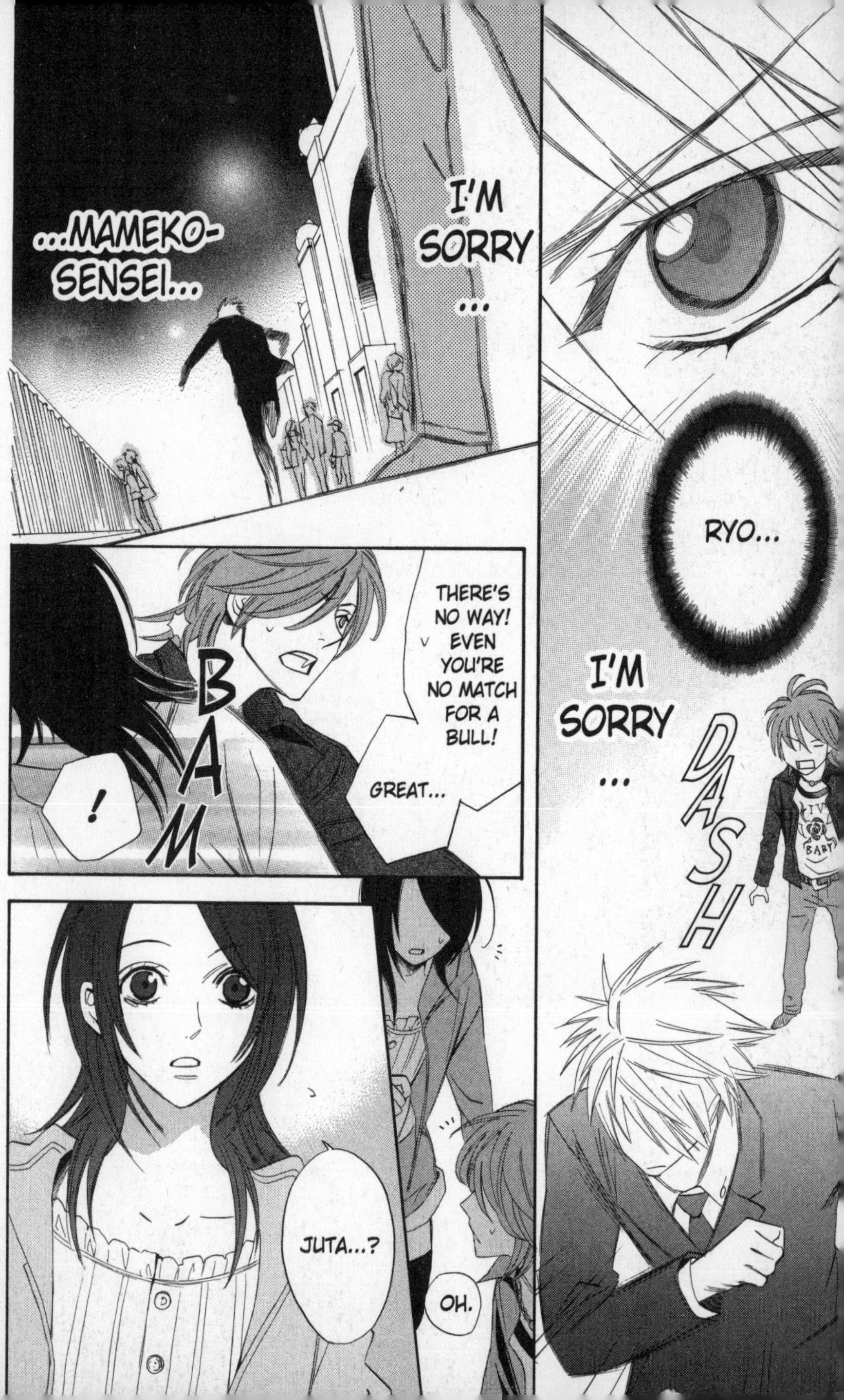

RYO...
I'M SORRY ...
DASH
I'M SORRY ...
...MAMEKO-SENSEI...
THERE'S NO WAY! EVEN YOU'RE NO MATCH FOR A BULL!
GREAT...
BAM
!
JUTA...?
OH.

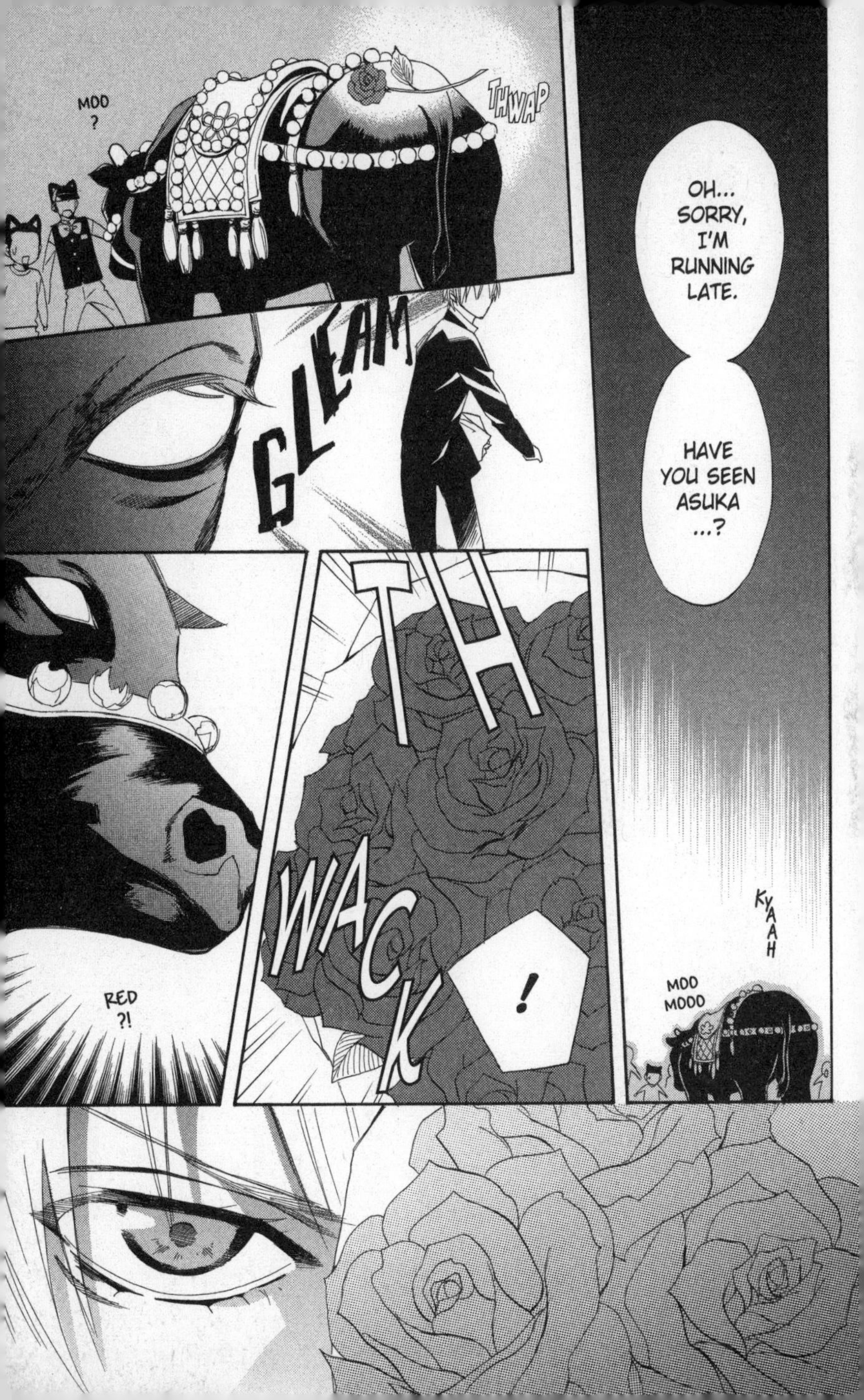
OH... SORRY, I'M RUNNING LATE.
HAVE YOU SEEN ASUKA ...?
THWAP
MOO ?
GLEAM
KYAAH
MOO MOODO
THWACK
!
RED ?!

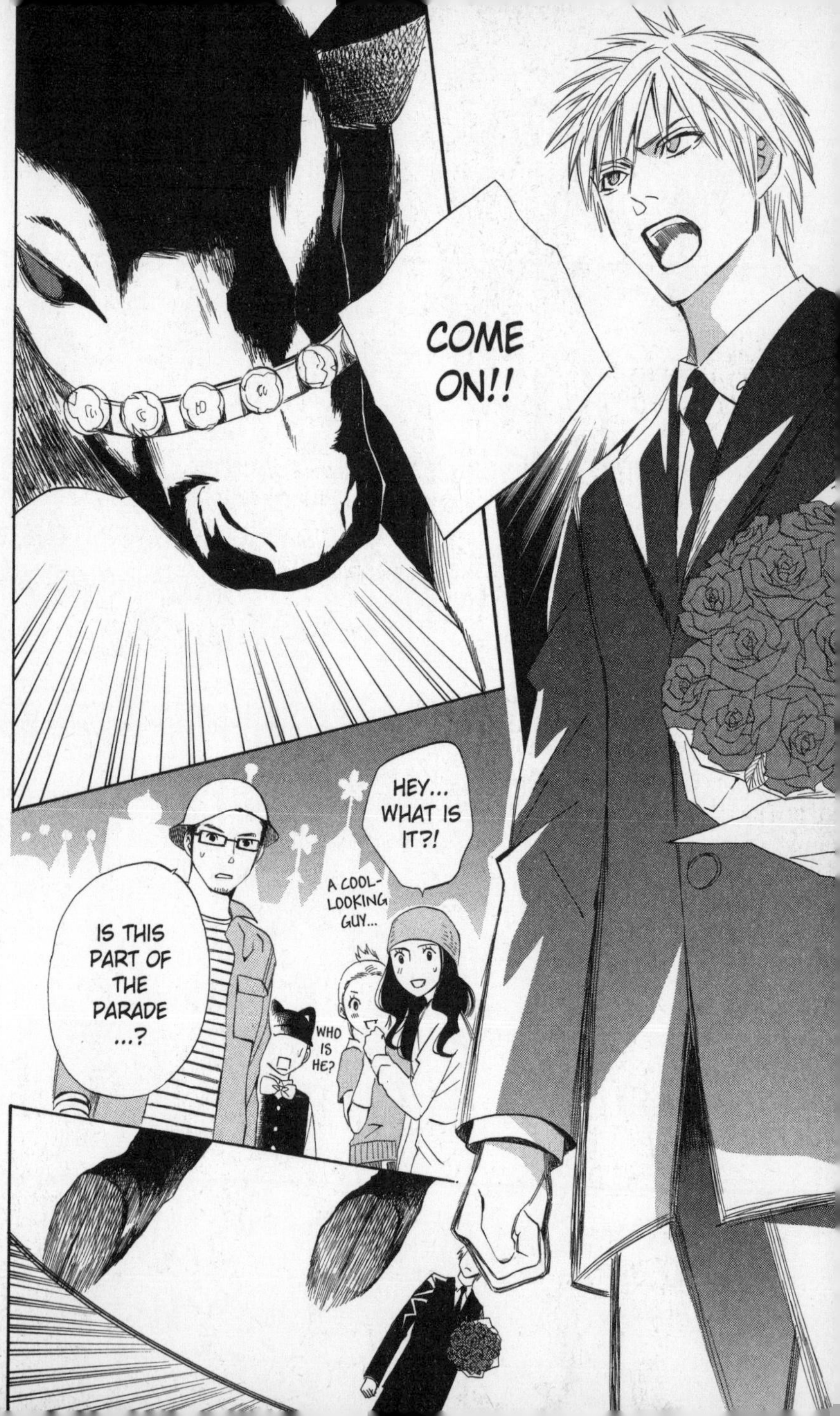
COME ON!!
HEY... WHAT IS IT?!
A COOL-LOOKING GUY...
WHO IS HE?
IS THIS PART OF THE PARADE ...?

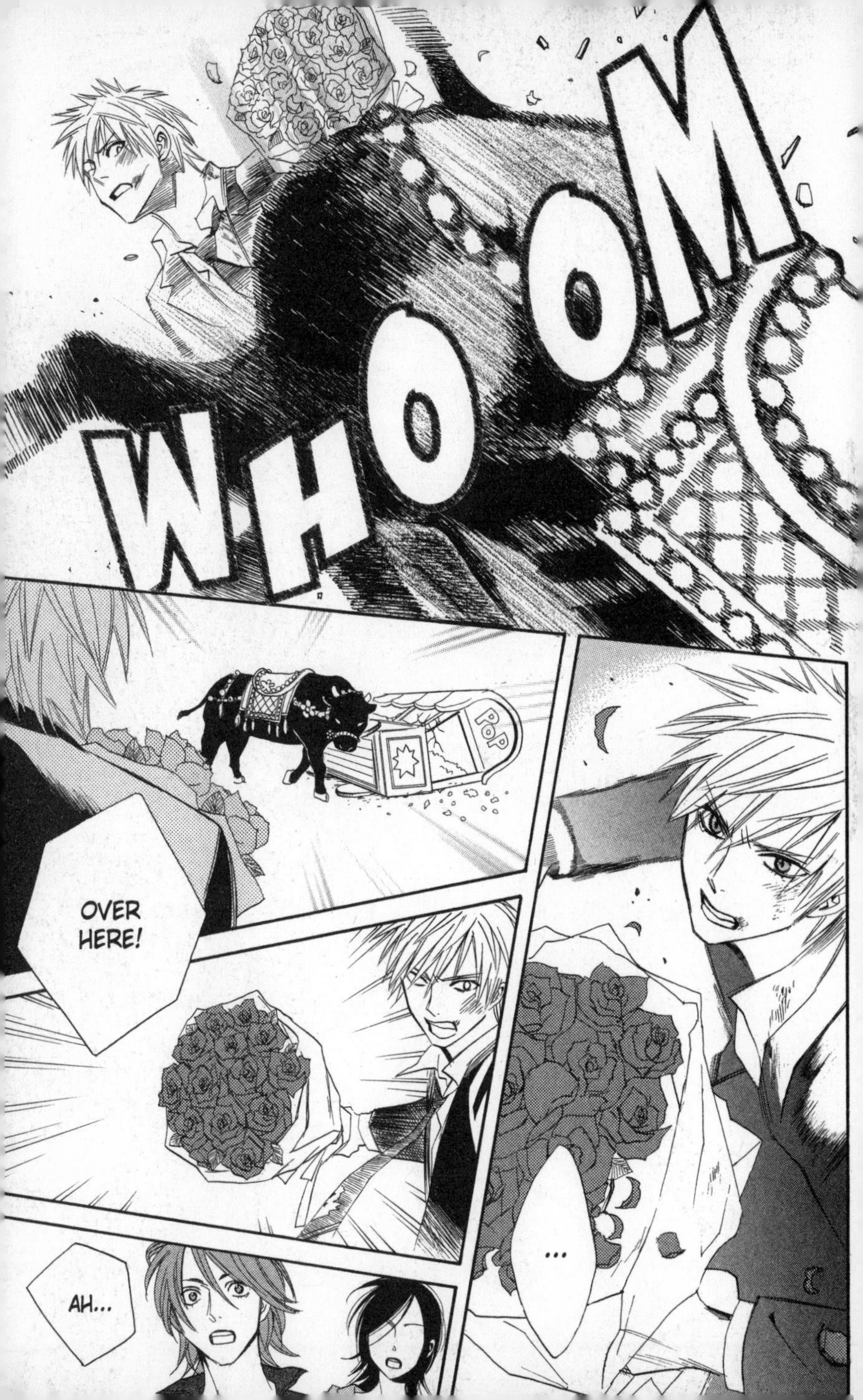
WHOOM
POP
OVER HERE!
...
AH...

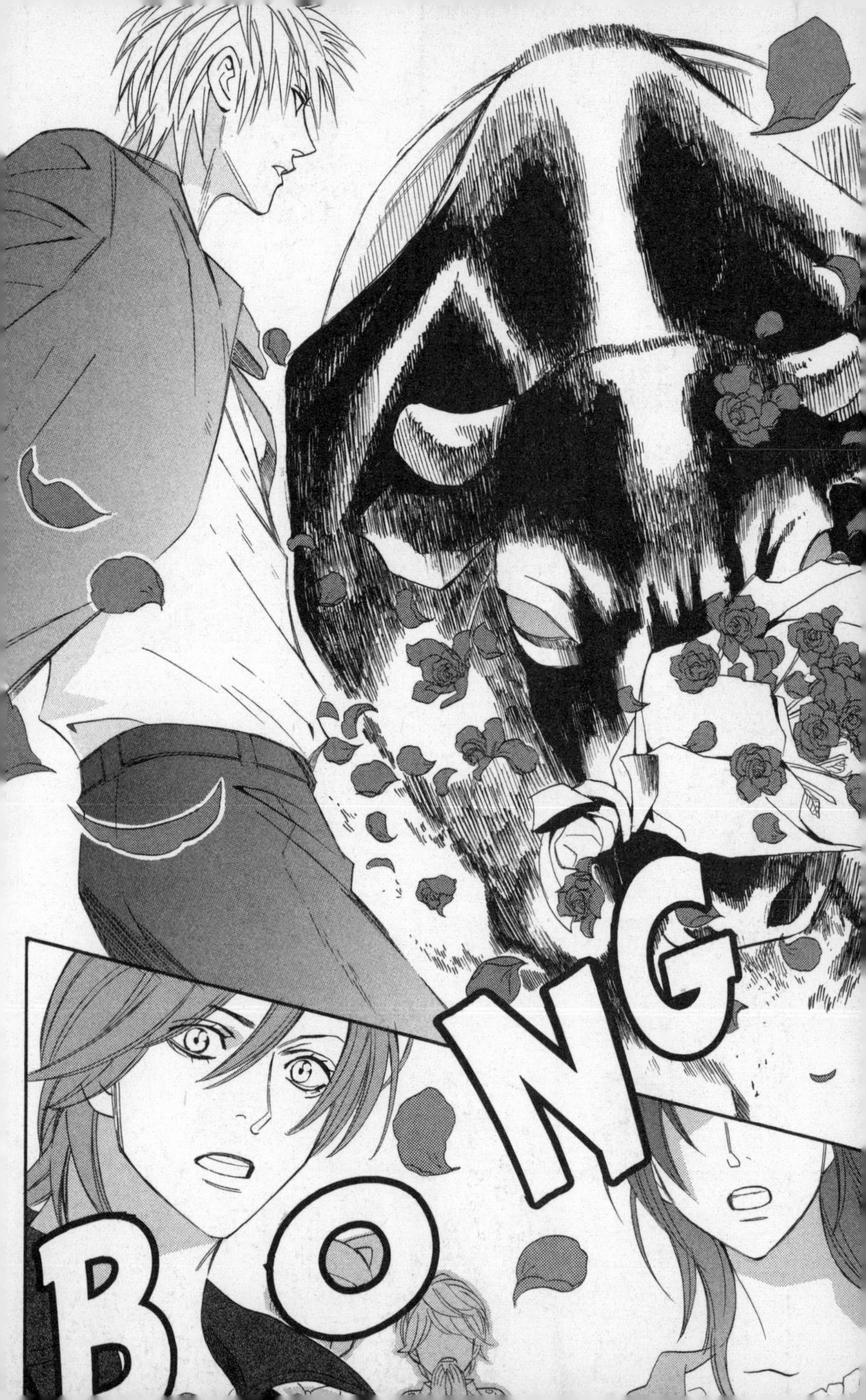
BOONG

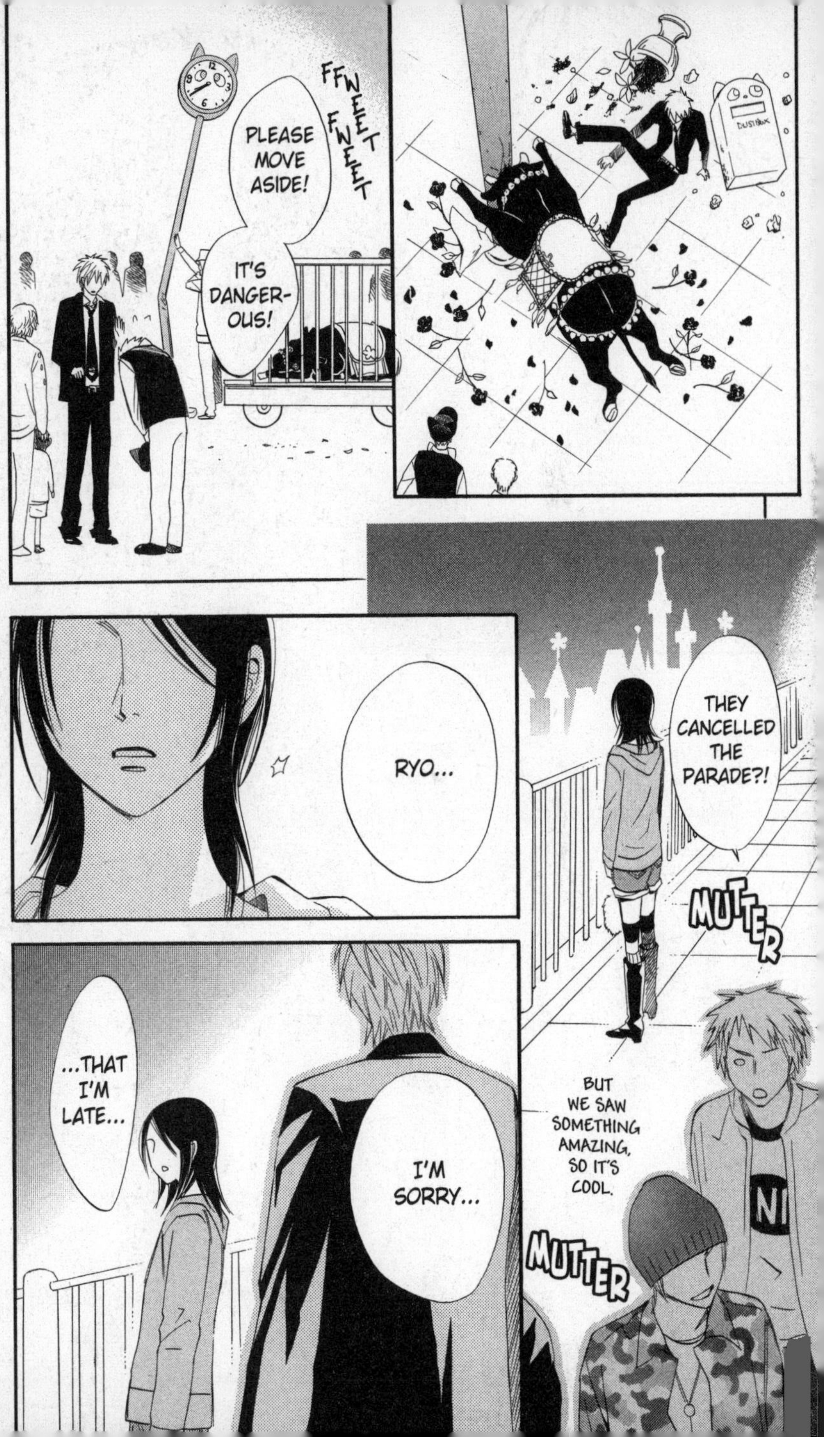
DUSTBOX
PLEASE MOVE ASIDE!
FFWEET FWEET
IT'S DANGER-OUS!
THEY CANCELLED THE PARADE?!
MUTTER
BUT WE SAW SOMETHING AMAZING, SO IT'S COOL.
MUTTER
RYO...
I'M SORRY...
...THAT I'M LATE...

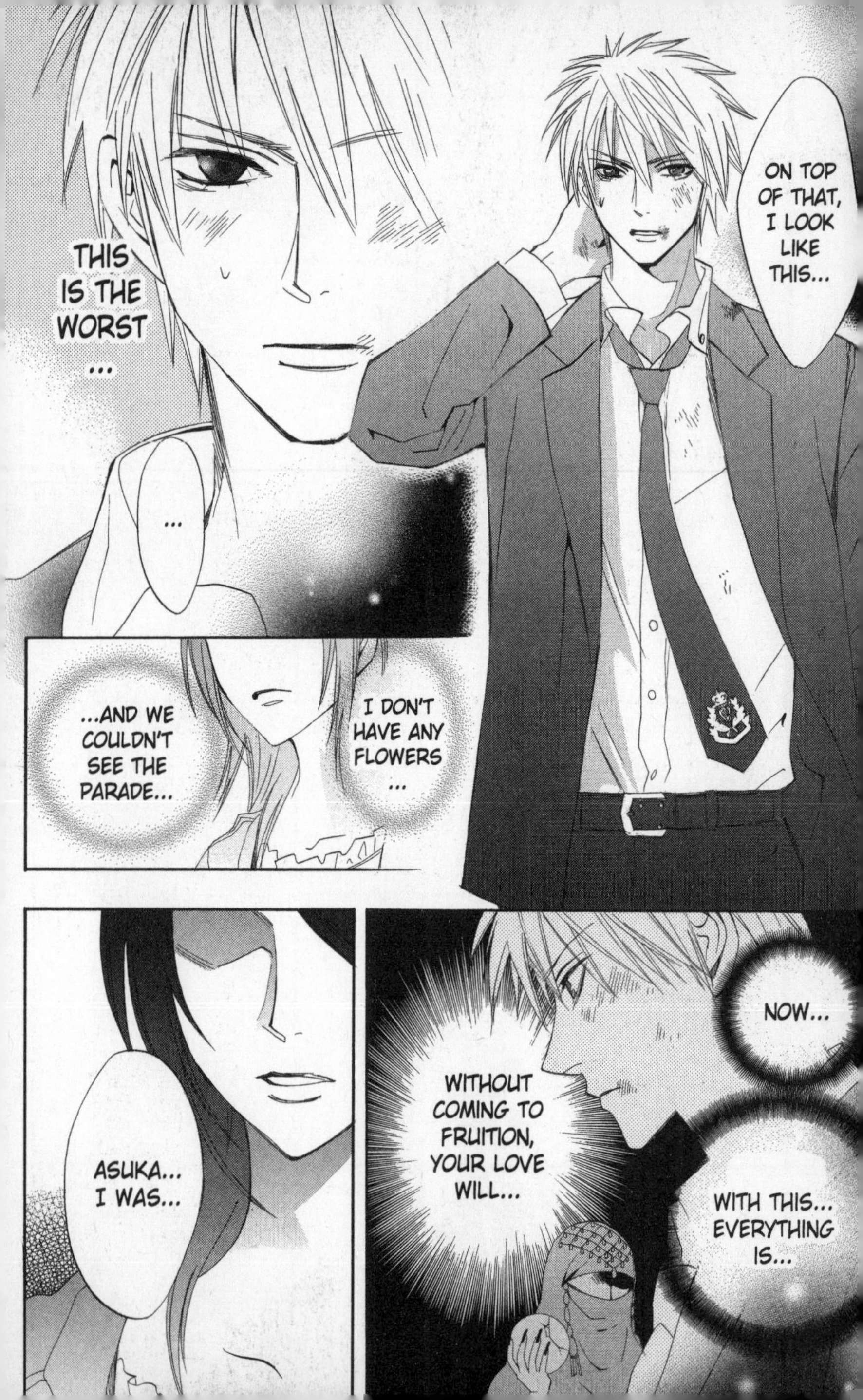
ON TOP OF THAT, I LOOK LIKE THIS...
THIS IS THE WORST...
...
I DON'T HAVE ANY FLOWERS...
...AND WE COULDN'T SEE THE PARADE...
NOW...
WITHOUT COMING TO FRUITION, YOUR LOVE WILL...
WITH THIS... EVERYTHING IS...
ASUKA... I WAS...

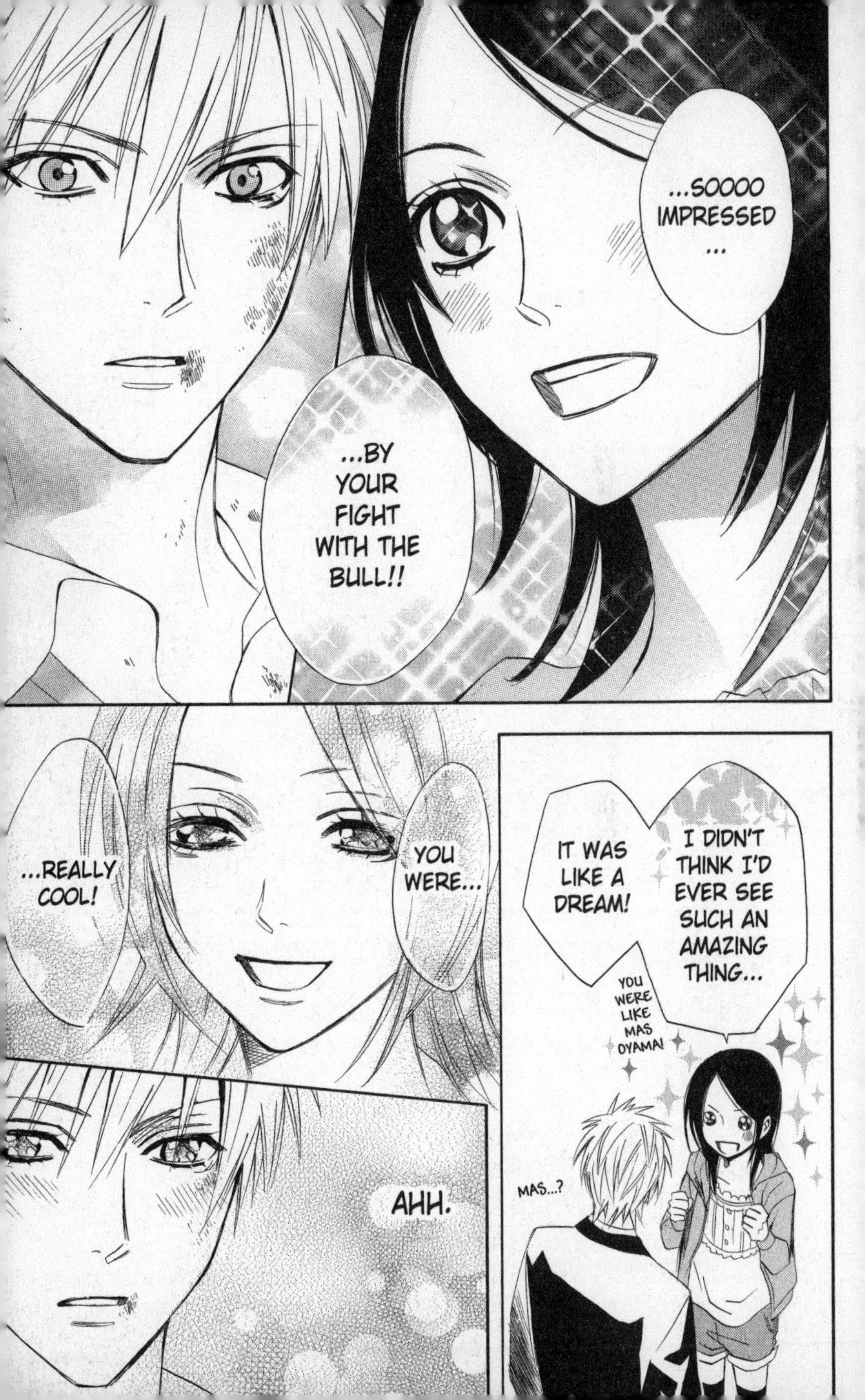
...SOOOO IMPRESSED ...
...BY YOUR FIGHT WITH THE BULL!!
I DIDN'T THINK I'D EVER SEE SUCH AN AMAZING THING...
IT WAS LIKE A DREAM!
YOU WERE LIKE MAS OYAMA!
MAS...?
YOU WERE...
...REALLY COOL!
AHH.

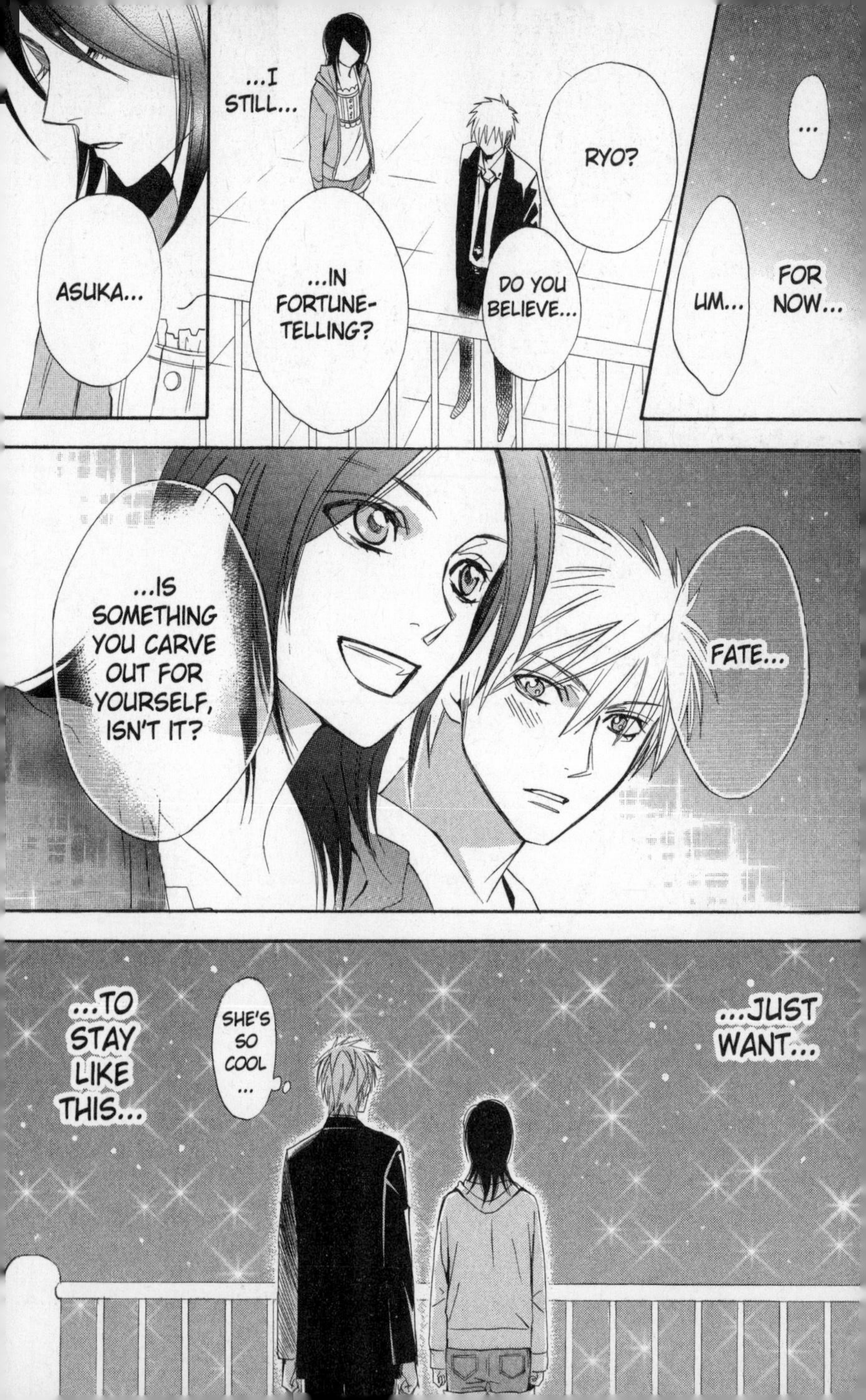
...
FOR NOW...
UM...
RYO?
DO YOU BELIEVE...
...I STILL...
...IN FORTUNE-TELLING?
ASUKA...
FATE...
...IS SOMETHING YOU CARVE OUT FOR YOURSELF, ISN'T IT?
...JUST WANT...
SHE'S SO COOL...
...TO STAY LIKE THIS...

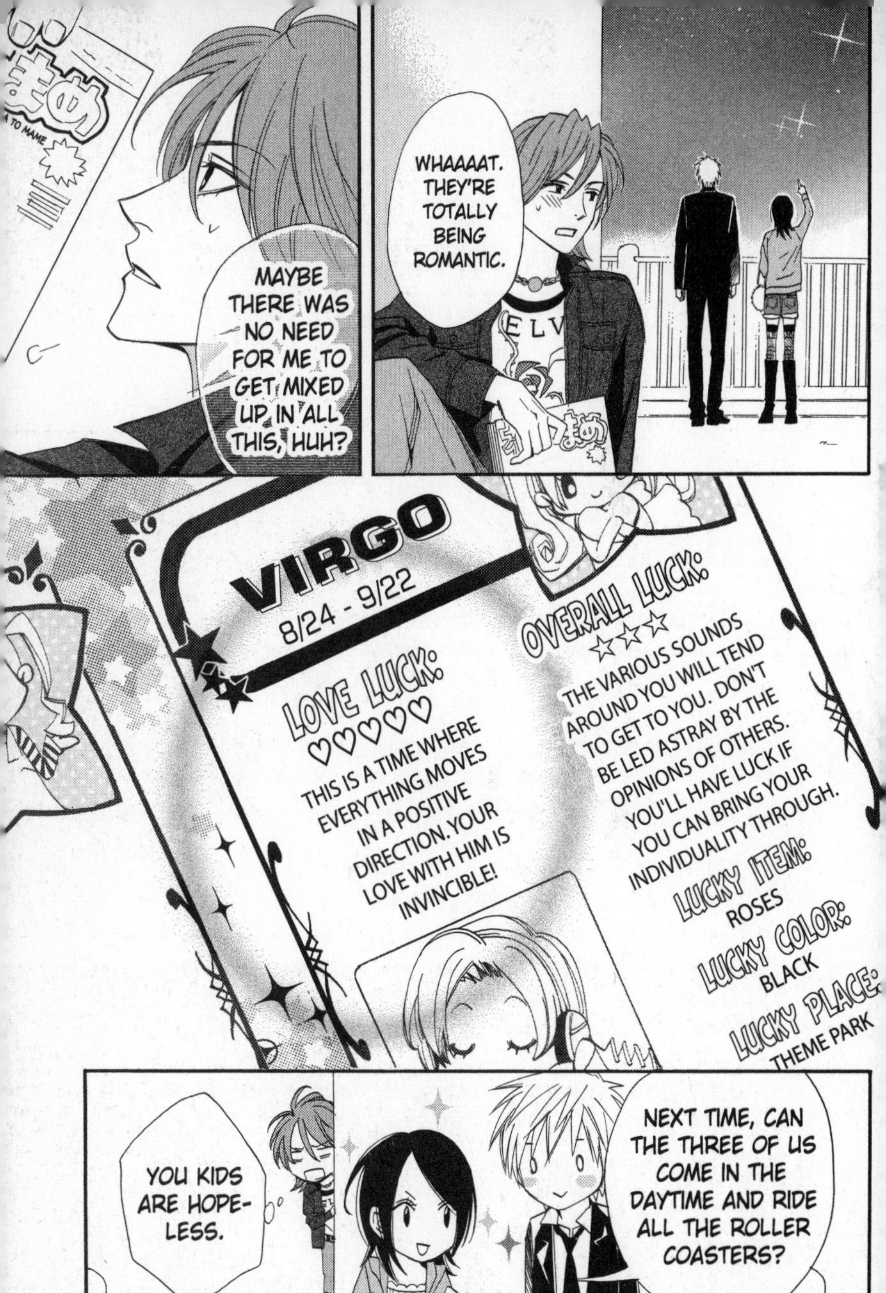
WHAAAAT. THEY'RE TOTALLY BEING ROMANTIC.
MAYBE THERE WAS NO NEED FOR ME TO GET MIXED UP IN ALL THIS, HUH?
VIRGO
8/24 - 9/22
OVERALL LUCK:
☆☆☆
THE VARIOUS SOUNDS AROUND YOU WILL TEND TO GET TO YOU. DON'T BE LED ASTRAY BY THE OPINIONS OF OTHERS. YOU'LL HAVE LUCK IF YOU CAN BRING YOUR INDIVIDUALITY THROUGH.
LUCKY ITEM:
ROSES
LUCKY COLOR:
BLACK
LUCKY PLACE:
THEME PARK
LOVE LUCK:
♡♡♡♡♡
THIS IS A TIME WHERE EVERYTHING MOVES IN A POSITIVE DIRECTION. YOUR LOVE WITH HIM IS INVINCIBLE!
NEXT TIME, CAN THE THREE OF US COME IN THE DAYTIME AND RIDE ALL THE ROLLER COASTERS?
YOU KIDS ARE HOPE-LESS.

OTOMEN 1 / THE END

Confused by some of the terms, but too MANLY to ask for help?

Here are some **cultural notes** to assist you!

Chan – an informal version of *san* used to address children and females. *Chan* can be used toward animals, lovers, intimate friends, and people whom one has known since childhood.

Kun – an informal honorific used primarily toward males. It can be used by people of more senior status addressing those junior to them or by anyone addressing boys or young men.

San – the most common honorific title. It is used to address people outside one's immediate family and close circle of friends.

Senpai – used to address one's senior colleagues or mentor figures. It is used when students refer to or address more senior students in their school.

Sensei – honorific title used to address teachers as well as professionals such as doctors, lawyers and artists.

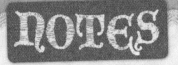

NOTES

Page 13, panel 1 | Hana to Mame
The manga magazine that Asuka reads is called *Hana to Mame* (Flowers and Beans), a play on the *shojo manga* (girls' comics) magazine *Hana to Yume* (Flowers and Dreams) published by Hakusensha. The manga *Love Chick* that Asuka enjoys is serialized in *Hana to Mame*.

1 花とまめ COMICS
2 らぶちっく
3 幸花 ジュエル 1

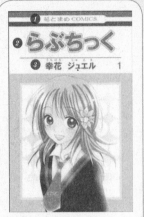

1. **Hana to Mame** (name of magazine that the manga is serialized in)
2. **Love Chick** (name of manga)
3. **Jewel Sachihana** (name of author/artist)

Page 27, panel 1 | Bushido
Bushido means "the way of the warrior" and is a code of conduct that emphasizes loyalty, martial arts mastery and honor unto death.

Page 28, panel 1 | Bento
A homemade lunch box that may contain rice, meat, pickles and an assortment of side dishes. Often the food is arranged in such a way as to resemble objects like animals, flowers, leaves, and so forth.

Page 69, panel 2 | Kyoshinhei
In the anime *Nausicaa of the Valley of the Wind*, a *kyoshinhei* (god warrior) is one of the lethal, giant, biological weapons used in an ancient war. Juta is remarking that Ryo's cake resembles a *kyoshinhei* during a scene in the movie.

Page 78, panel 7 | Ohmu
Gigantic, armored pillbug-like insects from the anime *Nausicaa of the Valley of the Wind*.

Page 94, panel 4 | Otōsan
Otōsan means "father" in Japanese. Asuka is using this term as a sign of respect rather than actually calling Ryo's father his own.

Page 166, panel 1 | Blood Type
In Japan, people believe that one's blood type can indicate one's personality. Similar to astrological signs, one can use blood type to gauge one's compatibility with others.

Page 172, panel 2 | Socrates in Love
Originally a novel entitled *Sekai no Chushin de, Ai o Sakebu* (Crying Out Love, In the Center of the World), the movie version of this story has a scene at the end where one of the characters in trouble yells out for help in the same way that Juta does here.

Page 197, panel 3 | Mas Oyama
Masutatsu Oyama, also known as Mas Oyama, was a famous karate master/instructor who founded an extremely influential style of full contact karate.

Aya Kanno was born in Tokyo, Japan.
She is the creator of *Soul Rescue* and *Blank Slate*
(originally published as *Akusaga* in Japan's
BetsuHana magazine). Her latest work, *Otomen*,
is currently being serialized in *BetsuHana*.

OTOMEN

Vol. 1

Shojo Beat Edition

This manga volume contains material that was originally published in English in *Shojo Beat* magazine, January 2009 issue. Artwork in the magazine may have been altered slightly from what is presented in this volume.

Story and Art by | **AYA KANNO**

Translation & Adaptation | **Lindsey Akashi**
Touch-up Art & Lettering | **Mark McMurray**
Design | **Fawn Lau**
Editor | **Amy Yu**

Otomen by Aya Kanno © Aya Kanno 2006
All rights reserved. First published in Japan in 2007 by HAKUSENSHA, Inc., Tokyo. English language translation rights arranged with HAKUSENSHA, Inc., Tokyo.

Printed in the U.S.A.

Published by VIZ Media, LLC
P.O. Box 77010
San Francisco, CA 94107

10 9 8 7 6
First printing, February 2009
Sixth printing, November 2014

PARENTAL ADVISORY
OTOMEN is rated T for Teen and is recommended for ages 13 and up. This volume contains suggestive themes.
ratings.viz.com

www.viz.com

www.shojobeat.com